W9-CWV-630

DISCOVERING EXODUS

Discovering Biblical Texts
Content, Interpretation, Reception

Comprehensive, up-to-date and student-friendly introductions to the books of the Bible: their structure, content, theological concerns, key interpretative debates and historical reception.

PUBLISHED

Iain Provan, *Discovering Genesis*
Ralph K. Hawkins, *Discovering Exodus*
Jerome F. D. Creach, *Discovering Psalms*
Ian Boxall, *Discovering Matthew*
Ruth B. Edwards, *Discovering John*
Anthony C. Thiselton, *Discovering Romans*
David A. deSilva, *Discovering Revelation*

DISCOVERING EXODUS

Content, Interpretation, Reception

Ralph K. Hawkins

WILLIAM B. EERDMANS PUBLISHING COMPANY

GRAND RAPIDS, MICHIGAN

First published 2021 in Great Britain by
Society for Promoting Christian Knowledge
36 Causton Street
London SW1P 4ST

This edition published 2021
in the United States of America by
Wm. B. Eerdmans Publishing Co.
4035 Park East Court SE, Grand Rapids, MI 49546
www.eerdmans.com

27 26 25 24 23 22 21   1 2 3 4 5 6 7

ISBN 978-0-8028-7262-3

Library of Congress Cataloging-in-Publication Data

A catalog record for this book is available from the Library of Congress.

To the blessed memory of

The Revd Dr Donald S. Armentrout
The Revd Dr Reginald H. Fuller
The Revd Marion J. Hatchett
The Very Revd Guy Fitch Lytle III

Contents

Contents

Contents

Contents

Acknowledgements

I would like to thank the excellent staff of the Blount Library over the last several years for their help with this project. Peggy Adkins and Jim Verdini have gone above and beyond the call of duty in helping me secure references. My appreciation goes to the students in my 'Discovering Exodus' classes in 2016 and 2018 who helped me think through many of the issues in the book of Exodus. I am grateful to the School of Theology at the University of the South, which invited me to be a Fellow-in-Residence in 2018, and to Romulus Stefanut, Director of the School of Theology Library, who provided me with an office, secured resources for me and extended his friendship. I would like to thank James Hoffmeier, Gordon Johnston, Paul Lawrence and Gary Rendsburg, all of whom discussed various aspects of the project with me. I appreciate their collegial support, while acknowledging that any deficiencies in the work are my responsibility. I am grateful to my wife, Cathy, and to our children, Hannah, Sarah, Mary and Adam, for their love and support. Finally, I would like to thank Philip Law and SPCK, as well as Andrew Knapp and Eerdmans, for the opportunity to write this volume. My prayer is that it might be a blessing to many. *Soli Deo gloria!*

Ralph K. Hawkins
Feast day of St Ambrose of Milan
Danville, Virginia

Abbreviations

Only abbreviations not currently found in the *SBL Handbook of Style* are included here.

Arab. Arch. Epig.	*Arabian Archaeology and Epigraphy*
AUSDDS	Andrews University Seminary Doctoral Dissertation Series
CSB	Christian Standard Bible
EAnth	*Encyclopedia of Anthropology.* 5 vols. Ed. H. James Birx. Thousand Oaks, CA: Sage, 2006.
ECNT	Exegetical Commentary on the New Testament
ETS	Evangelical Theological Society
EXB	Expanded Bible
GW	GOD'S WORD Translation
ISV	International Standard Version
KEL	Kregel Exegetical Library
LEB	Lexham English Bible
LGRB	Lives of Great Religious Books
MBI	Methods in Biblical Interpretation
NCV	New Century Version
NEASB	*Near East Archaeology Society Bulletin*
NOG	Names of God Bible
OEBI	*The Oxford Encyclopedia of Biblical Interpretation.* Ed. Steven L. McKenzie. Oxford: Oxford University Press, 2013.
PHSC	Perspectives on Hebrew Scriptures and Its Contexts
SBEC	Studies in the Bible and Early Christianity
SRA	Studies in Religion and the Arts
TatC	Texts @ Contexts
YLT	Young's Literal Translation

A note about style

All translations follow the New Revised Standard Version (NRSV) unless otherwise indicated in the text. All transliterations follow the General-Purpose Style presented in the *SBL Handbook of Style*. The project was completed during the 2020 COVID-19 quarantine, during which time library access was very limited, with the result that some of the references in the volume are to works earlier than their current editions. Finally, in this volume, I follow the NRSV's convention of rendering the divine name as 'the LORD'.

1

Introduction

Exodus is an individual book, but it is not meant to be read alone. Instead, it is a chapter in the broader story of the Pentateuch. Preceding the book of Exodus is the story of Abraham, whom God had called to leave his home and its gods and travel to a land he would show him (Gen. 12.1). God promised that he would build a great nation through Abraham's descendants and that, through it, he would bless all humankind (Gen. 12.2–3). In order to bring about these promises, God would give Abraham's descendants the land of Canaan, where they would eventually take root and grow into a nation (Gen. 12.4–7).[1] The promise that they would inherit the land of Canaan was reaffirmed to his descendants, Isaac and Jacob.[2]

The book of Exodus begins with multiple ironies. At the beginning of the book, the Israelites are living in Egypt rather than in the land that God had promised to them. And yet, one aspect of the Abrahamic promises *was* being fulfilled. When the family of Jacob migrated to Egypt in order to escape a famine that had struck Canaan, there were only 70 of them (Exod. 1.5). But these 70 'were fruitful and prolific' and 'multiplied and grew exceedingly strong, so that the land was filled with them' (1.7). God had promised Abraham that his descendants would grow into a great nation, and this was indeed happening. At the beginning of the book of Exodus, the Israelites are on the brink of becoming a nation, but in a foreign land.

However, the growth in number of the Israelites evoked the ire of the pharaoh, who enslaved them (Exod. 1.7–11) and, as they continued to multiply, implemented a policy of infanticide against their male children (1.15–22). This commences a theme that was first introduced in Genesis and continues throughout the book of Exodus: the threat to the Abrahamic promises. God had promised to provide Abraham with an heir in order to begin building him

---

1 Cf. Gen. 12.4–7. The psalmist likened Israel to a vine that God brought out of Egypt and planted in Canaan (Ps. 80.8).

2 Abraham repeats the Abrahamic promises to Eleazar, his servant, as part of his instructions about securing a wife for Isaac (Gen. 24.1–7) and then, later, God himself reaffirms those promises to Isaac (Gen. 26.3). Isaac echoes the Abrahamic promises in his deathbed blessing of Jacob (Gen. 27.27–29), and God himself affirms the promises to him in a dream at Bethel (Gen. 28.13–15).

into a great nation but, throughout the Abraham cycle (Gen. 11.27—25.11), the fulfilment of that promise came under threat in a series of crises.[3] In Exodus, those same promises are reiterated over and over,[4] but they continue to come under threat as 'Israel is repeatedly brought to the brink of failure and extinction, and then pulled out of it at the last minute by God's grace'.[5] Throughout the book of Exodus, God overcomes each obstacle and preserves Israel until he has built it into a nation and established his presence among its people.

The book of Exodus is, thus, a vital part of the larger story of the Pentateuch. Genesis gives an account of God's promise to build Abraham's posterity into a nation; Exodus recounts Israel's salvation and establishment as a nation in covenant with its God; and Exodus through Deuteronomy provide the details of the terms of its national covenant. Together, these books comprise the Pentateuch, the Magna Carta of early Israel and the *raison d'être* for Israel's national existence. As one of these, Exodus provides part of the foundation for the entire Bible.

The structure of Exodus

In the book of Genesis, a formula stands at the beginning of each section, marking the units off from one another throughout the book. The Hebrew formula *'elleh toledot* can mean 'these are the generations of', 'this is the family history of' or 'this is the account of', depending on the context. There are 11 of these *toledot* formulas in the book of Genesis and they thus divide the book into 11 sections. Conversely, the book of Exodus does not have any headings or titles marking any divisions in the book; instead, its narrative just continues from one event to the next. In the case of Exodus, its content rather than its form must provide the key for delineating its units.

Exodus can be divided into two main sections, chapters 1—18 and chapters 19—40, which 'might be called Liberation and Covenant', providing 'a compositional scheme that embraces the physical and spiritual birth of the people of Israel'.[6] While some commentators separate the chapters related to

---

3 Larry R. Helyer, 'Abraham's eight crises: the bumpy road to fulfilling God's promise of an heir', in *Abraham and Family: New insights into the patriarchal narratives*, ed. Hershel Shanks (Washington, DC: Biblical Archaeology Society, 2000), 41–52.

4 Cf. Exod. 3.8, 17; 6.4, 8; 12.25; 13.5, 11; 16.5; 20.12; 23.20–33; 32.13; 33.1–3; 34.11–16, 24.

5 Richard S. Hess, *The Old Testament: A historical, theological, and critical introduction* (Grand Rapids, MI: Baker Academic, 2016), 57.

6 J. P. Fokkelman, 'Exodus', in *The Literary Guide to the Bible*, ed. Robert Alter and Frank Kermode (Cambridge, MA: Belknap Press, 1987), 56. I follow Fokkelman's division of the book into these two

the tabernacle into a third section, it is the covenant that facilitates God's presence in the midst of the people. The instructions for building the tabernacle and the account of its construction therefore fall under the auspices of the covenant.

Part I: Liberation
Slavery and genocide (1.1–22);
Moses' birth and early life (2.1–22);
Moses' call and mission (2.23—4.31);
Confrontation with Pharaoh (5.1—7.13);
The ten plagues (7.14—11.10);
The exodus from Egypt (12.1—15.21);
The journey to Sinai (15.22—18.27).

Part II: Covenant
Revelation at Mt Sinai (19.1—20.21);
Laws and rules (20.22—23.33);
Establishment of the covenant (24.1–18);
Instructions for building the tabernacle (25.1—31.18);
The golden calf episode (32.1—34.35);
Construction of the tabernacle (35.1—40.38).

The story of Exodus

The author of the book of Exodus uses a timeless literary technique that Peter Ellis calls 'the obstacle story' to engage readers and keep the story moving. He explains that:

> Few literary techniques have enjoyed so universal and perennial a vogue as the obstacle story. It is found in ancient and modern literature from the Gilgamesh epic and the *Odyssey* to the *Perils of Pauline* and the latest novel. Its character is episodal. [The episodes are] not self-contained but find [their] *raison d'être* in relation to the larger story or narrative of which [they are] a part. [The] purpose is to arouse suspense and sustain interest by recounting episodes which threaten or retard the fulfillment of what the reader either suspects or hopes or knows to be the ending of the story.[7]

sections dealing with liberation and covenant. However, whereas he divides these sections into 1—15 and 16—40, I divide them into 1—18 and 19—40.

7 Peter Ellis, *The Yahwist: The Bible's first theologian* (Notre Dame, IN: Fides, 1968), 136. Cited in Helyer, 'Abraham's eight crises', 41.

The book of Exodus begins in crisis. While God had promised Abraham that his descendants would inherit the land of Canaan, the opening verses of Exodus find them settled in Egypt (1.1–7). Initially, it appears that the Abrahamic blessings were being fulfilled there since, while there were originally only 70 who had migrated to Egypt in the days of Joseph (1.5), they had 'multiplied and grew exceedingly strong, so that the land was filled with them' (1.7). In time, however, a new king, who did not know Joseph, came to power in Egypt, and observed that 'the Israelite people are more powerful than we' (1.8–9). In order to prevent them from ever overpowering the Egyptians and leaving their land, he enslaved them to build the supply cities of 'Pithom and Rameses' (1.10–11). When the Hebrews continued to grow, the pharaoh finally issued a decree that 'every boy that is born to the Hebrews you shall throw into the Nile, but you shall let every girl live' (1.22). Here is the first crisis: how can the Hebrew people flourish when they are trapped in slavery in a foreign land? How can the Israelites become a nation that can bring blessings to all humankind when the ruler of the mightiest nation on earth implements a policy of genocide against their children? It appears that, in the book of Exodus, the Abrahamic promises may crash and burn before leaving the runway.

Into this situation of crisis, a deliverer was born. A Levite couple had a child and, when his mother saw that he was a particularly 'fine' baby, she attempted to hide him (2.2). After three months, however, this became impossible, and it seemed that he too might fall victim to Pharaoh's genocidal machinations. Would crisis overtake Israel's deliverer even in his infancy?

The child's mother refused to allow this to happen. She hid him in a basket and placed it in the River Nile among the reeds outside Pharaoh's daughter's residence (2.1–3). When she discovered the basket, she had her maid take it out of the water. She realized that the baby must be one of the Hebrew children, and agreed that a Hebrew nursemaid should be sought out to breastfeed the child. Miriam, who was close at hand, brought the child's mother, who nursed him until he was weaned and then brought him back to the pharaoh's daughter (2.5–10a). She named him 'Moses', because she drew him out of the water (2.10b).

One day, after Moses had grown up, he went out to the camp of the Hebrew slaves and surveyed their situation. He saw an Egyptian taskmaster beating one of the Hebrews and, after looking around to make sure no one was watching, he killed the Egyptian and hid his body in the sand (2.11–12). The next day, he saw two Hebrews arguing and tried to arbitrate between them. They harshly rejected his efforts to mediate between them and made it clear that they knew he had killed an Egyptian the day before (2.13–14). When Pharaoh heard about what had happened, he tried to kill Moses (2.15a).

Faced with this new crisis, Moses fled into the desert of Midian, where he began a new life (2.15b). He married into the family of Jethro, a local Midianite priest. He and his wife, Zipporah, had a son, whom Moses named Gershom. And, while it may appear that, with these blessings of his new life, Moses was able to forget the situation in Egypt and put the past behind him, this was not the case. Moses named his son Gershom, based on the Hebrew word for 'alien' (gēr), as an illustration of the fact that he had not fully assimilated into Midianite society but viewed himself as an 'alien' (gēr) whose true home was in Egypt (2.22). Nonetheless, Moses spent the next 40 years as a shepherd for his father-in-law (2.23).

One day, while he was out tending sheep, Moses discovered a strange phenomenon – a burning bush that was not consumed by the flames (3.1–3). God spoke to him from the bush, calling him closer but commanding him to remove his shoes since he was on holy ground (3.5). He told Moses that he was going to liberate the Israelites and finally fulfil the promise he had made to Abraham to give them the land of Canaan, a land flowing with milk and honey (3.7–8). God told Moses that he could assure the Israelites that he was the same God their ancestors had known, and that he had sent him to accompany the elders of Israel to stand before the pharaoh and ask that he let the Israelites go a three days' journey into the wilderness to sacrifice to him (3.15–18). Moses resisted on the basis that he was unworthy to undertake such a momentous task (3.11), and this presents another crisis: would Moses' sense of inadequacy prevent him from answering God's call to serve as the deliverer of his people? The LORD overcame Moses' repeated protestations by assuring Moses that he would be with him, that he would empower him and that he would also send his brother Aaron along with him as his mouthpiece (3.11—4.17).

Moses and Aaron returned to Egypt and confronted Pharaoh, but he was unimpressed. He said, 'Who is the LORD, that I should heed him and let Israel go? I do not know the LORD, and I will not let Israel go' (5.2). Pharaoh was indignant and simply increased the Hebrews' workload (5.1–23). The LORD sent Moses and Aaron to Pharaoh again and, this time, they demonstrated the power of God by turning a staff into a snake (6.28—7.12). However, 'Pharaoh's heart was hardened, and he would not listen to them' (7.13).

God now launches a series of ten plagues against Egypt in order to impress upon the Pharaoh that he is the LORD (7.17). The first nine plagues were a series of disasters and climatological catastrophes that included: the waters of the Nile turning to blood; swarms of frogs, gnats, flies and locusts; the cattle being devastated by disease; an outbreak of boils; thunder and hail; and darkness (7.14—10.29). The plagues were God's judgement against Egypt, by which the LORD would make 'fools' of the Egyptians (10.2) and execute judgement against all their gods (12.12). Instead of leading the pharaoh to release the Hebrews, however, each plague simply triggered a new crisis when he responded by hardening his heart.[8]

The tenth and final plague was the culmination of the plagues and triggered the exodus. In this plague, the LORD himself would go throughout Egypt and smite the firstborn child of every household (11.4–6). The Hebrews would be saved from this plague by sacrificing a spotless lamb and painting the doorframes of their houses with its blood (12.1–6). When the angel of death passed through Egypt that night, he would 'pass over' those homes where he saw the doorframes painted with blood (12.13). When the death plague struck, 'there was a loud cry in Egypt, for there was not a house without someone dead' (12.30). In the middle of the night, Pharaoh summoned Moses and Aaron and told them that they could finally leave Egypt and go worship the LORD, and he asked that they would bring a blessing upon him too (12.31–32).

After the Israelites had left Egypt, however, a new crisis arose when the pharaoh changed his mind about having let them go, mustered a massive chariot force and set out after them. The Egyptians overtook the Israelites, who were camped by the sea (14.5–9). It appeared that this crisis might result in either the recapture or the destruction of Israel. The people cried out in desperation, afraid for their lives, but Moses assured them that the LORD would deliver them (14.13). At the LORD's prompting, Moses stretched out his hand over the sea and the waters were divided, so that the Israelites were able to cross on dry land. When the Egyptians pursued them into the sea, the waters returned to their normal depth and they were drowned (14.21–29). 'Thus the LORD saved Israel that day from the Egyptians' (14.30).

Moses led the Israelites deep into the desert, where they faced one crisis after another. From the beginning of their wilderness journey, they were in danger of getting lost in the desert. They could not find water (15.22–24; 17.1–3). There was no food (16.1–3). They were attacked by the Amalekites (17.8). And Moses himself nearly became overwhelmed with the judicial tasks required of him in his leadership of the Hebrew people (18.13–16). In each of these crises, however, the LORD intervened in order to save and preserve his people. The LORD led the Israelites in the form of a pillar of cloud by day and a pillar of fire by night (13.21–22). He led them to water (15.25a; 17.4–6) and provided food (16.4–36). He enabled the Israelites to defeat the Amalekites (17.9–16). And, through Jethro, he appointed judges to provide for a just and ordered society (18.17–27).

---

8   Cf. 8.15, 32; 9.7, 12, 34; 10.1, 20, 27; 11.10.

About two months after leaving Egypt,[9] the Israelites arrived at Mt Sinai (19.1–2). Moses ascended the mountain to meet God, who told him that, if Israel would obey his voice and keep his covenant, it would be his treasured possession out of all the peoples of the earth, 'a priestly kingdom and a holy nation' (19.5–6). Moses came down from the mountain and told the people what the LORD had said, and they agreed that they would enter into a covenant with him (19.7–9a). After the people's consecration, the LORD descended upon the mountain in the form of thunder, lightning and a thick cloud, and the people gathered around the foot of the mountain to meet him (19.16–17). Moses now ascends the mountain again and receives the covenant, and the text recounts a summary of its stipulations known as the Decalogue, or the Ten Commandments (20.1–17), as well as a selection of civil and religious laws (20.22—23.33) collected in a text known as the Book of the Covenant (24.7). Moses led the people in a ceremony to ratify the covenant. They swore that they would adhere to its stipulations (24.3, 7), and their commitment was sealed with blood (24.5–8) and followed by a theophany to Moses, Aaron, Nadab, Abihu and 70 of the elders of Israel (24.9–11).

The focus of the Sinai covenant and all of its laws and regulations was God's presence with his people, and the ensuing chapters recount how God himself gave instructions about several things that would facilitate it (25.1—31.18). First, God gave instructions for the construction of a portable sanctuary called the 'tabernacle', where he would dwell in the midst of the people. Second, he gave instructions for designing the vestments for the priests who would service the tabernacle. And, third, God repeated the command for a Sabbath rest. These institutions would facilitate God's continuing presence in the midst of the people.

During Moses' long absence while he was receiving these instructions from God, Israel faced its most profound crisis yet. The people demanded that Aaron 'make gods' for them (32.1). He cast an image of a calf, and the people proclaimed, 'These are your gods, O Israel, who brought you up out of the land of Egypt!' (32.4). They made sacrifices to the image, ate and drank, and 'rose up to revel' (32.6). God was furious and Moses had to plead for the lives of the Israelites (32.7–14). He descended Mt Sinai and smashed the tablets of the covenant at the foot of the mountain, ground the idol into powder, mixed it with water and made the people drink it, and commanded the Levites to kill those who had participated in the idolatry. In return for their faithfulness, the Levites were ordained for service to the LORD (32.15–29). Moses pleaded to God

---

9 Duane A. Garrett, *A Commentary on Exodus* (KEL; Grand Rapids, MI: Kregel Academic, 2014), 451, n. 82.

on behalf of Israel but, while the LORD affirmed that he would still lead the Israelites to the land he had promised to give them, he nonetheless sent a plague
among them because they had worshipped the golden calf (32.30–35). God
could not live in the midst of a sinful people; Israel must be a holy nation.

Moses pleaded for the Israelites again, and the LORD revealed himself to
him as a merciful and gracious, but also as a just, God (33.12—34.9). Despite
Israel's sin, God would renew the covenant and give the people the land of Canaan. God summoned Moses back up the mountain, made new tablets and
renewed the covenant with Israel (34.10–28). Moses descended the mountain
with his face shining from his encounter with God (34.29–35). The Israelites
observed the Sabbath, and then they built the tabernacle and its accoutrements
in the middle of the camp (35.1—40.33). In a dramatic conclusion, God's cloud
descended and the glory of the LORD filled the tabernacle before the eyes of all
Israel (40.34–38).

The distinctiveness of Exodus

In a 1991 lecture, Baruch Halpern stated that 'the closest parallel to the Book
of Exodus in the ancient West is Homer's *Odyssey*' and explained that 'both are
stories of migration – of identity suspended until the protagonist – Odysseus
or Israel – reaches a home'.[10] The comparison is apt. The *Odyssey* is focused on
the Greek hero Odysseus, king of Ithaca, and his journey home after the fall of
Troy. Although he had already fought for ten years in the Trojan War, his journey home proved to be just as difficult. He was waylaid by sorceresses, attacked
by one-eyed cannibals and lured off his path by sirens. His return journey took
another ten years. The book of Exodus is focused on the hero Moses and his
efforts to lead the Israelites to Canaan, a land flowing with milk and honey, after
liberating them from Egypt where they had been enslaved for 430 years. But the
journey to the promised land proved very difficult. The Israelites were in danger
of getting lost in the desert, had no food and water, and were attacked by desert
dwellers. It took them another 40 years to get there. However, Exodus is far more
than the epic journey of a nation that faces one obstacle after another in order
to reach the land where it can be planted. When the book's contents are closely
examined, it becomes clear that it is distinct in a number of profound ways.

First, Exodus recounts Ancient Israel's seminal salvation events, including
the Passover, the exodus from Egypt and the crossing of the Red Sea. Israel's

---

10   Baruch Halpern, 'The exodus from Egypt: myth or reality?', in *The Rise of Ancient Israel*, ed. Hershel
      Shanks (Washington, DC: Biblical Archaeology Society, 1992), 87.

very existence was accounted for by these formative events in its past. They provide the foundation of the Ten Commandments, which begin with the words 'I am the LORD your God, who brought you out of the land of Egypt, out of the house of slavery' (Exod. 20.2). Throughout the rest of Israel's history, both ancient and modern, its theological reflection, hymnody and liturgy have all focused on these events.[11]

Second, when the people of Israel agreed to the terms of the Sinai covenant, 'they became not simply a "nation" but a nation unlike any other'.[12] By accepting the covenant stipulations, they became the LORD's 'treasured possession out of all the peoples', and were to be 'a priestly kingdom and a holy nation' (Exod. 19.5–6). They 'were to behave toward all the other nations on earth as priests to the profane'.[13]

Third, the author of Deuteronomy viewed the laws associated with the covenant as more just than those of other societies. Deuteronomy 4.8 asks, 'What other great nation has statutes and ordinances as just as this entire law that I am setting before you today?' While a number of the laws of Exodus have parallels in other ancient law codes, many of them reflect ethical ideals unsurpassed in contemporaneous cultures.[14]

Fourth, the LORD's revelation of himself to Moses provides a central theme in the Old Testament. When the LORD passed before Moses, he proclaimed:

The LORD, the LORD,
a God merciful and gracious,
slow to anger,
and abounding in steadfast love and faithfulness,
keeping steadfast love for the thousandth generation,
forgiving iniquity and transgression and sin,
yet by no means clearing the guilty,
but visiting the iniquity of the parents
upon the children
and the children's children,
to the third and the fourth generation.
(Exod. 34.6–7)

---

11 This 'reception history' will be explored in later chapters.

12 Jan Assmann, *The Invention of Religion: Faith and covenant in the book of Exodus*, trans. Robert Savage (Princeton, NJ: Princeton University Press, 2018), 187.

13 Assmann, *Invention of Religion*, 187.

14 Some of these will be explored in later chapters.

This divine self-revelation provides a veritable vocabulary of mercy and grace. It is quoted or alluded to throughout the Old Testament and in intertestamental literature, and has come to serve as a creedal statement in Judaism known as the Thirteen Attributes of God. It is recited on festival days when the Torah scroll is taken from the Torah Ark, where it is housed in the synagogue. In addition, the emphasis on mercy and grace has certainly influenced Christian traditions about the nature and character of God.

Fifth, the fact that the LORD takes up residence among humankind, in the midst of the Israelites, is profoundly significant. In Genesis 3, when the first human couple sinned, they were irreversibly expelled from the Garden of Paradise. Christian theology understands their expulsion as having been predicated on the idea that sinful human beings cannot dwell with a holy God. A major result of the 'Fall', therefore, is the estrangement of humankind from God, a condition that persisted from that point forward, throughout the ages covered in the rest of the book of Genesis, up until God made provision to dwell in the midst of the Israelites in the tabernacle. Moshe Greenberg captures the profundity of the LORD's 'tabernacling' among the Israelites this way:

> It is possible to epitomize the entire story of Exodus in the movement of the fiery manifestation of the divine presence. At first the fire burned momentarily in a bush on the sacred mountain, as God announced his plan to redeem Israel; later it appeared for months in the sight of all Israel as God descended on the mountain to conclude his Covenant with the redeemed; finally it rested permanently on the tent-sanctuary, as God's presence settled there. The book thus recounts the stages in the descent of the divine presence to take up its abode for the first time among one of the peoples of the earth.[15]

Even though it was only the Israelites who had access to the tabernacle – and a quite restricted access at that – the LORD's condescension to dwell in the midst of people once again was an act of tremendous grace.

Sixth, God wants to be known by Egypt and all humankind, just as much as he wants to be known by Israel.[16] In roughly the first half of the book, God proclaims 'I am the LORD' five times to Israel,[17] but also five times to the Egyp-

---

15 Moshe Greenberg, *Understanding Exodus: A holistic commentary on Exodus 1–11* (2nd edn; Eugene, OR: Cascade, 2013), 14.

16 Fokkelman, 'Exodus', 64.

17 Cf. Exod. 6.2, 6, 7, 8, 29.

tians.[18] The proclamation appears at various points too in the second half of the book.[19] The repetition of this statement reflects the idea that the God of Israel is also the God of all peoples, even though other nations may not realize this. The vision of the Old Testament is that all people would eventually come to acknowledge the LORD as God.[20]

Each of these foci provides part of the rationale for Israel's existence. The nation of Israel existed because of what God had done for it in the Passover, the exodus and the crossing of the Red Sea. By accepting the terms of the covenant, Israel had become not only a nation, but also a priestly kingdom and a holy nation, brokers of the knowledge of God to all the earth. By living out its unique law, Israel was to create a just and equitable society. It was to share the message of the mercy and grace of the LORD. Israel was to live in fellowship with the God who tabernacled in its midst. And Israel was to disseminate knowledge of the LORD to the nations. In discussing Exodus in the context of the Torah, Greenberg points out that:

Israel's absorbing concern over its reason for being – which made the Torah so cherished a treasure – is unprecedented in antiquity. No Near Eastern analogues to a national literature like that of the Torah are available. Whether the literatures of the Arameans, the Moabites, or the Edomites once contained similar material is unknown. But the considerable remains of Egypt, Babylonia, the Hittites and Ugarit offer no parallels to the message of, and the national function served by, the Torah.[21]

The book of Exodus, as part of the larger Torah story, is certainly a very distinctive book.

---

18 Cf. Exod. 7.5, 17; 8.22; 14.4, 18.

19 Cf. Fokkelman, 'Exodus', 64.

20 Cf. the discussion of 'election' in Walter Brueggemann, *Reverberations of Faith: A theological handbook of Old Testament themes* (Louisville, KY: Westminster John Knox Press, 2002), 61–4.

21 Greenberg, *Understanding Exodus*, 9.

2

Reading Exodus as literature

The traditional approach to reading Exodus, as well as the rest of the Pentateuch, was as a single, unified work written by a single author, Moses. According to Jewish and Christian tradition, Moses wrote the book of Exodus in connection with the covenant experience at Mt Sinai.[1] Philo, a Hellenistic Jew who lived and wrote in Alexandria in the first century BC, began his study of the creation narratives with the observation that 'Moses says, "In the beginning"' (*Opif.* 26). Josephus likewise states that Moses wrote the first five books of the Pentateuch (*Ag. Ap.* 1.37–40). In the same way, the rabbis believed that Moses had written the Pentateuch (*B. Bat.* 14b) and that its origin was divine (*Sanh.* 99a).

Early Christian writers shared the view that Moses, under divine inspiration, had written the Pentateuch. Paul refers to it as the 'law of Moses' (e.g. 1 Cor. 9.9), and Luke refers to it simply as 'Moses'.[2] According to the Gospels, Jesus referred to it using both of these appellations.[3] The traditional approach generally prevailed until the eighteenth century, the Age of Enlightenment.

The Enlightenment and the rise of source criticism

The Enlightenment was an intellectual and philosophical movement that predominated in Europe throughout the eighteenth century. It was an age of rationalism and scepticism. During this period, the idea of deism became prominent. Deists believed that God existed and was even responsible for the initial creation of the universe, but that he does not continue to be involved with the created world nor does he intervene in it. This meant that miracles, predictive prophecy and even divine inspiration were all impossible by *definition*. The implication

---

1 Cf. Exod. 17.14; 24.4; 34.27.

2 Luke writes that the Jews had proclaimed 'Moses' for generations and had read him aloud every Sabbath (Acts 15.21). The distinctive Lukan formula, 'Moses and the prophets', makes it clear that his use of 'Moses' is a reference to the Pentateuch (cf. Luke 16.29, 31; 24.27; Acts 15.21; 26.22).

3 E.g. Mark 7.10; Luke 24.44.

was that natural explanations had to be sought not only for biological processes, but for supposedly supernatural ones as well. In the wake of the publication of Charles Darwin's *Origin of Species* (1859), anthropologists and scholars in various fields of religion began to reconceive of religion through evolutionary lenses. In this view, religion evolved from simple to complex forms.

The Documentary Hypothesis

In 1883, in the wake of these intellectual trends, Julius Wellhausen, who was then Professor of Old Testament at the University of Greifswald in Pomerania, wrote *A Prolegomena to the History of Israel*, in which he completely reconfigured the history of Israelite religion along developmental lines. The foundation of his understanding of Israel's history lay in his identification and separation of four literary sources, a theory that came to be known as the Documentary Hypothesis. He postulated that five features within the Pentateuch indicated that it was made up of multiple sources: (1) the use of different names for God; (2) variations in vocabulary and style; (3) contradictions and differences in viewpoint; (4) duplications and repetitions; and (5) indications of composite structure in the sections. On the basis of these literary indicators, Wellhausen identified four sources, which had been composed at different stages of Israel's history and woven together to form the Pentateuch.

In Wellhausen's original formulation, the four sources were J, E, D and P.[4] The J source was the earliest, and had been written in the tenth century BC by scribes of the court of Judah who referred to God using the divine name Yahweh, which in German (Wellhausen's mother tongue) begins with a 'J'. The E document was produced in the mid eighth century BC by their rivals in the northern kingdom of Israel, who referred to God as Elohim. After the fall of Samaria in 722 BC, a redactor combined these two disparate sources into a single document, JE. The D document, which was mainly the book of Deuteronomy, was composed in 622 BC by King Josiah's scribes as a tool for his religious reformation. The P document was written by priests early in the Second Temple period, after the Jews' return from exile, in the late sixth or early fifth century BC. All these sources were then combined in or around 450 or 400 BC to form the Pentateuch.[5]

---

4   Wellhausen was not the first to postulate that sources lay behind the Pentateuch. Others, going back as early as the seventeenth century, had also proposed to identify sources. Such proposals paved the way for Wellhausen's hypothesis. For a review of source-critical enquiry, see Joseph Blenkinsopp, *The Pentateuch: An introduction to the first five books of the Bible* (New York, NY: Doubleday, 1992), 1–30.

5   For the details of Wellhausen's source divisions, see S. R. Driver, *An Introduction to the Literature of the Old Testament* (repr.; Cleveland, OH and New York, NY: Meridian, 1956), 1–159.

The 'real novelty' of Wellhausen's conclusions was not so much his literary-critical conclusions, since others had been postulating since the seventeenth century that sources were used in the composition of the Pentateuch, as his use of source criticism to completely reconstruct Israel's history.[6] In his reconstruction, Wellhausen relegated the Priestly material, with all of its cultic laws and regulations, to the post-exilic period. While later redactors had retrofitted them to the time of Moses in order to fit their canonical portrayal of Israel's history, the reality was that written law was a later development of post-exilic Judaism. According to Wellhausen, J and E reflected a primitive stage of nature religion based on the kinship group. During this time, worship was spontaneous; it was simply the result of a person's yearning to respond to the divine. Worship was not regulated by cultic institutions and their laws, since these things only evolved later. Instead, Wellhausen believed that the prophets, disassociated from these later cultic institutions, stoked the fires of early Israel's ethical but non-institutional worship. When prophecy ceased in Ancient Israel, it was the death knell of Israel's spontaneous and free worship life. When the law developed in later periods, it distorted and stultified the primitive worship of Israel's earlier periods. Whereas early Israel had enjoyed free and uninhibited worship, the development of written cultic legislation represented the *de*volution to wooden or even dead religion. Wellhausen's *Prolegomena* is a reconstruction of Ancient Israel's history based on this hypothesis.

With regard to the book of Exodus, analysis of it on the basis of the Documentary Hypothesis was made available to English readers in S. R. Driver's 1897 *Introduction to the Literature of the Old Testament* and in his commentary on Exodus, published in 1911.[7] In this view, the final copy of the book of Exodus was the product of a basic J source having been combined with a more fragmentary and incomplete E account. This combined JE account was expanded with the addition of P material, which provided aetiological stories for many of Ancient Israel's cultic practices, including circumcision, the death of the firstborn, Passover, the Feast of Unleavened Bread, the giving of first fruits, Sabbath observance and the construction of the tabernacle with its associated cultic rituals. The narrative reached its final form when a post-exilic compiler arranged these materials into a clear and powerful story.

---

6 Rudolf Smend, *From Astruc to Zimmerli: Old Testament scholarship in three centuries*, trans. M. Kohl (Tübingen: Mohr Siebeck, 2007), 95–6.

7 Driver, *Introduction to the Literature of the Old Testament*; S. R. Driver, *The Book of Exodus* (Cambridge: Cambridge University Press, 1911).

Criticism, embrace and the fading of the traditional consensus

Wellhausen's publication of his *Prolegomena* caused pandemonium in theological circles. He was branded a heretic. In Germany, Franz Delitzsch criticized the Documentary Hypothesis as 'merely the application of Darwinism to the sphere of theology and criticism'.[8] In America, William Henry Green published a substantial tome refuting the hypothesis and defending the unity of the Pentateuch. Several of those who supported Wellhausen, including Charles Briggs, a Presbyterian minister and Professor of Hebrew and Cognate Languages at Union Theological Seminary, were defrocked, and William Robertson Smith, a theology professor at Aberdeen, was dismissed from his teaching position.

In the middle-to-final decades of the nineteenth century, archaeological excavations had begun to be conducted at Khorsabad, Nimrud and Nineveh in Mesopotamia, and at Tell el-Hesi in Israel. By the early decades of the twentieth century, a wealth of completely new data – which had not been available when Wellhausen constructed his four-source model – revealed problems with some of the main premises of the Documentary Hypothesis. For example, it became evident that deities in the Ancient Near East often had multiple names with different shades of meaning, and authors of ancient texts varied their usage of the names depending on which was more appropriate to the given context. In another example, it became clear from the study of Semitic literature that duplication was not an indication of multiple sources but rather a Semitic technique for emphasizing an idea. The author of Genesis uses this principle to explain Pharaoh's two dreams forecasting famine in the land: 'the doubling of Pharaoh's dream means that the thing is fixed by God, and God will shortly bring it about' (Gen. 41.32). One of the first to use this new data to mount a systematic refutation of the Documentary Hypothesis was Umberto Cassuto (1883–1951), Professor of Hebrew Language and Literature at the University of Florence, later Chair of Hebrew at the University of Rome and, finally, Chair of Bible Studies at the Hebrew University in Jerusalem.[9]

Despite the new archaeological and literary data being retrieved in the Near East, the four-source theory was quickly embraced. In fairly short order, it became the critical orthodoxy and was widely replicated, sometimes with some slight variations, in introductions to the Old Testament. By the mid twentieth century, nearly all introductions to the Old Testament presented

---

8 Rudolf Smend, 'Julius Wellhausen and his *Prolegomena to the History of Israel*', *Semeia* 25 (1982): 14.

9 Umberto Cassuto, *The Documentary Hypothesis and the Composition of the Pentateuch* (Jerusalem and New York, NY: Shalem Press, 2006). The eight lectures presented in this volume were originally presented by Cassuto in 1940.

the Documentary Hypothesis as 'the consensus opinion and the received wisdom'.[10] The most influential of all the twentieth-century introductions was probably *The Old Testament: An introduction*, by Otto Eissfeldt, which went through three editions.[11] In the twenty-first century, the standard introductions continue to present the Documentary Hypothesis as the normative model for understanding the formation of the Pentateuch.[12]

There has been a growing awareness, however, of the nineteenth-century ideological assumptions upon which the Documentary Hypothesis is based, some of which are no longer considered valid. In a survey of Pentateuchal scholarship, Joseph Blenkinsopp points out that, 'as closely argued and brilliantly original as it is, Wellhausen's historical reconstruction is very much a product of the intellectual milieu of the late nineteenth century'.[13] The influence of the nineteenth century upon his thought can be seen in at least three ways. First, as we have already noted, Wellhausen was heavily influenced by the concept of development. His model was not concerned with simply identifying multiple source documents, but with using them to reconstruct Israel's religious development in distinct theological stages. Second, he was heavily influenced by romanticism, in which every cultural phenomenon has primitive, classical and decadent stages. Wellhausen's J and E sources represented the more primitive stage of nature religion in early Israel; D brought the period of prophecy to an end by its production of a written law; and P marked the replacement of the natural religion with institutionalism, dead law and formalized worship.[14] Third, Wellhausen was influenced by nineteenth-century German Protestant theology, which could often be anti-Jewish.[15] In Wellhausen's reconstruction, the law was not a natural development in Ancient Israelite religion, but an imposition by a post-exilic religious sect. It was a later distortion of early Israel's primitive worship. Whereas the worship of early Israel

---

10 Blenkinsopp, *Pentateuch*, 19.

11 Otto Eissfeldt, *The Old Testament: An introduction* (3rd edn; New York, NY: Harper & Row, 1966).

12 E.g. Barry L. Bandstra, *Reading the Old Testament: Introduction to the Hebrew Bible* (4th edn; Belmont, CA: Wadsworth, 2008); Lawrence Boadt, *Reading the Old Testament: An introduction* (2nd edn; New York, NY: Paulist Press, 2012); John J. Collins, *Introduction to the Hebrew Bible* (3rd edn; Minneapolis, MN: Fortress Press, 2018); Michael D. Coogan, *The Old Testament: A historical and literary introduction to the Hebrew Bible* (4th edn; Oxford: Oxford University Press, 2017); Norman K. Gottwald, *The Hebrew Bible: A socio-literary introduction* (Minneapolis, MN: Fortress Press, 2002).

13 Blenkinsopp, *Pentateuch*, 11.

14 On German idealism, see Andrew Bowie, *Introduction to German Philosophy: From Kant to Habermas* (Cambridge: Polity Press, 2003), 41–93.

15 Cf. Lou H. Silberman, 'Wellhausen and Judaism', *Semeia* 25 (1982): 75–82. For a thorough study of this subject, see Anders Gerdmar, *The Roots of Theological Anti-Semitism: German biblical interpretation and the Jews, from Herder to Kittel and Bultmann* (Leiden: Brill, 2009).

had been free, natural and spontaneous, in post-exilic Israel it was 'banished into institutions'.[16] This is the opposite of the biblical view, in which the law is the Magna Carta of earliest Israel, not an invention of post-exilic Judaism.

In North America, the traditional Documentary Hypothesis remains the conventional wisdom. One recent monograph, for example, argues that the Documentary Hypothesis still provides the most persuasive explanation of the composition and meaning of the Pentateuch,[17] and another proposes to present its assured results.[18] However, the increasing recognition of the theory's commitment to nineteenth-century ideologies, along with the fact that its practitioners continue to produce contradictory results and even new sources, has led to some disillusionment with it.[19] Thomas Römer writes that, 'In the current debate about the formulation of the Torah, the traditional consensus built on the documentary hypothesis has faded away', and that 'in Europe, most scholars have given up the Wellhausen paradigm'.[20] There is in North America and Israel a so-called Neo-Documentarian movement, but it simply builds upon the Documentary Hypothesis.

Paradigm shift from source criticism to literary criticism

This is not to say that newer approaches should reject source criticism altogether. If there is one thing historical criticism has done, it has made it clear that no single individual, including Moses, was responsible for producing all the materials contained in the Pentateuch or, in our case, the book of Exodus. The internal evidence of the book of Exodus makes it clear that various materials came from different sources. Moses is said to have written down the instructions about holy war (17.14), recorded certain laws (24.4; 34.27–28) and composed the Song of Moses (15.1–18). Some of the contents, however, are directly

---

16 Julius Wellhausen, *Geschichte Israels* (Erster Band; Berlin: G. Reimer, 1878), 413. Quoted in Silberman, 'Wellhausen and Judaism', 77.

17 Joel S. Baden, *The Composition of the Pentateuch: Renewing the Documentary Hypothesis* (New Haven, CT and London: Yale University Press, 2012).

18 Richard Elliott Friedman, *The Bible with Sources Revealed: A new view into the five books of Moses* (New York, NY: HarperSanFrancisco, 2003).

19 For a recent critique, see Joshua A. Berman, *Inconsistency in the Torah: Ancient literary convention and the limits of source criticism* (Oxford: Oxford University Press, 2017).

20 Thomas Römer, 'The revelation of the divine name to Moses and the construction of a memory about the origins of the encounter between Yhwh and Israel', in *Israel's Exodus in Transdisciplinary Perspective: Text, archaeology, culture, and geoscience*, ed. Thomas E. Levy, Thomas Schneider and William H. C. Propp (New York, NY: Springer, 2015), 308.

attributed to God: the Ten Commandments are said to have been spoken by God himself (20.1); the contents of the Book of the Covenant (20.22—23.33) were first spoken by God, who then commanded Moses to write them down; and the instructions for the manufacture of the tabernacle and related matters are said to have been spoken by God to Moses (25—31), and oral or written accounts of these materials must have been preserved. Other portions are attributed to other parties. For example, the text seems to imply that Miriam composed the song that she sang in commemoration of the crossing of the Red Sea (15.21). In another example, the genealogical information given in Exodus 6.14–25 is unattributed, but it must have been drawn from family records.

The foregoing examples suggest that the ultimate author(s) of the book of Exodus utilized sources. Many additional examples could be cited. George Coats identifies 89 distinct genres in Exodus, along with 20 stereotyped formulas.[21] All of the texts reflecting these genres were preserved in either oral or written form (or both) after the events they record had occurred. With regard to passages dealing with cultic instructions, recent studies have shown that such materials were preserved by priestly communities.[22] Surely, other groups preserved other materials, such as families preserving their own genealogies, and so on. The author of Exodus collected all of these materials and wove them together to create the book of Exodus.

There are several clues that suggest that someone other than Moses compiled Exodus in its present form. Most of the book is comprised of third-person narratives, one of which praises Moses (11.3). Throughout the book, there are several parenthetical notes aimed at clarifying matters for later readers, one of which refers to events that occurred after the time of Moses (16.31–36; cf. Josh. 5.10–12). It is certainly possible that the materials attributed to Moses could have been preserved and assembled by someone contemporaneous with him, such as his acolyte Joshua or the priest Eleazar. The remaining third-person narrative accounts could have been preserved as oral tradition. These materials could have then been woven together, with some light editing to modernize archaic words and geographic place names (e.g. 15.23). Exodus and the rest of the Pentateuch may have existed in a primitive form as early as the days of the elders of Israel (Josh. 24.31), or the era of Samuel and the early monarchy (1 Sam. 3.19–21).

---

21   George W. Coats, *Exodus 1–18* (FOTL 2A; Grand Rapids, MI: Eerdmans, 1999), 155–78.

22   E.g. Bryan C. Babcock, *Sacred Ritual: A study of the West Semitic ritual calendars in Leviticus 23 and the Akkadian text Emar 446* (BBRSup 9; Winona Lake, IN: Eisenbrauns, 2014); Daniel E. Fleming, *Time at Emar: The cultic calendar and the rituals from the diviner's house* (Winona Lake, IN: Eisenbrauns, 2000).

In source criticism, however, identifying sources in a given book tends to be the focus. Introductions and commentaries that take a source-critical perspective often devote much – if not most – of their examination of the text to the identification and separation of sources. In William Propp's massive, two-volume commentary on Exodus, for example, he subjects every passage in Exodus to a highly detailed source analysis in which he identifies passages and their parts with the conventional sources J, E or P.[23] Thomas Dozeman, on the other hand, concludes that E does not feature in the compositional history of Exodus, and instead identifies a 'P History' and a 'Non-P History' as its chief sources.[24] This focus is a necessity to source criticism because, in this approach, the literary identification and separation of the sources is the means to a proper understanding of Israel's history of religion.

Beginning in the 1940s, a paradigm shift from source criticism to literary criticism had begun to occur.[25] It did not begin to gain traction, however, until the 1979 publication of Brevard Childs' *Introduction to the Old Testament as Scripture*, in which he urged that, in addition to dissecting the texts, we must also try to read and interpret them as they have come down to us, a process he called 'canonical interpretation'.[26] Childs was not calling for a departure from the historical-critical method, but rather a change in the focus. Whereas the traditional interest of historical-critical scholarship is in the presumed earlier stages of the text, Childs was arguing that the text also needs to be considered in its final form. He emphasized that the Old Testament was the sacred Scripture of a faith community and should be read as such.

Since the publication of Child's *Introduction*, the literary study of the Old Testament has burgeoned. In a popularly written 1989 article, Rolf Rendtorff wrote that 'recently, some of us have been asking, What about the *book* [of Exodus]? Should we not ask what the final author (or authors) of the *book* wanted to tell the readers?'[27] Indeed, more and more, scholars are focusing on the final form of the text, paying attention to the text as a carefully constructed whole. Handbooks like *The Art of Biblical Narrative, The Literary Guide to the Bible, Poetics and Interpretation of Biblical Narrative* and *The Poetics of Biblical*

---

23 William H. C. Propp, *Exodus 1–18: A new translation with introduction and commentary* (AB 2; New Haven, CT: Yale University Press, 1999); William H. C. Propp, *Exodus 19–40: A new translation with introduction and commentary* (AB 2A; New York, NY: Doubleday, 2006).

24 Thomas B. Dozeman, *Exodus* (ECC; Grand Rapids, MI: Eerdmans, 2009), 35–43.

25 The beginning of the paradigm shift could be associated with the lectures given by Umberto Cassuto in 1940 (see above, n. 8).

26 Brevard S. Childs, *Introduction to the Old Testament as Scripture* (Philadelphia, PA: Fortress Press, 1979).

27 Rolf Rendtorff, 'What we miss by taking the Bible apart', *BRev* 14.1 (1998): 44.

Narrative have shown that the Bible is a serious literary work, utilizes sophisticated literary techniques and warrants careful literary study.[28] Since the late 1960s, there have been a number of commentaries on Exodus published that focus on the literary analysis of the book in its final form.[29]

It should also be noted that, in its final form, the book of Exodus can be said to be 'Mosaic'. Whether or not a form of Exodus and the rest of the Pentateuch came into existence during the days of the elders of Israel, or the era of Samuel or later, their contents are Mosaic regardless. They are comprised of some materials that may have actually been composed by Moses, other materials that preserve the teachings of Moses, and accounts that conserve traditions about Moses. In this sense, when Philo, Josephus and the rabbis attributed the books of the Pentateuch to Moses, they were not wrong. When Jesus, Paul and Luke referred to the law as the 'law of Moses', or even simply as 'Moses', they were not mistaken. Indeed, the Pentateuch in general and the book of Exodus in particular contain the teachings of Moses.

Conclusions

There is a great deal more that could be said about reading the book of Exodus as literature.[30] In this chapter, however, we have focused on the rise of source criticism, its predominance in the academy, and the recent paradigm shift from source criticism to literary criticism. Whereas source criticism focuses on the identification of literary sources in a given book in an effort to reconstruct the history of Ancient Israel's religion, literary criticism studies the final form of the text, in the context of the whole canon of Scripture, in order to determine what its final author or authors wanted to tell its readers. In the ensuing chapters, we will relate to the book in its final form, rather than to its proposed constituent parts.

---

28 Robert Alter, *The Art of Biblical Narrative* (New York, NY: Basic, 1981); Robert Alter and Frank Kermode, eds, *The Literary Guide to the Bible* (Cambridge, MA: Belknap Press, 1987); Adele Berlin, *Poetics and Interpretation of Biblical Narrative* (Winona Lake, IN: Eisenbrauns, 1994); Meir Sternberg, *The Poetics of Biblical Narrative: Ideological literature and the drama of reading* (Bloomington, IN: Indiana University Press, 1985).

29 Walter Brueggemann, 'The book of Exodus', in vol. 1 of *The New Interpreter's Bible*, ed. L. Keck et al. (Nashville, TN: Abingdon Press, 1994), 676–981; Umberto Cassuto, *A Commentary on the Book of Exodus* (repr.; Jerusalem: Magnes Press, 1997); Brevard S. Childs, *The Book of Exodus: A critical, theological commentary* (Philadelphia, PA: Westminster Press, 1974); Nahum M. Sarna, *Exodus* (JPS Torah Commentary; Philadelphia, PA: Jewish Publication Society, 1991).

30 See, for example, the essays in Thomas B. Dozeman, ed., *Methods for Exodus* (MBI; Cambridge: Cambridge University Press, 2010).

3

The realia of Exodus

From the 1940s through the 1960s, there was an association of North American and European Protestant scholars who, although they acknowledged the legitimacy of historical criticism, held strongly to the idea that God had revealed himself in history. These scholars were part of what came to be known as the 'biblical theology movement'.[1] They read the Bible for the Church, wanted to recover it as a theological book, emphasized its unity and argued that God had revealed himself in history. With the publication of his monograph *God Who Acts: Biblical theology as recital*, G. Ernest Wright established himself as one of the key leaders of the biblical theology movement.[2] In it, he asserted that, 'In Biblical faith everything depends upon whether the central events actually occurred', and that 'to participate in Biblical faith means that we must indeed take history seriously as the primary data of the faith'.[3] For the members of the biblical theology movement, Old Testament theology presupposed the history of Israel.

By the mid 1960s, however, a crisis had begun to percolate in Israelite historiography.[4] Beginning with the patriarchs, critics began to challenge both traditional understandings of Israelite historiography and the historical accounts in the Old Testament.[5] Since that time, the fortunes of history within Old Testament theology have waxed and waned.[6] In this intellectual climate, the exodus traditions have not fared well, and numerous scholars have concluded that they are part of a fiction created by later Israelites that cannot

---

1   Gerhard F. Hasel, 'Biblical theology movement', in *Evangelical Dictionary of Theology*, 2nd ed.; ed. W. A. Elwell (Grand Rapids, MI: Baker, 2001), 163-66.

2   G. Ernest Wright, *God Who Acts: Biblical theology as recital* (SBT 8; London: SCM Press, 1952).

3   Wright, *God Who Acts*, 126-7.

4   Cf. the account in Brevard S. Childs, *Biblical Theology in Crisis* (Philadelphia, PA: Westminster Press, 1970).

5   E.g. Thomas L. Thompson, *The Historicity of the Patriarchal Narratives: The quest for the historical Abraham* (New York, NY: de Gruyter, 1974); John Van Seters, *Abraham in History and Tradition* (New Haven, CT: Yale University Press, 1975).

6   For an overview, see Elmer Martens, 'The oscillating fortunes of "history" within Old Testament theology', in *Faith, Tradition, and History: Old Testament historiography in its Near Eastern context*, ed. A. R. Millard, J. K. Hoffmeier and D. W. Baker (Winona Lake, IN: Eisenbrauns, 1994), 313–40.

be correlated with anything that occurred in Ancient Egypt.[7] William Dever concludes that 'there [is] no archaeological evidence for an exodus' and that 'the history of the Exodus [is] a dead issue'.[8] In their 2001 book, *The Bible Unearthed: Archaeology's new vision of Ancient Israel and the origins of its sacred text*, Israel Finkelstein and Neil Asher Silberman take for granted that the exodus traditions are simply a 'brilliant product of the human imagination'.[9]

Nevertheless, as others have already observed, scholars have not drawn these conclusions on the basis of new archaeological discoveries that have definitively proven that the events recounted in the book of Exodus did not occur. Instead, they seem to be based on the *lack* of direct archaeological evidence for those events. In this chapter, we will first consider the absence of evidence for the exodus, and then proceed to discuss the question of whether we might establish a broad time frame within which an exodus may have occurred. We will then discuss the one historical referent that we do have in the book of Exodus: the supply cities mentioned in 1.11. We will consider two issues that are often raised as the most serious obstacles for the believability of the exodus, including the number of those Israelites who left Egypt, and the lack of evidence for the Israelites in the wilderness of the Sinai. And, finally, we will consider what may be the most significant evidence for the exodus.

The absence of evidence for the exodus

The absence of direct evidence for the Israelite sojourn in Egypt, the exodus and the wilderness wanderings has certainly been among the leading reasons for rejecting the historicity of these events. There are several areas in which evidence has been lacking. First, there has never been any clear and indisputable reference to 'Hebrews' or 'Israelites' in any Egyptian records. However, as Joshua Berman points out, this should not be surprising. He notes that

---

7   E.g. William G. Dever, *Who Were the Early Israelites and Where Did They Come From?* (Grand Rapids, MI: Eerdmans, 2003); William Johnstone, *Exodus* (OTG; Sheffield: JSOT Press, 1990); Niels Peter Lemche, *Ancient Israel: A new history of Israelite society* (BibSem 5; Sheffield: JSOT Press, 1988), 109; Donald B. Redford, *Egypt, Canaan, and Israel in Ancient Times* (Princeton, NJ: Princeton University Press, 1992), 257–63; James Weinstein, 'Exodus and archaeological reality', in *Exodus: The Egyptian evidence*, ed. E. S. Frerichs and L. H. Lesko (Winona Lake, IN: Eisenbrauns, 1997), 87–103.

8   William G. Dever, 'Is there any archaeological evidence for the exodus?', in *Exodus* (ed. Frerichs and Lesko), 81.

9   Israel Finkelstein and Neil Asher Silberman, *The Bible Unearthed: Archaeology's new vision of Ancient Israel and the origins of its sacred texts* (New York, NY: Free Press, 2001), 8.

'the Egyptians referred to all of their West-Semitic slaves simply as "Asiatics," with no distinction among groups'.[10] This is typical of the way the Egyptians portrayed all foreigners, whom they 'depicted as strangers and generalized as an ethnic group with negative qualities'.[11] It is similar to how slaveholders in the New World related to their slaves, whom they did not identify by their specific provenance in Africa but simply called 'Negroes' after the colour of their skin.[12]

Second, there have never been any inscriptions found that make reference to any of the events in the book of Exodus. However, as Kenneth Kitchen points out, public stelae were designed to laud the pharaoh and his achievements, not highlight his gaffes. A pharaoh would not have commissioned a stele that acknowledged a failure on his part.[13] It should not be surprising, therefore, that no reference to an Israelite exodus has ever been found in any Ancient Egyptian inscription.[14]

And, third, there has never been any non-inscriptional evidence from the region of the Egyptian Delta that mentions 'Hebrews', 'Israelites' or anything connected with any of the events associated with the exodus. Not a single clay tablet, papyrus or even a fragment of a papyrus has ever been found mentioning anything to do with the events in the book of Exodus. However, as in the previous cases, this should not be a surprise. There are almost no papyri from dynastic times, and none at all have been found in the eastern Nile Delta where the Hebrews dwelled.[15] It is not that there are no papyri from the eastern Nile Delta that relate to the events in the book of Exodus; there are no papyri from the eastern Nile Delta at all.

This raises a very important methodological issue: the use of data *not* collected or *not* found as evidence. David Merling observes that, 'Generally speaking, such archaeological nonevidence . . . is given the same weight as collected data, as though they were of the same value.'[16] He points out, however, that non-evidence does not really exist but is 'the construct of an interpreter', who determines the meaning of that non-data.[17] Historian David Hackett

---

10   Joshua Berman, *Ani Maamin: Biblical criticism, historical truth and the Thirteen Principles of Faith* (Jerusalem: Maggid, 2020), 44.

11   Stuart Tyson Smith, 'People', *OEAE* 3:32.

12   As observed by Berman, *Ani Maamin*, 44.

13   Kenneth A. Kitchen, 'Exodus, The', *ABD* 2:707.

14   G. Wheeler, 'Ancient Egypt's silence about the exodus', *AUSS* 40 (2002): 257–64.

15   Cf. Bridget Leach and John Tait, 'Papyrus', *OEAE* 3:22–4.

16   David Merling, *The Book of Joshua: Its theme and role in archaeological discussions* (AUSDDS 23; Berrien Springs, MI: Andrews University Press, 1997), 240.

17   Merling, *Book of Joshua*, 241.

Fischer calls this approach the myth of 'negative proof', which he describes as 'an attempt to sustain a factual proposition merely by negative evidence'.[18] He argues that evidence must always be positive, and that 'Negative evidence is a contradiction in terms – it is no evidence at all.'[19]

Numerous cases could be cited in which the claims of a historical record cannot be verified by positive archaeological evidence. One of the most famous of such cases is that of the battle of Megiddo in 1457 BC, which occurred during Thutmoses III's first military campaign against Canaan. The battle is described in great detail in numerous ancient sources, including royal sources, private documents and the biographies of officers who participated in the battle.[20] In the course of the campaign, Thutmoses III's army went into battle against a coalition of Canaanites on a plain near Megiddo, some of whom ultimately took refuge in the city of Megiddo. Megiddo was heavily fortified, and so Thutmoses III built a siege ramp out of timbers in order to try to gain access to it. He besieged the city for seven months. Archaeologists, however, have not been able to find any evidence of the siege at all. They have not been able to find Late Bronze Age fortifications at Megiddo or any remains of Thutmoses III's siege ramp.

Despite the absence of evidence for the battle of Megiddo, no historian has ever questioned the reliability of the ancient texts that recount it. Despite the lack of corroborating data, historians give these ancient texts the benefit of the doubt. The texts are viewed as 'innocent until proven guilty'. Unfortunately, a double standard is often applied to the biblical texts, which are often treated as 'guilty until proven innocent'.[21] This 'hermeneutics of suspicion' preconditions some scholars to view any absences of evidence as negative proof. Adopting a consistent methodology, however, would require that we approach the biblical text using the same methodology as that which we apply to other Ancient Near Eastern texts. This means that we should view it as 'innocent until proven guilty' and give it the benefit of the doubt, unless we find compelling evidence to do otherwise.[22]

---

18 David Hackett Fischer, *Historians' Fallacies: Toward a logic of historical thought* (New York, NY: Harper & Row, 1970), 47.

19 Fischer, *Historians' Fallacies*, 62.

20 For a discussion of all the texts related to the campaign, see Donald B. Redford, *The Wars of Syria and Palestine of Thutmose III* (Leiden: Brill, 2003).

21 William G. Dever, *What Did the Biblical Writers Know and When Did They Know It? What archaeology can tell us about the reality of Ancient Israel* (Grand Rapids, MI: Eerdmans, 2002), 128.

22 For a discussion of criteria that are often used to disqualify biblical texts as historiographic in nature, see Ralph K. Hawkins, *How Israel Became a People* (Nashville, TN: Abingdon Press, 2013), 7–18.

The date of the exodus

The book of Exodus provides little data that can be used to determine an absolute date for the events recorded in its pages. There are no known extrabiblical texts that mention the exodus, and the book of Exodus provides few historical referents for identifying its historical setting. Nevertheless, scholars have proposed two main theories for the date of the exodus. The first, known as the 'early date', dates the exodus to 1446 BC, while the second, known as the 'late date', places it somewhere around 1280–1260 BC.

The early-date scenario is based primarily on a literal reading of 1 Kings 6.1, which states that Solomon began building the Temple in the fourth year of his reign, 480 years after the exodus. Thanks to Near Eastern synchronisms, we know that Solomon's fourth year was in 966 BC and, when that is combined with the number 480, it yields a date of 1446 BC for the exodus, right in the middle of Egypt's Eighteenth Dynasty (1550–1292 BC). Some Evangelical scholars refer to 1446 BC as the 'biblical date' of the exodus. However, Egypt continued to exercise hegemony over Canaan and Syria through the Late Bronze Age, until about 1250 BC. The idea that the Israelites could attack vital interests in Canaan without evoking a response from Egypt during this period seems unlikely. The biblical traditions associated with the conquest do not reflect such clashes with Egypt, nor does the archaeological evidence support a fifteenth-century Israelite emergence in Canaan, either by conquest or by peaceful immigration.

The late-date scenario, on the other hand, is based primarily on archaeological data from the thirteenth century BC, which points to a date for the exodus events sometime during Egypt's Nineteenth Dynasty (1292–1189 BC). These data include:[23]

1   *The city of Pi-Ramesses.* This can probably be identified with the supply city of 'Rameses' mentioned in Exodus 1.11. Pi-Ramesses only flourished from about 1270 to 1120 BC, in the Nineteenth Dynasty. There is no archaeological or textual evidence that the region was known as Ramesses or that there was a city known as Ramesses there during the previous Eighteenth Dynasty.[24]

---

23   For discussion of the sources relating to most of this data, see Hawkins, *How Israel Became a People*, 67–90.

24   Cf. further the discussion under 'The supply cities', below.

2 *The fact that Pharaoh resided in Rameses.* His residence here, which
  enabled Moses and Aaron to visit him so easily and regularly,[25] only
  occurred in the Ramesside era.[26]

3 *The 'Way of the Philistines'.*[27] The Israelites avoided this route when they
  left Egypt (Exod. 13.17). It was a system of stations and forts that had
  been built as part of the renewal of Egypt's military and administrative
  presence in north Sinai at the beginning of the Nineteenth Dynasty.[28]

4 *The Song of Moses.* The song is composed in archaic Hebrew, and most
  scholars agree that it dates to the thirteenth to twelfth centuries BC.[29]

5 *The form of the Sinai covenant.* This corresponds to that of suzerain–
  vassal treaties from the late second millennium, between about 1400 and
  1200 BC.[30]

6 *The Amarna texts.* These texts include 307 tablets that record
  correspondence between the Canaanite city-states of Syria-Palestine
  and Pharaoh Amenophis IV (1353–1337 BC), to whom they were vassals.
  The Canaanite tablets are from tributary rulers who address Pharaoh
  as 'my lord' and ask him to intervene in local power conflicts, and thus
  illustrate that Egypt was still viewed as having authority over Canaan in
  the fourteenth century BC.

7 *The crumbling of the Late Bronze Age system in the eastern
  Mediterranean world.* Along with Egypt's waning domination in

---

25 E.g. Exod. 5.1; 7.10, 20; 8.1–6, 8, 20–23, 25; 9.1–5, 8–10, 13–19, 27–33; 10.1–3, 16–18, 24–28; 11.1–8; 12.31–32.

26 Cf. Manfred Bietak, 'On the historicity of the exodus: what Egyptology today can contribute to assessing the biblical account of the sojourn in Egypt', in *Israel's Exodus* (ed. Levy, Schneider and Propp), 17–37; Kenneth A. Kitchen, 'Egyptians and Hebrews, from Ra'amses to Jericho', in *The Origin of Early Israel – Current Debate: Biblical, historical, and archaeological perspectives, Irene Levi-Sala Seminar, 1997*, ed. Shmuel Aḥituv and Eliezer D. Oren (Beer-Sheva: Ben-Gurion University of the Negev Press, 1998), 80–4; Eric P. Uphill, 'Pithom and Raamses: their location and significance', *JNES* 27.4 (1968): 291–316.

27 An anachronistic name for a route along the Mediterranean coast of Sinai known in the Egyptian sources as 'The Ways of Horus'.

28 Cf. Eliezer D. Oren, 'The "Ways of Horus" in north Sinai', in *Egypt, Israel, Sinai: Archaeological and historical relationships in the biblical period*, ed. Anson F. Rainey (Tel Aviv: Tel Aviv University Press, 1987), 69–119. More recently, see James K. Hoffmeier and Stephen O. Moshier, '"The Ways of Horus": reconstructing Egypt's east frontier defense network and the military road to Canaan in New Kingdom times', in *Excavations in North Sinai: Tell el-Borg I*, ed. James K. Hoffmeier (Winona Lake, IN: Eisenbrauns, 2014), 34–61.

29 Cf. Frank Moore Cross Jr, *Canaanite Myth and Hebrew Epic* (Cambridge: Cambridge University Press, 1973), 121–5; David Noel Freedman, 'Early Israelite history in the light of early Israelite poetry', in *Unity and Diversity: Essays in history, literature, and religion of the Ancient Near East*, ed. Hans Goedicke and J. J. M. Roberts (Baltimore, MD: Johns Hopkins University Press, 1975), 3–23.

30 Cf. Kenneth A. Kitchen and Paul J. N. Lawrence, *Treaty, Law and Covenant in the Ancient Near East*, 3 vols (Wiesbaden: Harrassowitz, 2012), Part 3: *Overall Historical Survey*, 117–213.

Canaan, this change left a political vacuum in the highlands of Canaan that created a window of opportunity for new settlement.

8 *A surge of new villages established in the highlands of Canaan.* This development, which occurred during the political vacuum mentioned above, represents a new demographic group in Canaan that shared a homogeneous culture and can be identified as 'Israelite'.[31]

9 *The Early Iron Age site on Mt Ebal.* A monumental structure, this appears to have served as a central cultic site for the early settlers. It was initially founded in about 1230 BC, remodelled at the end of the thirteenth or the beginning of the twelfth century BC, and continued in use until it was decommissioned in about 1140 BC. The structure may be associated with the altar of Joshua 8.30–35.[32]

10 *The Merneptah Stele.* This artefact contains a hymn that includes an account of a triumph over Asiatic peoples, including Israel, in its last poem. The stele commemorates an Egyptian campaign into Canaan that can be dated to the first few years of Merneptah's reign, *c.*1210 BC, and therefore attests that, by that date, the Israelites had settled there.

Since the Merneptah Stele, however, makes it clear that the Israelites were in Canaan by about 1210 BC, an exodus in the early decades of the Nineteenth Dynasty, possibly during the reign of Ramesses II, would not allow for 480 years to have elapsed between the exodus and Israel's emergence in Canaan. Those who hold to a late date for the exodus, therefore, must be willing to interpret the 480 years of 1 Kings 6.1 symbolically.[33] A date in the early-to-mid thirteenth century BC, in the Nineteenth Dynasty, has essentially become the consensus date for those who hold that a historical exodus occurred.[34]

The supply cities

Exodus 1.11 states that the Hebrews were put to forced labour and compelled to build supply cities for the pharaoh at 'Pithom and Rameses'. Storage facilities were important branches of temples, palaces or other administrative

---

31 For a summary of the discussion about identifying these highland sites as 'Israelite', see Hawkins, *How Israel Became a People*, 137–57.

32 Cf. the analysis of the structure in Ralph K. Hawkins, *The Iron Age I Structure on Mt. Ebal: Excavation and interpretation* (Winona Lake, IN: Eisenbrauns, 2012).

33 For a summary of this approach, cf. Hawkins, *How Israel Became a People*, 49–55.

34 Lawrence T. Geraty, 'Exodus dates and theories', in *Israel's Exodus* (ed. Levy, Schneider and Propp), 58–9.

buildings, and were often made of brick.[35] Since the names of Pithom and Ramesses are the only historical referents in the entire book of Exodus, their identification, nature and date are crucial for any discussion of the realia behind the exodus narratives.

Pithom

Pithom is named only once in the entire Old Testament, in Exodus 1.11. It is mentioned alongside Ramesses as being one of two 'supply cities' built by the Israelites. The name is known from the Ramesside period onwards.[36] There have been several places with the name Pithom in the Wadi Tumilat, but the only one with evidence of having been occupied in the Ramesside period is Tell el-Retaba.[37] This site is in a parallel situation with the supply city of Ramesses, and W. F. M. Petrie found substantial remains there from the Ramesside period.[38] These included the monumental temple-façade blocks of Ramesses, which included a relief and inscription that portrayed Ramesses II sacrificing enemies in front of the god Atum. This suggests that the temple was dedicated to Atum. Petrie also found a group statue of Ramesses II with Atum. Although it has not been excavated, if it is correctly identified, it would be consistent with a thirteenth-century BC exodus.[39]

Ramesses

It is well known that Ramesses II (1279–1213 BC) built a city named Pi-Ramesses, which means 'House of Ramesses', in the north-eastern delta.[40] Based on this information, scholars naturally concluded that the exodus occurred either late during the long reign of Ramesses II, or during the reign of Merneptah, his thirteenth son. Labib Habachi, a Coptic Christian Egyptologist, began investigating the site of Qantir in the 1950s, which he had concluded was to be identified as Pi-Ramesses, and, although it took a few decades, a consensus began to emerge that Qantir was indeed Pi-Ramesses.[41] A German team began excavating the site in 1980, and the picture that has emerged is of a city that flourished from about 1270 to 1120 BC, and that there was no city known as Ramesses

35 Cf. Edward Bleiberg, 'Storage', *OEAE* 3:327–9.
36 Bietak, 'On the historicity of the exodus', 26, n. 43.
37 Manfred Bietak, 'Comments on the "exodus"', in *Egypt, Israel, Sinai* (ed. Rainey), 168–9.
38 W. M. Flinders Petrie, *Hyksos and Israelite Cities* (London: Office of School of Archaeology University College and Bernard Quaritch, 1906), 29–30, pls 32A, 34, 35C.
39 Kitchen, 'Egyptians and Hebrews', 72–8.
40 A. H. Gardiner, 'The delta residence of the Ramessides pt. I', *JEA* 5 (1918): 127–271.
41 L. Habachi, 'Khatana-Qantir: importance', *ASAE* 52 (1954): 443–559.

there during the Eighteenth Dynasty.[42] These data have seemed to support the earlier supposition about an exodus during the Nineteenth Dynasty.

In 1925, Old Testament historian James Jack, who subscribed to an early-date exodus, recognized that the identification of the thirteenth-century Pi-Ramesses with the supply city of Ramesses in Exodus 1.11 presented a problem for an exodus in the fifteenth century BC. He sought to deal with this by arguing that the later editor of the text modernized the name in order to make it more easily identifiable for readers in his own day.[43] This position has continued to be held by many Evangelicals, including C. Aling, G. L. Archer, E. H. Merrill, M. F. Unger, B. G. Wood and L. J. Wood.[44] Editorial glossing did occur in the Hebrew Bible but, as James Hoffmeier observes, typically both the former name and the contemporary name occur together.[45] For example, Genesis 14.2 refers to 'Bela (that is, Zoar)'.[46] Longer descriptions of name changes also occur, such as when Jacob slept at a certain place and dreamed of the stairway to heaven when he was travelling to Haran. On this occasion, the text says that 'he called that place Bethel; but the name of the city was Luz at the first' (Gen. 28.19). While the place name Ramesses occurs five times in the Old Testament, the formula that includes the old name plus the new name is never used, nor is a longer explanation ever given. Hoffmeier concludes, therefore, that 'there is no evidence within these five passages to suspect that "Ramesses" is an editorial gloss'.[47] In sum, there is no archaeological or textual evidence to support the theory that the region was known as Ramesses or that there was a city known as Ramesses there during the Eighteenth Dynasty. Pi-Ramesses only flourished from about 1270 to 1120 BC, after which it was replaced by Zoan, which became the dominant city of the north-eastern delta for the next thousand years.[48]

---

42 See M. Bietak and E. Czerny, eds, *Tell El-Dab'a I: Tell El-Dab'a and Qantir, the site and its connections with Avaris and Piramesse* (Vienna: Austrian Academy of Sciences Press, 2001).

43 J. W. Jack, *The Date of the Exodus: In the light of external evidence* (Edinburgh: T&T Clark, 1925), 25–8.

44 Charles Aling, 'The biblical city of Ramses', *JETS* 25.2 (1982): 129–38; G. L. Archer, *A Survey of Old Testament Introduction* (rev. edn; Chicago, IL: Moody, 1994), 231–3; Eugene H. Merrill, *Kingdom of Priests: A history of Old Testament Israel* (rev. edn; Grand Rapids, MI: Baker, 2008), 26–88 (Merrill only considers this a possibility, while he is inclined towards other solutions); M. F. Unger, *Archaeology and the Old Testament* (4th edn; Grand Rapids, MI: Zondervan, 1960), 149; B. G. Wood, 'The rise and fall of the 13th-century exodus-conquest theory', *JETS* 48 (2005): 479; L. J. Wood, *A Survey of Israel's History* (rev. and enlarged by D. O'Brien; Grand Rapids, MI: Zondervan, 1986), 73–4.

45 James K. Hoffmeier, 'What is the biblical date for the exodus? A response to Bryant Wood', *JETS* 50.2 (2007): 233.

46 Additional examples cited by Hoffmeier include Gen. 14.3, 7, 17; 23.2.

47 Hoffmeier, 'A response to Bryant Wood', 234.

48 Ralph K. Hawkins, 'Zoan', *NIDB* 5:990.

The number of Israelites who left Egypt

One of the most serious obstacles to the believability of the exodus is the number of Israelites who purportedly left Egypt. John Laughlin writes:

> According to biblical tradition, several million people wandered around the Sinai Peninsula for forty years. Yet not a single trace of such a group has ever been recovered. Surely, if this event as described in the Bible actually happened, *something* of the presence of so many people would have turned up by now, if nothing more than camp sites with datable pottery.[49]

In this section, we will consider the number of the Israelites who participated in the exodus and, in the next, we will consider the lack of evidence for a large body of people travelling in the Sinai for 40 years.

The book of Exodus claims that 'six hundred thousand men on foot' left Egypt with Moses.[50] If each of these men had a wife and two children, the number of the exodus group would swell to 2,400,000. If a few of the 600,000 had three or four children, then the number would jump to three or even four million persons. There are at least four significant problems with these high numbers. First, such high numbers are not just unlikely, but literally impossible. George Mendenhall points out that, 'Marched twenty-five abreast, this many people would form a column almost two hundred miles [320 km] long, meaning that the front of the line would have reached Mount Sinai before the back of the line had left Egypt.'[51] Second, the high numbers do not make sense. If there were really three to four million Israelites who left Egypt in the exodus, why would they be terrified of an Egyptian chariot force that numbered only 600 chariots (Exod. 14.7)? Or, if there were really three to four million Israelites, how could they be overcome by wild animals once they had entered the land of Canaan (Exod. 23.29–30)? Third, the high numbers actually contradict the Bible. Moses told Israel that, when the LORD led them into the promised land, he would clear away 'the Hittites, the Girgashites, the Amorites, the Canaanites, the Perizzites, the Hivites, and the Jebusites, seven nations mightier and more numerous than you' (Deut. 7.1). He explained further that 'it was

---

49   John C. H. Laughlin, *Archaeology and the Bible* (New York, NY: Routledge, 1999), 91.

50   Exod. 12.37; see also Num. 1.46; 26.51.

51   George E. Mendenhall, *Ancient Israel's Faith and History: An introduction to the Bible in context*, ed. Gary A. Herion (Louisville, KY: Westminster John Knox Press, 2001), 52.

not because you were more numerous than any other people that the LORD set his heart on you and chose you – for you were the fewest of all peoples' (Deut. 7.7). Fourth, the high numbers also contradict the archaeological data from the Canaanite highlands, where there was a dramatic increase in settlements at the end of the Late Bronze Age (1550–1200 BC). Estimates based on the carrying capacity of the highland villages suggest that there were around 20,000 to 50,000 Israelites there in the twelfth century BC, and that this population grew to about 150,000 in the Iron Age I (1200–1000 BC).

At issue is the meaning of the Hebrew word *'eleph* (plural, *'elephim*), which has traditionally been translated as 'thousand' in English Bibles. If a text states that there were 10 *'elephim*, therefore, it would be translated 10,000; 20 *'elephim* would be 20,000; 30 *'elephim* would be 30,000; and so on. It is the translation of *'eleph* as a thousand and *'elephim* as thousands that leads to the extremely high numbers in Exodus and Numbers.

The term *'eleph* does not always mean 'thousand', but appears to sometimes mean something like 'unit'. For example, the judge Gideon complained that he could not join the military action against the Midianites because his *'eleph*, the military unit over which he had oversight, was too small (Judg. 6.10). The term may, depending on its context, refer to a 'unit' of soldiers rather than to the number 1,000. A cognate term appears in other Ancient Near Eastern texts and, when it occurs, it refers to a squad comprised of anywhere between six and 20 men. If such a meaning is valid for *'eleph* when it occurs in the lists of Exodus and Numbers, then the 600 squads enumerated therein could represent a total fighting force of only about 5,000 men on foot, representing the total fighting force of Israel. Some commentators argue that lowering the numbers reduces the wilderness wandering and its miraculous provision to naturalistic proportions. However, the miraculous nature of God's provision for the Israelites in the wilderness is not affected by whether their numbers were large or small.[52]

Hebrews in the wilderness

The other major objection to the historicity of the exodus is the lack of evidence for the Israelites in Sinai. There is plenty of archaeological evidence for

---

52 See further, Jerry Waite, 'The census of Israelite men after their exodus from Egypt', *Vetus Testamentum* 60 (2010): 487–91. Cf. also David Merling, 'Large numbers at the time of the exodus', *NEASB* 44 (1999): 15–27; Ralph K. Hawkins, 'The forty-thousand men of Joshua 4:13', in *Hebrew and Beyond: Studies in honor of Rodney E. Cloud*, ed. David Musgrave (Montgomery, AL: Amridge University Press, 2016), 150–8.

human occupation throughout Sinai in ancient times. That being the case, why is there no evidence of the *Israelite* presence in Sinai? In considering this question, there are several caveats that must be taken into account. First, the Bible reports that the Israelites lived in tents after the exodus and during the wilderness wandering.[53] This was certainly not unusual, and tent dwelling was deeply embedded in the consciousness of some peoples. Even after the Israelites had settled down in Canaan, there were some who continued to live in tents. There was a clan called the Kenites, who traced their ancestry to Jethro, who lived in tents in the Negev (Judg. 1.16). There was a conservative sect called the Rechabites who even continued to live in tents centuries after the wilderness period.[54]

In recent years, there has been much debate about whether nomads are discernible in the archaeological record. The general assumption has been that all people leave material remains, and therefore periods with no archaeological record represent periods of human absence. However, while it is true that sedentary people in settled areas usually leave a lot of archaeological evidence, in desert areas the opposite is true.[55] The archaeological evidence produced by nomadic societies is negligible, such that they are often archaeologically invisible. Israel Finkelstein, in his recent study of the Negev, provides a study of desert-dwelling nomads and the extent to which they register archaeologically.[56] He notes that they do not establish permanent houses, but live in tents which, by their very nature, leave virtually nothing for the archaeological record. He observes that there is very little rainfall in desert environments, which prevents nomadic peoples from developing significant agriculture and forces them to rely, instead, mainly on animal husbandry. The scarcity and seasonality of pasture, and the paucity of water sources, necessitates frequent relocation or at least seasonal migration. Observers of nineteenth-century bedouin reported that they moved their tent camps every 12 to 15 days in order to access new water sources as well as to pitch their tents on clean ground.[57] This constant migration allows them to take only minimal belongings. Furthermore, their limited resources do not facilitate the creation of a flourishing

---

53   E.g. Exod. 16.16; Num. 1.52; 9.17, 18, 20, 22, 23; Deut. 1.27.

54   Judg. 4.11–22; 5.24–26; Jer. 35.6–8.

55   For a survey of the issues, see C. Chang and H. A. Koster, 'Beyond bones: toward an archaeology of pastoralism', *Advances in Archaeological Method and Theory* 9 (1986): 97–148.

56   Israel Finkelstein, *Living on the Fringe: The archaeology and history of the Negev, Sinai and neighbouring regions in the Bronze and Iron Ages* (Sheffield: Sheffield Academic Press, 1995; repr. 2001), 23–30.

57   Eveline van der Steen, *Near Eastern Tribal Societies during the Nineteenth Century: Economy, society and politics between tent and town* (Sheffield: Equinox, 2013), 91–2.

material culture that would leave rich archaeological finds. Instead, it is based 'mostly on natural materials such as leather, textiles and wood that decompose over time'.[58]

Earlier in the chapter, I cited the objection of John Laughlin, who insists that, 'Surely,' if a large number of Israelites wandered in the desert for 40 years, '*something* of the presence of so many people would have turned up by now, if nothing more than camp sites with datable pottery'.[59] In a recent study entitled *To Your Tents, O Israel!*, Michael Homan examines the archaeology of tents and pastoral nomads to determine whether they would leave evidence of campsites.[60] He explains that 'tents by their very nature leave very little for the archaeological record, and the extent to which they were employed at settlements . . . cannot be determined'.[61] This is even the case in major military operations that utilized tent encampments. At the battle of Megiddo in 1457 BC, discussed above, Thutmoses III inhabited a tent throughout the seven-month campaign. However, no evidence of Thutmose III's encampment, his siege works or the battle itself have ever been recovered. Later, at the famous battle of Qedesh (1274 BC), Ramesses II inhabited a tent throughout the campaign. This battle was so famous that it was recorded numerous times. Homan summarizes:

> The profound impression made by the battle is evident from the fact that not only are the events of Qedesh captured for posterity epigraphically in ten different places, but they are artistically depicted on the walls of many Egyptian monuments. Scenes of the battle exist at Abydos, Karnak, Luxor, the Ramesseum, and Abu-Simbel, while depictions of the Egyptian camp adorn walls at Abu Simbel, Luxor, and twice at the Ramesseum.[62]

Despite the magnitude of this battle and the fact that it involved thousands of soldiers and hundreds of horses and chariots, no evidence of Ramesses II's encampment has ever been discovered, even after a century of exploration and excavation. In view of the lack of evidence for such massive military operations, it should come as no surprise that tent camps have not been found for the few thousand Israelites that wandered the Sinai after the exodus.

---

58 Finkelstein, *Living on the Fringe*, 25.

59 Laughlin, *Archaeology and the Bible*, 91.

60 Michael M. Homan, *To Your Tents, O Israel! The terminology, function, form, and symbolism of tents in the Hebrew Bible and the Ancient Near East* (Leiden: Brill, 2002), 47–59.

61 Homan, *To Your Tents*, 55.

62 Homan, *To Your Tents*, 66.

As far as finding datable pottery that might be associated with Israelites wandering in the Sinai, travellers in the Ancient Near East typically used skins to transport liquids instead of pottery. Pottery is heavy and impractical for travel, whereas skins are lightweight and, once they have been emptied, can easily be folded up and stored among the gear. The Beni Hasan tomb painting illustrates the use of skins for carrying liquids.[63] It portrays 15 persons, whom the caption refers to as 'Asiatics', coming to Egypt to trade, and several of them have skins of water slung over their shoulders. Similarly, the Old Testament contains numerous accounts of people carrying skins of water.[64] Again, it is no surprise that hoards of pottery that can be identified with the Israelites have not been found in the Sinai.

There are types of evidence that may be found in arid zones. These include hunting installations, cemeteries, cult places, rock drawings and rock inscriptions, and even settlements.[65] However, these typically represent periods when peoples have settled down. It is when people settle down that they begin to produce tangible remains. When they live nomadically, 'they may not leave traceable remains behind them'.[66]

The location of Mt Sinai

One of the most important sites in the book of Exodus is Mt Sinai. After the exodus, the Israelites travelled to the foot of this mountain, where they entered into a covenant with the LORD and received the law (Exod. 19.1—40.38). The location of this important mountain, however, is not precisely known. The main Sinai expanses are called the 'wilderness of Paran',[67] and the mountain is even referred to twice as 'Mount Paran'.[68] However, in Exodus, Leviticus and Numbers it is usually (though not always) referred to as 'Mount Sinai', although in other places the name Horeb is often used.[69] These two names appear to refer to the same site and were apparently interchangeable. The site

---

63 *ANEP*, 3.

64 E.g. Gen. 21.14, 19; Judg. 4.19; 1 Sam. 1.24; 16.20.

65 Finkelstein, *Living on the Fringe*, 15–21.

66 Finkelstein, *Living on the Fringe*, 15. See also the recent article by Thomas W. Davis, 'Exodus on the ground: the elusive signature of nomads in Sinai', in *'Did I Not Bring Israel Out of Egypt?' Biblical, archaeological, and Egyptological perspectives on the exodus narratives*, ed. James K. Hoffmeier, Alan R. Millard and Gary A. Rendsburg (Winona Lake, IN: Eisenbrauns, 2016), 223–39.

67 E.g. Num. 10.12; 12.16; 13.3.

68 Deut. 33.2; Hab. 3.3.

69 'Horeb' is used 17 times in the Old Testament, in: Exod. 3.1; 17.6; 33.6; Deut. 1.2, 6, 19; 4.10, 15; 5.2; 9.8; 18.16; 28.69; 1 Kings 8.9; 19.8; 2 Chron. 5.10; Ps. 106.9; Mal. 3.22.

is also sometimes called 'the mountain of God'[70] or 'the mountain of the LORD' (Num. 10.33). The location of this mountain has been one of the most vigorously debated questions in the historical geography of the Old Testament.

There have been at least a dozen proposals for the identification of Mt Sinai in three main regions: (1) north-west Saudi Arabia or southern Jordan; (2) the northern Sinai Peninsula; or (3) the steppes of the southern Sinai Peninsula. Those who hold to a location in north-west Saudi Arabia or southern Jordan have proposed Gebel Biggir, Gebel el-Lawz and Hallat el-Badr as possible identifications. Those who argue for a location in the northern Sinai Peninsula have proposed Gebel Helal and Har Karkom as viable contenders. And those who prefer a location in the steppes of the southern Sinai Peninsula have proposed Gebel Musa, Gebel Serbal and Gebel Katherina as the best candidates.[71]

While they do not provide enough information for us to identify the exact mountain that features so prominently in the book of Exodus, the corresponding travel itineraries of Exodus 15—19 and Numbers 33 do enable us to identify the region and therefore rule out several of the aforementioned proposals. Once they had crossed the sea, the Israelites entered Sinai, travelled three days into the wilderness and then stopped to camp in several different locations before they reached Mt Sinai. Another piece of the puzzle is found in Deuteronomy 1.2 which, reflecting on the journey out of the wilderness and through Edom, states that, 'By way of Mount Seir it takes eleven days to reach Kadesh-barnea from Horeb.' Since Kadesh-barnea was probably just inside Israel's southern border, an 11-day journey from there to Mt Sinai 'can only point to a place in southern Sinai and rules out most alternatives'.[72]

Early Christian tradition recognized Mt Sinai as Gebel Musa, meaning 'Mount Moses', which is located in the southern Sinai Peninsula, and this identification has a lot to commend it. It dates back to at least the early fourth century, when Helena, the mother of Constantine, ordered that the Chapel of the Burning Bush be built in the valley below the mountain, at the site where Moses was supposed to have encountered the LORD at the burning bush. A few decades later, in AD 360, a Syrian monk named Julianus Sabus, along with some of his disciples, built another chapel on the peak of the mountain. In the

---

70 E.g. Exod. 4.27; 18.5; 24.13.

71 For a detailed consideration of all of these possible identifications, see Barry J. Beitzel, *The New Moody Atlas of the Bible* (Chicago, IL: Moody, 2009), 109–13.

72 Anson F. Rainey and R. Steven Notley, *The Sacred Bridge: Carta's atlas of the biblical world* (Jerusalem: Carta, 2006), 120.

sixth century, Emperor Justinian I (reigned 527–65) ordered that a monastery be built to enclose the Chapel of the Burning Bush. The monastery was later named after a virgin named Catherine who, according to tradition, was martyred at Alexandria in the early fourth century. While this location has been the destination of thousands of pilgrims over the years, there are four other Christian monasteries in the area, which points to the early Christian belief that this was the vicinity where the Israelites encamped around a mountain. While there is no direct archaeological evidence to connect the Israelites with any specific mountain in the region, the distances from Egypt and Kadesh-barnea, along with early Christian tradition, fit best with a location for Mt Sinai in the southern Sinai Peninsula.

The exodus tradition

The most significant evidence for the exodus as a whole is probably its embeddedness in the Israelite consciousness. The LORD's liberation of the Israelites from Egypt and his presence with them in the wilderness is viewed as the core of Israel's distinctive identity. God had told the Israelites that they were his 'treasured possession out of all the peoples' of the earth (Exod. 19.5), and the proof of this was that God had liberated them from slavery in Egypt and established his presence with them in the wilderness. After the golden calf episode, when the LORD's presence with the Israelites came under threat, Moses implored God, saying:

> For how shall it be known that I have found favour in your sight, I and your people, unless you go with us? In this way, we shall be distinct, I and your people, from every people on the face of the earth.
> (Exod. 33.16)

Forty years later, as the Israelites stood on the brink of the promised land, Moses reminded them of how unique the exodus events were. He said:

> Ask from one end of heaven to the other: has anything so great as this ever happened or has its like ever been heard of? Has any people ever heard the voice of a god speaking out of a fire, as you have heard, and lived? Or has any god ever attempted to go and take a nation for himself from the midst of another nation, by trials, by signs and wonders, by war, by a mighty hand and an outstretched arm, and by terrifying displays of power, as the LORD your God did for you in Egypt before your very eyes?

(Deut. 4.32–34)

These questions are rhetorical, and their implied answer is a categorical no! No other god has ever manifested himself in the way that God manifested himself to the Israelites at Mt Sinai. No other god has ever plucked a people from the midst of another nation in the way that God brought the Israelites out of their slavery in Egypt, by levelling the ten plagues against their oppressor, and by protecting them and preserving them in such dramatic and powerful ways. The Israelites viewed the exodus events as the core of their identity and uniqueness. The exodus made them who they were.

Over and over, throughout the Old Testament, its authors repeat that the LORD brought Israel 'up from the land of Egypt' and 'redeemed' it 'from the house of slavery'. The Israelites were not native to the land of Canaan, but had come 'out of Egypt'. Allusions to the exodus and its themes in the Old Testament are beyond counting. The story of the exodus events is *the* central story of the Old Testament. It is *the* foundational act of salvation in the Old Testament. The exodus and wilderness narratives shape the religion of later Israel. They serve as the historical prologue to the Sinai covenant and provide the foundation for laws, religious festivals, observances and rituals. Even foreigners like Jethro, Balaam and Rahab acknowledged the exodus from Egypt. The salvation that occurred in the exodus events is the subject of Israel's hymns and the starting point of many of the sermons of the prophets. It provides the paradigm for God's future redemption of Israel and, indeed, the world.[73]

How did the story of the exodus attain such status in Israelite society? Scholars have put forward many hypotheses. For example, Ronald Hendel, who believes that the Israelites were never in Egypt but evolved from the Canaanites, postulates that they transformed their memories of Egyptian domination in Canaan into a memory of liberation from Egyptian bondage.[74] In another case, Donald Redford proffers that the book of Exodus represents later Israelite co-opting of the story of the Hyksos occupation of the Nile Delta, their rule of a large part of Egypt and their expulsion after a reign of 108 years.[75] And,

---

73   These and other examples will be discussed in Chapters 11 and 12.

74   Ronald Hendel, 'The exodus as cultural memory: Egyptian bondage and the Song of the Sea', in *Israel's Exodus* (ed. Levy, Schneider and Propp), 65–77.

75   Donald B. Redford, 'The great going forth: the expulsion of West Semitic speakers from Egypt', in *Israel's Exodus* (ed. Levy, Schneider and Propp), 437–45.

in yet another instance, William Dever concludes that it is a foundation myth whose basic elements were simply invented.[76]

None of these hypotheses, however, adequately accounts for the pervasive belief among the Ancient Israelites that they had been slaves in Egypt and that God had liberated them. This belief spans from the Song of the Sea (Exod. 15), which may date as early as the twelfth century BC,[77] to the post-exilic prophet Haggai (Hag. 2.5). From the book of Exodus until the end of the Old Testament, the exodus and its associated events are constant themes that shape every aspect of Israelite identity. The idea that the Israelites would invent a fictitious history of an ignominious past in which they had been slaves in a foreign land stretches credulity. Foundation myths are designed to edify the noble – sometimes even divine – origins of a people, not embarrass them. And yet the story of Israel's experience in Egypt is anything but noble. The Israelites are enslaved and oppressed for 430 years and, after their liberation, they do nothing but complain in the wilderness. When their God establishes a covenant with them, they immediately disregard the stipulations of the covenant by worshipping a golden calf. It is only by the sheer grace of God that the Israelites are saved and fashioned into 'a kingdom of priests and a holy nation' in whose midst God himself condescends to dwell. Those who believe that the exodus is a fabrication must provide an explanation for this. In lieu of such an explanation, the persistence of the exodus traditions themselves provides their own best evidence.

Conclusions

In the past, Jewish and Christian readers accepted the story of Exodus, or at least its basic outline, at face value. In recent decades, however, traditional understandings of historiography have changed and the historical accounts contained in the book of Exodus have come into question. The primary reason for rejecting the historicity of the Exodus accounts has been a lack of evidence for them. In this chapter, we discussed the absence of evidence for the exodus, and concluded that it is not unusual that it has no extrabiblical attestation. We considered the milieu in which an exodus may have occurred, and found that a date in the late thirteenth century BC, in the Nineteenth Dynasty, has

76 William G. Dever, 'The exodus and the Bible: what was known; what was remembered; what was forgotten?', in *Israel's Exodus* (ed. Levy, Schneider and Propp), 399–408.

77 Frank Moore Cross Jr and David Noel Freedman, 'The Song of Miriam', *JNES* 14 (1955): 237–50; Frank Moore Cross Jr and David Noel Freedman, *Studies in Ancient Yahwistic Poetry* (SBLDS; Missoula, MT: Scholars Press, 1975; repr. Grand Rapids, MI; Eerdmans, 1995), 1–45.

essentially become the consensus date for those who hold that a historical exodus occurred. We saw that the identification of Qantir as the supply city of Pi-Ramesses bolsters that date. We also discussed the number of Israelites who left Egypt and the question of whether or not we should expect to find their archaeological footprint in the Sinai wilderness. In the end, we saw that the persistence of the exodus traditions themselves may be the most significant evidence for the realia behind the book of Exodus, for they became the basis on which the nation of Israel's existence was predicated. It was because they had seen what the LORD had done to the Egyptians, and because God had brought them safely through the wilderness to Mt Sinai, that they entered into covenant with him and became his 'treasured possession', 'a priestly kingdom and a holy nation' (Exod. 19.5–6).

4
Beginnings

People of every tribe and nation throughout human history have wanted to know who they are and where they came from. Most cultures have stories of origins that answer such questions. Such stories are foundational to their societies, providing what the famous anthropologist Bronislaw Malinowski called a 'foundation myth', and serving as a 'sacred charter' that legitimizes their political and religious identity.[1] The book of Exodus is such a book. It 'contains what may well be considered the most grandiose and influential story ever told', which is the beginning of 'the shift from polytheism to monotheism'.[2] As such, it is not only the 'founding myth' of Ancient Israel, but also 'that of monotheism as such, a key constituent of the modern world'.[3] The book of Exodus recounts a number of profound beginnings that are formative for Ancient Israel. These include the early life and call of Moses, the so-called revelation of the divine name, the first Passover and the founding of Israel as a nation by means of the Sinai covenant.

The early life and call of Moses

The story of Moses has resonated with people throughout the generations. A story of a child born into slavery who became a prince, but who eventually gave up his privileged position to side with the slaves, it has inspired the admiration of many people. It has provided the inspiration for Jewish midrash, Christian sermons, African spirituals and even modern films. Part of the reason the Moses story has had such enduring appeal may have to do with the mystery associated with it. How did a Hebrew child, the son of slaves, become a prince of Egypt? Did either he himself or the Egyptians know he was a Hebrew? Why did he eventually come to sympathize with the Hebrews? And why,

---

1   E.g. Bronislaw Malinowski, *A Scientific Theory of Culture* (Chapel Hill, NC: University of North Carolina Press, 1944).

2   Jan Assmann, *The Invention of Religion: Faith and covenant in the book of Exodus* (Princeton, NJ: Princeton University Press, 2018), 1.

3   Assmann, *Invention of Religion*, 1.

after killing an Egyptian taskmaster, who was certainly of lower rank than he, did Moses flee Egypt and remain in a self-imposed exile for 40 years? And how did he come to return to Egypt to liberate the Hebrews at the end of that time? We will examine these and other questions in the course of reviewing Moses' early life and call.

The book of Exodus begins by recalling that the family of Jacob had migrated to Egypt during a period of famine in Canaan. Joseph had risen to the position of vizier in Egypt, and he was able to facilitate the immigration of his family to what had become his homeland. The Hyksos kings (1750–1570 BC), who were Asiatic immigrants themselves, had probably put Joseph into his prominent position. However, they were driven out of Egypt by Ahmose, the founder of the Eighteenth Dynasty, at the end of that period, and eventually 'a new king arose over Egypt, who did not know Joseph' (Exod. 1.8). As the Israelites increased in number, Pharaoh came to fear them and eventually enslaved them for the building of the supply cities Pithom and Ramesses (Exod. 1.11). The oppression did nothing to quell the growth of the Hebrew people, and their numbers continued to increase. Pharaoh ordered that the Hebrew midwives should allow female children to be born, but were to kill male children (1.15–16). The midwives feared God, however, and would not obey the king of Egypt, and the Hebrews continued to multiply (1.17–20). The pharaoh finally issued a decree that, 'Every boy that is born to the Hebrews you shall throw into the Nile, but you shall let every girl live' (1.22).

It was into this situation that Moses was born. A Levite couple had a baby boy, 'and when she saw that he was a fine baby, she hid him for three months' (2.2). When it became impossible to hide him, she built a papyrus basket sealed with pitch, hid the baby in it and 'placed it among the reeds on the bank of the river' (2.3). His sister, Miriam, 'stood at a distance, to see what would happen to him' (2.4). While she was bathing in the Nile, Pharaoh's daughter noticed the basket and sent a servant to retrieve it from the water (2.5).

When she opened it, the child was crying and she took pity on it, observing, 'This must be one of the Hebrews' children' (2.6). This verse has sparked a great deal of debate: how could Pharaoh's daughter have known that the baby belonged to the Hebrews? The rabbis inferred that she must have seen that he was circumcised.[4] This is an interesting possibility, since it would indicate that the Hebrews faithfully maintained the mark of circumcision during their oppression in Egypt. It is also possible that the pharaoh's daughter simply assumed that he was one of the Hebrews' children, since she knew that her

---

4   Cf. *b. Soṭah* 12b; *Exod. Rab.* 1, 24. Cf. also Pseudo-Philo, 9.15.

father had decreed that all Hebrew male children were to be thrown into the Nile. The text itself does not provide an answer to how she would have known the child was a Hebrew, but it does heighten the suspense: knowing what she knows, how will she respond?[5] Will she have her father's decree enforced and have the child drowned on the spot? Or will she save him?

The pharaoh's daughter's response is revealed when the child's sister offered to find a Hebrew woman to act as a nursemaid, and she agreed (2.7). Miriam fetched Moses' Levite mother, and what happened next raises a host of questions:

> Pharaoh's daughter said to her, 'Take this child and nurse it for me, and I will give you your wages.' So the woman took the child and nursed it. When the child grew up, she brought him to Pharaoh's daughter, and she took him as her son.
> (Exod. 2.9–10)

It appears that Moses' mother took him back to the Hebrew slave camp in order to nurse him. Although the text does not say how long she kept the child, it does say that, when he had grown up, she brought him back to the princess. This probably means that she kept him until he had been weaned which, according to the Egyptian text Instructions of Ani, would have been about three years.[6] However, since the text does not say that she kept him until he was weaned, but simply until he had grown up, Greenberg concludes that Moses' mother kept him until he had reached boyhood.[7] In either case, during those years, he would have experienced the influence of Hebrew culture. His mother would have surely told him the stories of Abraham, Isaac, Jacob and Joseph. She would have told him about the promises that the LORD had made to the ancestors of Israel. She would have sung to him the songs of the LORD. She would have held him as she and her family participated in family and communal worship of the LORD. When she returned him to the pharaoh's daughter as a young boy, surely he would have had some awareness of his Hebrew identity.

After the child's mother brought him back to the pharaoh's daughter, the narrator reports that the princess gave him the Hebrew name 'Moses' (*mōsheh*), explaining that it was because 'I drew him (*meshîtihû*) out of the water' (2.10).

---

5 As observed in Cornelis Houtman, *Exodus*, Vol. 1 (Leuven: Peeters, 1993), 284.

6 *ANET*, 420d.

7 Moshe Greenberg, *Understanding Exodus: A holistic commentary on Exodus 1–11* (2nd edn; Eugene, OR: Cascade, 2013), 35–6.

There has been a great deal of controversy over the etymology of the Hebrew name Moses, which does not precisely match the explanation given by the princess. The Hebrew *mōsheh* actually means 'he who *draws* out', while it is the form *māshūy* that means 'he who *is drawn* out'. This should not be construed as misleading or as evidence against the historicity of Exodus, however, but simply as an example of the Israelite tendency to invent creative but imprecise etymologies.[8]

What is even more peculiar, though, is that an Egyptian princess should give her child a Hebrew name at all and, while it is certainly possible that she understood Hebrew or that a later editor translated her Egyptian words into Hebrew, most interpreters today view the name as Egyptian in origin.[9] The consensus today is that Moses derives from the Egyptian root *mss*, 'to be born', which features in many Egyptian theophoric names. For example: 'Ptahmose' means 'born of [the god] Ptah'; Ramesses means 'born of [the god] Ra'; and Thutmose means 'born of [the god] Thoth'. In this case, the name Moses is actually the final element in a longer theophoric name, with the initial god-element missing. If this view is correct, the princess may have given the child a full theophoric name that included the name of an Egyptian deity. Since he was pulled from the Nile, it could have been something like 'Hapimose', which would mean 'born of [the god] Hapi', who was god of the Nile.

If the name really does derive from Egyptian, however, why would the author say that the princess had named him Moses and explained it on the basis of a Hebrew pun (2.10)? Greenberg suggests several possible explanations, one of which is that the Hebrew passage may have been a translation from Egyptian, in which the name was different.[10] If that were the case, the princess may have originally given the child a theophoric name ending in -*mose* but, when he grew up, Moses himself dropped its god-component in order to distance himself from Egypt and its religion. Then, he transposed his Egyptian name Mose into Hebrew Moshe, and the popular Hebrew etymology – 'he who *is drawn* out' – came to be associated with it. The Hebrew author of the book of Exodus then attributed the popular etymology to the princess, who had first named him.

Incidentally, the prophet Isaiah later understood the Hebrew name Moses according to its correct meaning, 'he who *draws* out'. In Isaiah 63.11, he said

---

8 Cf. Yair Zakovitch, 'A study of precise and partial derivations in biblical etymology', *JSOT* 15 (1980): 31–50.

9 J. Gwyn Griffiths, 'The Egyptian derivation of the name Moses', *JNES* 12 (1953): 225–31.

10 Greenberg, *Understanding Exodus*, 36.

that, in a moment of penitence, the Israelites 'remembered the days of old, of Moses (*mōsheh*) his servant', and asked, 'Where is the one who brought (*mōsheh*) them up out of the sea with the shepherds of his flock?' If the name was originally Egyptian, its popular Hebrew etymology eventually replaced its previous Egyptian meaning.

In any case, regardless of the background of his name, the pharaoh's daughter took Moses 'as her son' (2.10). Whether this refers to legal or de facto adoption, it clearly means that he was assimilated into the royal family, which literally made him a prince of Egypt. Despite the protestations of some interpreters,[11] this means that he was raised as an Egyptian. The book of Exodus does not provide any details about Moses' early years, but being raised in the royal court would have certainly provided Moses with all the advantages of any son of a princess. He would have received a thorough education that would have included Egyptian religion, history, language and culture. He would have been taught court protocol, leadership and military strategy. Jewish and Christian traditions supplement the biblical data about Moses' early years with stories that demonstrate his princely honour and training.[12] Later legends portray him as performing all kinds of supernatural acts during these years, but these are probably apocryphal.[13] Without additional data, these 'silent years' must remain a mystery. What we can know is that Moses was raised as an Egyptian prince who would certainly have been comfortable in a royal setting.

The narrator passes over the next several decades and picks up the story in Moses' adulthood. The author of Exodus sets the stage generally in the time 'after Moses had grown up' (Exod. 2.11), while the New Testament (NT) specifies that it was 'when he was forty years old' (Acts 7.23).[14] In any case, when the story resumes, it continues to raise the question of Moses' identity. The account in Exodus states that he 'went out to his people and saw their forced labour' (Exod. 2.11). Did Moses recall his early years among the Hebrews and know that they were 'his people'? Or is this simply the narrator's observation that, when Moses the Egyptian went out and looked upon the Israelites, he was, even though he did not realize it, looking upon his own people?

---

11   E.g. Benno Jacob, *The Second Book of the Bible: Exodus*, trans. Walter Jacob (Hoboken, NJ: Ktav, 1992), 30–2.

12   Josephus, *Ant.* 2.9.6–10.2; Acts 7.22; *Shem. Rab.* 1.26.

13   Cf. S. R. Driver, *The Book of Exodus* (Cambridge: Cambridge University Press, 1911), 11–12; Louis Ginzberg, *The Legends of the Jews*, 6 vols (Philadelphia, PA: Jewish Publication Society, 1928): 2.269–89; Philo, *Mos.* 1.18–31.

14   Stephen's identification of Moses as 'forty' divides his life of 120 years into three clearly demarcated periods of 40 years each.

There are two accounts of the story in the NT that may hint at an answer. The first is in the speech given by Stephen, one of the early Church's first deacons. After he was arrested and hauled before the Sanhedrin for preaching that Jesus was the Messiah, he was allowed to respond to the accusations made against him. In his defence, he made a review of Hebrew history leading up to the death of Jesus (Acts 7.2–53).[15] As he reviewed Hebrew history, he made a brief summary of the story of Moses. After recounting his early years, Stephen said that, 'When he was forty years old, it came into his heart to visit his relatives, the Israelites' (Acts 7.23). Stephen seems to say that Moses knew the Israelites were 'his relatives', and that it 'came into his heart' to visit them. Maybe, when he was adopted into the princess's family, he was no longer allowed to associate with the Hebrews. Or, it could be that, as the years passed and he was immersed in Egyptian life and culture, he forgot them. Or possibly, as he grew, he came to view himself as an Egyptian and no longer wanted to associate with them.

In the second account, an early Christian synagogue homily that came into the New Testament as the book of Hebrews,[16] its author states that, 'By faith Moses, when he was grown up, refused to be called a son of Pharaoh's daughter, choosing rather to share ill-treatment with the people of God than to enjoy the fleeting pleasures of sin' (Heb. 11.24–25). Although they are sparse, these remarks make at least four claims about how Moses' views changed when he grew up. They indicate that, when Moses reached maturity: (1) he came to identify with the Hebrews; (2) he came to view Egyptian life and culture – or at least the Egyptian treatment of the Hebrews – as sinful; (3) he rejected his relationship with the pharaoh's daughter and therefore his position in the court; and (4) he chose to share in the Hebrews' ill-treatment. This may mean that, at some point after he had reached maturity, he either discovered or remembered that he was a Hebrew, [17] went out and looked upon his people, and felt sympathetic towards them. Something may have caused him to develop an affinity

---

15 The speech is made by Stephen, a Hellenist, to Jews. For a discussion of all aspects of the speech, see: Joseph A. Fitzmyer, *The Acts of the Apostles: A new translation with introduction and commentary* (AB 31; New York, NY: Doubleday, 1998), 361–88; Luke Timothy Johnson, *The Acts of the Apostles* (SP 5; Collegeville, MN: Liturgical Press, 1992), 122–38.

16 For a detailed discussion about the authorship and date of the book, as well as the identification of the book as a 'Christian synagogue homily', see Gareth Lee Cockerill, *The Epistle to the Hebrews* (NICNT; Grand Rapids, MI: Eerdmans, 2012), 2–16.

17 Fitzmyer writes that these remarks indicate that, 'Despite his Egyptian upbringing, Moses never forgot his background and his own people.' Cf. Fitzmyer, *Acts of the Apostles*, 376.

with them, and he rejected his position in the Egyptian court, and moved out of the royal residence and into the Hebrew slave community in Goshen.[18]

In any case, at some point, 'he saw an Egyptian beating a Hebrew, one of his kinfolk' and, after looking around to make sure no one was watching, 'he killed the Egyptian and hid him in the sand' (2.11–12). Stephen's speech provides another interesting assessment of Moses' actions. He explains that, 'He supposed that his kinfolk would understand that God through him was rescuing them, but they did not understand' (Acts 7.25). When Stephen's statement is taken into account, it appears that Moses had shifted his allegiance from the Egyptian court to the Hebrews, and was trying to interject himself into Hebrew society as a revolutionary leader.

The next day, Moses came across two Hebrews who were fighting, and he tried to arbitrate between them. They rejected him harshly, demanding, 'Who made you a ruler and judge over us? Do you mean to kill me as you killed the Egyptian?' (Exod. 2.14). One or both of these Hebrews viewed Moses as trying to impose himself as a 'ruler' (*śar*) and a 'judge' (*šōpēṭ*) among the Hebrews. A ruler was a royal official, and a judge was a magistrate or military leader. Both of these positions were part of earliest Israel's local leadership, and these Hebrews clearly resented Moses trying to posture in either role. Maybe they viewed him as an Egyptian and resented his attempts to lord his Egyptian authority over them. Or, if they understood that he was a Hebrew, maybe they resented the fact that he had been raised as a prince of Egypt, and they thought he had betrayed his heritage and no longer had a place in Hebrew society.

What happened next raises profound questions. The text states that, 'When Pharaoh heard of it, he sought to kill Moses' (2.15). What did Pharaoh hear about? Was it that Moses had killed an Egyptian taskmaster? This is extremely unlikely. Moses was a member of the royal house, a prince of Egypt. An Egyptian taskmaster would probably have been little more than a slave and may even have been a slave himself.[19] If the fact that Moses killed an Egyptian taskmaster was all that Pharaoh had heard about, this, in and of itself, would surely not have been enough for the Pharaoh to seek his life. If, however, Pharaoh had heard that Moses had renounced his Egyptian identity and sided instead with the Hebrews, that he had moved out of the palace and into the Hebrew slave camp, and that he sought to rally the Hebrews against him, then

---

18 However, neither Exodus, Acts nor Hebrews fills in the blanks for this episode in Moses' life. This inference makes sense, however, based on further developments in the story. Other legends elaborate extensively on Moses' actions. Cf. Eusebius, *Praep. ev.* 9.27.1–37; Philo, *Mos.* 1.32; and Josephus, *Ant.* 2.10.1–2 §238–53.

19 Cf. Kenneth A. Kitchen, 'From the brickfields of Egypt', *TynBul* 27 (1976): 137–47.

that would have been treason. And that would have certainly evoked the ire of the pharaoh. These were the things Moses found out that Pharaoh had heard about, and this was why he fled away from Egypt and into the desert of Midian.

The text says that, after having fled from Egypt, Moses 'settled in the land of Midian, and sat down by a well' (2.15). While he sat there, the daughters of Jethro, the priest of Midian, came to draw water, but some shepherds came and drove them away. Moses defended them, drove the shepherds away and watered their flocks (2.16–17). They went home and told their father that 'an Egyptian' had saved them from the shepherds and drawn water for them and their flocks (2.19). Apparently, even though Moses had shifted his allegiance from the house of Pharaoh to the Hebrews, so much of his life had been spent among the Egyptians that there was still something distinctively Egyptian about him. Maybe he still dressed like an Egyptian. Or maybe he either spoke Egyptian or spoke with an Egyptian accent. The text does not give any explanation but simply says that there was something about him that caused Jethro's daughters to identify him as an Egyptian. Moses' identity is still ambiguous.

Jethro invited Moses to dine with his family, and then to live among his people, the Midianites. Moses did so and, eventually, the priest gave Moses his daughter, Zipporah, in marriage. She bore a son, and Moses named him 'Gershom', based on the Hebrew word for 'sojourner' (*gēr*), with the explanation, 'I have been an alien residing in a foreign land' (2.22). The fact that Moses gave his son this name further illustrates his continuing identity crisis and 'betrays [his own] consciousness of his ambiguous status'.[20] Despite the fact that he had fled Egypt and had now married into the family of Jethro, a Midianite, he still thought of Egypt as his native land.

Moses became a shepherd, keeping the flocks of Jethro, his father-in-law (Exod. 3.1). This was yet another beginning for Moses. While Moses had arrived in Midian as an Egyptian prince who had been pampered as a child and raised with all the privileges of royalty, he was surely transformed by his 40-year sojourn in the desert among the Midianites. Living and working among a bedouin people was a major change from the urban life he had experienced as an Egyptian prince. Spending his days quietly among the flocks and herds, leading them to pasturage, providing them with water and taking care of their physical needs was a far cry from learning to read and write in hieroglyphic, studying the ancient history and religion of Egypt, and being trained in court protocol and military strategy. Moses' 40 years as a shepherd in the desert of

---

20   William H. C. Propp, *Exodus 1–18: A new translation with introduction and commentary* (AB 2; New York, NY: Doubleday, 1999), 177.

Midian served well to prepare him for the leadership tasks that lay ahead of him. In fact, the work of the shepherd was a common metaphor for leadership, both human and divine, in the Ancient Near East.[21] In the Old Testament, Israel's ideal king, David, first learned leadership by caring for his father's flocks and herds.[22] In Moses' case, the skills of a shepherd would be important during the 40 years of wilderness wandering after the exodus and en route to the promised land.

The last major beginning for Moses was God's call to him to return to Egypt to liberate the Hebrews and lead them to the promised land. This occurred 'a long time' after Moses had fled Egypt (2.23), 40 years, according to Stephen (Acts 7.30). The pharaoh of Moses' youth had died, and yet the Hebrews remained enslaved. They cried out to God for help, and he heard their cries. God 'remembered his covenant with Abraham, Isaac, and Jacob', 'looked upon the Israelites, and . . . took notice of them' (Exod. 2.23–25). God took action on behalf of the Hebrews by calling Moses. It happened one day, while he was tending sheep, that he discovered a strange phenomenon – a burning bush that was not consumed. God spoke to him from the bush, calling him closer but commanding him to remove his shoes since he was on holy ground. Then God announced that he was the God of his ancestors, Abraham, Isaac and Jacob (3.6).

What follows is a 'call narrative', an account in which God commissions Moses to return to Egypt on his behalf and liberate his people (3.1—4.31). The biblical call narrative is a standard genre which typically follows a set literary structure that contains six elements, including: (1) divine confrontation; (2) introductory word; (3) commission; (4) objection; (5) reassurance; and (6) sign.[23] The call of Moses is the most elaborate of any of the call narratives in the Bible. While it is typical of call narratives for those receiving God's call to resist, Moses resists repeatedly, raising five different objections over two chapters![24] In each case, God responds that he will be with Moses and help him to overcome any and every obstacle.[25]

Moses finally agreed to do what God asked of him, and he returned to the camp to speak with his father-in-law about it. If there was ever any doubt in

---

21 The Mesopotamian kings Lipit-Ishtar (*ANET*, 159c), Hammurabi (*ANET*, 164c, 165c, 178a) and Esarhaddon (*ANET*, 289a), for example, were all described as shepherds of their people. In the divine realm, the Egyptian sun god (*ANET*, 368a), Ptah (*ANET*, 371d) and Shamash (*ANET*, 388a), for example, were all described as shepherds.

22 David's ascent from the sheepfolds to the throne is summarized in poetic form in Ps. 78.70–72.

23 Norman Habel, 'The form and significance of the call narratives', *ZAW* 77 (1965): 298.

24 Exod. 3.11, 13; 4.1, 10, 13.

25 Exod. 3.12, 14–22; 4.2–9, 11–12, 14–17.

his mind about whether he was an Egyptian or a Hebrew, his words to Jethro show that he had finally resolved them. He said, 'Please let me go back to my kindred in Egypt and see whether they are still living' (4.18). The Hebrew word translated as 'kindred' is literally 'brothers'. Moses finally identified the Hebrews as his own family, distinguishing himself from the Egyptians and the Midianites. In his confrontation with the LORD, Moses' identity crisis has finally been resolved.

Several aspects of the story of Moses' early years have been said to be legendary features. The first of these is the tale of Moses being put in a basket in the Nile. Propp writes that:

> The historical Moses is most unlikely to have endured so traumatic an infancy . . . [and] any folklorist recognizes the tale of an imperiled child of illustrious lineage, abandoned by its natural parents and raised in obscurity by foster parents, only at length to come into its own. This is, more or less, the biography of Oedipus, Romulus, King Arthur, Snow White, Tarzan, Superman and innumerable less familiar heroes.[26]

He proposes that this aspect of the Moses story is a myth based on the trope of the 'floating foundling', for which he provides several parallels.[27] The most commonly cited parallel is that of the so-called 'Legend of Sargon'. Sargon was king of Akkad for 55 years during the third millennium BC. He was originally a cupbearer to the king of Kish, whom he overthrew in order to take the throne. He founded a new capital called 'Agade', which has never been found, though it may be in the vicinity of Babylon. He pushed east into Elam and west into Lebanon, and eventually controlled all Mesopotamia. According to the birth legend, Sargon was born to the high priestess, who was apparently not supposed to have children. She placed him in a basket and floated him down the river, where he was eventually picked up by 'Akki the Drawer of Water', who adopted him and raised him as his son. Eventually, he grew up to be king of Akkad.

Although the Sargon legend recounts events purported to have occurred in the third millennium BC, the earliest copies we have are found on tablets that date to the first millennium BC. The story of the birth of Sargon is often derided as a fabrication. Werner Keller famously writes that:

---

26 Propp, *Exodus 1–18*, 155.
27 Propp, *Exodus 1–18*, 155–8.

> The basket-story is a very old Semitic folk-tale. It was handed down by word of mouth for many centuries . . . It is nothing more than the frills with which prosperity has always loved to adorn the lives of great men.[28]

Some scholars assume that later Pentateuchal authors simply borrowed the details of the Sargon birth story and added them to the story of Moses' birth in order to give it the aura of a heroic tale. However, James Hoffmeier has conducted a thorough study of the narrative of Moses' birth (Exod. 2.1–10) and shown that many of its details are indisputably Egyptian.[29] Specifically, he demonstrates that much of the key vocabulary in Exodus 2.3, which provides the core features of the Moses birth narrative that are typically compared with the Sargon legend, consists of Hebrew words that either derive from or are transliterations of Egyptian words used in Egypt during the New Kingdom period, including 'basket', 'bulrushes', 'pitch', 'reeds', 'river' and 'bank'. Hoffmeier concludes that this substantial cluster of Egyptian terms points to an Egyptian rather than a Mesopotamian setting for the composition of the narrative. He also points out that it is unlikely that a scribe writing during the late Judean monarchy or in the exilic period would have been familiar with these Egyptian terms.[30]

In the end, both the Legend of Sargon and the story of the birth of Moses do share a common theme, which is that both children are 'exposed', or left to the elements. It is true that, in the Ancient Near East, the 'exposed child' was a common trope. In a thorough study of the topic, Donald Redford collected 32 examples of Near Eastern stories that draw on it.[31] But does the fact that it was common mean that it is necessarily mythical? Hoffmeier writes that:

> In the end, the reason for the multitude of stories from across the Near East and Mediterranean of casting a child into the waters is that it may reflect the ancient practice of committing an unwanted child, or one needing protection, into the hands of providence. A modern parallel would be leaving a baby on the steps of an orphanage or at the door of a church.[32]

28 Werner Keller, *The Bible as History* (2nd rev. edn; New York, NY: Morrow, 1981), 123.

29 James K. Hoffmeier, *Israel in Egypt: The evidence for the authenticity of the exodus tradition* (New York, NY: Oxford University Press, 1997), 138–40.

30 Hoffmeier, *Israel in Egypt*, 140.

31 Donald B. Redford, 'The literary motif of the exposed child (cf. Ex. ii 1–10)', *Numen* 14 (1967): 209–28.

32 Hoffmeier, *Israel in Egypt*, 138.

Another aspect of the story that is often said to be a legendary feature is that of Moses being reared in court as a prince of Egypt. However, data from the New Kingdom period (1550–712 BC) reveal that foreigners from the lowest to the highest social classes were sometimes raised in court and even adopted into the royal household. With regard to foreigners from the lowest social classes, a papyrus from the time of Ramesses XI (1107–1078/1077 BC) provides an example. The text recounts how Nebnūfer, the royal stable-master, and his wife, Rennūfer, purchased a female slave named Diniḥetiri and later adopted her children. Nebnūfer and Rennūfer wrote a declaration stating that Diniḥetiri and her children were no longer slaves, but that they were free persons of the land of Pharaoh with full inheritance rights.[33] With regard to higher social classes, there are records going back to at least the time of Thutmose III (1457–1425 BC) that recount how the princes of subject kings throughout western Asia were brought to Egypt for training. This would both ensure their fathers' loyalty as vassals and indoctrinate the next generation of vassal leadership.[34] Kitchen writes that, 'If indeed Moses was brought up at the Egyptian court in the E delta, he would have had plenty of other West-Semitic speaking colleagues to chat with.'[35]

Yet another aspect of the story that comes under question is the likelihood that an Egyptian prince would flee Egypt and settle among a bedouin people in the desert.[36] However, the 'Tale of Sinuhe' provides a literary parallel with striking similarities. This was a very popular Egyptian story, as attested by the discovery of numerous copies of it (five papyri and at least 17 ostraca) ranging in date from the Twelfth to the Twenty-first Egyptian Dynasty. The story is about a high-ranking Egyptian named Sinuhe who fell out of favour with Pharaoh and fled to Syria-Palestine, where he heard people speaking in his own language. He settled among tent-dwelling bedouin and eventually married the chieftain's eldest daughter. After many years, the pharaoh with whom he had fallen out died, and the new pharaoh sent a message to him that he should return home and appear before him.[37] The parallels are obvious, and they demonstrate that the movement of peoples back and forth from Egypt to Syria-Palestine, and vice versa, was not unusual at all.

---

33   Alan H. Gardiner, 'Adoption extraordinary', *JEA* 26 (1941): 23–9.

34   Kenneth A. Kitchen, 'Exodus, The', *ABD* 2:704.

35   Kitchen, 'Exodus, The', 704.

36   Cf. John Van Seters, *The Life of Moses: The Yahwist as historian in Exodus-Numbers* (Philadelphia, PA: Westminster John Knox Press, 1994), 29–33.

37   Miriam Lichtheim, 'Sinuhe', *COS* 1:77–82.

The revelation of the divine name

When Moses encountered God at the burning bush, and God said he was going to send him back to Egypt to liberate the Hebrews, Moses asked God to clarify his name. He said, 'If I come to the Israelites and say to them, "The God of your ancestors has sent me to you", and they ask me, "What is his name?" what shall I say to them?' (Exod. 3.13). In reply, God said, 'I am who I am' (*'ehyeh 'asher 'ehyeh*) (v. 14a). He went on to say:

> Thus you shall say to the Israelites, 'The LORD, the God of your ancestors, the God of Abraham, the God of Isaac, and the God of Jacob, has sent me to you':
>> This is my name for ever,
>> and this my title for all generations.
>
> (Exod. 3.15)

The name that God told Moses that he should use for him when he spoke to the Israelites consists of four consonants, *y-h-w-h*, and is therefore known as the 'Tetragrammaton', literally 'the four letters'. Most scholars think this name was probably pronounced 'Yahweh',[38] but the name does not appear in most English translations, which usually follow ancient precedent and render it as 'LORD' in capital letters.[39]

The divine name Yahweh may be a verbal form based on the Hebrew root *hwyh*, 'to be'.[40] Most scholars believe that it is a third-person imperfect of *hwyh*, though there is disagreement about whether it is in the simple stem (Qal) or the causative stem (Hiphil). In the simple stem, it could mean 'he was', 'he is' or 'he will be'. If the name Yahweh is in fact in the simple stem, its intended meaning would be something like 'he was, is and will be'. Such a name would powerfully convey the timelessness of God, who not only existed in the past but also exists in the present, and will always exist in the future.

---

38 Tropper makes a strong argument that the divine name should be rendered as 'Yahwa'. Cf. Josef Tropper, 'The divine name *Yahwa*', in *The Origins of Yahwism*, ed. Jürgen van Oorschot and Markus Witte (Berlin: de Gruyter, 2017), 1–21.

39 For a brief explanation of this tradition, see Bruce M. Metzger, 'To the reader', in *The New Interpreter's Study Bible: New Revised Standard Version with the Apocrypha*, ed. Walter J. Harrelson (Nashville, TN: Abingdon Press, 2003), xvii–xx.

40 Some have argued that, instead of explaining the name Yahweh using West Semitic etymology, we should look to Arabic etymology. Cf. Karel van der Toorn, 'Yahweh', *DDD*: 915. This argument, however, is based on the argument that Yahweh originated in Edom, or even further south, a theory known as the Kenite Hypothesis, which will be discussed later in this section.

In the causative form, Yahweh would mean something like 'he [who] causes [things] to be'.[41] In this case, the name would emphasize that not only is Yahweh the God who was, is and always will be, but he is also the causative force behind everything else that ever was, is or will be.

Both the timelessness of Yahweh and his nature as the causative force behind everything else that exists are emphasized in the Latter Prophets. Isaiah, for example, emphasizes that idols are temporal, while God is eternal. While they were formed of wood, stone or iron at a fixed point in time (e.g. Isa. 44.9–20),[42] Yahweh is eternal. God says, 'Before me no god was formed, nor shall there be any after me' (Isa. 43.10c), and he asks, 'Is there any god besides me? There is no other rock; I know not one' (Isa. 44.8b). Likewise, Jeremiah too emphasizes this difference. While idols are inanimate, Yahweh is alive and timeless. He explains that 'the LORD is the true God; he is the living God and the everlasting King' (Jer. 10.10a). At the same time, Jeremiah also stresses that Yahweh is the causative force behind everything that exists. 'It is he who made the earth by his power, who established the world by his wisdom, and by his understanding stretched out the heavens' (10.12). Yahweh 'is the one who formed all things' (v. 16a).

Whether the Tetragrammaton is in the simple stem or the causative stem, both aspects of Yahweh's character are certainly true. Yahweh is both timeless, in that he was, is and always will be, and he is also the causative force behind everything else that ever was, is or will be. The divine name is clearly intended to be viewed as expressing the complete distinctiveness of Yahweh. As Jeremiah exclaims, 'There is none like you, O LORD' (Jer. 10.6a).

God's existence and power are inherent in the powerful name Yahweh, which is certainly related to the stipulation in the Decalogue, 'You shall not make wrongful use of the name of the LORD your God', as well as the warning that 'the LORD will not acquit anyone who misuses his name' (Exod. 20.7). The name Yahweh took on extraordinary significance in later Judaism and, by the Achaemenid period, the custom had developed of not even pronouncing it. When Jews encountered the divine name in the liturgy, and even in everyday life, they would substitute expressions like 'the LORD' or 'the Name' in its place. Such traditions, including prohibitions against writing or erasing the divine name, were eventually enshrined in the *Sifrei*, the Mishnah and the Talmud.[43]

---

41   Hess points out that causatives of the verb *hyh* do occur in Aramaic, which supports the possibility that 'Yahweh' may be understood as a causative form. Cf. Richard S. Hess, *Israelite Religions: An archaeological and biblical survey* (Grand Rapids, MI: Baker Academic, 2007), 175.

42   Cf. also Isa. 40.18–20; 41.6–7, 21–24, 28–29; 42.8, 17; 45.16–17, 20–25; 46.1–13.

43   Cf. Louis Isaac Rabinowitz, 'God, Names of: in the Talmud', *EncJud* 7:676–7.

These religious customs are based on the extraordinary significance attached to the personal name of God.[44]

Moses responded to God's call, returned to Egypt and confronted the pharaoh (Exod. 4—5). However, not only did Pharaoh not agree to let the Hebrews go but he also increased their workload, and they were furious with Moses because of it (5.20–21). Moses turned to the LORD in desperation and asked God why he had ever sent him back to Egypt in the first place (vv. 22–23). God replied with assurances that Moses would see what he would do to Pharaoh and that he would indeed liberate the Hebrews (6.1). Furthermore, he spoke to Moses and said, according to the NRSV, 'I am the LORD. I appeared to Abraham, Isaac, and Jacob as God Almighty, but by my name "The LORD" I did not make myself known to them' (vv. 2–3). This passage seems to say that God had not been known by the name Yahweh until this point in time. This presents an extremely vexing question since, after its first appearance in Genesis 2.4b, the Tetragrammaton appears repeatedly throughout Genesis. In fact, the author of Genesis claims that people began to call on the name of the LORD in the primordial period, in the days of Cain and Enosh (Gen. 4.17–26a). The writer says that, 'At that time people began to invoke the name of the LORD' (v. 26b). From that point forward, it appears repeatedly in the patriarchal narratives, as well as in the first five chapters of Exodus, and in the call of Moses, right up until Exodus 3.15. Naturally, this raises at least two profound questions. First, how are we to understand the relationship between Exodus 3.15 and 6.2–3, which seem so clearly to be in tension? Second, how are we to understand the relationship between Exodus 6.2–3, Genesis 4.26 and other passages in the patriarchal narratives which suggest that they knew the name Yahweh? And third, what was the religion of the Hebrews who worshipped God before the time of Moses?

The apparent tension between Exodus 3.15 and 6.2–3 was important for the development of early source criticism. Source critics viewed these two passages as a doublet and explained the tension between them on the basis of the Documentary Hypothesis. They assigned Exodus 3.15 to J (c.850 BC), whose author believed that the divine name was known and used in the patriarchal period, and Exodus 6.2–3 to P (c.400 BC), whose author believed that it was

---

44 It seems clear, however, that the name of God was spoken among the Ancient Hebrews. The Priestly Benediction (Num. 6.24–26), for example, which was to be spoken over the people, includes three pronouncements of the name of Yahweh. Furthermore, the name was spoken not just by the priests but also by ordinary Israelites. For example, when the landowner Boaz passed through the fields, he greeted the reapers by saying, 'The LORD be with you', and they answered with the reply, 'The LORD bless you' (Ruth 2.4). The cessation of pronouncing the Tetragrammaton was a later development.

unknown prior to its revelation to Moses. Whenever the divine name Yahweh occurs in Genesis, those passages were attributed to J, while those that only use God (*Elohim*) were attributed to E (*c.*750 BC). According to the basic form of the Documentary Hypothesis, a Priestly author living at the end of the fifth century BC took these sources, along with D (*c.*622 BC), and synthesized them into the Pentateuch as we know it (*c.*400 BC). As he edited the final document, he freely used the Tetragrammaton in the narrative and put it in the mouths of the patriarchs. From the perspective of the Documentary Hypothesis, however, these are all anachronisms. They are retrojections from the Priestly author who assembled the Pentateuch as a final product.

Accordingly, most source critics assume that Moses' question about the name of the deity who called him means that the Tetragrammaton was unknown up until his day. Thomas Römer, for example, explains that, in Exodus 6, 'the revelation of the divine name is something new'.[45] Similarly, Mark Smith explains that 'this passage shows that Yahweh was unknown to the patriarchs'.[46] Moberly explains that the patriarchs did not know the divine name Yahweh. It was first revealed to Moses and then, when the later compilers of the Pentateuch sources edited them into a single work, they reworked the patriarchal traditions through the lens of Mosaic Yahwism.[47] While many interpreters continue to use source-critical methods to elucidate these issues, others have sought solutions along different lines of enquiry, and it is to these that we will now turn.

When looking at the question of the beginnings of Yahwism, we must take note of the statement in Exodus 6.2–3 that Yahweh originally revealed himself as El Shaddai, a compound of *'el*, which means 'God', and *shaddai*, which has been variously interpreted as 'strength', 'mountains' or even 'breasts'. It has been traditionally translated 'God Almighty', as in the NRSV.[48] The compound raises an important point of debate in Old Testament scholarship, because its first element, *'el*, could function simply as a noun meaning 'god' but,

45 E.g. Thomas Römer, 'The revelation of the divine name to Moses and the construction of a memory about the origins of the encounter between Yhwh and Israel', in *Israel's Exodus in Transdisciplinary Perspective: Text, archaeology, culture, and geoscience*, ed. Thomas E. Levy, Thomas Schneider and William H. C. Propp (New York, NY: Springer, 2015), 310.

46 Mark S. Smith, *The Origins of Biblical Monotheism: Israel's polytheistic background and the Ugaritic texts* (Oxford: Oxford University Press, 2001), 141.

47 R. W. L. Moberly, *The Old Testament of the Old Testament: Patriarchal narratives and Mosaic Yahwism* (Minneapolis, MN: Fortress Press, 1992), 36–78.

48 As noted, however, it may also mean 'God of the Mountains' or even 'God of the Breasts'. Its meaning is intensely debated.

in numerous ancient texts reflecting the Ugaritic Canaanite culture, it also served as the proper name of the chief god of the pantheon.[49]

When the Old Testament uses '*el* for the deity of the patriarchs, it is not clear whether it is intended to be understood as a proper noun or a simple noun. Most scholars assume that when '*el* appears in Genesis, it was being used as a proper noun and that the patriarchs worshipped the Canaanite god named El.[50] However, the designation '*el* rarely occurs by itself in Genesis and, when it does, it may be that the patriarchs are using it as a generic word for their god, or even as a generic name. If the patriarchs used '*el* this way, as a 'name' for God, that does not necessarily mean that they equated their God with the Canaanite El. Today, Jews, Christians, Muslims, Buddhists, Hindus and many others all use the term 'God', but it would be extreme naivety to suggest that they all mean the same thing in their use of the term. In Genesis, the term '*el* rarely occurs by itself;[51] it is usually part of an epithet such as 'god almighty' ('*el-shaddai*), 'god most high' ('*el-'elyon*) or 'god who sees' ('*el-roi*). These are not names, but epithets. They are adjectival phrases by which the speaker intends to identify the deity.

Clearly, there are cases in the Pentateuch where the speaker seems to equate the God of the Hebrews with the Canaanite god El. This seems to be the case in the Balaam prophecies (Num. 22—24), where the prophet extols the qualities of '*el*. Note that Balaam is a foreigner. There are also cases where '*el* clearly appears to refer to the Canaanite god El. For example, when Melchizedek sought to bless Abraham by 'God Most High' ('*el-'elyon*) (Gen. 14.19), he was probably referring to El, the head of the Canaanite pantheon. When Abraham replied to the priest, however, he clarified that El was really 'the LORD, God Most High' (YHWH, '*el-'elyon*) (v. 22). Note that in this case, too, Melchizedek was a foreigner, and Abraham corrected him in his misconception that the Hebrew deity was El. It may be that some of the ancestors worshipped El but, if that was the case, the authors of Genesis stress that they equated him with Yahweh.

In terms of the origin of Yahwism, there has been a great deal of speculation. One popular idea builds on poetic verses that refer to Yahweh as 'the One of Sinai' (Judg. 5.5), 'the God of Sinai' (Ps. 68.8b), or the one having come

49   Cf. W. Herrmann, 'El', *DDD*: 274–80.

50   E.g. André Lemaire, *The Birth of Monotheism: The rise and disappearance of monotheism*, trans. André Lemaire and Jack Meinhardt (Washington, DC: Biblical Archaeology Society, 2007), 11–17; P. Kyle McCarter Jr, 'The patriarchal age: Abraham, Isaac and Jacob', in *Ancient Israel: From Abraham to the Roman destruction of the Temple* (3rd edn; ed. Hershel Shanks; Washington, DC: Biblical Archaeology Society, 2011), 21–4; Smith, *Origins of Biblical Monotheism*, 135–94.

51   There are passages that refer to "*el*, the god of Israel' (Gen. 33.20) and "*el*, the god of your father' (Gen. 46.3) (literal translations).

from Sinai (Deut. 33.2), or the one having gone out from Seir and marched forth from Edom (Judg. 5.4), or having come from Teman (Hab. 3.3) or Midian (Hab. 3.7). In this view, Jethro, Moses' father-in-law, who was a priest of Midian,[52] is identified as a priest of Yahweh who served at a shrine where Yahweh revealed himself to Moses. Jethro blessed Yahweh, proclaimed that he was greater than all other gods and offered burnt offerings to him (Exod. 18.10–12). Lemaire concludes that Yahweh was clearly 'the principal deity of those Midianites who lived in the mountainous area of the central Negev'.[53] Moses must have learned about Yahweh from these Midianites, and from there he took the message about Yahweh back to the Hebrews in Egypt. Since Jethro was a Kenite/Midianite, the idea that Yahweh was a north Arabian deity who was adopted by the Hebrews has come to be known as the 'Kenite Hypothesis'. This proposition continues to draw wide support.[54]

However, there are many reasons why the Kenite Hypothesis seems unlikely. First, there is no basis for the argument that Jethro was a priest of Yahweh. He is introduced as a 'priest of Midian' and not as a 'priest of Yahweh' (Exod. 3.1). The second name by which he is known, Reuel, is a theophoric name that includes the divine element *'el* and not *Yah* (an abbreviation for 'Yahweh'). He only recognized Yahweh and made sacrifices to him after he had heard of the exodus events and not before (Exod. 18.1, 8, 9). And the mountain where Moses encounters Yahweh was not called the 'Mountain of Yahweh' but the 'Mountain of *'el*'. It appears that Jethro learned about Yahweh from Moses, and not the other way around. Second, the biblical passages used to connect Yahweh with southern locations like Teman, Seir and Mt Paran do not provide any information about the origin of Yahweh, but simply point to his manifestation at these locations.[55] Yahweh passed through these locations on his way from Sinai to Canaan.

---

52 Cf. Exod. 2.16–21; 3.1.

53 Lemaire, *Birth of Monotheism*, 26.

54 E.g. Joseph Blenkinsopp, 'The Midianite-Kenite Hypothesis revisited and the origins of Judah', *JSOT* 33.2 (2008): 131–53; Lemaire, *Birth of Monotheism*, 19–28; Nadav Na'aman, 'The "Kenite Hypothesis" in the light of the excavations at Ḥorvat 'Uza', in *Not Only History: Proceedings of the conference in honor of Mario Liverani*, ed. Gilda Bartoloni and Maria Giovanna Biga with the assistance of Armando Bramanti (Winona Lake, IN: Eisenbrauns, 2016), 171–82; Römer, 'The revelation of the divine name to Moses', 312–14; Mark S. Smith, 'YHWH's original character: questions about an unknown god', in *The Origins of Yahwism* (ed. van Oorschot and Witte), 25–9; van der Toorn, 'Yahweh', 911–12.

55 Henrik Pfeiffer, 'The origin of YHWH and its attestation', in *The Origins of Yahwism* (ed. van Oorschot and Witte), 139. There are a couple of sanctuaries in the region where Yahweh may have been worshipped in some form or fashion. At Kuntillet 'Ajrud, some graffiti bearing the epithet 'Yahweh of Teman' were found. However, the site dates to about 800 BC and there is nothing about it

Another fascinating new data set includes recent discoveries of forms of the name Yahweh in a number of ancient texts that trace the name back into the Late Bronze Age (1550–1200 BC) or even the Middle Bronze Age (2000–1550 BC). A topographical list in Ramesses II's thirteenth-century Hypostyle Hall at 'Amrah West, which was copied from Amenhotep III's earlier temple at Soleb, which dates to around 1400 BC, contains a group of six names, all of which are preceded by the words 'Shasu land of'. The first interpreter of the list, Bernard Grdseloff, identified all of the lands as being located in Edom and northern Transjordan and identified the fifth 'Shasu land' as associated with the name *yhwz*, which he did not hesitate to identify with Yahweh. He located the 'Shasu land of Yahwa' in the region of Edom and used this identification as support for the Kenite Hypothesis. There has been great scepticism among scholars, however, about identifying the Egyptian *yhwz* with the Hebrew YHWH,[56] and it also appears that the geographical context in which the name occurs was located in Middle Syria rather than Edom.[57] More recently, Egyptologist Thomas Schneider has identified what he believes may be the first documented occurrence of the name Yahweh in the name of the ancient owner of a papyrus of the Egyptian Book of the Dead.[58] The copy, which is housed in the Princeton University Library, dates to *c*.1330–1230 BC. Schneider believes the owner's name, translated 'My lord is the shepherd of Yah', means that the god was the shepherd of the region called Yah, short for Yahweh, which occurs here as a place name. Schneider's claim, however, has gained little traction.[59] To date, the Egyptian evidence for the name Yahweh does not seem especially convincing.[60]

A more promising discovery comes from a cuneiform archive in a collection dated to around 1500 BC, during the First Sealand Dynasty in Babylonia, which was published in 2009. Two personal names have been found in the collection that contain the divine element 'Yau' and may be translated: 'Servant of Yau' and 'Yau is my god'. Since this is the spelling of Yahweh in cuneiform

that suggests it was the birthplace of Yahweh worship. Instead, it simply attests that someone venerated Yahweh at the site.

56 E.g. Hans Goedicke, 'The Tetragrammaton in Egyptian?', *Society for the Study of Egyptian Antiquities* 24 (1994): 24–7; Gösta Ahlström, *Who Were the Israelites?* (Winona Lake, IN: Eisenbrauns, 1986), 57–60.

57 For an overview of the discussion, see Ralph K. Hawkins, *How Israel Became a People* (Nashville, TN: Abingdon Press, 2013), 70–2.

58 Thomas Schneider, 'The first documented occurrence of the god Yahweh? (Book of the Dead Princeton "Roll 5")', *JANER* 7.2 (2008): 113–20.

59 See the criticisms in Faried Adrom and Matthias Müller, 'The Tetragrammaton in Egyptian sources – facts and fiction', in *The Origins of Yahwism* (ed. van Oorschot and Witte), 108–9.

60 For a detailed overview of the data and its analysis, see Adrom and Müller, 'The Tetragrammaton in Egyptian sources', 93–113.

texts, Stephanie Dalley argues that these 'may be identified with the later Hebrew god Yahweh'.[61] The thousands of cuneiform texts from Mesopotamia contain the names of myriads of people who lived there, some of whom were from other places or whose ancestry was in other locations. Apparently, 'men who acknowledged the cult of Yau lived in lower Mesopotamia during the sixteenth/early fifteenth centuries BC'.[62] If Dalley is correct, this would be the earliest occurrence of the name Yahweh. These fascinating data would mean that the name Yahweh was known prior to the time of Moses.

One final line of enquiry that may shed light on whether or not the Tetragrammaton was known before the time of Moses is the translation of the second half of Exodus 6.3. While it is conventionally rendered, 'but by my name "The LORD" I did not make myself known to them', Sir Godfrey Rolles Driver argues that this is a mistranslation based on a failure to recognize a common Hebrew colloquialism, which might be dubbed the 'emphatic interrogative', in which a negative particle is used to express affirmation. The Webster's Bible, following the King James Version (KJV), renders it as such, with Exodus 6.2–3 reading as follows:

> And God spoke to Moses, and said to him, I am the LORD: And I appeared to Abraham, to Isaac, and to Jacob, by the name of God Almighty, but by my name JEHOVAH was I not known to them[?][63]

Although the Hebrew idiom is easily missed, Driver is able to provide numerous examples of it in the Old Testament.[64] If he is correct, the translation of Exodus 6.3 as an emphatic interrogative would mean that the patriarchs indeed knew the name Yahweh.

With the conventional focus on this passage as revealing something new, some interpreters may have missed the real point of the text. The real focus in Exodus 6.2–3 is on the continuity between the covenant promises that God made to Abraham and what God was about to do in the exodus events. This was not a different deity doing something new and unrelated to what he had done in the patriarchal period. Instead, it was the same God, Yahweh, being

---

61 Stephanie Dalley, 'Gods from north-eastern and north-western Arabia in cuneiform texts from the First Sealand Dynasty, and a cuneiform inscription from Tell en-Naṣbeh, c.1500 BC', *Arab. Arch. Epig.* 24.2 (2013): 182.

62 Dalley, 'Gods from north-eastern and north-western Arabia', 183.

63 The ISV also translates the second half of Exod. 6.3 as an emphatic interrogative.

64 The examples he provides include: Exod. 8.22; 1 Sam. 14.30; 20.9; 2 Sam. 5.23; 2 Kings 5.26; 1 Chron. 14.14; Isa. 11.3; Jer. 4.27; 5.18; Lam. 3.36–38; Ezek. 7.11; 16.43, 47; Zech. 14.18; Ps. 50.8–9; Job 8.12; 11.11; 14.16; 29.24; 37.23.

faithful to the covenant promises he had made to Abraham.[65] The focus is not on novelty, but on continuity.

There is one thing that would be new for the Hebrews, and it was that, through the exodus events, they would truly come to '*know*' the LORD (Exod. 6.7, emphasis mine). This does not mean they would learn about the LORD for the first time, nor is it referring to cognitive knowledge or mental assent. The Hebrew word for 'know' (*yada'*) has to do with experiential knowledge of the most intimate kind. The usage here is similar to that in Isaiah 52.6, which says that when the exile comes to an end, 'my people shall know my name'. In this case, it obviously does not mean that they would come to know the divine name for the first time. Instead, it means that they would *really* know it in an experiential sense. They would come to know and appreciate Yahweh in a new way.[66] This would be the case for those Hebrews languishing in bondage in Egypt.

But how would they come to know and appreciate Yahweh in a new way? Yahweh makes himself known by his actions of defending and redeeming Israel.[67] These are the proofs of his power (cf. Ps. 98.1-3), and he becomes known through these powerful acts of salvation. Rolf Rendtorff points to numerous hymnic celebrations of the ways in which the LORD has made himself known by his saving acts.[68]

Helmut Utzschneider and Wolfgang Oswald point out that, after the LORD states that he has remembered his covenant (Exod. 6.5) and tells Moses to proclaim to the Hebrews that he is Yahweh (v. 6), there are seven verbal clauses in verses 6-8 that 'fill the name YHWH with content'.[69] This God who calls himself Yahweh will: (1) *free* them from the burden of the Egyptians; (2) *deliver* them from slavery to them; (3) *redeem* them with an outstretched arm and with mighty acts of judgement; (4) *take* them as his people; (5) *be* their God; (6) *bring* them into the land he swore to give to Abraham, Isaac and Jacob; and (7) *give* it to the Hebrews for a possession.[70]

---

65   See further, John I. Durham, *Exodus* (WBC 3; Waco, TX: Word, 1987), 77.

66   Allen P. Ross, 'Did the patriarchs know the name of the LORD?', in *Giving the Sense: Understanding and using Old Testament historical texts*, ed. David M. Howard Jr and Michael A. Grisanti (Grand Rapids, MI: Kregel, 2003), 336-7.

67   Rolf Rendtorff, 'The concept of revelation in Ancient Israel', in *Revelation as History*, ed. Wolfhart Pannenberg et al.; trans. David Granskou (New York, NY: Macmillan, 1968), 31.

68   E.g. Exod. 9.16; Deut. 3.24; Pss. 77.14ff.; 78.11ff.; 98.2ff.; 145.12.

69   Helmut Utzschneider and Wolfgang Oswald, *Exodus 1-15* (IECOT; Stuttgart: Kohlhammer, 2015), 159.

70   Utzschneider and Oswald, *Exodus 1-15*, 159. I have modified their list to reflect the order and translation of the NRSV.

The point to the entire oracle of Exodus 6 is not deciphering a new revelation from God about the divine name. Instead, it is God's assurance to Moses that he was the same God that the patriarchs had known. He was the LORD of the patriarchs, and he would be the LORD of the Hebrews in bondage. Duane Garrett affirms that

> the whole purpose of this oracle is to vindicate Moses, to reassure him, and to reassure the nation . . . in terms of actual content, there is nothing at all here that is new. In fact, the oracle does little more than repeat what YHWH had already told Moses on Mt. Sinai (see 3:6–10, 12, 15–22). And this is the whole point; Moses did not need some new information about God, he needed assurance. The reassurance was a repetition of the words of faith he had already heard.

And the key to interpreting Exodus 6.3 is the verb 'to know'.[71] Yahweh assured Moses that he would fulfil the promises he had made to the patriarchs but, more importantly, he promised that they would come to know him experientially as LORD through his actions as he fulfilled them. In this sense, the revelation of the divine name to Moses in Exodus 3.15 was indeed a new beginning.

Passover

The Passover festival finds its beginnings in the book of Exodus. It started as the crescendo of the so-called 'ten plagues' and provided the impetus for the exodus. It all began when the LORD sent a series of plagues upon Egypt in order to impress upon Pharaoh that he was the LORD (7.17). These plagues were a series of disasters and climatological catastrophes. The author of Exodus understood them as God's judgement against Egypt, by which the LORD would make 'fools' ('ālal) of the Egyptians (Exod. 10.2). God himself said that, in the plagues, he would execute judgements against all the gods of Egypt (Exod. 12.12), and each of the plagues was directed against one of the gods of Egypt.

In Chapter 6, we will examine all of the plagues. At this point, however, we will focus on the tenth plague, since it was the culmination of all the plagues. It is described as a 'disease' (nega') that would strike down every firstborn son in Egypt (Exod. 11.5). It was primarily directed against the pharaoh, who was viewed as a god in Egypt, and against pharaonic succession, which was the way

---

71 Ross, 'Did the patriarchs know the name of the LORD?', 337.

he maintained perpetual rule over the land. The LORD explained to Moses how the plague would be administered:

> I will go throughout Egypt. Every firstborn son in Egypt will die, from the firstborn son of Pharaoh, who sits on the throne, to the firstborn son of the female slave, who is at her hand mill, and all the firstborn of the cattle as well. There will be loud wailing throughout Egypt – worse than there has ever been or ever will be again.
> (Exod. 11.4–6 NIV)

This plague of death would demonstrate the absolute sovereign power of the God of whom the pharaoh had denied all knowledge.

If the plague was to strike down the firstborn in every house in Egypt, then how were the Hebrews to be saved from its effects? The LORD explained to Moses that, in preparation for the night of the final plague, each man was to take a lamb for his family. The lamb should be a year old and without defect – spotless, with no broken bones. At twilight, the Hebrews were to slaughter the lamb, take some of its blood, and put it on the sides and tops of the doorframes of their houses (Exod. 12.1–6). They were to prepare the lamb and eat it as a meal inside the home, dressed and ready to go – with 'your loins girded, your sandals on your feet, and your staff in your hand; and you shall eat it hurriedly' (12.11). That night, the LORD would come through Egypt and strike down the firstborn, thereby bringing judgement on all the gods of Egypt (Exod. 12.12).

'The blood', however, 'will be a sign for you on the houses where you are, and when I see the blood, I will pass over you' (v. 13 NIV). In Israel, blood was viewed as constituting the life essence. In Leviticus 17.11, the LORD explains that 'the life of a creature is in the blood, and I have given it to you to make atonement for yourselves on the altar'.[72] A life had to be poured out in substitution in order to provide atonement. The Passover lamb was understood as a sacrifice (Exod. 12.27). And when the LORD saw the blood of the lamb painted on to the doorways of the Israelite houses, the English translations say that he would 'pass over' them, and they would be spared from death.

According to the text, that is exactly what happened. That night, the angel of death passed through Egypt, and all the firstborn of Egypt were slain (Exod. 12.29–30). This was an attack on the religion of the Egyptians and their very identity. In the death of Pharaoh's firstborn, the Egyptian cycle of dynastic succession was interrupted, which demonstrated the LORD's total superiority

---

72   Cf. also Gen. 9.4; Lev. 17.14; Deut. 12.23; Ps. 72.14.

over the pharaoh and the Egyptian gods. With this last plague, the pharaoh finally agreed to let the Hebrews go (vv. 31–32). Pharaoh, his officials and all the Egyptians urged the Israelites to leave the land of Egypt, and they left after living in Egypt for 430 years (12.31–36).

The fact that the Passover triggered the exodus events is paramount, since they led to the Israelites' freedom, to their becoming a nation. As a result, instructions were given for a Passover festival to be celebrated annually in every Hebrew home. During this festival, a ritual meal would be eaten while the events of the first Passover were rehearsed. The Passover meal was fashioned into a catechism, a question-and-answer format in which children ask their parents about the events of the first Passover so that the story can be retold around the table (12.24–27). It is a festive meal that celebrates early Hebrew independence.

The beginnings of the Israelite nation

The tenth plague triggered the exodus of the Hebrew slaves from Egypt. But who were the Hebrews? When they went out from Egypt, they were a loose network of landless tribes. Their ancestral land was far away, in Mesopotamia. When Abraham arrived in Canaan, the native peoples referred to him as a 'Hebrew' (Gen. 14.13). The very name 'Hebrew' may come from the Hebrew verb 'ābar, which means 'to cross over' or 'beyond', and would thus refer to someone who has come from the other side of the River Euphrates (Josh. 24.3).[73] The term is typically used by Canaanites, Philistines, Egyptians or others who are differentiating the Israelites from their own native ethnic group.[74] In these cases, it may therefore mean something like 'foreigner' or 'immigrant'.[75]

When the Hebrews went out from Egypt, the text also states that a 'mixed crowd' (Exod. 12.38), which Everett Fox translates as 'riffraff',[76] went out with them. Like many Ancient Near Eastern peoples, when the Egyptians defeated their enemies in battle, they often brought back some of those whom they had subjugated as slaves. Any and all captives became a royal resource. They could be resettled in colonies to provide labour, assigned to temples, and given to

---

73 The Septuagint version of Gen. 14.13 confirms this view. It renders 'Abram the Hebrew' as 'Abram, the one who crossed over'.

74 The term is used 33 times in the OT. E.g. Gen. 14.13; 39.14, 17; 40.15; 41.12; 43.32; Exod. 1.19; 2.6–7, 11–14; 3.18; 5.3; 7.16; 9.1.

75 P. Kyle McCarter Jr, *1 Samuel: A new translation with introduction and commentary* (AB 8; New York, NY: Doubleday, 1980), 240–1.

76 Everett Fox, *Genesis and Exodus: A new English rendition with commentary and notes* (New York, NY: Schocken, 1990), 299.

meritorious individuals or even to soldiers who had distinguished themselves in battle.[77] Apparently, when the Hebrews prepared to depart Egypt, some of these other enslaved peoples joined them. There are also Hellenistic Egyptian writers who claim that even many Egyptians allied themselves with Moses in departing from Egypt.[78] In any case, it would appear that, when the exodus actually occurred, those who departed from Egypt made up a great ethnic salad.

When this mixture of people arrived at Mt Sinai, they entered into a covenant with the LORD. The Sinai covenant is so significant that Chapter 7 will be entirely devoted to it. Here, we will simply observe the critical role of the covenant in forming the nation of Israel. In the Ancient Near East, a covenant was a legal agreement that bound two parties to take on certain obligations towards each other. A covenant could serve as the foundation of a new legal community by sealing relations between originally separate groups.[79] When this great amalgam of people who had experienced the exodus gathered around Mt Sinai and entered into a covenant with the LORD, they swore fealty to God as their king and to one another as his subjects. When God inaugurated the covenant, he said that, if the Hebrews would obey his voice and keep his covenant, they would be 'a priestly kingdom and a holy nation' (Exod. 19.6). The covenant at Mt Sinai was where those who had experienced the exodus were formed into a people. It was the beginning of the Israelite nation.

Conclusions

The beginnings we have considered in this chapter were paramount to the formation of early Israelite identity. The story of Moses' early life and call is central, since he would be Israel's leader par excellence. His identity crisis – his struggle with deciding whether to identify with the Hebrews or the Egyptians – foreshadowed the crises that threatened the fulfilment of the Abrahamic promises.[80] God would ransom the Hebrews from their enslavement in Egypt and enter into a covenant with them, and if they adhered to that covenant, they would be for the LORD 'a priestly kingdom and a holy nation' (Exod. 19.6). However, many crises threatened to prevent this from happening, including the Israelites' own lack of faithfulness (e.g. Exod. 32). And yet, just as Moses finally made the decision to be the LORD's ambassador to Egypt and

---

77   S. Allam, 'Slaves', *OEAE* 3:294.
78   E.g. Manetho claims that 80,000 lepers and other diseased persons sided with Moses and the Jews. Cited in Josephus, *Ag. Ap.* 1.234.
79   Cf. George E. Mendenhall and Gary A. Herion, 'Covenant', *ABD* 1:1179–83.
80   See 'The story of Exodus' in Chapter 1.

return to his kindred in Egypt (Exod. 4.18), the Israelites ultimately repented of their sin and entered into a renewed covenant with the LORD (34.10ff.), who took up residence among them in the tabernacle (40.34–38).

The oracle of Exodus 6 is also paramount. When God told Moses that he was the LORD, it affirmed that this was the same God whom the patriarchs had known. This was not some new deity calling on Moses to liberate the Hebrews, but it was the same LORD whom the patriarchs had known. This crucial passage establishes continuity between Genesis and Exodus. In Exodus, this was not a new God doing a new thing, but it was the God of Abraham, Isaac and Jacob faithfully working out the promises he had made to them long ago.

The Passover and the Sinai covenant, which are inextricably intertwined, are also of vital importance. The events of the first Passover triggered the exodus itself and made it possible for the Israelites to travel to Mt Sinai, where they entered into a covenant with the LORD and became a nation. The Passover ordinance ensured that this event would be celebrated in perpetuity as a festive meal that celebrates both the Passover itself as well as the covenant it made possible.

Each of these beginnings contributes to the totality of the 'foundation myth' of the exodus, which tells how God liberated the people of Israel from Egyptian bondage, singled them out from all the peoples of the world (19.5), and made them into a 'priestly kingdom and a holy nation' (19.6), through whom all the families of the earth could be blessed (Gen. 12.3).

5

The portrayal of Moses as a leader in the book of Exodus

From a Jewish perspective, Moses is the dominant figure in the Pentateuch and in the entire Old Testament. While Abraham was the ancestor of Israel, it was Moses who mediated the covenant with God, delivered its laws, organized the people and led them in the wilderness for 40 years. During this time, Moses served as a prophet, a priest and almost a king as he directed every facet of national life. The Pentateuch comes to an end when, after the wilderness wandering, Moses led the people in a renewal of the covenant (Deut. 29.9—30.20). After Moses' death, there are no new laws or conditions given throughout the rest of the Old Testament to regulate Israel's existence as a nation. Instead, from that point on, Israel's history is understood as an outgrowth of the covenant that God made with Israel through Moses. He is so closely associated with the law that he is sometimes used as a symbol for it. At the Transfiguration, for example, Moses and Elijah appear with Jesus in order to symbolize that the Law and the Prophets testify to Jesus.[1]

Moses' importance is indisputable, but the complexity of his character has often been overlooked. He is often portrayed as a powerful figure, such as in Michelangelo's sculpture of Moses, housed in the Church of San Pietro in Vincoli, in Rome, which depicts Moses as young and muscular. This may be attributed, in part, to Stephen's description of Moses as 'powerful in speech and action' (Acts 7.22 NIV). The Pentateuch itself, however, described Moses as 'very humble, more so than anyone else on the face of the earth' (Num. 12.3). Moses himself insisted that he was 'slow of speech and slow of tongue' (Exod. 4.10). And yet he was raised in the royal court as a prince of Egypt (2.10), conducted himself in an authoritative manner (2.13–14) and was able to overpower others in one-on-one combat (2.12, 15b–19). In this chapter, by reviewing the several ways that the author of Exodus depicts Moses, we will seek to understand how he intended his readers to perceive him.

---

1   Matt. 17.3–8; Mark 9.2–13; Luke 9.28–36.

The traditional portrayal of Moses as a prophet

Most readers of the Pentateuch, Jewish and Christian alike, probably think of Moses as a prophet. This traditional understanding of Moses stems from several passages. The first of these is Exodus 7.1, in which God tells Moses that he would make him 'like God' to Pharaoh, and that he had designated Aaron to be his prophet. Moses would 'speak all that I command you' (v. 2). This would include confronting Pharaoh on God's behalf, and speaking to Israel on God's behalf, including mediating the covenant, delivering its laws and regulations, and giving the instructions for the building of the tabernacle and its furniture. Since the basic function of a prophet was to speak on behalf of God, Moses was in all these ways indeed a prophet.[2]

Later passages confirm this identification. When the Israelites stood on the plains of Moab, on the brink of entering the promised land, God assured them that he would raise up a prophet like Moses from among them, and that the people should heed that prophet (Deut. 18.15). Similarly, the concluding scene in Deuteronomy specifically calls Moses a 'prophet'. The text states that:

> Never since has there arisen a prophet in Israel like Moses, whom the LORD knew face to face. He was unequalled for all the signs and wonders that the LORD sent him to perform in the land of Egypt, against Pharaoh and all his servants and his entire land, and for all the mighty deeds and all the terrifying displays of power that Moses performed in the sight of all Israel.
> (Deut. 34.10–12)

The idea that Moses had known God 'face to face' implies that he had known God as fully as was possible for a human being. This set him apart from all other prophets, who only knew God through visions and dreams (Num. 12.6–8). Later Jewish interpreters embellished Moses' role as a prophet, claiming that he had secret knowledge and that he had ascended into heaven.[3]

---

2 David L. Peterson, 'Prophet, prophecy', *NIDB* 4:622–3.

3 E.g. Philo, *Mos.*; *As. Mos.*; *Jub.*

Other portrayals of Moses in Exodus

While it is certainly clear that the author of Exodus did intend to portray Moses as a prophet, there are a number of other ways in which he is characterized in the book of Exodus (and in the rest of the Pentateuch). These include portrayals as a shepherd, divine figure, military leader, judge, mediator of the covenant and giver of the law, priest and sanctuary builder. We will discuss each of these in turn, consider their implications and then examine the ways in which the author of Exodus portrays Moses as particularly unique.

Moses as shepherd

After Moses had left Egypt and settled among the Midianites, he became a shepherd, keeping the flocks of his father-in-law, the priest of Midian (Exod. 3.1). The ownership of vast quantities of cattle – typically sheep and goats in Syria-Palestine and the Near East[4] – was a symbol of power and wealth. The role of a shepherd was to feed and protect the owner's flocks, which meant helping them to find enough food and water and protecting them from predators.[5] A good shepherd took special care of the flocks. Because of the tasks and responsibilities associated with shepherding, an extensive store of shepherd and flock imagery accumulated throughout the Ancient Near East. The image of shepherd often served as a metaphor for a king. In the Code of Hammurabi, for example, the king was referred to as 'Hammurabi, the shepherd'.[6] In another example from Greece, the sceptre of Agamemnon, as well as those of other kings, is frequently mentioned in conjunction with the expression 'shepherd of the host'.[7]

In Egypt, where the Hebrews were enslaved, the image of the shepherd as a metaphor for the leadership of the pharaoh was both ancient and prominent. It appears to have originated with the god Osiris, who is always portrayed holding a flail and crook, and is sometimes called a shepherd. The crook symbolized his power and importance, as well as his role in providing leadership to his flock, the people of Egypt. Similarly, the pharaohs were typically also portrayed holding a flail and a shepherd's crook,[8] and inscriptions repeatedly refer to them as the shepherds of the people of Egypt. After he fled Egypt and

---

4   Ralph K. Hawkins, 'Cattle', *EBR* 4:1069.

5   Jack W. Vancil, 'Sheep, shepherd', *ABD* 5:1187.

6   He is referred to by this term at several points in both the prologue and the epilogue of his law code. Cf. *ANET*, 164.

7   *Iliad* 2.75–109; *Odyssey* 3.156.

8   E.g. *ANEP*, 379.

settled among the Midianites, Moses became shepherd of his father-in-law's flocks. He spent 40 years in this role (Acts 7.30) and received his call from God while he was with the herd (Exod. 3.1). While Bible readers have traditionally viewed the 40 years of Moses' sojourn among the Midianites as a period of preparation for his future role as leader of the Hebrew people,[9] it may also be that it served to put Moses on a par with Pharaoh. Just as Pharaoh held the shepherd's crook, passed down from the god Osiris, and wielded its authority, so too Moses held a shepherd's crook and wielded the authority of the LORD.

Moses as a divine figure

In the midst of Moses' call story, God tells the reluctant prophet that Aaron will speak for him and he will serve 'as God for him' (Exod. 4.16).[10] Later, God affirmed his elevation of Moses' status, saying: 'See, I have made you *like* God to Pharaoh, and your brother Aaron shall be your prophet' (7.1).[11] In both of these cases, the qualifiers 'as' and 'like', which are not in the Hebrew text, have been added to the English translation in order to avoid the uncomfortable portrayal of Moses as divine. Gary Rendsburg, however, points out that 'the background for comprehending the import of these passages is the very essence of Egyptian religion'.[12] In Egypt, the pharaoh was considered divine[13] – the human manifestation of Horus – and so the author of Exodus describes God as having done for Moses what he had never done for another human being. God elevated Moses to divine status so that he could confront Pharaoh on equal terms.

This theme is developed throughout the Moses story. In the tale of his birth, which parallels the Horus birth story, Moses is presented as equal to Pharaoh.[14] Later, when Moses' staff had been turned into a snake, God told Moses to reach out his hand and 'seize it by the tail' (Exod. 4.4). While the typical way of grabbing a snake is by the neck, just behind the head, numerous Ancient Egyptian objects of art have been found on which Horus is portrayed holding snakes (and sometimes other creatures) by the tail. If Pharaoh's divine counterpart, Horus, is able to handle snakes by the tail, then so is Moses, his

---

9   This is a very ancient view. E.g. Louis H. Feldman, *Philo's Portrayal of Moses in the Context of Ancient Judaism* (Notre Dame, IN: University of Notre Dame Press, 2007), 73.

10   Italics mine.

11   Italics mine.

12   Gary A. Rendsburg, 'Moses as equal to Pharaoh', in *Text, Artifact, and Image: Revealing Ancient Israelite religion*, ed. Gary M. Beckman and Theodore J. Lewis (Providence, RI: Brown University Press, 2006), 201.

13   Cf. D. O'Connor and D. P. Silverman, eds, *Ancient Egyptian Kingship* (Leiden: Brill, 1995).

14   See the discussion of Moses' birth story in Chapter 4.

equal.[15] The 'shining' of Moses' face (Exod. 34.29–30) probably provides another feature of divinity. The meaning of the Hebrew version of this passage has been heavily debated over the centuries, and English translations have traditionally followed Jewish interpreters in rendering the phrases in question as 'the skin of his face shone' (v. 29) and 'the skin of his face was shining' (v. 30). However, Jerome was probably correct when he translated them in the Vulgate as 'the skin of his face was horned'.

Horns and being horned were signs of divinity and power in the Ancient Near East.[16] Since the pharaoh was divinized, one of his many titles was 'the horned one'.[17] Numerous Eighteenth and Nineteenth Dynasty pharaohs are portrayed with a ram's horn curled around the ear and extending alongside the cheek, probably in order to represent divinity. It is not clear what it would have looked like for the skin of Moses' face to be 'horned', and interpretations have ranged from the literal to the figurative.[18] What seems evident, however, is that the author of Exodus portrayed Moses with horns in order to validate his identification with God (Exod. 7.1) and depict him as equal or superior to Pharaoh.[19]

Moses as a military leader

The book of Exodus also portrays Moses as a military leader and the people of Israel as his army. From Israel's departure from Egypt until their entrance into the promised land, the Israelites are described as a structured militia under the leadership of Moses.[20] Their situation is similar to those of other Ancient Near Eastern cultures, which viewed warfare as fundamentally religious. Kings typically went to war at the command of their gods.[21] They would typically

---

15 Rendsburg, 'Moses as equal to Pharaoh', 213–15.

16 Ruth Mellinkoff, *The Horned Moses in Medieval Art and Thought* (Berkeley, CA: University of California Press, 1970), 3.

17 Benjamin E. Scolnic, 'Moses and the horns of power', in *Judaism: Festschrift in honor of Dr. Robert Gordis*, ed. Eugene B. Borowitz (New York, NY: American Jewish Congress, 1991), 575–6.

18 As an example of a literal interpretation, during the Renaissance, Michelangelo crafted literal horns as part of the sculpture of Moses he prepared for the tomb of Pope Julius II. On the other hand, as an example of a figurative interpretation, in the late eleventh to the twelfth century Rashi interpreted the 'horns' as emanations of light taking the shape of horns as they radiated from Moses' face.

19 Herbert R. Broderick, *Moses the Egyptian in the Illustrated Old English Hexateuch* (Notre Dame, IN: University of Notre Dame Press, 2017), 53–78.

20 Exod. 13.18; Num. 33.1. The author of Exodus consistently uses the military term 'hosts' to describe the people of Israel (Exod. 6.26; 7.4; 12.17, 37, 41, 51).

21 Cf. Bustanay Oded, '"The command of the god" as a reason for going to war in the Assyrian royal inscriptions', in *'Ah, Assyria . . .': Studies in Assyrian history and Ancient Near Eastern historiography presented to Hayim Tadmor*, ed. Mordechai Cogan and Israel Eph'al (Scripta Hierosolymitana 33; Jerusalem: Magnes Press, 1991), 223–30.

receive a prophetic word from the god assuring the results of the battle in advance, be given a special weapon from the god for use in the battle and see their hand in battle.[22]

Moses' experience was similar in many ways. God called him to confront Pharaoh (Exod. 3.7–13). He consecrated Moses' shepherd's staff as the divine weapon by which Moses would perform a series of signs, inaugurate the plagues, part the Red Sea and produce water from a rock.[23] Before the Israelites left Egypt, they plundered the Egyptians by taking their jewellery and clothing (12.31–36). They went out 'prepared for battle' (13.18) and are continually referred to as the LORD's 'company' or 'companies', terms with militaristic overtones.[24] When Pharaoh and his army went out after them, the Israelites were 'going out boldly' (14.8), which translates an expression that suggests that they were ready to fight and eager to prevail.[25] Before crossing the Red Sea, Moses pronounced a war oracle (14.13–14) and, afterwards, he and Miriam both sang victory hymns (15.1–18, 21). In the wilderness, when the Amalekites attacked the Israelites, Moses stood on the top of a nearby hill and held his shepherd's staff aloft as a banner that seemed to secure victory (17.8–11a).

On the other hand, Moses' experience was very dissimilar to that of Ancient Near Eastern kings. While God commissioned Moses to confront Pharaoh, he warned him that Pharaoh would *not* let the Israelites go 'unless compelled by a mighty hand' (3.19). While the Israelites departed Egypt 'prepared for battle' (13.18), they were terrified by the prospect of a battle with the Egyptians (14.10–12). Moses told the people that, in fact, it was the LORD who would fight for the Israelites, and they only needed to keep still (14.14). At the battle with the Amalekites, while the Israelites did prevail whenever Moses held his staff aloft, they began to suffer defeat whenever he lowered it, so that he had to have assistance in order to hold it up throughout the course of the battle (17.11b). Since the shepherd's crook symbolized the power of God, the need to keep it elevated represented the Israelites' complete dependence on God for the outcome of the battle. In fact, throughout the book of Exodus, it is the LORD himself who fights for Israel.[26] Moses was a military leader, but he was a military

---

22 See the chapter on 'Divine warriors' in Charlie Trimm, *Fighting for the King and the Gods: A survey of warfare in the Ancient Near East* (Atlanta, GA: SBL Press, 2017), 553–625.

23 Exod. 4.2–4; 4.17, 20; 7.15, 17, 19, 20; 8.5, 16, 17; 9.23; 10.13; 14.16; 17.5.

24 Cf. Exod. 6.26; 7.4; 12.17, 41, 51.

25 C. J. Labuschagen, 'The meaning of *bĕyād rāmâ* in the Old Testament', in *Von Kanaan bis Kerala: Festschrift für J. P. M. van der Ploeg*, ed. W. E. Delsman et al. (AOAT 211; Neukirchen-Vluyn: Neukirchener, 1982), 146.

26 Cf. Charlie Trimm, *'YHWH Fights for Them!' The Divine Warrior in the Exodus narrative* (Piscataway, NJ: Gorgias Press, 2014).

leader who was completely dependent upon the sovereign and almighty God, the LORD.

Moses as a judge

Another way that the book of Exodus portrays Moses is as a judge, like the later charismatic leaders of Israel.[27] After Moses had grown up and, for whatever reason, become sympathetic to the Israelites, he sought to interject himself into Hebrew society.[28] He tried to arbitrate between two Hebrews who were engaged in a dispute, but one of them snidely asked, 'Who made you a ruler and judge over us?' (Exod. 2.14). Throughout the wilderness period, among other things, Moses mediated between the LORD and the people, prophesied, and settled disputes among the Hebrew populace. All of these activities are described using the term 'judge' (18.13). Due to the size of the Hebrew community and the number of people who brought requests to enquire of God or disputes to be settled, Moses found himself involved in the tasks of judging 'from morning until evening' (18.13). His father-in-law, Jethro, finally suggested that he appoint 'able men' from among the people to serve as 'officers' over the people, and 'let them sit as judges for the people at all times; let them bring every important case to you, but decide every minor case themselves' (18.22). In 1970, Rudolf Smend proposed that Moses may have been the first of the 'major judges'.[29] Robert Boling notes that several parallels between the stories of the judges and that of Moses, including the birth, enlistment and diplomatic functioning of Moses in Exodus 1—13, strengthen this premise.[30] Boling overlooks Moses' burial report (Deut. 34.6), which is another parallel between his story and those of most of the judges. Like the later charismatic judges, the author of Exodus clearly intended to portray Moses as the highest authority among the Hebrew people.

In the Ancient Near East, it was the king who was understood to be the highest source of justice. The earliest known law code, the so-called Code of Ur-Nammu (2112–2095 BC), contains a prologue followed by legal prescriptions.[31] The prologue mentions the institutions of new divine offerings, the revitalization of agricultural activities, the reopening of the Gulf trade,

---

27 Rudolf Smend, *Yahweh War and Tribal Confederation: Reflections upon Israel's earliest history*, trans. M. G. Rogers (Nashville, TN: Abingdon Press, 1970), 128.
28 See the discussion in Chapter 4.
29 Smend, *Yahweh War*, 128.
30 R. G. Boling, *Judges: A new translation with introduction and commentary* (AB 6A; New York, NY: Doubleday, 1975), 6.
31 *ANET*, 523–5.

the establishment of 'freedom' for some cities and the creation of new weight-standards. It also presents the king as the guarantor of all justice. The legal prescriptions are comprised of 40 short paragraphs dealing with punishable acts, which are ranked from minor infractions to serious crimes, with punishments that correspond to the nature of the crime. The later Code of Hammurabi (c.1750 BC) follows the same outline, with a prologue followed by legal prescriptions, and it, too, presents the king as the guarantor of all justice.[32] This attribution of justice to the king was also a feature of the Israelite monarchy from its earliest days. The inscription on the Khirbet Qeiyafa ostracon, which probably dates to the time of King David, seems to suggest that the king may have personally been involved in adjudicating on behalf of the poor and the widow.[33] A famous episode about Solomon, in which he judged between two mothers, each of whom claimed custody of a child (1 Kings 3.16–28), would seem to support this conception of the king as the guarantor of justice. The author of the book of Exodus would have us understand that, during the period of the exodus and the wilderness wandering, Moses was the highest source of authority and the arbiter of justice in Israel.

Moses as the mediator of the covenant and giver of the law

One of Moses' most central roles in the book of Exodus is as the mediator of the covenant at Mt Sinai. The Sinai covenant was a standard suzerain–vassal treaty, in which a people committed themselves to being subject (vassals) to a potentate (the suzerain). In this case, the Hebrews pledged fealty to the LORD as their suzerain and the LORD declared them to be his people (Exod. 19.5–6). As their suzerain, the LORD gave the Israelites laws. In the book of Exodus, Moses served as the mediator of these laws, including the Ten Commandments (Exod. 20.1–17) and the Book of the Covenant (20.22—23.33), as well as various legal and cultic instructions.[34]

In the Ancient Near East, covenant making and the giving of laws were the activities of kings. A king entered into a covenant relationship with another king, either as an equal or as a vassal, in order to establish peace and ensure stability between their nations.[35] In extant law codes, the king is always spe-

---

32 *ANET*, 163–80.

33 Cf. Yosef Garfinkel and Saar Ganor, *Khirbet Qeiyafa*, Vol. 1: *Excavation Report, 2007–2008* (Jerusalem: Israel Exploration Society, 2009), 243–60.

34 E.g. Exod. 15.26; 16.1–36; 18.16, 20.

35 Cf. George E. Mendenhall and Gary A. Herion, 'Covenant', *ABD* 1:1179–83.

cifically said to be the source of the law.[36] By emphasizing Moses' role as the mediator of the covenant and the giver of the law, the author of Exodus is attributing to him the authority of a king.

Moses as a priest

There are hints in the book of Exodus, as well as in the rest of the Pentateuch, that Moses may have been an Egyptian priest. He did not require a mediator but, like a priest, communicated with God directly (e.g. Exod. 33.11). He also mediated between God and the people of Israel (Exod. 20.18–21) and sought pardon for them (e.g. Exod. 34.9). Although God later commanded Moses to consecrate Aaron as high priest (Lev. 8.1–12), this would seem to imply that Moses was the first high priest. In addition, as noted in Chapter 4, he was highly educated, having been brought up as a prince of Egypt, and is the first person described in the Bible as writing (Exod. 24.4–8). He wrote down the law and gave it to the priests (Deut. 31.9). When he descended Mt Horeb, found the Israelites had built a golden calf and threw down the tablets of the Ten Commandments so that they shattered, this may have been the ritual act of a priest.[37]

One of the most intriguing pieces of evidence that may provide a link between Moses and the Egyptian priesthood is the description of Moses with 'horns' (Exod. 34.29–30).[38] Among the various ranks of Egyptian priests was the 'Khery-heb', or chief lector-priest (Gk *hierogrammateus*), who was both a sacred scribe and a magician. The lector-priest was sometimes known as a 'feather bearer', because of the distinguishing two-feathered headband he wore.[39] In visual representations of lector-priests, these feathers could easily be mistaken for horns.[40]

There is a strong tradition in Greco-Roman Egyptian texts that Moses was an Egyptian priest. The tradition is attested by the Greek-speaking Egyptian priest Manetho (third century BC), Apion, Chaeremon, the Greek historian Strabo, and Philo, who presented Moses as the ideal high priest in his *Life of Moses*.[41] The book of Acts states that Moses was 'instructed in all the wisdom

---

36 Cf. Martha T. Roth, *Law Collections from Mesopotamia and Asia Minor* (2nd edn; Atlanta, GA: Society of Biblical Literature, 1997).

37 Michael S. Donahou, *A Comparison of the Egyptian Execration Ritual to Exodus 32:19 and Jeremiah 19* (PHSC 8; Piscataway, NJ: Gorgias Press, 2010), 137–201.

38 Broderick, *Moses the Egyptian*, 93–102.

39 Cf. Broderick, *Moses the Egyptian*, fig. 34.

40 Cf. Broderick, *Moses the Egyptian*, figs 29, 30, 31.

41 Cf. John G. Gager, *Moses in Greco-Roman Paganism* (Nashville, TN: Abingdon Press, 1972), 40.

of the Egyptians' (Acts 7.22), which certainly would have included Egyptian religion and magic. It may be that he was schooled as a lector-priest, and the author of Exodus modelled the description of him descending the mountain, with his featherlike horns, on the Egyptian chief lector-priest. The magicians of Pharaoh who replicated Moses' signs (Exod. 7.11) were lector-priests. They were able to replicate his signs (Exod. 7.11), as well as some of the plagues, including the plague of water turned to blood (7.22) and the plague of frogs (8.7). However, they were stymied when it came to the plague of gnats (8.18–19), and they, too, were afflicted with the plague of boils (9.11). If Moses had indeed been educated as a lector-priest, only to return and trump the lector-priests of the pharaoh, it would be dramatically ironic.

Moses as a sanctuary builder

The occupation of Moses that receives the most attention in Exodus is his building and staffing of the tabernacle. Victor Hurowitz has shown that the construction of a sanctuary is one of the quintessential functions of a king in the Ancient Near East.[42] In reviewing the stories of Near Eastern kings who built temples, including those of Gudea of Lagash (ruled c.2144–2124 BC), Tiglath-pileser I, king of Assyria (1115–1077 BC), Nabonidus (ruled 556–539 BC) and others, he demonstrates that accounts of temple building follow a standard literary pattern that includes: (1) divine command to speak to a selected builder, who is to collect building materials and build the sanctuary; (2) messenger goes to recipient; (3) messenger recites command to collect building materials and build sanctuary; (4) builder follows order and gathers building materials; (5) skilled artisans are appointed; (6) additional building materials are gathered; and (7) building is constructed.[43]

The present form of the story of the building of the tabernacle follows this standard literary pattern. God gave Moses the plan for the tabernacle on Mt Sinai (Exod. 24.15—31.18). He collected the materials and recruited labourers and skilled craftsmen for its construction (35.20—36.7). He erected the tabernacle, installed its equipment and dedicated it (40.1–33). The book of Leviticus records Moses' subsequent installation of Aaron and his sons as priests to serve in the tabernacle (Lev. 8—9). The author's use of this literary pattern establishes the validity of the tabernacle as the house of the LORD, Israel's God, and the fact that he chose to dwell in the midst of his people.

---

42 Victor Hurowitz, 'The Priestly account of building the tabernacle', *JAOS* 105 (1985): 21–30; Victor Hurowitz, *I Have Built You an Exalted House: Temple building in the Bible in light of Mesopotamian and Northwest Semitic writings* (JSOTSup 115; Sheffield: JSOT Press, 1992).

43 Hurowitz, 'The Priestly account of building the tabernacle', 29.

Moses as equal to Pharaoh

As we have noted above, there are clearly a number of ways in which Moses is characterized in the book of Exodus besides that of prophet. Danny Mathews has recently proposed that the author(s) of the Pentateuch specifically utilized these tropes,[44] as well as a number of others, because they were 'traditional features of royal portraiture' and he wanted to portray Moses as a quasi-royal figure.[45] Many of these themes do appear in the stories of royal figures like Hammurabi, Esarhaddon, Nabonidus and Cyrus, and Mathews contends that these similarities establish Moses' identity 'as a royal figure without claiming that Moses functioned as an actual king'.[46] While Mathews is certainly correct that many of the characterizations of Moses in Exodus do feature aspects shared by Ancient Near Eastern kings, I do not think that the author's main purpose is to portray him as a royal figure. Gary Rendsburg is probably correct that these various tropes are all part of a strategy to portray Moses as equal to Pharaoh, not just in royalty, but in every respect.[47] After Moses had returned from his 40-year exile from the land of Egypt, confronted Pharaoh with signs and instigated nine of the ten plagues, the text says that 'the LORD gave the people favour in the sight of the Egyptians' and, 'moreover, Moses himself was a man of great importance in the land of Egypt, in the sight of Pharaoh's officials, and in the sight of the people' (Exod. 11.3). While Pharaoh himself continued to deny Moses' request to let the Hebrews go, the plagues had vindicated him in the eyes of his own officials and those of the Egyptian people at large. All Egypt had come to see Moses as equal to Pharaoh.

The uniqueness of Moses

While the characterizations of Moses discussed above do indeed converge to form a picture of Moses as equal to Pharaoh, the author(s) of Exodus, as well as the rest of the Pentateuch, clearly wanted to portray Moses as completely unique. During the year and a half or so that the Israelites spent at Mt Sinai, Moses spent two periods of 40 days and nights atop the mountain, surrounded by the glory of God.[48] The text states that 'the LORD used to speak to Moses face

---

44 Except for Moses as priest.

45 Danny Mathews, *Royal Motifs in the Pentateuchal Portrayal of Moses* (New York, NY: T&T Clark International, 2012), 85.

46 Mathews, *Royal Motifs*, 100.

47 Rendsburg, 'Moses as equal to Pharaoh', 201–19.

48 Exod. 24.18; 34.28.

to face, as one speaks to a friend' (Exod. 33.11). Later, during the wilderness sojourn, when Aaron and Miriam claimed that God spoke through them as well as through Moses, God replied that he spoke with Moses face to face, not through dreams and visions (Num. 12.6–8). Of all God's leaders in the Pentateuch, Moses was unique.[49]

The exalted status of Moses is made clear by the application to him of the title 'the servant of the LORD'.[50] Modern readers may tend to think of 'servant' (*'ebed*) as a title of low status, like a household servant or even a slave, and the Hebrew word certainly can have this meaning. However, in Hebrew, with its relatively limited vocabulary,[51] 'servant' has a broad range of meanings that must be determined by context. The servant of the king who hosts foreign dignitaries and speaks on the king's behalf is not a lowly slave, but an 'officer', 'minister' or 'ambassador'.[52] In his capacity as servant of the LORD, Moses represented God to the pharaoh and mediated between God and his people. These roles are certainly not those of a lowly servant or slave, but are more akin to those of a high-ranking officer, a minister, an ambassador or a vice-regent.

The title of 'servant' is applied to Moses only once in Exodus (14.31), and the title 'servant of the LORD' only three times in the Pentateuch, twice in Numbers and once in Deuteronomy.[53] However, the author of Joshua applied the term to Moses at least 16 times[54] and, from that point forward, it became the customary title for Moses throughout the Old Testament.[55] It was understood as an exalted title for the man who was probably the most revered human leader in the Old Testament. Mathews emphasizes that, as the servant of the LORD, 'Moses acts in the role of a "vice-regent" exercising temporal sovereignty on the LORD's behalf to establish Israel as a discrete nation'.[56]

---

49 The uniqueness of Moses and the authoritative nature of his teaching became the basis of all subsequent leadership positions in Israelite society. See S. Dean McBride Jr, 'Transcendent authority: the role of Moses in Old Testament traditions', *Int* 44 (1990): 229–39.

50 Moses is referred to as 'his servant' in Exod. 14.31, and as 'servant of the LORD' in Deut. 34.5; Josh. 1.1, 2, 7, 13, 15, etc.

51 There are only 8,679 unique words in biblical Hebrew, at least as far as it is represented in the Old Testament, compared with, for example, French, which contains up to 100,000 words, or German, with more than 200,000.

52 E.g. 1 Kings 1.47; 2 Kings 22.12; 2 Chron. 34.20; Neh. 2.10–19.

53 Num. 12.7, 8; Deut. 34.5.

54 Josh. 1.1, 2, 7, 13, 15; 8.31, 33; 9.24; 11.12, 15; 12.6; 13.8; 14.7; 22.2, 4, 5.

55 E.g. 2 Kings 8.53, 56; 1 Chron. 6.34; 2 Chron. 1.3; 24.6, 9; Ps. 105.26; Dan. 9.11; Neh. 1.8; 9.14; 10.30; Mal. 3.2.

56 Mathews, *Royal Motifs*, 147–8.

Conclusions

This chapter has explored the complexity of the portrayal of Moses in the book of Exodus. While Jewish and Christian traditions have both emphasized the characterization of Moses as a prophet, the book of Exodus includes numerous other portrayals of Moses. He is also represented as shepherd, divine figure, military leader, judge, mediator of the covenant and giver of the law, priest and sanctuary builder. Cumulatively, these depictions render Moses as equal to Pharaoh. However, the author of Exodus wants his readers to understand that, not only was Moses equal to Pharaoh, but he was completely unique. Moses knew God as fully as was possible for a human being and was given the title 'servant of the LORD'. This did not identify Moses as a lowly servant, but as God's ambassador or vice-regent. The portrayal of Moses in the book of Exodus identifies him as probably the most important human leader in the entire Old Testament.

6

The power of God in Exodus

In Chapter 5, we considered the portrayal of Moses as a leader in the book of Exodus, and showed that it intends to represent him as equal to Pharaoh and probably also as the most important human leader in the entire Old Testament. When God first called Moses, he told him that, through him, God would strike Egypt with 'all my wonders' (Exod. 3.20). Moses would become known as the greatest prophet in Israel, who

> was unequalled for all the signs and wonders that the LORD sent him to perform in the land of Egypt, against Pharaoh and all his servants and his entire land, and for all the mighty deeds and all the terrifying displays of power that Moses performed in the sight of all Israel.
> (Deut. 34.11–12)

In this chapter, we will explore the three primary miracles of Exodus and their interpretation, consider how scholars have responded to these accounts of the miraculous and, finally, examine the theological meaning of these miracles in the book of Exodus.

The weakness of Moses and the power of God

While Moses would come to be known as probably the most important human leader in the entire Old Testament, his beginning was one of false starts. As discussed in Chapter 4, when Moses was 40 years old, he shifted his allegiance from the Egyptian court to the Hebrews and tried to interject himself into Hebrew society as a revolutionary leader. These attempts were rejected by the Hebrews and, even worse, Pharaoh heard about it and sought to kill Moses (Exod. 2.14–15). Moses fled to Midian, where he settled among the Midianites and lived for 'a long time' (2.23).

One day, as he tended his father-in-law's sheep, he discovered a bush that was on fire but did not burn up (3.2). God spoke to him from the bush, told him to remove his sandals because he was on holy ground, and explained that he was the God of his ancestors, Abraham, Isaac and Jacob (3.4–6). In the ensuing 'call narrative', God commissioned Moses to return to Egypt on his behalf and liberate his people (3.1—4.31). In the dialogue that follows, Moses raised five different objections over two chapters, including: 'Who am I that I should go to Pharaoh?' (3.11); 'What shall I say to them?' (3.13); 'But suppose they do not believe me or listen to me, but say, "The LORD did not appear to you"' (4.1); 'I am slow of speech and slow of tongue' (4.10); and 'Please send someone else' (4.13). God rebuked Moses, but responded to his objections by appointing Aaron as his mouthpiece (4.14–17). Moses and Aaron returned to Egypt, secured an audience with Pharaoh and asked that he release the Hebrews so that they could celebrate a festival to the LORD (5.1). Pharaoh, however, answered that he did not know the LORD, scoffed at their request and increased the Hebrews' workload (5.2–14).

Moses was deeply distraught and complained to God, saying:

O LORD, why have you mistreated this people? Why did you ever send me? Since I first came to Pharaoh to speak in your name, he has mistreated this people, and you have done nothing at all to deliver your people. (Exod. 5.22–23)

The LORD reassured Moses that he would indeed use him to liberate the Hebrews but, once again, Moses objected. He insisted that 'The Israelites have not listened to me; how then shall Pharaoh listen to me, poor speaker that I am?' (6.12). A few verses later, the narrative says that, when the LORD spoke to Moses in the land of Egypt and reiterated his instructions, Moses objected yet again. He asked, 'Since I am a poor speaker, why would Pharaoh listen to me?' (6.30).

This brings the number of objection–reassurance cycles in Moses' call narrative to a total of eight. As discussed in Chapter 4, the 'call narrative' is a standard biblical genre which normally follows a set literary structure with six elements, including: (1) divine confrontation; (2) introductory word; (3) commission; (4) objection; (5) reassurance; and (6) sign.[1] Typically, these elements feature in a single episode[2] and, in fact, they all do appear in Moses' initial encounter with the LORD (Exod. 3.1–12), which ends with the giving of

---

1 Norman Habel, 'The form and significance of the call narratives', *ZAW* 77 (1965): 298.
2 In the cases of Isaiah and Jeremiah, for example, the formula is completed in just seven verses (Isa. 6.1–7; Jer. 1.4–10). In the case of Ezekiel, there is no mention of an objection on his part, but the other elements of the call narrative are included in a single vision (Ezek. 1.1–3.15).

a sign in verse 12.[3] Objections continue to appear, however, through the end of chapter 6, making the call of Moses the most elaborate of any of the call narratives in the Bible.

Interpreters have tried to explain this in a variety of ways. Traditional interpreters have suggested that the repeated objections are simply to emphasize Moses' sense of humility or sense of inadequacy.[4] Source critics, on the other hand, have explained this as the expansion of the original call of Moses to include additional materials. Brevard Childs, for example, writes that, 'In its present form a series of objections has been appended which allows a variety of divergent traditions to be incorporated within the narrative framework', and that 'the questions reflect widely differing concerns and point to a development of tradition over a considerable length of time'.[5] In a recent monograph, however, Amy Balogh observes that

> even if they belong to different sources, Moses's string of objections is carefully crafted, as he moves from questioning his identity as the proper messenger, to questioning the message itself, then the message's recipients, and, finally, the faculty by which this message is to be delivered, his lips . . . it is this final issue that becomes central and intensifies the longer it goes unresolved.[6]

She concludes that 'Moses's questions are not presented as a collection or list of disconnected traditions, but work together to present an argument that is tailored to a specific problem having to do with the status of Moses's mouth'.[7]

Indeed, Moses' objections do culminate in a focus on his mouth. He insisted, 'I have never been eloquent, neither in the past nor even now . . . but I am slow of speech and slow of tongue' (4.10). After his initial return to Egypt in which

---

3 The identification of the sign is disputed. Meyers writes: 'It is not clear what the sign is – it could be the miraculous burning bush, the very presence of God, the fact that God is sending him, or even the ultimate outcome of the mission, in which Moses effects the miraculous deliverance of his people from Egypt. Perhaps the language is intentionally ambiguous, allowing for all these possibilities, which encompass past, present, and future events, as one might expect in mnemohistory.' Cf. Carol Meyers, *Exodus* (Cambridge: Cambridge University Press, 2005), 56.

4 E.g. Walter C. Kaiser, 'Exodus', in *Expositor's Bible Commentary*, ed. Frank E. Gaebelein; 12 vols (Grand Rapids, MI: Zondervan, 1990), 2:318–29.

5 Brevard S. Childs, *The Book of Exodus: A critical, theological commentary* (Philadelphia, PA: Westminster Press, 1974), 54.

6 Amy L. Balogh, *Moses among the Idols: Mediators of the divine in the Ancient Near East* (Lanham, MD: Lexington/Fortress Academic, 2018), 40.

7 Balogh, *Moses among the Idols*, 40–1.

he failed to secure release for the Hebrews, he objected that, 'The Israelites have not listened to me; how then shall Pharaoh listen to me, poor speaker that I am?' (6.12). A few verses later, Moses is said to have repeated the argument, asking God, 'Since I am a poor speaker, why would Pharaoh listen to me?' (6.30). In the first objection, that Moses was 'slow of speech and slow of tongue', the Hebrew literally says that he was 'heavy of mouth and heavy of tongue' (4.10) and, in the second and third objections, Moses actually said he was 'uncircumcised of lips' (6.12, 30). Both of these phrases have been discussed by generations of commentators.[8] Both expressions are usually understood as: (1) a language barrier; (2) a physical disability; or (3) a metaphor for a general feeling of being unqualified. A speech impediment seems to be the most likely explanation, since Hebrew often calls flawed bodily organs 'heavy'.[9]

The LORD responded to Moses' objections with three assurances: (1) he appointed Aaron to be his spokesman (4.14–16; 7.1–2), and Aaron served in this capacity through the time of the plagues and, according to the Pentateuchal narratives, throughout the period of the exodus and the wilderness wandering;[10] (2) he promised to 'harden Pharaoh's heart' (7.3); and (3) he promised to multiply his signs and wonders in the land of Egypt (7.3). The LORD assured Moses that the result would be that the Egyptians would know that he was the LORD, and that he would bring the Israelites out from among them (7.5).

The point of the extended call narrative, with all of Moses' objections, along with Aaron's appointment as his spokesman and God's assurances that he would be with him, is to emphasize that Moses could not and would not be able to fulfil the commission to liberate the Hebrews on his own. The task of liberating the Hebrews did not depend on Moses' skill or ability, but on God. It was God who would liberate the Hebrews and, if Moses was to play a part in the exodus events, it would only be by depending on him. It would be God's power at work through Moses that would bring success.

The first thing that God told Moses and Aaron to do was to secure an audience with Pharaoh and, when he asked them to perform a wonder, Aaron was to throw his staff before Pharaoh and it would become a snake (7.8–9). They carried out the LORD's instructions, but Pharaoh's wise men and sorcerers

---

8 See the brief overview of interpretative options in William H. C. Propp, *Exodus 1–18: A new translation with introduction and commentary* (New York, NY: Doubleday, 1999), 210–11, 273–4.

9 Jeffrey H. Tigay, '"Heavy of mouth" and "heavy of tongue": on Moses' speech difficulty', *BASOR* 231 (1978): 57–67.

10 Alan Millard, 'Moses, the tongue-tied singer!', in *'Did I Not Bring Israel Out of Egypt?' Biblical, archaeological, and Egyptological perspectives on the exodus narratives*, ed. James K. Hoffmeier, Alan R. Millard and Gary A. Rendsburg (Winona Lake, IN: Eisenbrauns, 2016), 133–42.

seemed to be able to replicate the miracle 'by their secret arts' (7.11). Although Aaron's staff swallowed up their snakes, 'Pharaoh's heart was hardened' and, therefore, he would not listen to Moses and Aaron (7.12–13).

Since the pharaoh's heart was hardened and he refused to let the Israelites go, Moses and Aaron were to return in the morning and announce to the pharaoh that the LORD was going to 'strike the water that is in the Nile' so that it would be 'turned to blood' (7.17). Moses had Aaron lift up his staff and stretch out his hand over the waters of Egypt, 'and all the water in the river was turned into blood, and the fish in the river died' (7.20–21). Once again, however, the magicians of Egypt were able to mimic this miracle, so that 'Pharaoh's heart remained hardened, and he would not listen to them' (7.22). Pharaoh went into his house, and the Egyptian people had 'to dig along the Nile for water to drink, for they could not drink the water of the river' (7.23–24).

Seven days passed, and the LORD sent Moses and Aaron back to threaten Pharaoh with a plague of frogs. When he was unresponsive, Aaron 'stretched out his hand over the waters of Egypt; and the frogs came up and covered the land of Egypt' (8.6). Although the magicians seemed to be able to replicate the phenomenon, Pharaoh seemed to relent, called for Moses and Aaron, and asked them to pray to the LORD for the frogs to be taken away (8.8–11). However, once there was a respite from the frogs, Pharaoh once again hardened his heart and would not listen to Moses and Aaron (8.15).

The third plague was an infestation of gnats, and Pharaoh's magicians were not able to replicate it. Gnats covered humans and animals throughout Egypt (8.18). Although Pharaoh's magicians announced to him that this was evidence of 'the finger of God', he hardened his heart yet again and would not listen to Moses and Aaron (8.19). Plagues of flies (8.20–32), disease upon the livestock (9.1–12), thunder and hail (9.13–35), locusts (10.1–20) and darkness (10.21–27) followed but, in every case, Pharaoh hardened his heart and would not listen to Moses and Aaron.[11]

Finally, God announced that he would send one final plague upon Egypt that would break Pharaoh's will and cause him to let the Israelites go (11.1). At midnight, he would go throughout Egypt and strike down the firstborn in the land, 'from the firstborn of Pharaoh who sits on his throne to the firstborn of the female slave who is behind the handmill, and all the firstborn of the livestock' (11.4–5). When it came to pass, 'there was a loud cry in Egypt, for there was not a house without someone dead' (12.30). Pharaoh summoned Moses

---

11 Exod. 7.22; 8.15, 19, 32; 9.7, 12, 34, 35; 10.20, 27; 11.10. In 9.12; 10.20, 27 and 11.10, the text states that it was the LORD who hardened Pharaoh's heart.

and Aaron and told them to take the Israelites and leave Egypt (12.31–32) and, finally, after having lived in Egypt for 'four hundred and thirty years', 'all the companies of the LORD went out from the land of Egypt' (12.40–41).

However, the LORD warned Moses that it would not be long before Pharaoh concluded that the Israelites were lost and wandering aimlessly in the wilderness (14.3). Furthermore, he told Moses that he would harden Pharaoh's heart so that he would set out in pursuit of the Israelites, in order that he could 'gain glory for myself over Pharaoh and all his army; and the Egyptians shall know that I am the LORD' (v. 4). In short order, Pharaoh indeed regretted having let Israel go and he 'took six hundred picked chariots and all the other chariots of Egypt with officers over all of them', and 'the LORD hardened the heart of Pharaoh king of Egypt and he pursued the Israelites' (vv. 7–8). When the Egyptians came upon the Israelites camped by the Red Sea, the Israelites were trapped and it looked as if they were doomed. They would have been, except that the 'pillar of cloud moved from in front of them and took its place behind them' (v. 19), preventing the Egyptian army from approaching.

The LORD told Moses to command the Israelites to go forward, and that he should lift up his staff and stretch out his hand over the sea and divide it, so that 'the Israelites may go into the sea on dry ground' (v. 16). Furthermore, he would harden the hearts of the Egyptians so that they would go in after them (v. 17). Moses stretched out his hand over the sea, and 'the LORD drove the sea back by a strong east wind all night, and turned the sea into dry land; and the waters were divided' (v. 21). The Israelites 'went into the sea on dry ground, the waters forming a wall for them on their right and on their left' (v. 22). When the Egyptians went into the sea after them, the LORD threw them into a panic, and caused the wheels of their chariots to get clogged so that they only turned with difficulty (vv. 23–25). Finally, the LORD commanded Moses to once again stretch out his hand over the sea and, when he did so, the sea 'returned to its normal depth', drowning Pharaoh's army (vv. 26–29).

That day, the LORD saved Israel from the Egyptians, 'and Israel saw the Egyptians dead on the seashore' (v. 30). The crossing of the Red Sea caused the people to fear and believe in the LORD, and to put their trust in the LORD's servant, Moses (v. 31). In the wake of this exhilarating experience of salvation, Moses and the Israelites sang a victory ode that celebrates the breathtaking power and unsurpassed supremacy of God over Pharaoh and his army (15.1–18). The focus of the song is on the LORD, whose name appears ten times in these 18 verses. It celebrates the LORD's overthrow of the Egyptian forces (vv. 1b–12) and looks forward to Israel's entrance into the promised land (vv. 13–18). Afterwards, Moses and Aaron's sister, Miriam, led the women out 'with tambourines and with dancing' (Exod. 15.20), and she sang to them: 'Sing to the LORD, for he has triumphed gloriously; horse and rider he has thrown into the sea' (v. 21). Miriam's song follows the form of hymns of praise and thanksgiving,[12] inviting her audience to sing with her, and then giving the reason for raising the hymn. By throwing the Egyptian chariot forces into the sea, the LORD has 'triumphed gloriously' (v. 21). He has eliminated the Egyptian threat and liberated the former Israelite slaves.

Miracles and the modern mind

Miracles are usually understood as 'events, actions, and states taken to be so unusual, extraordinary, and supernatural that the normal level of human consciousness finds them hard to accept rationally'.[13] Biblical Hebrew does not have a direct equivalent for the English word 'miracle', but the terms 'wonder' (*pele*') and 'signs' ('*otot*) are clearly used to refer to events that are understood as miraculous.[14] 'Wonders' are extraordinary and marvellous, and 'evoke a reaction of astonishment and praise from their beholders'.[15] When God first called Moses, he told him that, through him, he would strike Egypt with 'all my wonders' (Exod. 3.20), and later biblical authors referred back to the exodus events as 'wonders'.[16] 'Signs' are 'extraordinary and surprising events which God brought about in order to demonstrate His power and will in particular situations, when men had to be convinced'.[17] Jacob Licht identifies the most important signs in the Old Testament as those that occurred in Egypt, especially the transformation of the staff into a serpent (Exod. 4.1–7) to establish Moses as God's representative, and the ten plagues by which the LORD 'coerced Pharaoh to accept the divine command to let the people go'.[18]

However, the idea of materialism as an adequate explanation for all things began to develop among several classical Greek thinkers, was developed by Aristotle (384–322 BC) and burgeoned in the period of the Enlightenment.[19] In 1748, David Hume (1711–76), a Scottish philosopher, historian, economist and

---

12 The technical term for the hymn of praise, *tehilla*, occurs in the title to Ps. 145.1.

13 Manuba Waida, 'Miracles: an overview', *ER* 9:6049.

14 Wendy Cotter, 'Miracle', *NIDB* 4:100.

15 Jacob Licht, 'Miracle', *EncJud* 14:305.

16 E.g. Ps. 78.12ff.; Mic. 7.15.

17 Licht, 'Miracle', 305.

18 Licht, 'Miracle', 305.

19 The Enlightenment was an intellectual and philosophical movement that dominated the world of ideas in Europe from the seventeenth to nineteenth centuries. Cf. Allen W. Wood, 'Enlightenment, The', *ER* 4:2795–9.

essayist, published a study, *Of Miracles*, in which he espoused a system of radical philosophical empiricism, scepticism and naturalism.[20] Hume insisted that the world functions according to laws of nature, which have been established by 'firm and unalterable experience', demonstrating that they are unbreakable. Since people have experienced nature as unchangeable, this, in and of itself, is 'the proof against a miracle'. Hume understood miracles as a violation of the laws of nature and, therefore, impossible. This world view, which considers all miracles to be misperceptions based on ignorance, superstition or the failure to grasp the purely physical causes of the phenomenon, has come to dominate intellectual and academic life in the West. William Propp, for example, explains that 'the modern historian's method precludes acknowledgment of supernatural phenomena, onetime suspensions of physical law', and that 'it is only prudent to credit human imagination with the majority of "miracles"'.[21] He concedes that 'a small proportion may be based on direct observation or secondhand knowledge of real events', but that these represent 'misunderstood natural phenomena or ordinary occurrences of unusual magnitude or timeliness'.[22] With regard to the study of the book of Exodus, this approach has certainly influenced critical scholars to conclude that the stories of the serpent confrontation, the ten plagues, and the crossing of the Red Sea can be explained by natural causation or misunderstood observation, or as the mythologizing of ordinary events.

There are certainly those who take a more traditional view with regard to the miraculous in the Old Testament. Ernest Lucas, for example, argues that

> a theist cannot accept Hume's narrow definition of 'miracle,' because accepting it amounts to adopting a semideistic worldview in which God is outside of, and inactive within, his creation except on those rare occasions when he 'violates' the laws of nature, which he created, and 'intervenes' in the world.[23]

He suggests that contemporary theists can instead adopt 'a nuanced version of the ancient Hebrew worldview', in which God created the world and continues to maintain it.[24] Lucas goes on to explain that:

---

20 David Hume, *Of Miracles* (repr.; Chicago, IL: Open Court, 1985).

21 William H. C. Propp, *Exodus 1–18: A new translation with introduction and commentary* (AB 2; New York, NY: Doubleday, 1999), 347.

22 Propp, *Exodus 1–18*, 347.

23 E. C. Lucas, 'Miracles', in *Dictionary of the Old Testament: Historical books*, ed. B. T. Arnold and H. G. M. Williamson (Downers Grove, IL: InterVarsity Press, 2005), 700.

24 Lucas, 'Miracles', 700.

> The 'natural laws' that scientists discover are one of God's 'normal' ways
> of working in the world [and] it is not surprising, therefore, that God
> sometimes uses these natural laws to produce a 'wonder' that becomes a
> sign that says something to his people.[25]

In this approach, even if the 'wonders' or 'signs' of the book of Exodus occurred in conjunction with 'natural causes', this would not be viewed as having eliminated the miracle. Instead, the 'natural causes' may be viewed as
the means by which the LORD sent the plagues and, later, parted the waters
of the Red Sea.

Efforts to provide a natural explanation for the plagues go back at least to
the early nineteenth century.[26] Johann Gottfried Eichorn (1752–1827), an early
Protestant theologian of the Enlightenment, was one of the first to try to
work out a rationalistic explanation, which he published as *De Aegypti anno
mirabili*.[27] In the early twentieth century, the Egyptologist William Matthew
Flinders Petrie wrote that, 'The order of the plagues was the natural order of
such troubles on a lesser scale in the Egyptian seasons', and that this had been
'pointed out long ago'.[28] Petrie seems to take the idea for granted, and summarizes it in just one paragraph.[29] In more contemporary times, Greta Hort
(1903–67) has examined the various proposals and provided a compelling syn-
thesis.[30] In her reconstruction, an unusually high inundation of the Nile was
the precipitating factor. This was caused by excessive rains, which brought
down large amounts of red sediment from Ethiopia, turning the Nile blood
red and killing fish. A week later, frogs, infected with *Bacillus anthracis*, went
ashore to escape the polluted Nile. Eventually, the piles of dead frogs all over
the land led to the cattle disease of the fifth plague. The high floodwaters created an abundant breeding ground for the gnats and flies of the third and fourth

---

25 Lucas, 'Miracles', 700.

26 Even ancient interpreters explored the idea that God worked through nature in the plagues. For
example, Philo argued that God marshalled the 'elements of the universe . . . into a state of hostility'
against the Egyptians, 'in order to exhibit the height of the authority which God wielded, who had
also fashioned those same elements at the creation of the universe, so as to secure its safety, and who
could change them all whenever he pleased, to effect the destruction of impious men' (*Mos.* 1.96). The
idea that the plagues could be explained as completely natural phenomena, however, appears to date
to the Enlightenment.

27 Like most scholarly works written between the Early Renaissance and the end of the eighteenth century, it was written in Latin.

28 W. M. Flinders Petrie, *Egypt and Israel* (London: SPCK, 1911), 35.

29 Petrie, *Egypt and Israel*, 35–6.

30 Greta Hort, 'The plagues of Egypt', *ZAW* 69 (1957): 84–103; Greta Hort, 'The plagues of Egypt, II',
ZAW 70 (1958): 48–59.

plagues, and these could have caused the boils or skin anthrax of plague six. The hailstorm of the seventh plague would have occurred several months later, in January or February, destroying the flax and barley but not the wheat and spelt, which would have been left for the locusts of the eighth plague. The ninth plague was the first *khamsin* of the year, which would have whipped up the deep layer of red earth that had been left after the plague of hail.[31] Since a *khamsin* in Egypt normally lasts two to three days, these fine particles of red earth would have created an enormously thick darkness.

Hort views the tenth plague as 'very different . . . from the account of all the other plagues', since it 'has been worked and re-worked, and integrated into the account of the origin of [Passover]'.[32] She proposes that it did not originally refer to the slaying of the firstborn (Heb. *bkr*) but to the destruction of the first fruits (*bkrym*). This destruction was the natural consequence of the ninth plague but, whether through a substitution or accidentally, it became 'an aetiological explanation of [Passover]'.[33] She admits that her explanation for the tenth plague is 'no more than a suggestion' but, if correct, would also follow as a natural consequence from the ninth plague.[34] In the end, she concludes that

> each of the plagues in its essential features describes correctly a natural phenomenon, which, though far from common, may yet happen in Egypt from time to time . . . these conclusions prove that the Bible gives us an historically accurate account of the ten plagues.[35]

A number of influential scholars have found her reconstruction compelling.[36]

Contemporary interpreters continue to look for a cause-and-effect chain that would explain the ten plagues. In one recent example, Cambridge University physicist Colin Humphreys proposes an alternative chain-reaction that might provide a natural explanation for the ten plagues.[37] In this reconstruction, the plagues were triggered by a 'red tide', due to a bloom of toxic red

---

31 The *khamsin* is an oppressively hot, dust-laden, southerly wind.

32 Hort, 'The plagues of Egypt, II', 54.

33 Hort, 'The plagues of Egypt, II', 54. An aetiology is a story that explains the origins of a phenomenon.

34 Hort, 'The plagues of Egypt, II', 54–5.

35 Hort, 'The plagues of Egypt, II', 58.

36 J. Finegan, *Let My People Go: A journey through Exodus* (New York, NY: Harper & Row, 1963), 47–57; James K. Hoffmeier, *Israel in Egypt: The evidence for the authenticity of the exodus tradition* (New York, NY: Oxford University Press, 1997), 149; Kenneth A. Kitchen and Paul J. N. Lawrence, 'Plagues of Egypt', *NBD*: 1001–3.

37 Colin J. Humphreys, *The Miracles of Exodus: A scientist's discovery of the extraordinary natural causes of the biblical stories* (New York, NY: HarperSanFrancisco, 2003).

algae.[38] In such a case, the algae grow very fast and accumulate into dense visible patches near the surface of the water, which can kill fish and other animals. This 'red tide' triggered the rest of the plagues.

A favourite suggestion is that either the ten plagues or the parting of the Red Sea, or both, were caused by the eruption of the great volcano on the island of Santorini, located 70 miles (112 km) north of Crete, in the Aegean Sea. In this scenario, the eruption could have caused the flooding of low coastal lands in Egypt, which facilitated the exodus and the crossing of the Red Sea. The plume, which was visible from the Nile Delta, was interpreted by the Israelites as a pillar of fire, which they followed into the wilderness. Variations on these theories have been advocated by scholars and popular writers alike. Scholars who have argued in favour of versions of it have ranged from the famous Egyptologist Hans Goedicke to the geologist Barbara Sivertsen.[39] Popular writers who have connected the exodus events with the eruption of the Santorini volcano have included Ian Wilson in *Exodus: The true story behind the biblical account*, Rian Booysen in *Thera and the Exodus: The exodus explained in terms of natural phenomena and the human response to it* and many others.[40] This view has also been promoted over and over in television documentaries, most recently *The Exodus Decoded* by Simcha Jacobovici.[41]

Could the eruption of the Santorini volcano have triggered the plagues? Could its plume have been visible from the Nile Delta and interpreted as a pillar of fire? Could its effects have facilitated the crossing of the Red Sea? The answer to all of these questions must be negative, for several reasons. First, the effects of the eruption on Santorini would not have had the kinds of

---

38 Humphreys, *Miracles of Exodus*, 114–18.

39 In 1981, Hans Goedicke proposed that the eruption of the Santorini volcano caused the flooding of low coastal lands in Egypt, which facilitated the exodus and the crossing of the Red Sea. Cf. Hershel Shanks, 'The exodus and the crossing of the Red Sea, according to Hans Goedicke', *BAR* 7.5 (1981): 42–50. He later presented his arguments in scientific publications. See Hans Goedicke, *The Speos Artemidos Inscription of Hatshepsut and Related Discussions* (Oakville, CT: Halgo, 2004); Hans Goedicke, 'The chronology of the Thera/Santorini explosion', in *High, Middle, or Low? Acts of the Second International Colloquium on Absolute Chronology, Schloß Haindorf/Lanlois, 12–15 August 1990* (Ägypten und Levante 3; Vienna: Austrian Academy of Sciences Press, 1992), 57–62. Barbara Sivertsen has written a comprehensive study of the exodus, in which she ties the plagues, the exodus and the crossing of the Sea to the Santorini eruption. Cf. Barbara J. Sivertsen, *The Parting of the Sea: How volcanoes, earthquakes, and plagues shaped the story of the exodus* (Princeton, NJ: Princeton University Press, 2009), 35–45.

40 Ian Wilson, *Exodus: The true story behind the biblical account* (New York, NY: HarperCollins, 1986); Rian Booysen, *Thera and the Exodus: The exodus explained in terms of natural phenomena and the human response to it* (Winchester: O-Books, 2012). For discussion of these and other accounts, see Mark Harris, 'The Thera theories: science and the modern reception history of the exodus', in *Israel's Exodus in Transdisciplinary Perspective: Text, archaeology, culture, and geoscience*, ed. Thomas E. Levy, Thomas Schneider and William H. C. Propp (New York, NY: Springer, 2015), 91–9.

41 Simcha Jacobovici, *The Exodus Decoded* (Toronto: Syndicado, 2016).

dramatic effects that have been imagined. Several scientists recently simulated the tsunami that followed the Thera eruption, and their replication 'does not show impressive waves along the coasts of the Nile Delta and Northern Sinai'.[42] Second, the date of the Santorini eruption does not coincide with the exodus events. In the early-to-mid 1980s, the Santorini eruption was redated using Carbon-14 to about 1628 BC,[43] although there are some who argue that it should be dated to about 1525 BC.[44] In either case, however, there can be no connection with the Santorini eruption, because historical and archaeological evidence put the date of the exodus somewhere between about 1275 and 1250 BC.[45] In the end, there could not have been a connection between the exodus events and the Santorini eruption.

There may have been some kind of cause-and-effect process at work in the ecological disasters that engulfed Egypt in the plagues but, if the Israelites even considered this possibility, they had no interest in it. Whatever it was that they experienced, Roland de Vaux insists, they 'regarded it as a miraculous intervention on the part of their God'.[46] When they produced the account of the plagues that is recorded in Exodus, their interest was in this divine dimension and not in the production of a scientific account that explored cause and effect. This is evident in the fact that, in other biblical accounts of the ten plagues, their number and order varies.[47] Ziony Zevit explains that, 'These differences can be taken to indicate that the specific number and order of the plagues was less important to Israel than the fact of the plagues and what was revealed to Israel through them.'[48]

Just as the ten plagues have evoked efforts to provide a rational explanation, so has the crossing of the sea. Discussions of the event focus on two questions: which body of water was involved and what happened there? The identification of the body of water involved is uncertain. In Hebrew, the name of the body of water is *yam sûp*, which most English translations render as the

---

42 Amos Salamon, Steve Ward, Floyd McCoy, John Hall and Thomas E. Levy, 'Inspired by a tsunami? An earth sciences perspective of the Exodus narrative', in *Israel's Exodus* (ed. Levy, Schneider and Propp), 126.

43 Cf. S. W. Manning, *A Test of Time: The volcano of Thera and the chronology and history of the Aegean and East Mediterranean in the mid-second millennium BC* (Oxford: Oxbow, 1999); S. W. Manning, 'Eruption of Thera/Santorini', in *The Oxford Handbook of the Bronze Age Aegean*, ed. E. H. Cline (New York, NY: Oxford University Press, 2010), 457–74.

44 Malcolm H. Wiener, 'Dating the Theran eruption: archaeological science versus nonsense science', in *Israel's Exodus* (ed. Levy, Schneider and Propp), 131–43.

45 See Chapter 3, this volume.

46 Roland de Vaux, *The Early History of Israel* (Philadelphia, PA: Westminster Press, 1978), 608.

47 Cf. Ps. 78.44–51 and Ps. 105.28–36.

48 Ziony Zevit, 'Three ways to look at the ten plagues', *BRev* 6.3 (1990): 23.

'Red Sea' (e.g. Exod. 13.18). The Hebrew term *sûp*, however, corresponds to Egyptian *tjuf*, which means 'reed', and *yam sûp* should therefore correctly be translated as 'Reed Sea'. Knowing that the Hebrew name does not refer to the 'Red Sea' does not help to pinpoint the body of water, however, since *yam sûp* is not only used for the Sea through which the Israelites passed,[49] but also for the Gulf of Suez[50] and the Gulf of Aqaba.[51] Lake Timsah and the Bitter Lakes, north of the Gulf of Suez, also have abundant supplies of reeds and papyrus, so one of these bodies of water could have been the 'Reed Sea'. The term could also apply to the marshy lakes in the Isthmus of Suez. It has also been proposed that *yam sûp* was the proper name of a marshy region of the eastern delta, east of the Hebrew slave camp.[52] The biblical data simply do not allow for a clear identification of the *yam sûp*.[53]

The identification of the body of water, however, certainly affects how interpreters have understood the events that followed. When the Israelites arrived at the *yam sûp*, with the Egyptian army approaching from behind, they were terrified and cried out to the LORD (Exod. 14.10). God commanded Moses to raise his staff and stretch it out over the sea (14.16), and then

> the LORD drove the sea back by a strong east wind *all night*, and turned the sea into dry land; and the waters were divided. The Israelites went into the sea on dry ground, the waters forming a wall for them on their right and on their left.
> (Exod. 14.21–22, italics mine)

Popular imagination has pictured the Israelites crossing through a massive body of water, with trembling walls of water towering above them on either side, such as in the film adaptations *The Ten Commandments* and *The Prince of Egypt*. If the crossing took place through the centre of a large body of water, such as the Gulf of Suez, it certainly would have required some kind of dramatic displacement of water. If the crossing was through a smaller body of water, or at the tongue of a body of water, a sustained east wind (14.21), a sirocco, could have shifted the waters so that at this place the seabed was exposed. If it was through a marshy region or a papyrus swamp, the Israelites could have

---

49 E.g. Exod. 13.18; 15.4; Josh. 24.6.

50 Cf. Num. 33.10, 11.

51 Cf. Exod. 23.31; Deut. 1.40, 2.1; 1 Kings 9.26.

52 Manfred Bietak, 'Comments on the "exodus"', in *Egypt, Israel, Sinai: Archaeological and historical relationships in the biblical period*, ed. Anson F. Rainey (Tel Aviv: Tel Aviv University, 1987), 163–70.

53 For a detailed study, see Hoffmeier, *Israel in Egypt*, 199–222.

simply waded across.[54] It has also been explained as a historical event that has been greatly embellished through poetic licence or a religio-nationalist agenda, or even as a historicized myth, in which case there was no crossing at all.[55]

Assuming that these texts are trying to describe some kind of historical events, reconstructing them may not be possible. We may have to conclude, with Noth, that 'it must remain uncertain what [the author(s) of Exodus] meant to express when he said that "the sea was driven back" and with what phenomenon from what realm of experience he connected it'.[56] The biblical writers viewed both the ten plagues and the crossing of the Sea as 'wonders' and 'signs', and were primarily interested in their theological meaning, to which we will now turn.

Theological meaning of the miracles of Exodus

The serpent confrontation

In discussing the miracles of Exodus, many interpreters focus on the ten plagues and the crossing of the Red Sea and overlook the serpent confrontation of Exodus 7.8–13. However, John Currid argues that this story is 'critical for our understanding of what follows because it is a paradigm of the plague narratives' and, as such, 'it foreshadowed Yahweh's humiliation of Egypt through the plagues and at the Red Sea'.[57] He explains that the serpent confrontation and the Red Sea crossing are like bookends for the entire narrative of the exodus, emphasizing its primary themes. The repetition of the word 'swallow' supports this thematic unity. At the beginning of the exodus narratives, Aaron's rod 'swallowed' the magicians' rods (7.12) and, at the end, the Egyptian army was 'swallowed' by the Red Sea (15.12). As Currid points out, these parallels 'establish Exodus 7:8–13 as a microcosmic prototype of the imminent national catastrophe of Egypt'.[58]

The serpent confrontation also defines the real issues at stake in the whole struggle to secure the Israelites' freedom from bondage in Egypt. The battle to

---

54 See the discussion in Childs, *Book of Exodus*, 228.

55 See the discussion and references in Bernard F. Batto, 'Mythic dimensions of the exodus tradition', in *Israel's Exodus* (ed. Levy, Schneider and Propp), 187–95.

56 Martin Noth, *Exodus: A commentary* (Philadelphia, PA: Westminster Press, 1962), 116.

57 John D. Currid, *Ancient Egypt and the Old Testament* (Grand Rapids, MI: Baker, 1997), 85.

58 Currid, *Ancient Egypt*, 85–6.

secure their freedom was not primarily a confrontation between two peoples (Israel and Egypt) or between two men (Moses and Pharaoh). Instead, it was a battle between the God of the Hebrews and the deities of Egypt. The serpent confrontation introduces us to this theological issue. It is based on the Egyptian fear of snakes, which were ever present and justly feared.[59] The many charms and spells found in the Pyramid Texts, as well as the many amulets used to ward off venomous snakes that have been found in excavations, confirm Ancient Egyptians' dread of poisonous bites. This fear resulted in the rise of various cults that worshipped certain snakes. Harmless snakes, on the other hand, were viewed as protectors. Some Egyptian myths, therefore, describe snakes as protectors or as escorts on journeys.[60] Snakes were therefore both feared and honoured in Ancient Egyptian society.

The most important example of serpent worship in Ancient Egypt was probably that of the cobra goddess Wadjet, whose cult was based in the ancient towns of Pe and Dept, in the north-western delta, where her shrine is attested as early as predynastic times.[61] Wadjet was the personification of the cobra, which represents strength, power and sovereignty, and became the tutelary deity of Lower Egypt. Nekhbet, the vulture goddess, was the tutelary deity of Upper Egypt. The two deities were often portrayed as seated together, or even as a single figure consisting of parts of both deities.[62] Since the pharaoh had the power of both Wadjet and Nekhbet, he was able to control both Upper and Lower Egypt.

The power that these two gods conveyed to the pharaoh was represented by the uraeus, the stylized upright cobra on the front of his crown.[63] The actual device of the uraeus came to be considered the source of Pharaoh's power. The Egyptians believed that the uraeus would strike fear into the hearts of Pharaoh's enemies in the same way that a real snake would. Hymns were actually composed to the pharaoh's crown, and these sometimes describe the uraeus as wreaking havoc against the pharaoh's enemies in battle.[64] It was as effective as a physical weapon.[65] It was also viewed as investing the pharaoh with magical powers.

---

59 Nicole B. Hansen, 'Snakes', *OEAE* 3:296–9.

60 For examples, see Currid, *Ancient Egypt*, 88.

61 Richard H. Wilkinson, *The Complete Gods and Goddesses of Ancient Egypt* (London: Thames & Hudson, 2003), 227.

62 Wilkinson, *Complete Gods and Goddesses*, 227.

63 The English word 'uraeus' comes from *ouraios*, the Greek word for 'cobra'.

64 For examples, see Currid, *Ancient Egypt*, 90.

65 Cf. *ARE* 4:77, where the uraeus is in parallel with the pharaoh's mace.

Viewed in this light, the serpent confrontation is clearly polemical. When Moses and Aaron threw down their staffs (Exod. 7.8), it was a direct 'challenge to the power of Egyptian magic as described in numerous mythological texts'.[66] Many Egyptian sources recount amazing feats performed by Egyptian magicians.[67] Of particular relevance to the serpent confrontation is the Westcar Papyrus, a series of stories that recounts the wondrous deeds of Egyptian lector-priests in the age of Cheops.[68] One of these stories tells about a lector-priest named Webaoner who made a wax crocodile that came to life when he threw it into a lake. Later, he bent down and picked it up, and it became wax again.[69] The story has certain similarities to the biblical serpent confrontation, in which Aaron threw down his staff and it turned into a snake (Exod. 7.10). Currid suggests that the Exodus writer(s), 'by narrating a historical event in which a priest actually transformed an inanimate object into an animal, may be subtly pointing to the fictional character of the Egyptian mythological texts'.[70] When Aaron threw down his staff and the LORD turned it into a snake, and that snake devoured those of the court magicians, it was demonstrating that the LORD was superior to the powers of Egyptian magic. Not only that, but the LORD's snake devoured the court magicians' snakes right in front of the uraeus coiled on the front of Pharaoh's crown. Wadjet and Nekhbet, the gods of Upper and Lower Egypt, were powerless before Yahweh.

The ten plagues

The ten plagues, whose number represented perfection and completion,[71] have fascinated interpreters for generations. There have been four main approaches to interpreting the plagues. The first, as natural phenomena, was discussed above. The second approach has been to view the plagues as polemical attacks on the gods of Egypt.[72] In this method, each plague is aimed at a specific deity

---

66 Currid, *Ancient Egypt*, 92.

67 Robert K. Ritner, 'Magic: an overview', *OEAE* 2:321–6.

68 Cf. William Kelly Simpson, *The Literature of Ancient Egypt: An anthology of stories, instructions, stelae, autobiographies, and poetry* (3rd edn; New Haven, CT: Yale University Press, 2003), 13–24.

69 This is the Second Tale in the Westcar Papyrus, entitled 'The Marvel Which Happened in the Time of King Nebka'. Simpson, *Literature of Ancient Egypt*, 14–16.

70 Currid, *Ancient Egypt*, 93.

71 Ellen Frankel and Betsy Platkin Teutsch, *The Encyclopedia of Jewish Symbols* (Northvale, NJ: Jason Aronson, 1992), 173.

72 Leading advocates for this view include: Charles Aling, *Egypt and Bible History* (Grand Rapids, MI: Baker, 1981), 103–10; John J. Davis, *Moses and the Gods of Egypt* (2nd edn; Grand Rapids. MI: Baker, 1986), 98–153; Peter Enns, *Inspiration and Incarnation: Evangelicals and the problem of the Old Testament* (Grand Rapids, MI: Baker, 2005), 100–1; G. A. F. Knight, *Theology as Narration* (Grand

or at that deity's control over some aspect of nature. The first plague is seen as an attack on the River Nile. The Nile was critical to the Egyptians and, in its inundation, was designated as Hap or Hapy (*H'py*) and deified as the god of the Nile and the father of all beings.[73] Ancient Egyptian texts do refer to the Nile by this divine name,[74] and the Egyptians even wrote hymns to the Nile.[75] When Moses and Aaron lifted up the staff and struck the water in the Nile, 'all the water in the river was turned into blood, and the fish in the river died. The river stank so that the Egyptians could not drink its water, and there was blood throughout the whole land of Egypt' (Exod. 7.20–21). This first plague has traditionally been understood literally, but it could also be symbolic.[76] In the 'Admonitions of Ipuwer', a prophet uses blood as a metaphor to describe the Nile during a particularly difficult period in the Middle Kingdom (2040–1782 BC):

> Why really, the River is blood. If one drinks of it, one rejects (it) as human and thirsts for water . . . [Why] really, the desert is (spread) throughout the land. The nomes are destroyed. Barbarians from outside have come to Egypt . . . There are really no people anywhere . . . Why really, the entire Delta marshland will no (longer) be hidden: the confidence of the Northland is (now) a beaten path . . . Why really, grain has perished on every side . . . Everybody says: 'There is nothing!' The storehouse is stripped bare . . .[77]

The Nile had not really turned to blood during the Middle Kingdom, but this text uses blood as a metaphor for what it had become like.[78] The rest of the text suggests that its water levels had become low, since the marshland had become visible and desert conditions had spread throughout the region. Maybe there had been a particularly poor inundation or the waters had become contaminated, or both.[79] In any case, blood made a powerful symbol for whatever

Rapids, MI: Eerdmans, 1976), 62–79; and Nahum Sarna, *Exploring Exodus: The origins of biblical Israel* (New York, NY: Schocken, 1986), 78–80.

73 Karl W. Butzer, 'Nile', *OEAE* 2:550.

74 E.g. S. A. B. Mercer, *The Pyramid Texts*, 4 vols (New York, NY: Longmans, Green, 1952), 4:65.

75 E.g. 'Hymn to the Nile', trans. John A. Wilson (*ANET*, 372–3).

76 I first encountered this idea in James K. Hoffmeier, 'Egypt, Plagues in', *ABD* 2:377.

77 'The Admonitions of Ipu-Wer', trans. John A. Wilson (*ANET*, 441–4).

78 Throughout the ancient world, blood was a powerful symbol of both life and death and, as such, was often taboo. Ancient Egypt was no exception, and blood was often connected with pollution, impurity and danger. Paul John Frandsen, 'Taboo', *OEAE* 3:345–6. More generally, see Mary Douglas, *Purity and Danger: An analysis of the concepts of pollution and taboo* (New York, NY: Frederick A. Praeger, 1966).

79 As suggested in Hoffmeier, 'Egypt, Plagues in', 377.

conditions had crippled the Nile. In the same way, when the LORD turned the Nile into 'blood', he rendered Hap/Hapy powerless to sustain Egypt's people.[80]

In the second plague, masses of frogs fled from what had become an uninhabitable Nile (Exod. 8.1–15). This plague is viewed as having been directed against the frog goddess Heket, whose iconography portrays her as a human female with a frog's head.[81] She was a birth deity who assisted in the creation and birth of human children. Heket was seen as a deity with life-giving power but, if this plague was directed at her, she had clearly lost control when the reproduction of life became a disaster and frogs 'came up and covered the land of Egypt' (8.6).

Plagues three and four both involved flying insects of some kind. The third plague involved *kinnim*, a Hebrew word whose meaning is uncertain (Exod. 8.16–19). It may refer to gnats, lice or maggots. The fourth plague involved the *'arob* (Exod. 8.20–32), which may have been a stinging fly or a mosquito. There were several invertebrate and insect deities in Egypt but, in this approach, this plague is usually seen as having been directed against Khepry, who was a form of the sun god. Khepry was represented by the form of the scarab beetle, an association that probably resulted from observation of dung beetles rolling a ball of mud or dung along the ground in a way that seemed to mirror the god rolling the solar disc across the sky. Female scarab beetles also laid their eggs in a similar ball and, when the young eventually emerged, it seemed as if they had emerged spontaneously. Because of these behaviours, the scarab became the hieroglyph for 'to become', or 'to come into existence', and images of Khepry sometimes had a beetle in place of a head to convey the idea that he was the god of creation.[82] In the third plague, the gnats seemed to spontaneously generate from out of the dust (8.17) and, in the fourth, the flies seemed to come out of nowhere (8.24). The polemical approach would stress that it was the LORD, not Khepry, who raised up the gnats and flies against Egypt, and it was the LORD, not Khepry, who removed them (8.32).

---

80 If the blood of the first plague is a metaphor, that does not make it any less 'true'. The use of metaphor is a normal feature of biblical narrative. Cf. Robert Alter, *The Art of Biblical Narrative* (New York, NY: Basic, 1981); V. Philips Long, *The Art of Biblical History* (Grand Rapids, MI: Zondervan, 1994); Jean-Louis Ska, *Our Fathers Have Told Us: Introduction to the analysis of Hebrew narratives* (Rome: Pontifical Biblical Institute, 1990); and Meir Sternberg, *The Poetics of Biblical Narrative: Ideological literature and the drama of reading* (Bloomington, IN: Indiana University Press, 1985). For the issue of the conveyance of 'truth' in narrative, see especially chapters 1–4 in C. John Collins, *Reading Genesis Well: Navigating history, poetry, science, and truth in Genesis 1–11* (Grand Rapids, MI: Zondervan, 2018).

81 Wilkinson, *Complete Gods and Goddesses*, 229.

82 Wilkinson, *Complete Gods and Goddesses*, 23–33.

The fifth plague consisted of a disease upon Egypt's cattle (Exod. 9.1–7). This is viewed as having been directed at the veneration of cattle in Egyptian society, which went back to Late Palaeolithic to Neolithic times. This reverence probably stemmed from the importance of cattle in Egyptian society. They provided many necessities, including food, milk, clothing and transportation, and thus 'a special human/cattle relationship existed in the Nile Valley'.[83] When and how Egypt's various cattle cults developed is debated, but the Egyptian pantheon eventually did come to include a variety of bull, cow and calf divinities who were among the most important of all of Egypt's gods. Apis, the most important of the bull deities in Egypt, was first known as the representative and later as the very image of the god Ptah. The Mnevis bull was the son and representative of the god Re. Hathor was one of Egypt's greatest goddesses. She was the mother or wife of Horus, the sky goddess, the wife or daughter of Re, and the goddess of women, female sexuality and motherhood. She was also the mother or wife of the king, goddess of foreign lands and their goods, goddess of the afterlife, and the goddess of joy, music and happiness. Due to the wide variety of her manifestations and associated activities, Hathor was one of the most important and popular members of the Egyptian pantheon.[84] There were numerous other bovine deities as well, including Bat, Buchis, Hesat, Mehet-Weret, Mnevis, Shentayet and the Sky Bull (Bull of the West). The bovine deities touched on almost every aspect of the Egyptians' lives, and were also strongly tied to aspects of kinship and monarchial ideology. The plague upon Egypt's cattle could certainly have shaken this ideology.

The sixth plague, which consisted of 'festering boils' that broke out on both humans and animals throughout Egypt (Exod. 9.9), has been interpreted as a polemic against Sekhmet, the most important of Egypt's leonine deities. Sekhmet was the daughter of Re and, among her many other abilities, she had the power to ward off pestilence and to heal. For these reasons, she was sometimes known as the 'mistress of life'. Her main cult centre was at Memphis, but she had temples in many other places as well.[85] When festering boils broke out upon people and animals throughout Egypt, this could certainly have undermined belief in Sekhmet's ability to ward off pestilence and to heal.

The seventh plague consisted of a hailstorm that is described in harrowing detail. The text recounts that 'the LORD rained hail on the land of Egypt' and that 'there was hail with fire flashing continually in the midst of it, such heavy

---

83 Douglas J. Brewer, 'Cattle', *OEAE* 1:242.

84 Wilkinson, *Complete Gods and Goddesses*, 139–45, 170–2, 174–5.

85 Wilkinson, *Complete Gods and Goddesses*, 181–2.

hail as had never fallen in the land of Egypt since it became a nation' (Exod. 9.23–24). The hail ravaged the landscape, killing people and animals who failed to come in out of the fields, and also destroyed many plants and trees (v. 25). This plague is seen as having lampooned the inadequacy of Egypt's sky gods, including: Nut, the personification of the vault of the heavens; Shu, the god of air and sunlight; and Tefnut, the goddess of moisture.[86] The destructiveness of the hail could have also shown the inadequacy of Isis to protect life, as well as Seth's inability to protect the crops.[87]

The eighth plague was a swarm of locusts (Exod. 10.1–20), a chronic threat throughout the Ancient Near East. A ton of locusts, which is just a tiny part of the average swarm, can eat the same amount of food in a single day as 10 elephants, 25 camels or 2,500 people. A locust swarm could leave a country barren within days. In this eighth plague, locusts 'covered the surface of the whole land, so that the land was black', and 'they ate . . . all the fruit of the trees that the hail had left; nothing green was left, no tree, no plant in the field, in all the land of Egypt' (10.15). This plague has been regarded as directed at one or all of a number of deities, including: Seth, a god of strength, cunning and protective power; Min, a fertility deity associated with the eastern desert regions; the locust-headed god Senehem; Neper, god of grain; Renenutet, a goddess of the harvest; and Thermuth.[88] The inability of these and other gods to prevent the devastation caused by the locust swarm would certainly have demonstrated their powerlessness before the Lord.

The ninth calamity, the plague of darkness (Exod. 10.21–29), has been regarded as a polemic against Amun (Amun-Re), the king of the gods of Egypt. Amun was considered to be the creator god and, although he had several traits, his solar aspect was the most important. A complex theology developed in association with his identity as the solar god. Amun's daily rising symbolized new life and resurrection, and his setting symbolized death and the underworld. The 'Hymn to Amon-Re' calls for universal reverence to him.[89] The ninth plague, however, brought about 'dense darkness in all the land of Egypt for three days', so that 'people could not see one another, and for three days they could not move from where they were' (10.22–23). In the light of the Egyptians' belief in the supremacy of the sun god, this prolonged abject darkness would have been terrifying.

---

86 Wilkinson, *Complete Gods and Goddesses*, 129–30, 160–3, 83.

87 Wilkinson, *Complete Gods and Goddesses*, 146–9, 197–9.

88 Wilkinson, *Complete Gods and Goddesses*, 115–17, 197–9, 225.

89 'A Hymn to Amon-Re', trans. John A. Wilson (*ANET*, 365–7).

Finally, in this approach, the tenth plague (Exod. 11.1—12.36) is seen as having targeted Pharaoh as a god and the system of dynastic succession as the means of maintaining the reign of the deity. In the Thirteenth and Fourteenth Dynasties (1786–c.1665 BC), the king was viewed as the representative of god on earth and, from the Second Intermediate period (c.1664–c.1081 BC) on, he was viewed as the very image of god. In late predynastic times (5500–3100 BC), the first title of the king was Horus and, from the Fourth Dynasty (c.2649–2513 BC) on, the kingship came to be associated with Re and Osiris.[90] Horus was one of the earliest of Egyptian deities and was the great sky god who preceded all other gods. Re was the sun god, who eventually merged with several other solar and cosmic gods to become what may have been Egypt's most important deity. He was a cosmic god who acted in the heavens, on earth and in the underworld. Osiris was another extremely important deity associated with monarchial ideology, as well as death, resurrection and fertility.[91] As the representative of these and all the gods of Egypt, Pharaoh was the 'son of the gods and their permanent representative in the world . . . for he belonged to the same sphere as they'.[92] The continuity of his reign was maintained through dynastic succession, with his firstborn son as heir apparent. The tenth plague, however, was not directed at the pharaoh alone, but against 'all the firstborn in the land of Egypt, from the firstborn of Pharaoh who sat on his throne to the firstborn of the prisoner who was in the dungeon' and, as a result of it, 'Pharaoh arose in the night, he and all his officials and all the Egyptians; and there was a loud cry in Egypt, for there was not a house without someone dead' (Exod. 12.29–30). So, while this plague certainly undercut the power of Pharaoh as a god, it clearly had a much broader reach.

Some scholars reject the idea that each plague was directed against a specific Egyptian deity. Victor Hamilton, for example, insists that 'the biblical text gives no indication that the plagues are to be associated with the Egyptian religion and deities', and that 'the similarities may, therefore, be

---

90 Ulrich H. Luft, 'Religion', *OEAE* 3:143–5.

91 Wilkinson, *Complete Gods and Goddesses*, 118–23, 200–3, 205–9.

92 Françoise Dunand and Christiane Zivie-Coche, *Gods and Men in Egypt: 3000 BCE to 395 CE* (Ithaca, NY: Cornell University Press, 2004), 100. There are Egyptologists who argue that 'the current image of the god-king is excessive'. Cf. Marie-Ange Bonhême, 'Kingship', trans. Elizabeth Schwaiger, *OEAE* 2:243. See, however, the discussion in David P. Silverman, 'Divinity and deities in Ancient Egypt', in *Religion in Ancient Egypt: Gods, myths, and personal practice*, ed. Byron E. Shafer (Ithaca, NY: Cornell University Press, 1991), 58–87.

coincidental'.[93] However, the idea that the plagues were an attack on the gods of Egypt reflects the Bible's own view of these events, as well as those of later Jewish traditions. According to the book of Exodus, the LORD told Moses and Aaron that, through the plagues, he would make 'fools' of the Egyptians (Exod. 10.2). Later, he told them that he would 'execute judgements' on 'all the gods of Egypt' (12.12). The author(s) of the book of Numbers shared this view that, through the plagues, 'the LORD executed judgements even against their gods' (Num. 33.4). This idea is also reflected in later Jewish traditions, such as the pseudepigraphal book of *Jubilees* (*c*.160–150 BC), which teaches that

> the LORD executed a great vengeance on them for Israel's sake, and smote them through blood and frogs, lice and dog-flies, and malignant boils breaking forth in blains; and their cattle by death; and by hail-stones, thereby He destroyed everything that grew for them; and by locusts which devoured the residue which had been left by the hail; and by darkness; and by the first-born of men and animals, and on all their idols the LORD took vengeance and burned them with fire.[94]

Similarly, the author of the apocryphal Wisdom of Solomon (written between 100 BC and AD 50), wrote of the Egyptians that:

> In return for their foolish and wicked thoughts, which led them astray to worship irrational serpents and worthless animals, you sent upon them a multitude of irrational creatures to punish them, so that they might learn that one is punished by the very things by which one sins.
> (Wisd. 11.15–16)

On the other hand, identifying specific deities against which each of the plagues may be directed is problematic.[95] It may be that each plague was more generally directed at any or all deities associated with the realm affected by the plague. Or the meaning of the plagues may even be broader than that, and reflect the Ancient Near Eastern idea that the defeat of a nation must have

---

93 Victor P. Hamilton, *Handbook on the Pentateuch* (2nd edn; Grand Rapids, MI: Baker Academic, 2005), 160.

94 R. H. Charles, *The Book of Jubilees* (Jerusalem: Makor, 1972), 205.

95 For a detailed critique of this approach, see Duane A. Garrett, *A Commentary on Exodus* (KEL; Grand Rapids, MI: Kregel Academic, 2014), 291–301.

meant that its gods had been defeated.[96] Indeed, in the ancient world, defeat meant subjection to the god or gods of the conquerors.[97] In this latter view, the plagues demonstrated the LORD's mastery over all the gods of Egypt.

The third main interpretation of the plagues has been as decreation. In this view, first proposed by Ziony Zevit, each of the plagues represents a reversal of God's original creation.[98] Over the course of the seven days of creation, God: (day 1) created light; (day 2) separated the waters; (day 3) uncovered the dry land and brought forth vegetation; (day 4) created the luminaries; (day 5) created birds, fish and sea creatures; and (day 6) created land animals and humans (Gen. 1.1–31). In the plagues, the LORD either destroys or removes each of the elements of the natural order, beginning with water, then moving to animals, plants, sunlight and, finally, human beings. Zevit argues that other accounts of the plagues, in liturgical texts that contained seven plagues rather than ten, mirrored the seven days of creation.[99] The account in Exodus was expanded to ten in order 'to correspond to the ten divine utterances by which the world was created and ordered (Genesis 1.3, 6, 9, 11, 14, 20, 24, 26, 28, 29)'.[100] While some have embraced this view,[101] others remain unconvinced. Propp argues that 'the Plagues narrative is so complicated, so studded with features extraneous to anti-Creation, that the theme's very existence becomes conjectural', and he concludes by asking whether any act of destruction is not, 'in a sense, "anti-Creation"'.[102]

A fourth approach to the ten plagues views them as an attack on the pharaoh's ability to maintain *ma'at*.[103] The meaning of the Egyptian term *ma'at* is wide-ranging and includes the ideas of 'truth', 'order' and 'cosmic balance', in

---

96 As suggested by Garrett, *Commentary on Exodus*, 301.

97 Cf. Bertil Albrektson, *History and the Gods: An essay on the idea of historical events as divine manifestations in the Ancient Near East and in Israel* (Winona Lake, IN: Eisenbrauns, 2011), 98–114; Daniel Block, *The Gods of the Nations: Studies in Ancient Near Eastern national theology* (2nd edn; Grand Rapids, MI: Baker, 2000), 113–34; Bustanay Oded, '"The command of the god" as a reason for going to war in the Assyrian royal inscriptions', in *'Ah, Assyria . . .': Studies in Assyrian history and Ancient Near Eastern historiography presented to Hayim Tadmor*, ed. Mordechai Cogan and Israel Eph'al (Scripta Hierosolymitana 33; Jerusalem: Magnes Press, 1991), 226.

98 Ziony Zevit, 'The Priestly redaction and interpretation of the plague narrative in Exodus', *JQR* 66 (1975–6): 193–211; Zevit, 'Three ways to look at the ten plagues'.

99 These liturgical texts were Ps. 78.44–51 and Ps. 105.28–36.

100 Zevit, 'Three ways to look at the ten plagues," 23.

101 E.g. Currid, *Ancient Egypt*, 113–17; Terence E. Fretheim, *Exodus* (Interpretation; Louisville, KY: John Knox Press, 1991): 110; Terence E. Fretheim, 'The plagues as ecological signs of historical disaster', *JBL* 110 (1991): 385–96.

102 Propp, *Exodus 1–18*, 345.

103 Hoffmeier, 'Egypt, Plagues in', 377.

contrast to disorder and chaos.[104] At the beginning of time, Re replaced chaos with *ma'at*. It 'is manifest in nature in the normalcy of phenomena; it is manifest in society as justice; and it is manifest in an individual's life as truth'.[105] The concept was so important that it was personified as the goddess Ma'at, the daughter of Re, who was portrayed as a woman with a large feather on her head, which symbolized lightness and perfection.[106] One of the main duties of Egypt's pharaoh was 'to maintain the order of the cosmos, effected by upholding the principle of *maat* through correct and just rule and through service to the gods'.[107] At his accession, in order to symbolize his role in the maintenance of *ma'at*, each pharaoh would ritually present a small figure of Ma'at in the temples of the gods and, from the time of Seti I onwards, most pharaohs would also combine their regnal name with *ma'at* in order to equate themselves with it. When the LORD afflicted Egypt with the ten plagues, he turned *ma'at* into total disorder and chaos. He showed that Pharaoh had no power over the natural world, and that the God of the cosmos was the LORD alone.

A fifth approach to the plagues interprets them as weapons used by the LORD as Divine Warrior (Exod. 15.3) in his battle against Egypt. The narrative of the exodus events is about a confrontation of wills between the LORD and Pharaoh, and the primary tension in the story is whether the LORD has the power to prevail over Pharaoh. Thomas Dozeman argues that, 'The plagues are afflictions of growing intensity that [the LORD] brings to bear on Pharaoh to overcome his resistance.'[108] They were literally nature weapons in the hands of the Divine Warrior.[109] Just as those gods identified as storm gods in the Ancient Near East were thought to be able to use hail, thunder and lightning as weapons, so the LORD used these elements, and more, against Pharaoh. When the final plague, the death of the firstborn, failed to stop Pharaoh's oppression of the Israelites and achieve their liberation, the story reaches its crescendo as the LORD destroys the Egyptian army at the Red Sea, achieving his desired goal. In this view, the plagues were nature weapons in the hands of the Divine Warrior, who used them to vanquish Pharaoh.

---

104 Emily Teeter, 'Maat', *OEAE* 2:319.

105 Henri Frankfort, *Ancient Egyptian Religion: An interpretation* (Mineola, NY: Dover, 2011), 63.

106 Erik Hornung, *Conceptions of God in Ancient Egypt: The one and the many*, trans. John Baines (Ithaca, NY: Cornell University Press, 1982), 213.

107 Teeter, 'Maat', 319.

108 Thomas B. Dozeman, *God at War: Power in the exodus tradition* (New York, NY: Oxford University Press, 1996), 26.

109 Cf. Charlie Trimm, *'YHWH Fights for Them!' The Divine Warrior in the Exodus narrative* (Piscataway, NJ: Gorgias Press, 2014), 47–53.

In the end, there is probably some truth to each of the interpretative approaches to the plagues. The plagues certainly portray God as working through nature and, at the same time, they also provide a polemic against the gods of Egypt. While the theme of decreation in the plagues may be on shaky ground, there is no doubt that the chaos of the plagues undermined the view of Pharaoh as the upholder of *ma'at*. Ultimately, the plagues were weapons in the hands of the Divine Warrior, who used them to overcome Pharaoh and manifest his sovereignty over all (Exod. 7.5).

The parting of the Red Sea

The account of the parting of the Sea is not a scientific account that intends to answer modern questions about how it could have occurred. Its author(s) was not interested in explaining how the waters parted scientifically, but theologically. The text states that 'the LORD drove the sea back by a strong east wind . . . and turned the sea into dry land; and the waters were divided' (14.21). Gary Rendsburg points to two Egyptian texts that relate to the splitting of the sea and the drowning of the Egyptians.[110] One of these, known as 'Setne I' and dated to the Ptolemaic period (305–30 BC), is about a magician-prince named Na-nefer-ka-ptah who wanted to locate a book written by Thoth, which was now in a box in the middle of the Nile. He built a model boat, complete with rowers and sailors, and brought it to life with a spell. He had them row out to the middle of the Nile, where the book was lying on the riverbed below. He then recited a spell that split the river, whereupon the book was retrieved. The story illustrates the belief that an Egyptian wise man could part the waters.

Another story relevant for the parting of the sea is from the Westcar Papyrus (*c.*1600 BC) and is entitled 'The Boating Party Story'. It tells about a time when the royal family was enjoying leisure on the lake, when one of the princesses dropped her pendant into the water. Her father, Pharaoh Seneferu (*c.*2600 BC), commanded that the chief lector-priest be summoned. When he arrived, he cast a spell that split the water, found the pendant lying on a shard and returned it to the princess. He pronounced another spell, and the water returned to its place. In this Egyptian tale, the dividing of the water saves the day while, in the biblical account, it serves to outwit the Egyptians and allow the Israelites to escape. In both of these stories, Egyptian magicians divide waters, and Rendsburg concludes that the biblical account was polemicizing against

---

110 For detailed discussions of both stories, as well as bibliography, see Gary A. Rendsburg, 'Moses the magician', in *Israel's Exodus* (ed. Levy, Schneider and Propp), 243–58.

the belief in Egyptian magic. He suggests that, in the biblical account, it is *as if* the author was saying that, 'if you Egyptians believe that magician-priests are capable of such praxes, we will use those very same actions to bring about your ruin and defeat'.[111]

While these Egyptian tales surely provide background, the biblical story of the parting of the Sea includes a focus on the role of divine wind that may provide a more direct theological explanation. In the narrative account, the LORD controls and uses wind to part the waters. The text states that 'the LORD drove the sea back by a strong east wind all night, and turned the sea into dry land; and the waters were divided' (14.21). In the poetic account in the Song of Moses, the text proclaims that, 'At the blast of your nostrils the waters piled up, the floods stood up in a heap; the deeps congealed in the heart of the sea' (15.8). It seems clear that the biblical author intended for the wind that parted the waters to be understood as the breath of God. Scott Noegel points out that blowing, which could be symbolic of the transfer of the breath of life, was an essential ingredient of Egyptian magic. He points to several examples of Egyptian texts that mention blowing in the context of rituals, funerals, healing and creation.[112] What happened at the sea surpassed all Egyptian magic when God himself blew upon the waters and caused them to part in order to both save his people and vanquish the Egyptians.

The parting of the sea must also be understood through the lens of holy war, which shapes much of the Exodus narrative.[113] The LORD announced to Moses that he was going to stretch out his 'mighty hand' (3.19) against Egypt and redeem Israel with his 'outstretched arm' (6.6).[114] In the plagues, the LORD launched his assault against Egypt and its Pharaoh. Before the Israelites left Egypt, they plundered the Egyptians by taking their jewellery and clothing (12.31–36). They went out 'prepared for battle' (13.18) and are continually referred to as the LORD's 'company' or 'companies', terms with militaristic overtones.[115] The LORD led the Israelites with a pillar of cloud by day and of fire by night (13.21), similar to the way that Alexander the Great had used a smoke signal by day and a fire signal by night to alert his troops that it was

---

111 Rendsburg, 'Moses the magician', 252.

112 Scott B. Noegel, 'Moses and magic: notes on the book of Exodus', *JANES* 24 (1996): 58.

113 Cf. Dozeman, *God at War*, 1–14.

114 These terms echo New Kingdom royal terminology and are used repeatedly in the exodus narratives for the LORD's actions against Egypt and the pharaoh. The expression 'mighty hand' features in Exod. 3.19; 13.3, 14, 16; 32.11, while the 'outstretched arm' occurs only in Exod. 6.6. For a detailed discussion, cf. James K. Hoffmeier, 'The arm of God versus the arm of Pharaoh in the exodus narratives', *Bib* 67 (1986): 378–87.

115 Cf. Exod. 6.26; 7.4; 12.17, 41, 51.

time to take up camp.[116] When Pharaoh and his army went out after them, the Israelites were 'going out boldly' (14.8), which translates an expression that suggests they were ready to fight and eager to prevail.[117] Before they crossed the Red Sea, Moses pronounced a war oracle (14.13–14). The 'blast' of the LORD's breath split the sea (15.8), and the military confrontation that would follow was 'an epiphany of divine power'.[118] At the third watch, the LORD threw the Egyptian army into a panic by clogging their chariot wheels so that they only turned with great difficulty (14.24–25). He blew upon the waters again so that they would return to their place and kill the Egyptians (14.10). It was when they were destroyed in the sea that the LORD 'gain[ed] glory for [himself]' over Pharaoh . . . his chariots, and his chariot drivers' (14.17). Finally, after the destruction of the Egyptian army in the sea, both Moses (15.1–18) and Miriam (15.21) sang victory hymns.

In a recent study, Joshua Berman has proposed that the Exodus sea account (13.17–15.19) has strong affinities with a specific military record, that of the Kadesh inscriptions of Ramesses II, which records a battle between the Egyptians and the Hittites.[119] In it, Ramesses' army was on the march, when the Hittites launched a surprise attack against it, which frightened the troops and caused them to scatter (P72–4). Having been abandoned by his frightened soldiers, Pharaoh fought the Hittites on his own. He appealed to Amun (P92–122), who came to his aid (P123–5). From that point forward, Ramesses was endowed with divine power and was enabled to vanquish the Hittites. At the morning watch, he fought them, and they acknowledged the power of his gods (P285–7). He defeated them and hurled them into the River Orontes, where there were no survivors (P128–42). When Ramesses' army saw the Hittite army dead on the seashore, they raised up a hymn of triumph in which they praised his prowess and the salvation he had brought them (P224–49) by the power of his 'strong arm'.[120] He led the army home in peace, since all lands now feared him (P332–6). He arrived peacefully, rested

---

116 As observed in Michael M. Homan, *To Your Tents, O Israel! The terminology, function, form, and symbolism of tents in the Hebrew Bible and the Ancient Near East* (CHANE 12; Leiden: Brill, 2002), 115.

117 C. J. Labuschagen, 'The meaning of *bĕyād rāma* in the Old Testament', in *Von Kanaan bis Kerala: Festschrift für J. P. M. van der Ploeg*, ed. W. E. Delsman et al. (AOAT 211; Neukirchen-Vluyn: Neukirchener, 1982), 146.

118 Dozeman, *God at War*, 22.

119 Joshua Berman, 'The Kadesh inscriptions of Ramesses II and the Exodus sea account (Exodus 13:17–15:19)', in *'Did I Not Bring Israel Out of Egypt?'* (ed. Hoffmeier, Millard and Rendsburg), 93–112.

120 References are repeatedly made to Ramesses' 'strong arm', 'his arms' and his 'valiant arm'. Cf. P236, 241, 242, 257, 276.

in his palace (P338–9) and was greeted by the gods of Egypt, who 'granted him a million jubilees and eternity upon the throne of Re, all lands and all foreign lands being overthrown and slain beneath his sandals, eternally and forever' (P340–3).

The Exodus sea account of Exodus 14—15 mirrors the Kadesh Poem very closely. When the Israelites left Egypt, they were 'prepared for battle' (Exod. 13.18) and marching 'with a raised arm' (14.8, my translation). They were surprised by Pharaoh's army and became frightened (14.10–12). Moses assured the Israelites that, if they would just 'keep still', their king, the LORD, would fight on their behalf (14.14). At dawn, the LORD threw the Egyptian army into a panic (14.24), and its troops recognized that it was the LORD who was fighting for the escaped slaves (14.25). The Egyptians were completely vanquished when they were submerged in the sea (15.4, 5, 10), and there were no survivors (14.28). When the Israelites saw the Egyptians dead on the seashore, they acknowledged their fear of the LORD (14.30–31) and offered up a hymn of praise and victory (15.1), celebrating how the LORD's 'right hand' had shattered his foes (15.6). The Song of the Sea concludes with the LORD leading his people back to the place where he made his abode, where he would reign 'for ever and ever' (15.17–18).

The two poems share a common plot and have many clear parallels. These parallels are of 'highly distinct motifs' that are unique to both works, and they largely occur 'in common sequence'.[121] These factors suggest to Berman that 'the Exodus account incorporates and adapts the valorous deeds of Ramesses'[122] in order to venerate the LORD over Pharaoh.

Like the exodus itself, the parting of the Red Sea was a foundational experience for the Israelites, and its importance did not lie in the scientific details of its occurrence, but in its profound theological meaning. It was the means by which the LORD vanquished Pharaoh and his armies, and the Israelites experienced his 'deliverance' (Exod. 14.13). Its impact was so profound that it was preserved in both narrative (14.1–31) and song (15.1–21). It made such a deep impression upon the Israelites that its echoes can be found throughout both the Old and New Testaments,[123] and it came to be viewed as a paradigm for later salvation events, such as the return from exile (Zech. 10.10–11) and Christian baptism (1 Cor. 10.1–4).

---

121 Berman, 'The Kadesh inscriptions', 106.
122 Berman, 'The Kadesh inscriptions', 108.
123 Cf. Chapters 11–12 of this volume.

The hardening of Pharaoh's heart

While it is not usually viewed as a miracle, one of the main themes of the exodus narrative is the hardening of Pharaoh's heart so that he would not let the Israelites go. Language associated with this hardening is used 20 times in Exodus 4—14, with three different words used to describe the hardening. The first word, kābēd, means 'to be heavy'. The second, ḥāzaq, means 'to be strong' or 'to be hard'. And the third, qāšâ, means 'to be hard' or 'difficult'. The roots ḥāzaq and qāšâ are both used to describe Pharaoh's stubborn commitment to his plan, while the root kābēd is used to convey the idea that his heart did not work properly and that he could not therefore make the right decisions. In some cases, Pharaoh is said to have hardened his own heart,[124] and in others the narrator simply observes that his heart was hardened.[125] Most often, however, it says that God hardened his heart[126] and, in the cases where the narrator simply observes that Pharaoh's heart was hardened, it is probably implied that it was the LORD who had hardened it.[127] The cumulative effects of the hardening of Pharaoh's heart prevented him from responding positively to Moses' and Aaron's initial appeal to let the Israelites go (7.13), from relenting in the wake of the plagues[128] and even from giving up his pursuit of the Israelites at the sea (14.4). The hardening of his heart eventually led to his defeat and the destruction of his army (14.26–31).

Generations of Bible readers have struggled with the idea that God hardened Pharaoh's heart. Did God suspend Pharaoh's free will and literally force him to continue oppressing the Israelites so that he could punish him? How could Pharaoh have been blamed for refusing to free the Israelites if God in fact hardened his heart? How could God condemn someone for doing what he forced that person to do? Hamilton tries to mitigate the problem by pointing to several ways in which God seemingly 'attempted to soften his [Pharaoh's] heart' throughout the Exodus narrative.[129] Several commentators also note that there seems to be a progression in the hardening of Pharaoh's heart, in which he is responsible for the hardening of his heart up until the fifth

---

124 Exod. 8.15 [11], 32 [28]; 9.34.
125 Exod. 7.14; 8.19 [15]; 9.7, 35.
126 Exod. 9.12, 34; 10.1, 20, 27; 11.10.
127 Lexical studies of each occurrence of the terminology can be found in: Garrett, *Commentary on Exodus*, 370–5; Hamilton, *Handbook on the Pentateuch*, 161–7; Trimm, 'YHWH Fights for Them!', 201–6.
128 Exod. 7.22; 8.15, 19, 32; 9.7, 12, 35; 10.20, 27.
129 Hamilton, *Handbook on the Pentateuch*, 165.

plague, and that it was only with the sixth plague that God began to harden his heart.[130]

The phenomenon of God hardening Pharaoh's heart, however, did not present a moral problem to the author of Exodus. He is not viewed in the text as a victim of the Israelites and their God, but as 'mean-spirited, obstinate, and implacably hateful toward Israel'.[131] In the exodus events, God was at war with Pharaoh, and the theme of the hardening of his heart, therefore, is a key part of the Divine Warrior motif in Exodus.[132] By hardening Pharaoh's heart, the LORD overcame him completely, proving his incomparability and demonstrating that all of creation belonged to him, even the land of Egypt.

Conclusions

This chapter has explored the emphasis on the power of God in the exodus events. While Moses would become the premier human figure in the entire Old Testament, the story of his call in Exodus intentionally emphasizes his inadequacy for fulfilling the commission to liberate the Hebrews on his own. Although Moses would serve as God's agent, it was God alone who would liberate the Hebrews. The LORD would accomplish this when he stretched out his mighty hand and struck Egypt with all the wonders he would perform there. These wonders occurred in the natural realm and demonstrated the LORD's mastery over nature and, indeed, all of creation. They were nature weapons in the hand of nature's God. After having liberated the Israelites from Egypt, the LORD led them through the sea, which he used to finally vanquish the armies of Pharaoh. There, as declared in the Song of Moses, the LORD demonstrated his superiority over Pharaoh and the so-called gods of Egypt:

> You blew with your wind, the sea covered them;
>   they sank like lead in the mighty waters.
> 'Who is like you, O LORD, among the gods?
>   Who is like you, majestic in holiness,
>   awesome in splendour, doing wonders?
> You stretched out your right hand,
>   the earth swallowed them.'
> (Exod. 15.10–12)

---

130 E.g. Garrett, *Commentary on Exodus*, 372–3; Hamilton, *Handbook on the Pentateuch*, 164.
131 Garrett, *Commentary on Exodus*, 374.
132 Dozeman, *God at War*, 118–20; Trimm, 'YHWH Fights for Them!', 201.

7

The law of God in Exodus

When God first called Moses, he told him to ask Pharaoh to release the Israelites so that they could go into the wilderness to worship the LORD (Exod.
3.18). This request was the subject of Moses' and Aaron's repeated talks with
Pharaoh up until the exodus occurred.[1] Although the location where they
would worship is never stated in their negotiations with Pharaoh, it is clear
that the destination of their pilgrimage was to be Mt Sinai. In Moses' encounter with God at the burning bush, the LORD had told him that, 'when you have
brought the people out of Egypt, you shall worship God on this mountain'
(3.12). Once the Israelites left Egypt, they headed into the wilderness and, after
three months, they arrived at Mt Sinai (19.1). There they experienced a powerful theophany. After the people had consecrated themselves, the mountain
was engulfed in thunder, lightning and a thick cloud (19.9b–15). Then 'the
LORD . . . descended upon it in fire', and 'the smoke went up like the smoke
of a kiln, while the whole mountain shook violently' (19.18). Following this
theophany, the book of Exodus reports the giving of the Ten Commandments
and various other laws and ordinances. Afterwards, it recounts the ratification
of the covenant with a cultic ceremony. In this chapter, we will look at the laws
that were given to the Israelites in the context of this covenant. We will begin
by studying the Ancient Near Eastern background of covenants and the issue
of whether or not this form is present in the book of Exodus. Next, we will
examine the major groups of laws given within the context of the covenant,
including the Ten Commandments, the Book of the Covenant, and the promise of the conquest of Canaan. Finally, we will conclude with some reflections
on the implications of these laws for Ancient Israel.

---

1 Exod. 5.1–3; 7.16; 8.21, 25–28; 9.1, 13; 10.3, 7–11, 24–26; 12.31–32. On the question of whether the
   LORD had given a command to mislead Pharaoh, see Cornelis Houtman, *Exodus*, Vol. 1 (HCOT:
   Leuven: Peeters, 1993), 375–7.

Ancient Near Eastern background of the covenant concept

After it recounts the Ten Commandments, along with various laws and ordinances, the text describes the foregoing laws as part of the covenant that God had made with Israel (24.1–8). Wellhausen recognized that the Hebrew word for covenant, *berit*, is connected with treaty making.[2] It was used for contractual agreements between two parties, which were originally sealed with blood. Wellhausen believed, however, that the idea of covenant was a late development in Israelite history. He attributed most of the material in Exodus 19—24 to the J and E sources, which he dated to the tenth and mid eighth centuries BC, respectively. He assigned the ascent of Moses (19.20–25), the revelation of the Book of the Covenant (20.23–26; 21—23) and the covenant ceremony (24.3–8) to J. He attributed the theophany at Mt Sinai (19.10–19), the giving of the Ten Commandments (20.1–20) and the command that Moses write the law (24.1–2, 11–14; 31.18) to E. In his view, these materials were all expanded and woven together by a later redactor.[3]

What Wellhausen did not know when he published his source-critical analysis was that covenants were well known throughout the Ancient Near East as early as the third millennium BC. It was not until about a decade after the publication of his *Prolegomena to the History of Ancient Israel* that the Amarna tablets were discovered, which contained the correspondence of Amenhotep III and Akhenaten with their covenant partners, including both their equals and subjects.[4] More than a century has passed since then and, in that time, over a hundred treaty, law and covenant documents have been found from across the Ancient Near East, ranging in date from the third to the first millennium BC. Among these covenants, there were two main types. The first was the Parity Treaty, which was a covenant between kings of equal status. In this case, the two kings would negotiate the terms of their agreement. The second type was the Suzerain–Vassal Treaty, which was a covenant between the king of a ruling nation and a subject nation. In this case, the suzerain would simply dictate the terms of the covenant, and the vassal was required to comply.

---

2 Julius Wellhausen, *Prolegomena to the History of Ancient Israel* (Gloucester, MA: Peter Smith, 1878; repr. New York, NY: Meridian, 1957), 392.

3 See the overview of Wellhausen's literary study of these materials in Thomas B. Dozeman, *Exodus* (ECC; Grand Rapids, MI: Eerdmans, 2009), 421–2.

4 Cf. William L. Moran, ed. and trans., *The Amarna Letters* (Baltimore, MD: Johns Hopkins University Press, 1992).

The most comprehensive study of these covenants so far is Kenneth Kitchen and Paul Lawrence's *Treaty, Law and Covenant in the Ancient Near East*.[5] In it, they analyse all known ancient covenants on the basis of any number of the following components.

1 Preamble. This consisted of an opening line that introduced the suzerain with all of his or her elaborate titles. Its purpose was to establish his supreme authority over the vassal with whom he or she was entering into a covenant. In the covenant between Mursilis of the Hittites (*c.*1370–1330 BC) and Duppi-Tessub, king of the vassal kingdom of Amurru, for example, Mursilis introduces himself as 'the great king' and 'the king of the Hatti land', followed by various other epithets that laud his greatness.[6]

2 Historical prologue. This section reviewed the previous history between the suzerain and the vassal(s), and there was typically a strong emphasis on the benevolent deeds which the suzerain had performed for the benefit of the vassal. The section was not made up of stereotyped formulae, but was a careful description of actual events that had occurred in the previous relationship between the two powers. It was an especially important part of the covenant, because it evoked the gratitude of the vassal for the prior benevolence of the suzerain. It demonstrated how beneficial it had been for the vassal to be in a covenant relationship with the suzerain in the past, and made the vassal want to renew the covenant out of gratitude. In the example of the covenant between Mursilis and Duppi-Tessub, the historical prologue recounts the good relationship that had existed between the Hittites and the kingdom of Amurru for the past two generations. Duppi-Tessub's father, and his father before him, had been faithful vassals of the Hittites, and the suzerain–vassal relationship had been good for them and the kingdom of Amurru. The Hittite suzerain reviews how his own father had been loyal to the kingdom of Amurru; he never undertook any unjust action against its people or incited their anger. He ensured the perpetuation of their dynasty and promised that, if Duppi-Tessub continued to be loyal to the covenant, he would be loyal to him, too, and make sure that his son ascended the throne after him. The historical prologue ends by urging Duppi-Tessub to maintain exclusive loyalty to Mursilis as his suzerain.

---

5 Kenneth A. Kitchen and Paul J. N. Lawrence, *Treaty, Law and Covenant in the Ancient Near East*, 3 vols (Wiesbaden: Harrassowitz, 2012).

6 'Treaty between Mursilis and Duppi-Tessub of Amurru', trans. Albrecht Goetze (*ANET*, 203–5).

3 Stipulations or laws. This part of the covenant document spelled out in detail the requirements that the suzerain imposed upon the vassal. These typically focused on: (a) the prohibition of foreign relationships outside the suzerain's domain; (b) the requirement that the vassal be singularly devoted to the suzerain; (c) the vassal's willingness to answer a call to arms from the suzerain; (d) the need for the vassal to have complete faith and trust in the suzerain; (e) the vassal's obligation to refuse asylum to foreign refugees; (f) the requirement that the vassal appear before the king once a year to present his tribute; and (g) the need for any conflicts between vassals to be presented to the suzerain for judgement. The stipulations of the covenant between Mursilis and Duppi-Tessub deal primarily with military matters and relationships with foreigners. Mursilis pronounces, 'With my friend you shall be friend, and with my enemy you shall be enemy.' The stipulations give examples of how the kingdom of Amurru should relate to the enemies of the Hittites. If any of the vassals decide to rebel against the Hittites, for example, and try to recruit the people of Amurru to join them, they should reply that they cannot, since they are loyal vassals of Mursilis. If the Hittites need their military help, the people of Amurru should not hesitate to provide it. Mursilis emphasizes his own loyalty to the kingdom of Amurru and states that, if anyone should seek to oppress its people, he would dispatch foot soldiers and charioteers to defend them. Similarly, the stipulations dealing with foreigners are clearly intended to contribute to the security of the Hittite Empire and the reputation of its king.

4a Deposit of the document. The covenant document was deposited in the sanctuary of the vassal state. In the case of our example of the covenant between Mursilis and Duppi-Tessub, no deposit clause is included.

4b Public reading. The document was to be brought out for periodic public reading. This would ensure that the people heard about the benevolence the suzerain had shown to their own king and his kingdom, and it would also guarantee that they were aware of what was expected of them as subjects of the great king. In the case of the covenant between Mursilis and Duppi-Tessub, the provision for public reading is not included.

5 List of gods as witnesses. In a similar manner to the way in which legal contracts today are attested by witnesses, so the gods served as witnesses to international covenants. The list of gods included the deities of both states, those of the suzerain and the vassal. The fact that the gods of the vassals served as witnesses to the covenant showed that they themselves approved of and supported the covenant. In the case of the covenant between Mursilis and Duppi-Tessub, numerous gods are invoked. These include deities that would have been recognized by both the Hittites and the kingdom of Amurru.

6a Blessings. If the vassal adhered to the covenant, his kingdom would flourish. Since the covenant was viewed as a sacred treaty, the blessings were viewed as the actions of the gods, but it was the king, as the agent of the god, who would ensure the stability of the vassal kingdom. In the case of the covenant between Mursilis and Duppi-Tessub, the blessings are stylized and without detail. They simply say that, 'If Duppi-Tessub honours these words of the treaty and the oath that are inscribed on this tablet, may these gods of the oath protect him together with his person, his wife, his son, his grandson, his house (and) his country.'

6b Curses. If the vassal violated the covenant, the suzerain, as the agent of the gods, would take military action against the vassal. In the covenant between Mursilis and Duppi-Tessub, the curses are simply the reversal of the blessings.

7 Oath(s). The vassal would swear allegiance to the suzerain and promise to adhere to the covenant stipulations. In the case of the covenant between Mursilis and Duppi-Tessub, the oath is not recorded.

8 Solemn ceremony. The taking of the oath was marked by appropriate rituals, sometimes described in the covenant documents. The solemn ceremony is not recounted in the covenant between Mursilis and Duppi-Tessub.

9 Epilogue. A concluding statement is sometimes found in law collections.

10 Additional items. These may include colophons or labels, but are not regular features of covenants.

11 Sanctions. These are statements of sanctions applied by a deity or deities. They are not a standard feature of covenants and are found only in reports about covenants, not in the covenants themselves.

12 Historical report and/or archaeological flashback. This is a reference to previous conditions, former peoples, an artefact or a recent event, inserted by the one initiating the covenant or by another speaker. These are like footnotes or endnotes.

No single covenant document contains all of these components, since the covenant format varied from one century to the next. In some periods, certain features would be present, while in other periods, those same features would fall out and be replaced by others. However, the composition of covenants in various periods is so consistent that Kitchen and Lawrence have been able to establish a typology that can be used to date covenants to their respective periods on the basis of their components.

Regardless of when a suzerain–vassal covenant was made, its primary purpose was to establish a relationship of mutual support between the two parties. On the surface, it may appear that the covenant was unilateral and that it benefited only the suzerain. However, as noted above, the treaty repeatedly promises to provide help and support to the vassal. This only makes sense, since the interests of his vassals were also the interests of the suzerain. By entering into a covenant relationship, groups that were originally separate would be grafted into a new legal community.

The suzerain–vassal covenant form in Exodus

In a revolutionary article first published in 1954, George Mendenhall (1916–2016) proposed that the Sinai covenant mirrored Late Bronze Age Hittite suzerain–vassal covenants and established the LORD as king and Israel as his vassal.[7] A number of critics, however, argued that the similarities between the Sinai covenant traditions and the Late Bronze covenants are incomplete, and that the real source of inspiration for the biblical idea of covenant must be sought in later periods, either monarchic or post-monarchic.[8] It is true that the exodus narrative is sparse in terms of specific references to the covenant. The term itself does not appear until after the so-called Book of the Covenant (Exod. 20.22—23.19) and at the end of a section in which the conquest of Canaan was promised (23.20–32). There Israel was prohibited from making covenants with the Canaanites and their gods (23.32). Afterwards, the narrative resumes, and Exodus 24 recounts how representatives of Israel met with the

---

7 George E. Mendenhall, 'Covenant forms in Israelite tradition', in *The Cultural and Religious Creativity of Ancient Israel: The collected essays of George E. Mendenhall*, ed. Gary A. Herion and Herbert B. Huffmon (University Park, PA: Eisenbrauns, 2018), 209–33. The original article was published in 1954.

8 E.g. Eberhard Gerstenberger, 'Covenant and commandment', *JBL* 84 (1965): 38–51; D. J. McCarthy, *Treaty and Covenant: A study in form in the ancient oriental documents and in the Old Testament* (repr. of 3rd edn; Winona Lake, IN: Eisenbrauns, 1981); John Thompson, *The Ancient Near Eastern treaties and the Old Testament* (London: Tyndale Press, 1963).

LORD, but the text never explicitly states that this was a covenant-making ceremony. It does say that Moses read the 'book of the covenant' to the people (24.7), but it seems to refer to the making of the covenant as having already occurred.

The trend in critical scholarship has been to approach the whole of Exodus 19—24 as a composition of the late monarchial, exilic and post-exilic periods, with a multiplicity of authors and sources involved.[9] Similarities between second-millennium covenants and the Sinai covenants are downplayed, while those with first-millennium covenants are emphasized.[10] The Ten Commandments are viewed as post-exilic, and their relationship to the Sinai covenant is viewed as late redactional work on the Exodus narrative.[11] The Covenant Code (Exod. 20.22—23.19) is viewed as the oldest law code in the Pentateuch, but one made up of various legal traditions that may have been operative in early Israelite villages.[12] The promise of the conquest of Canaan (23.20–33) is usually left out of the Covenant Code altogether and assigned to a later source.[13] The covenant ceremony (24.1–11) was attributed to JE in the conventional Documentary Hypothesis but, more recently, is attributed to a 'Non-P History' in the early monarchial period.[14] In short, contemporary scholarship tends to view Exodus 19—24 as a hodge-podge of disparate sources ranging in date from the early monarchial to the post-exilic period.

However, while many scholars continue to view the Sinai covenant as a patchwork of late and disparate sources, Kitchen and Lawrence's exhaustive study of *Treaty, Law and Covenant in the Ancient Near East* demonstrates that it mirrors late second-millennium BC covenants precisely. This can be illustrated (see Table 1 overleaf).[15]

---

9   Cf. the overview in Wolfgang Oswald, 'Lawgiving at the mountain of God (Exodus 19–24)', in *The Book of Exodus: Composition, reception, and interpretation*, ed. Thomas B. Dozeman, Craig A. Evans and Joel N. Lohr (Leiden: Brill, 2014), 169–92.

10 For an overview of the scholarship on this subject, see John Van Seters, *A Law Book for the Diaspora: Revision in the study of the Covenant Code* (New York, NY: Oxford University Press, 2003).

11 See the overview in Thomas B. Dozeman, *The Pentateuch: Introducing the Torah* (Minneapolis, MN: Fortress Press, 2017), 334–43.

12 Douglas A. Knight, 'Village law and the Book of the Covenant', in *'A Wise and Discerning Mind': Essays in honor of Burke O. Long*, ed. Saul M. Olyan and Robert C. Culley (Brown Judaic Studies 325; Providence, RI: Brown Judaic Studies, 2000), 174–8; Saul M. Olyan and Robert C. Culley, *Law, Power, and Justice in Ancient Israel* (Louisville, KY: Westminster John Knox Press, 2011), 115–56.

13 E.g. David P. Wright, 'The origin, development, and context of the Covenant Code', in *Book of Exodus* (ed. Dozeman, Evans and Lohr), 220–44.

14 Thomas B. Dozeman, *Exodus* (ECC; Grand Rapids, MI: Eerdmans, 2009), 428–32.

15 This chart is based on the outline in Kitchen and Lawrence's *Treaty, Law and Covenant in the Ancient Near East*, 3:137–9. The numbers in the left-hand column identify which elements of known ancient covenants are included in the Sinai covenant.

Table 1 The elements of the Sinai covenant in Exodus-Leviticus

	Covenant element	Biblical text	Narrative
1	Preamble	Exod. 20.1	
2	Historical prologue	Exod. 20.2	
3	Laws (basic)	Exod. 20.3–17 Exod. 20.18–21	Decalogue Sinai phenomena
3	Laws (detailed)	Exod. 21—23	
8	Solemn ceremony	Exod. 24.1–11	
5	List of witnesses	Exod. 24.4	
4b	Reading of the text	Exod. 24.7	
3	Laws (continued)	Exod. 25.1–8	
4a	Deposit of text	Exod. 25.16, 21 Exod. 25—31 Exod. 32—34	Notation of deposit Instructions for tabernacle Rebellion, etc.
3	Laws (tabernacle)	Exod. 35 Exod. 36—40 Lev. 1—10	Commands for building tabernacle Tabernacle and accoutrements Tabernacle and accountrements
3	Laws (continued)	Lev. 11—15 Lev. 16—17	Various laws Setting up the cult
3	Laws (continued)	Lev. 18—20 Lev. 21—22	Regulations for holiness Holiness of priests and conduct of offerings
3	Laws (continued)	Lev. 23—25	Public feasts
6b	Blessings	Lev. 26.1–13	
6c	Curses	Lev. 26.14–45	
10	Colophon	Lev. 26.46	
3	Laws	Lev. 27	Additional law
10	End-colophon	Lev. 27.34	

The implications of the correspondence between the Sinai covenant and the Late Bronze Age covenant form are profound. For Mendenhall, it is evidence that the Sinai covenant dates to the late second millennium BC.[16] It also discredits an evolutionary model for interpreting the development of Ancient Israel's conception of the idea of covenant. Instead of developing in later periods and then being retrojectively inserted into the story of early Israel, the traditions about the covenant were actually derived from the Late Bronze/ early Iron Age by a biblical writer who was familiar with them. In addition, it points to the literary unity of the entire account of the Sinai covenant, in which case the so-called Book of the Covenant (20.22—23.19) and the promise of the conquest of Canaan (23.20–32), which have been viewed as separate sources, would be considered part of the original covenant, as outlined above.

If these conclusions are correct, it begs the question of how a covenant format that was only valid from c.1400 to 1200 BC, and that would have only been known in detail among the governing classes of late-Eighteenth to Nineteenth Dynasty Egypt, Egypt's neighbours in the Levant, and the courts of other major states like Hatti and Mesopotamia, could have been drawn up by uneducated Israelite slaves. Kitchen and Lawrence conclude that:

> The only realistic conduit from court politics to a slave-group would be a rebel courtier in the Egyptian foreign office who cast in his lot with them, and guided the escape, the cohesion and the binding covenant – of contemporary type! – for and on this early Hebrew group. Then, all would be clear, logical, and realistic. Inscriptionally, we have no independent data for such a proceeding at present; but, then, 99% of all Delta and Memphite administrative records (papyri and ostraca) are irremediably lost to us forever, so no light will reach us from that source. Within the Hebrew tradition, a leader *Mashu (trad. text: Moshe) is posited; he would fit the bill completely, if he could be viewed more dispassionately and detachedly than is commonly the case.[17]

Kitchen and Lawrence's recent analysis of extant covenants shows that the treaty between Hattusili III and Ramesses II represents the classic pattern of second-millennium BC covenants.[18] Gordon Johnston suggests that Moses

---

16   George E. Mendenhall and Gary A. Herion, 'Covenant', *ABD* 1:1185–8.

17   Kitchen and Lawrence, *Treaty, Law and Covenant*, 3:136.

18   Kitchen and Lawrence, *Treaty, Law and Covenant*, 1:573–94.

may have actually seen this covenant.[19] The prologue to its Egyptian version reports that the pharaoh was residing at the royal residence at Pi-Ramesses when ambassadors arrived from Hattusa to visit him in the twenty-first year of his reign, which would have been *c*.1259 BC. The Hittite ambassadors brought a silver tablet upon which was inscribed the Hittite version of the treaty that the two kings had agreed to enter into. Hieroglyphic versions of the treaty were later inscribed upon the walls of the Amun temple at Karnak, in Lower Egypt, and the mortuary temple of Ramesses II at the Ramesseum in Thebes, in Upper Egypt. Johnston points out that, according to the biblical text, Moses was serving at the court of pharaoh in the royal city of Pi-Ramesses, where the Israelites were enslaved (Exod. 1), and therefore could have actually seen the account of this covenant portrayed on the temple walls.[20] If 1295 BC is too late, the Egyptian account also mentions that there had been previous covenants with Suppiluliuma I (1358–1322 BC) and Muwatalli II (*c*.1295–1272 BC).[21] As a member of the royal household, Moses would have received an education in preparation for a supervisory role in administration, building projects, temple cults or some other professional capacity.[22] Such an education could have included foreign policy and exposed him to such covenants.[23]

The Ten Commandments

Once the Israelites had reached Mt Sinai, God instructed Moses to have the people consecrate themselves because, on the third day, he would descend upon it (Exod. 19.10–11). On the third day, God spoke the Ten Commandments. These were the stipulations of the suzerain–vassal covenant and the heart of what God expected from his vassal people. There has been some dispute as to how to count the commandments, and Jewish, Roman Catholic, Anglican, Lutheran, Orthodox and Reformed traditions number them differently.[24] There is no doubt, however, that ten were intended, since the author

---

19 Gordon Johnston, 'What biblicists need to know about Hittite treaties' (paper presented at the Annual Meeting of the ETS, San Antonio, TX, 16 November 2016), 15–36. Mendenhall had already observed that this covenant had been established 'about the same time as the exodus out of Egypt' (Mendenhall, 'Covenant forms in Israelite tradition', 214, n. 13).

20 Johnston, 'What biblicists need to know', 23.

21 Kitchen and Lawrence, *Treaty, Law and Covenant*, 1:587.

22 Hans W. Fischer-Elfert, 'Education', *OEAE* 1:438–42.

23 Acts 7.22 mentions Moses' Egyptian education.

24 Cf. Jason S. DeRouchie, 'Counting the ten: an investigation into the numbering of the Decalogue', in *For Our Good Always: Studies on the message and influence of Deuteronomy in honor of Daniel I. Block*, ed. Jason S. DeRouchie, Jason Gile and Kenneth J. Turner (Winona Lake, IN: Eisenbrauns), 93–125.

of Exodus later refers to them as the 'Ten Commandments' (Exod. 34.28) or, literally, the 'ten words'.[25] The number of the commandments is certainly not incidental, as some have concluded,[26] but stems from the symbolic value attributed to the number ten by ancient people. It represented perfection and completion, for which it is used as a symbol frequently in the Old Testament.[27] The Ten Commandments can be broken into two halves, with the first four dealing with the people's relationship to God, and the remaining six with relationships in the covenant community. It is significant that the commandments about how to conceive of and relate to God preceded those that regulate relationships between people. Among the Ancient Israelites, a right conception of God and a right relationship with him was supposed to provide the foundation for personal and communal ethics.

The Ten Commandments were given in the context of a covenant, introduced by a preamble in which God introduced himself, saying, 'I am the LORD your God' (Exod. 20.2a). This is followed by a very brief historical prologue that recounts how he saved Israel from oppression. He 'brought [the Israelites] out of the land of Egypt, out of the house of slavery' (20.2b). This is a very significant theological idea, that the LORD's salvation of Israel provided the basis for his invitation to enter into a covenant relationship with him. The Ten Commandments were not given to a people outside of a relationship with God, so that they might earn access to God. They were not requirements that must be met in order for the people to initiate a positive relationship with God. They were not provided as a way for the Ancient Israelites to earn their salvation. Instead, the covenant was the LORD's gracious initiative, established with a people whom he had already 'redeemed' (Exod. 20.1). God's covenant with Ancient Israel was his own gracious initiative.

After the preamble and the historical prologue, the Ten Commandments provide the stipulations for the covenant, as follows:

1 'You shall have no other gods before me' (Exod. 20.3). In the same way that Ancient Near Eastern suzerain–vassal treaties called upon vassals to give exclusive loyalty to their suzerain, so the first commandment calls upon Israel to give its exclusive loyalty to the LORD. Many scholars believe that monotheism was a late development in Israel and argue that

---

25 The expression also occurs in Deut. 4.13 and 10.4.

26 E.g. Eduard Nielsen, *The Ten Commandments in New Perspective: A traditio-historical approach* (SBT 2.7; London: SCM Press, 1968), 6–10.

27 Ellen Frankel and Betsy Platkin Teutsch, *The Encyclopedia of Jewish Symbols* (Northvale, NJ: Jason Aronson, 1992), 173.

this command is henotheistic rather than monotheistic. In this view, the first command acknowledged the existence of other gods but prohibited the worship of them for the Israelites.[28] However, Richard Elliott Friedman points out that, in the Hebrew, God prohibits having any other gods 'before my face', and that everywhere is before God's face, 'so the commandment means that one simply cannot have any other gods'.[29] While some may balk at the idea that Moses could have called early Israel to monotheism in the Late Bronze Age, the monotheistic revival in Egypt in the Amarna age (1353–1336 BC) provides an analogy for this early date.[30]

2 'You shall not make for yourself an idol, whether in the form of anything that is in heaven above, or that is on the earth beneath, or that is in the water under the earth. You shall not bow down to them or worship them; for I the LORD your God am a jealous God, punishing children for the inequity of parents, to the third and fourth generation of those who reject me, but showing steadfast love to the thousandth generation of those who love me and keep my commandments' (Exod. 20.4–6). The English word 'idol' translates the Hebrew *pesel*, which refers to a carved image.[31] Throughout the Ancient Near East, from at least as early as the mid third millennium BC, idols were the focus of worship.[32] Today, scholars generally aver that 'people did not believe that the idol itself was a god or goddess', but that it 'simply represented the presence of the god or goddess'.[33] Recent studies, however, make a compelling case that in the Ancient Near East, idols were not viewed as symbols but as actual deities.[34] In either case, portraying God as a statue would reduce him

28 E.g. Bob Beking, 'More than one god? Three models for construing the relations between YHWH and the other gods', in *Divine Doppelgängers: YHWH's ancient look-alikes*, ed. Collin Cornell (University Park, PA: Eisenbrauns, 2020), 68–9.

29 Richard Elliott Friedman, *Commentary on the Torah with a New English Translation* (San Francisco, CA: HarperSanFrancisco, 2001), 236.

30 Jan Assmann, *From Akhenaten to Moses: Ancient Egypt and religious change* (Cairo: American University in Cairo Press, 2014), 61–8; James K. Hoffmeier, *Akhenaten and the Origins of Monotheism* (Oxford: Oxford University Press, 2015), 193–266; Donald B. Redford, 'The monotheism of Akhenaten', in *Aspects of Monotheism: How God is one*, ed. Hershel Shanks (Washington, DC: Biblical Archaeology Society, 1997), 26; Donald B. Redford, *Akhenaten: The heretic king* (Princeton, NJ: Princeton University Press, 1984), 169–81.

31 John C. H. Laughlin, 'Idol', *NIDB* 3:8.

32 William W. Hallo, 'Cult statue and divine image: a preliminary study', in *Scripture in Context II*, ed. W. Hallo, J. C. Moyer and L. G. Perdue (Winona Lake, IN: Eisenbrauns, 1983), 1–17.

33 John C. H. Laughlin, 'Idolatry', *NIDB* 3:11.

34 Amy L. Balogh, *Moses among the Idols: Mediators of the divine in the Ancient Near East* (Lanham, MD: Lexington/Fortress Academic, 2018), 8.

from what he was, the infinite God, and identify him with something
finite in this world.

3 'You shall not make wrongful use of the name of the LORD your God,
for the LORD will not acquit anyone who misuses his name' (Exod.
20.7). In the Ancient Near Eastern world, naming was a way of claiming
authority over others.[35] Deities, therefore, sometimes had hidden or
secret names, 'so as to emphasize their otherness and to guard against
improper invocation by devotees'.[36] The LORD's name was not a secret,
but its misuse was prohibited in this third command. Although the
tradition developed of avoiding pronouncing the divine name,[37] this was
clearly not the original meaning of this command, since the divine name
was used in spoken blessings, greetings and ordinary conversation.[38]
The Name Command has been interpreted as prohibiting: (a) taking
false oaths in the name of God;[39] (b) profane use of God's name;[40] (c) the
use of God's name in magic;[41] and (d) claiming allegiance to the LORD
without carrying out his will.[42] Baker observes that 'the language of the
third commandment is quite general, which is perhaps deliberate because
it permits a range of application, covering all kinds of misuse of God's
name'.[43]

4 'Remember the Sabbath day, and keep it holy. Six days you shall labour
and do all your work. But the seventh day is a Sabbath to the LORD your
God; you shall not do any work – you, your son or your daughter, your
male or female slave, your livestock, or the alien resident in your towns.
For in six days the LORD made heaven and earth, the sea, and all that is in
them, but rested the seventh day; therefore the LORD blessed the Sabbath

35 George W. Ramsey, 'Is name-giving an act of domination in Genesis 2:23 and elsewhere?' *CBQ* 50 (1988): 24–35.

36 H. B. Huffmon, 'Name', *DDD*: 610.

37 By the first century, speaking the name of the LORD had become taboo. The Mishnah forbade it, except under special circumstances (*b. Soṭah* 7.6; Sanh. 7.5; 10.1).

38 In conferring blessing upon the people, the priests would pronounce the divine name (Num. 6.22–27), but it was also used by ordinary Israelites as a form of greeting (e.g. Ruth 2.4) and in conversation (e.g. 1 Sam. 14.6).

39 Cf. Lev. 19.12. This was the interpretation of Josephus, in *Ant.* 3.91.

40 Cf. Exod. 22.28; Lev. 24.10–16.

41 As suggested by Sigmund Mowinckel. Cf. Brevard S. Childs, *The Book of Exodus: A critical, theological commentary* (Philadelphia, PA: Westminster Press, 1974), 411.

42 This 'representational' interpretation of the Name Command is most clearly articulated in Carmen Joy Imes, *Bearing YHWH's Name at Sinai: A reexamination of the Name Command of the Decalogue* (University Park, PA: Eisenbrauns, 2018).

43 David L. Baker, *The Decalogue: Living as the people of God* (Downers Grove, IL: IVP Academic, 2017), 64.

day and consecrated it' (Exod. 20.8–11). In the Ancient Near East, there were no laws that made provision for holidays. In the Sabbath command, however, the Israelites were instructed to consecrate the seventh day of the week and spend it in rest and worship. The command served several purposes, including to: (a) provide rest and refreshment after the week's work; (b) recall the liberation of the exodus (Deut. 5.15); (c) sanctify people's labour, in that they worked towards the Sabbath each week; (d) remind the Israelites that the LORD was their creator (Exod. 20.8–11); (e) serve as a 'sanctuary in time' in which they could worship the LORD;[44] and (f) teach the Israelites that their holiness was rooted in God, rather than law or ritual. The Sabbath was intended to be 'a delight', a day when 'you shall take delight in the LORD' (Isa. 58.13–14).

5 'Honour your father and your mother, so that your days may be long in the land that the LORD your God is giving you' (20.12). This command serves as a bridge between the foregoing commands that focus on the relationship with God, and those that follow, which deal with relationships in the community. Throughout the Ancient Near East, the family was viewed as the foundation of a stable society, and law codes often included provisions to protect it.[45] In the case of the Ten Commandments, several of the commands that follow are designed to reinforce and protect it.[46] This command promotes family stability by establishing domestic authority with parents, who were to be honoured. 'Honour' translates the Hebrew verb *kabbēd*, 'to make heavy', and means to regard someone as weighty, in the sense of great importance. There are at least two foci of this commandment, including honouring parents and caring for them in their old age. Honouring parents was understood to mean showing them respect in public, obeying their teaching, bringing them joy by embracing wisdom, and not bringing harm upon them.[47] Caring for and supporting one's parents in their old age is also modelled and lauded in Scripture. Two notable examples of biblical figures who cared for their senior parents are Joseph, who brought his

---

44 Abraham Joshua Heschel, *The Sabbath: Its meaning for modern man* (New York, NY: Farrar, Straus & Young, 1952).

45 Gerald L. Mattingly, 'Family', *Dictionary of the Ancient Near East*, ed. Piotr Bienkowski and Alan Millard (Philadelphia, PA: University of Pennsylvania Press, 2000), 113–14.

46 Christopher J. H. Wright, 'The Israelite household and the Decalogue: the social background and significance of some commandments', *TynBul* 30 (1979): 120–4.

47 In Ancient Israel, one would rise before the elderly (Lev. 19.32). The Wisdom literature contains repeated references to the ways that one would show respect to one's parents; e.g. Prov. 1.8–9; 6.20; 10.1; 15.5, 20; 17.21, 25; 19.26; 20.20; 23.22–25; 28.24; 30.11, 17.

father and all his extended family to Egypt (Gen. 45.9–11), and Ruth, who
restored Naomi's life and nourished her in her old age (Ruth 4.14–15).
The intertestamental book of Sirach urges God's people to follow suit
by helping their parents in their old age, even if their minds fail, and
explains that kindness to parents will not be forgotten and will even serve
as a credit against one's sins (Sir. 3.12–16). How could such great respect
and care for parents provide the foundation for a stable society? How
adult children treated their own fathers and mothers became 'a model
by which their own children [would] learn to keep the commandment
and what its keeping entails'.[48] Venerating one's parents would build
intergenerational respect and ensure a stable and long-lived society.

6 'You shall not murder' (20.13). This command forbids illegal killing,
which was prohibited in the law codes of most Ancient Near Eastern
societies. There are kinds of killing that were certainly viewed in Ancient
Israel as warranted, such as in cases of self-defence, war and capital
punishment. The prohibition in the sixth commandment, however, uses a
relatively rare Hebrew word that connotes unauthorized killing.[49] While
subsequent laws distinguish between murder and other kinds of killing,
this prohibition enshrines the principle of the sanctity of human life.[50]
Human life is sacred and can never be replaced. Its value is enshrined in
the sixth commandment.

7 'You shall not commit adultery' (20.14). Throughout human history,
marriage has been the foundational relationship of every society,[51] and
laws prohibiting adultery can be found in most Ancient Near Eastern
law collections.[52] In these commandments, the sanctity of marriage is
enshrined immediately following that of human life, and its protection
comes in the form of a prohibition of adultery, which refers to sexual
relations between a married person and someone other than his or
her spouse. Some have argued that the Israelite prohibition of adultery

---

48 Patrick D. Miller, *The Ten Commandments* (Interpretation; Louisville, KY: Westminster John Knox Press, 2009), 204.
49 The Hebrew uses the second-person imperfect of the verb *rāṣaḥ*, which is rendered in some translations as 'kill' (e.g. KJV, RSV) and as 'murder' in others (e.g. NJPS, NRSV). More recent translations tend towards the latter option, since some forms of killing were clearly viewed as justified in the Old Testament.
50 The Covenant Code provides some immediate elaboration on the sixth commandment in Exod. 21.12–14. Lev. 24.10–23 deals with certain cases for which the death penalty is prescribed, and Deut. 19.1–22.8 considers numerous aspects of and cases that may arise related to the sixth commandment. Num. 35 provides places of asylum for those who have killed another person accidentally.
51 Maria Velioti-Georgopoulos, 'Marriage', *EAnth* 4:1536.
52 Gerald L. Mattingly, 'Adultery', *Dictionary of the Ancient Near East* (ed. Bienkowski and Millard), 4–5.

stemmed from the patrilineal nature of its society, where mistaken paternity could result in the bequeathal of the family inheritance to an illegitimate heir.[53] Wright, however, sees this as another command designed to reinforce and protect the family as the foundation of Israelite society. He explains that, in the same way that the fifth commandment reinforced societal stability by reinforcing the integrity of the family, so the seventh commandment did so by protecting the sexual integrity of the marriage at the heart of the household.[54]

8 'You shall not steal' (20.15). Property ownership is a standard feature of most societies, and virtually all known law codes from the Ancient Near East had laws that protected it.[55] Penalties range from monetary fines to capital punishment, depending on the crime and the social class of those involved.[56] In the eighth commandment, the prohibition against stealing applies to everyone, irrespective of social status. The prohibition also establishes the viability of property ownership. Like the fifth and seventh commands, the eighth command upholds the economic viability of the family by protecting its property.

9 'You shall not bear false witness against your neighbour' (20.16). This prohibition requires that witnesses tell the truth when called upon to testify in court. The use of witnesses in court was common in the Ancient Near East and, if the truth were to be established, it was imperative that witnesses be reliable. Giving false testimony in court was a considered a serious crime, and the punishments for perjury in Ancient Near Eastern society ranged from fines to capital punishment.[57] The same principles applied in Ancient Israel, where witnesses might be called either by the prosecution or the defence to testify in court.[58] Since witnesses would often provide the primary evidence for bringing a conviction, their honesty was vital for guaranteeing justice in Ancient Israelite society.

10 'You shall not covet your neighbour's house; you shall not covet your neighbour's wife, or male or female slave, or ox, or donkey, or anything that belongs to your neighbour' (20.17). This law is completely unique

---

53 Cf. Elaine Adler Goodfriend, 'Adultery', *ABD* 1:82.

54 Wright, 'The Israelite household and the Decalogue', 101–24.

55 Alan Millard, 'Property ownership and inheritance', *Dictionary of the Ancient Near East* (ed. Bienkowski and Millard), 235.

56 E.g. law 8 in 'Code of Hammurabi', trans. Theophile J. Meek (*ANET*, 166), and laws 93–9 in 'The Hittite laws', trans. Albrecht Goetze (*ANET*, 193).

57 E.g. laws 1–4 in 'Code of Hammurabi', trans. Meek.

58 E.g. 1 Kings 21.10, 13; Prov. 14.25; Isa. 43.9, 10, 12.

in the Ancient Near East in that it prohibits thoughts. The prohibited thoughts are those of covetousness, the desire for something that belongs to someone else.[59] Some interpreters have argued that what is really being prohibited is acting on one's unethical desires, but there is nothing in the command that suggests such an interpretation and so it should be read straightforwardly as actually prohibiting thoughts and desires.[60] This does not lessen the seriousness of the command, however, since desire could very well lead to the breaking of all the other commands. For example, David's desire for Bathsheba led to his committing adultery, lying and committing murder to cover it up and, in the end, stealing her for his wife (2 Sam. 11). In another example, Ahab's desire for Naboth's vineyard led him to lie, murder and steal his property for his own (1 Kings 21). Since all the crimes prohibited in the commandments stem from illicit desire, its prohibition may have been intended as a help to avoid breaking them.[61]

The Ten Commandments are succinct and general, and obviously a whole host of questions could be raised about how each one should be applied in different situations. The Decalogue itself, however, is not meant to be comprehensive. Instead, the application of each of the commands is elaborated upon in subsequent texts. There is some elaboration in the book of Exodus itself, as well as in Leviticus and Numbers, but the primary expansion comes in Deuteronomy, the name of which literally means 'second law'. Virtually the entire book of Deuteronomy follows the covenant format, and its longest section, the second speech of Moses, is an elaboration of the Ten Commandments.[62] The relationship of the Ten Commandments to Israelite law, therefore, is like the relationship of the Constitution of the United States to American law. The Constitution, which contains the Bill of Rights and 17 additional amendments, is the supreme law of the United States of America. Its 27 amendments, however, could not possibly address every possible situation that might arise, and so it is supplemented by a large body of constitutional law, which continues to be interpreted and supplemented.

---

59 The Hebrew verb is *ḥamad*, 'to covet', which refers to unjust desire.

60 For a review of the history of this interpretation and the arguments for rejecting it, see David L. Baker, 'Last but not least: the tenth commandment', *HBT* 27 (2005): 3–24.

61 Friedman, *Commentary on the Torah*, 239.

62 Meredith Kline, *The Treaty of the Great King: The covenant structure of Deuteronomy* (Grand Rapids, MI: Eerdmans, 1963), 27–49. Cf. also S. Dean McBride Jr, 'Polity of the covenant people: the book of Deuteronomy', in *Constituting the Community: Studies on the polity of Ancient Israel in honor of S. Dean McBride, Jr.*, ed. John T. Strong and Steven S. Tuell (Winona Lake, IN: Eisenbrauns, 2005), 17–33.

The Ten Commandments were written down on two stone tablets.[63] These tablets were placed inside the ark of the covenant, which was installed in the tabernacle.[64] Meredith Kline points out that these two copies fulfil the deposit clause of the standard suzerain–vassal covenant, which called for depositing one copy of the treaty document in the sanctuary of the vassal and another in the sanctuary of the suzerain.[65] Israel's copy served as a witness to remind the people of their covenant obligations (Deut. 31.26), while the LORD's copy reminded him of their commitment, as well as of his own role as their suzerain.

The Book of the Covenant

After the account of the Ten Commandments, additional laws are given in Exodus 20.22—23.19.

As noted above, this section has been designated the Covenant Code, with the idea that some or all of it originally formed an independent law code that was later incorporated into the Sinai narratives. However, as discussed above, the correspondence between the Sinai covenant and the Late Bronze Age covenant form points to the literary unity of the account of the Sinai covenant, in which case the Book of the Covenant would be considered part of the original covenant.

J. M. Sprinkle demonstrates that the laws in the Book of the Covenant echo and apply the Ten Commandments.[66] The first command (Exod. 20.3) is echoed in the prohibition against sacrificing to any other god (22.20), invoking the names of other gods (23.13), or worshipping them or entering into a covenant with them (23.24, 32). The third command (20.7) provides the background for cases of disputed ownership (22.7–9). The fourth commandment (20.8) is repeated (23.12) and expanded into a Sabbatical Year observance (23.10–11). The fifth commandment (20.12) is shown to be violated in examples of crimes against parents (21.15, 17), while an additional example shows its observance (22.16–17). The sixth commandment (20.13) is elaborated upon in various regulations about violence (21.12–14, 20, 23, 29; 22.2). The seventh commandment (20.14), while not explicitly repeated, provides the backdrop for laws connected with the seduction of a virgin (22.16–17). The eighth command (20.15) is applied in a variety of laws prohibiting the stealing of animals (21.37—22.4),

---

63 Exod. 31.18; 34.1, 4, 29; Deut. 4.13; 5.22; 9.10–11.

64 Exod. 25.16, 21; 40.20; Deut. 10.2.

65 Meredith G. Kline, *The Structure of Biblical Authority* (2nd edn; Eugene, OR: Wipf & Stock, 1997), 121.

66 J. M. Sprinkle, *'The Book of the Covenant': A literary approach* (JSOTSup 174; Sheffield: JSOT Press, 1994), 25–6.

attempted theft (22.2–3), accusation of theft (22.7–8), disputed ownership of animals (22.9–13) and kidnapping (21.16). The ninth command (20.16) is repeated and elaborated upon (23.1–3). And the tenth command (20.17) underlies several cases that deal with taking care of a neighbour's possessions (22.7–13). These interconnections reinforce the continuity of the Book of the Covenant with the Sinai covenant.

The conquest of Canaan promised

The promise of the conquest of Canaan (23.20–33), which comes immediately after the Covenant Code, is usually assigned to a later source.[67] The land theme, however, was one of the most basic themes derived from Israel's earliest history.[68] The original Abrahamic promises implied land (Gen. 12.1–3), and their reaffirmation made it explicit that the land to be inherited was the land of Canaan (Gen. 15.18–21). This promise was repeated to Jacob (Gen. 28.15), who instructed his sons to bury his body in Canaan once they had returned there from Egypt, where they had migrated during a famine (Gen. 49.29–32). Many years later, after the Israelites had endured centuries of slavery in Egypt, God spoke to Moses and told him that he had heard the Israelites' cry and was about to

> deliver them from the Egyptians, and to bring them up out of that land to a good and broad land, a land flowing with milk and honey, to the country of the Canaanites, the Hittites, the Amorites, the Perizzites, the Hivites, and the Jebusites.
> (Exod. 3.8)

In order to make these promises a reality, the Canaanites would have to be displaced (Exod. 23.20–26). The LORD would send his 'terror' ahead of the Israelites (v. 27) and a 'hornet' (v. 28) to drive out Canaan's indigenous inhabitants.[69]

The theme of the inheritance of land is implicit in the exodus theme. The guidance out of Egypt required a destination. After the exodus and the

---

67 E.g. Wright, 'Origin, development, and context of the Covenant Code', 220–44.

68 Martin Noth, *A History of Pentateuchal Traditions*, trans. Bernhard W. Anderson (Englewood Cliffs, NJ: Prentice-Hall, 1972), 46–62.

69 In 1931, John Garstang proposed that the hornet was a metonymy for Egypt. His theory is based on the fact that the symbol for Lower Egypt was a hornet, and that Egypt's various military campaigns into Canaan softened it up, making it ripe for the invasion of the Israelites. Cf. John Garstang, *Joshua and Judges* (London: Constable, 1931), 258–61.

crossing of the sea, the idea of the conquest of Canaan features in the Song of Moses (15.13–18), a poem composed in archaic Hebrew that most scholars date to the thirteenth to twelfth centuries BC.[70] The conquest theme reoccurs later in the book of Exodus in the midst of a discussion of the covenant commands (34.10–28). In this latter passage, undertaking the conquest is viewed as part and parcel of being faithful to the suzerain and his covenant, in which the land is bequeathed.

The ratification of the covenant

The covenant was ratified in a solemn ceremony, which consisted of at least three components.[71] First, the members of the entire assembly gave their verbal assent and affirmed that 'All the words that the LORD has spoken we will do' (24.3). Second, there was an animal sacrifice, the blood of which was dashed upon an altar and upon the people (24.5–8). The spattering of the people with the blood of the sacrificed animal was probably a symbolic way of affirming that, if they failed to adhere to the covenant, they would share its fate.[72] Through the animal sacrifice and by being spattered with its blood, the people promised their very lives as a guarantee that they would abide by the covenant. Third, the ratification ceremony included a banquet in the presence of the LORD (24.9–11), another common element of Ancient Near Eastern covenant ceremonies.[73] The suzerain–vassal covenant at Sinai formed a new society when all those in attendance, both Hebrew and non-Hebrew, accepted the LORD as their suzerain and bound themselves to live in sacred truce with one another under his lordship.

An important factor in the success of the Sinai covenant as a model was its timing. It was easy for the Israelites to understand and implement the Sinai covenant 'because it corresponded to ways of thinking and decision making that were not only potentially universal throughout the West Semitic linguistic region but also probably a thousand years old already by the time of Moses'.[74]

---

70 See Chapter 3.

71 Mendenhall, 'Covenant forms in Israelite traditions', 221.

72 For the slaughter of animals as a feature of Ancient Near Eastern covenants, see D. J. McCarthy, *Old Testament Covenant: A survey of current opinions* (Richmond, VA: John Knox Press, 1972), 30–1.

73 McCarthy, *Treaty and Covenant*, 253–4.

74 George E. Mendenhall, 'The suzerainty treaty structure: thirty years later', in *Cultural and Religious Creativity of Ancient Israel* (ed. Herion and Huffmon), 313. The article was originally published in 1990.

Conclusions

The Sinai covenant was an epochal event in the early history of Israel. When the Israelites were delivered from bondage in Egypt, they were a loose network of Hebrew tribes, accompanied by a 'mixed crowd' (Exod. 12.38) of other ethnic groups. Together, they journeyed to Mt Sinai, where Moses mediated a covenant between them and the LORD. In the covenant, God established laws, regulations for life, and religious ceremony. While some of its laws were similar to those of other cultures, others were entirely unique and distinguished Israel from all other peoples in the region. The most exceptional law was the first of the Ten Commandments, which called upon the covenant people to recognize the LORD alone as their God. Through the Sinai covenant, this ragtag band of former slaves became 'a priestly kingdom and a holy nation' (Exod. 19.6). This new status, however, was not an end in itself, but a means to a greater end. God fashioned Israel as a priestly kingdom so that, ultimately, 'all the families of the earth shall be blessed' (Gen. 12.3).

8

The presence of God in Exodus

The Lord chose Israel to be his 'treasured possession out of all the peoples
. . . a priestly kingdom and a holy nation' (Exod. 19.5–6). In order to facilitate that relationship, he established a covenant with its people at Mt Sinai.
After the ratification of the covenant (Exod. 24.1–8), therefore, the Lord revealed the plan for a portable sanctuary, comprised of an enclosure, in which
stood a tent and an altar (Exod. 25—31; 35—40). In this sanctuary the Lord
would 'tabernacle' in the midst of the Israelites[1] and go with them through
the desert on their way to the promised land.[2] The tabernacle texts begin with
a breathtaking theophany, in which the cloud that represented the very presence of God descended upon Mt Sinai (Exod. 24.15–18). Moses climbed Mt
Sinai, entered the cloud, and spent 40 days and nights in the presence of God
(Exod. 24.18). During that time, God gave him instructions for the building
of the tabernacle and its furnishings (Exod. 25—31). Moses conveyed the instructions to the people, who manufactured all of its components, and then he
assembled the tabernacle and set it up (Exod. 35—40). When the tabernacle
was completed, the cloud descended upon it and the glory of the Lord filled
it (Exod. 40.34). This chapter will provide an overview of the content of the
tabernacle texts, a discussion of the historicity of the tabernacle and the ark of
the covenant, and an exploration of their theology.

The tabernacle texts

The Lord gave Moses the instructions for the tabernacle and all of its components in a series of speeches.[3] In the first and longest speech, God gave Moses
instructions for the building of the sanctuary and its sacred furniture (Exod.
25.1—27.21), the design and manufacture of the priestly vestments (Exod. 28),
for their consecration and installation, and for the daily offerings (Exod. 29).
The speech began with the request for a voluntary collection of materials,

---

1 Cf. Exod. 25.8; 29.45–46; 40.35.

2 Cf. Exod. 40.36–38; Num. 9.15–23; 10.11; etc.

3 These occur in Exod. 25.1—30.10; 30.11–16; 30.17–21; 30.22–33; 30.34–38; 31.1–11; and 31.12–17.

including: gold, silver and copper; a variety of textiles; acacia wood; lamp and anointing oil; and precious stones (Exod. 25.1–9). In calling for a collection, the LORD explained that it was 'so that I may dwell among them' (Exod. 25.8). Brevard Childs identifies this as the purpose statement for the building of the tabernacle.[4]

Instructions were given for the installation of the sacred objects inside the tabernacle (Exod. 25.10–40), most notably the ark of the covenant. The ark is described as a wooden box that would serve, in part, as a repository for the covenant document (Heb. *'eduth*, Exod. 16). It was to be two and a half cubits long, a cubit and a half wide and high,[5] and overlaid with gold foil inside and out. It should have rings, through which carrying-poles could be inserted in order to make it transportable. A cover (*kapporet*), made of pure gold and adorned with two cherubim, was to be fashioned as a cover for the ark. Two cherubim were to be positioned on opposite ends of the lid, facing each other and with their wings outstretched towards each other across it. The Hebrew word for this top (*kapporet*) comes from a verb (*kapar*) that means 'to provide reconciliation' or 'to make atonement'.[6] It was therefore not just a 'lid' or 'cover', as it is rendered in some translations,[7] but the very place where God would be present and from which he would extend mercy. This is why the NRSV and many other translations render it as the 'mercy seat' (Exod. 25.17, 22).[8]

A table measuring two cubits long, one cubit wide, and a cubit and a half high[9] and laminated in gold foil was to be made for the bread of the Presence (Exod. 25.23–30).[10] Like the ark, it was also to be fixed with rings so that it would be portable. Its plates, dishes, flagons and bowls were all to be made of pure gold. A lampstand with six branches going out of its sides, three on each side, was to be made of pure gold (Exod. 25.31–40). Its size is not specified in the text, although it does say that it was to be fashioned using a talent of pure gold, which would have weighed about 34 kilograms (75 lb).

---

4 Brevard S. Childs, *The Book of Exodus: A critical, theological commentary* (Philadelphia, PA: Westminster Press, 1974), 540.

5 1.2 m (4 ft 2 in.) long, 76.2 cm (30 in.) wide and 76.2 cm (30 in.) high.

6 William L. Holladay, *A Concise Hebrew and Aramaic Lexicon of the Old Testament* (Grand Rapids, MI: Eerdmans, 1988), 163.

7 E.g. CEB, NCV, NLT.

8 The LEB and NIV render it as 'atonement cover', while many others, such as the CSB, ESV, HCSB, KJV and NASB, translate it as 'mercy seat'.

9 0.9 m (3 ft) long, 0.4 m (1 ft 6 in.) wide and 0.7 m (2 ft 3 in.) high.

10 Cf. Paul V. M. Flesher, 'Bread of the Presence', *ABD* 1:780–1.

The instructions for the tabernacle itself (Exod. 26.1–30) begin with details about the design for four tent coverings that were to be laid one on
top of the other in order to form the sanctuary's roof. Each covering was
to be made of a different material. The innermost curtain should be made
of 'twisted linen, and blue, purple and crimson yarns', with 'cherubim skil-
fully worked into them' (26.1). The next curtain was to be made of goat hair
(26.7), the third of rams' skins and the outermost covering of 'fine leather'
(26.14). The tabernacle should be stabilized on three sides by 'upright frames
of acacia wood', which were to be fastened together by pegs and supported by
a series of crossbars (26.15–30). The frames and bars were all to be overlaid
with gold foil (26.29).[11] The height of the tabernacle can be deduced from its
framework, which suggests that it would have been 10 by 30 cubits (*c*.5.25 x
15.75 m/ *c*.17 x 51 ft).

A special curtain (*paroket*) was to be designed to divide the interior of the
tabernacle into two rooms, the 'holy place' and the 'most holy place' (26.31–35).
The curtain was to be made of blue, purple and crimson yarns, along with fine
twisted linen, all with cherubim worked into them (26.31), just like the innermost covering. The tabernacle tent would be entered through the holy place,
which would include the table of the Presence and the lampstand. The most
holy place, enclosed behind the curtain, contained the ark of the covenant. A
screen served as the entrance to the tabernacle on its east side (26.36–37).

An altar for burnt offering was to be built to stand in front of the tabernacle
(27.1–8). Although its description is brief, it is complicated and its interpretation is the subject of some controversy. It was to be a hollow structure built of
acacia wood, measuring approximately 2.25 by 2.25 by 1.5 metres (7.5 x 7.5 x
4.5 ft), with horns on its four corners. The whole thing was to be overlaid with
bronze. On the inside, there was to be 'a grating, a network of bronze' (27.4).
This may have been a system of gratings inside the altar, one of which may
have been located halfway up from ground level, on which wood for the fire
would be placed, and another, situated farther up, where the meat would be
barbecued. The upper grating would have allowed for the oxygenation of the
fire below, as well as for fat and ashes to drip down.[12] Its accompanying sacrificial equipment, including pots, shovels, basins, forks and firepans, were all
to be made of bronze.

---

11 For a detailed study of the instructions for the construction of the tabernacle, see Richard Elliott
Friedman, 'Tabernacle', *ABD* 6:292–300.

12 Cf. Ralph K. Hawkins, *The Iron Age I Structure on Mt. Ebal: Excavation and interpretation* (Winona
Lake, IN: Eisenbrauns, 2012), 157–9.

Around the tabernacle and its altar, the Israelites were to create a court-yard by setting up an enclosure of linen hangings fastened to columns, which would be stood in copper bases (27.9–19). When everything was in place, the courtyard would measure 100 by 50 cubits, or about 45 by 23 metres (150 x 75 ft). The enclosure would be five cubits, or about 2.3 metres (7 ft 6 in.) high.

The instructions for the manufacture of the tabernacle conclude with brief instructions for the installation of a lamp, just in front of the curtain before the most holy place (27.20–21). The light was to burn 'regularly' or 'continual-ly' (*tāmîd*). It is not entirely clear from the text whether it was kindled regular-ly or kept burning continually. There are indications in various biblical texts that it was kindled on a regular basis each evening.[13] In later Judaism, howev-er, it was understood to be an 'eternal light' that symbolized the presence of God, who was always with his people.

The tabernacle texts next describe the vestments for ordination of its priests (28.1—29.46). Much of the text is devoted to describing Aaron's 'sacred vest-ments' (28.2), which were clearly very different from ordinary clothing. They indicated that his role set him apart to the LORD. His vestments were to include 'a breastpiece, an ephod, a robe, a chequered tunic, a turban and a sash' (28.4). The ephod was like an apron, which was held over the shoulders by suspend-ers and around the waist with tied strips.[14] It was to be made of the same col-ourful blend of fabrics as the curtain of the tabernacle (28.6). Precious stones with the names of the 12 tribes were to be affixed to the ephod on the shoul-ders, so that, when he wore them, he would 'bear their names before the LORD on his two shoulders for remembrance' (28.12). The 'breastpiece' was a sort of pocket, fastened to the front of the ephod, which held four rows of three pre-cious stones on which the names of the tribes were engraved, so that he would have them over his heart any time he went before the LORD (28.29–30). In addition, the Urim and the Thummim, two dice-like objects that were used by the priest to discern the will of the LORD, were to be kept in the ephod.[15] Together, the breastpiece and the ephod are referred to as the 'breastpiece of judgement' (28.15), which attests to the priest's role in discerning God's will for the people.[16]

---

13 Both Exod. 27.21 and Lev. 24.3 explicitly state that the lamp was to burn from evening until morning, and 1 Sam. 3.3 suggests that it burned out on its own.

14 Carol L. Meyers, 'Ephod', *ABD* 2:550.

15 Cornelis Van Dam, *The Urim and Thummim: A means of revelation in Ancient Israel* (Winona Lake, IN: Eisenbrauns, 1997), 140–53.

16 Patrick D. Miller, *The Religion of Ancient Israel* (London and Louisville, KY: SPCK and Westminster John Knox Press, 2000), 165–70.

The high priest's vestments were also to include 'the robe of the ephod', whose lower hem was decorated with 'pomegranates of blue, purple and crimson yarns, all around the lower hem, with bells of gold between them all around – a golden bell and a pomegranate alternating all around the lower hem of the robe' (28.33–4). The design of the high priest's vestments mirrored that of the sacred space of the tabernacle exactly, so that he blended in with it. The bells woven into his robe may have had an apotropaic function.[17] Finally, a rosette engraved with the words 'holy to the LORD' was to be fastened to the front of the high priest's turban (28.36–37). Aaron was to wear this when he presented Israel's offerings, so that he could 'take on himself any guilt incurred in the holy offering that the Israelites consecrate as their sacred donations; it shall always be on his forehead, in order that they may find favour before the LORD' (28.38–39). The liturgical clothing of the ordinary priests was to include tunics, sashes and headdresses, along with linen undergarments (28.40–43).

The speeches that follow supplement the instructions for the sanctuary. There are instructions that outline the process of ordaining the priests (29.1–37) and explain how the daily offerings were to be conducted (29.38–46). There are also details about the design of another piece of tabernacle furniture, the altar of incense, which was to be positioned in front of the curtain that separated the holy place from the most holy place (30.1–10). There are also instructions about a half-shekel offering that should be made to the sanctuary by every Israelite (30.11–16), the construction of a bronze basin in which the priests should wash their hands and feet before performing their duties either in the tent of meeting or at the altar (30.17–21), the making and use of anointing oil and incense (30.22–38), and the calling of two craftsmen to draft plans for the carrying out of all the foregoing instructions (31.1–11). The tabernacle texts conclude with a repetition and expansion of the Sabbath commandment (31.12–17). Even though the building of the tabernacle and its furnishings was a sacred task, it did not preclude the observation of the Sabbath. Conversely, even while the Israelites were occupied with the fabrication of the sanctuary and its parts, they must still pause every seventh day to observe the Sabbath. By observing the Sabbath, the Israelites would be patterning the rhythm of their work on that of the LORD in creation (31.17). It would allow tired workers to rest and be refreshed (31.15, 17), and it would also serve as a sign for the Israelites that their sanctification would not come

---

17 For a review of this and other interpretations, see Cornelis Houtman, *Exodus*, Vol. 3 (HCOT; Leuven: Peeters, 2000), 511–12.

about through their work on the tabernacle and its furnishings, but directly from the LORD himself (31.13).

Historicity of the tabernacle and the ark of the covenant

With the emergence of 'higher criticism', belief in the tabernacle declined and even, in some cases, disappeared. In Wellhausen's reconstruction of Israelite history, early Israelite worship, reflected in the J and E documents, was a primitive stage of nature religion that was spontaneous and came from a person's yearning to respond to the divine. Although he believed there were some early traditions that attested to the existence of the ark of the covenant, there was no tabernacle and there were no cultic laws and regulations. These kinds of materials were developed in the exilic or post-exilic period by priests. Later redactors retrofitted the institution of the tabernacle, and all of the cultic laws and regulations, to the time of Moses in order to fit their canonical portrayal of Israel's history.[18] While there may have been some kind of a tent for the ark, according to Wellhausen, the Priestly tabernacle was a 'historical fiction'.[19] He argues that:

> At the outset, its very possibility is doubtful. Very strange is the contrast between this splendid structure, on which the costliest material is lavished and wrought in the most advanced style of Oriental art, and the soil on which it rises, in the wilderness amongst the native Hebrew nomad tribes, who are represented as having got it ready offhand, and without external help. The incompatibility has long been noticed, and gave rise to doubts as early as the time of Voltaire.[20]

He asserts that the earliest traditions of the Hebrews knew 'nothing at all about it', and that it ultimately arose out of the Temple of Solomon and was projected into the Mosaic period 'to give pre-existence to the temple and to the unity of worship'.[21] Wellhausen believed there were some early traditions about the ark, but that it, too, was simple, and that P derived 'its inner

---

18 See Chapter 2 of this volume.

19 Julius Wellhausen, *Prolegomena to the History of Ancient Israel* (Gloucester, MA: Peter Smith, 1878; repr. New York, NY: Meridian, 1957), 39.

20 Wellhausen, *Prolegomena*, 39.

21 Wellhausen, *Prolegomena*, 39, 45.

character and its central importance for the cultus as well as its external form' from the Temple.[22]

Wellhausen's reconstruction charted the direction for source-critical studies after him.[23] Martin Noth, for example, explained that, in P, the Temple was changed into a movable tent sanctuary, and its most holy place, the holy of holies, was furnished with the ark, since 'P was neither willing nor able to conceive of the arrangement of the central sanctuary except in terms of the facts, conceptions, and cultic requirements of his own time'.[24] P's purpose for retrojecting the tabernacle into the past was 'to present a program for the future'.[25] Contemporary scholars continue to be heavily influenced by this approach, and even those who believe there was an actual tabernacle accept the idea that it could not have been as elaborate as the description in the tabernacle texts. Ralph Klein asserts that 'no critical scholar accepts that the account in Exodus is a literal account of the desert shrine' and that its complexity is 'unrealistic'.[26] Menahem Haran argues that it was 'largely imaginary and never existed in Israel'.[27] Even Ziony Zevit insists that the idea of the tabernacle 'as described in Exodus as a structure constructed by any group in Sinai' is ahistorical.[28] 'The working hypothesis in critical scholarship has been the assumption that the "historical" experience at Sinai did not include instructions concerning the tabernacle.'[29]

While Wellhausen's fifth-century dating of the wilderness tabernacle has had a lasting influence on biblical scholarship, it did not convince everyone. In 1947 Frank Moore Cross Jr wrote an article in which he examined the tabernacle in the light of tent shrines from Phoenicia, Ugarit, Egypt and Mesopotamia. His comparative study led him to conclude that the author of P must not have invented the idea of the tabernacle, but rather based it on written documents from the archives of the First Temple that described the tent David had erected for the ark (2 Sam. 6.17; 1 Chron. 16.1).[30] Since Cross's seminal work,

---

22 Wellhausen, *Prolegomena*, 45.

23 See the survey of scholarship in Thomas B. Dozeman, *The Pentateuch: Introducing the Torah* (Minneapolis, MN: Fortress Press, 2017), 351–5.

24 Martin Noth, *A History of Pentateuchal Traditions*, trans. Bernhard W. Anderson (Englewood Cliffs, NJ: Prentice-Hall, 1972), 243.

25 Noth, *Pentateuchal Traditions*, 243.

26 Ralph W. Klein, 'Back to the future: the tabernacle in the book of Exodus', *Int* 50 (1996): 264.

27 Menahem Haran, 'Shiloh and Jerusalem: the origin of the Priestly tradition in the Pentateuch', *JBL* 81 (1962): 14.

28 Ziony Zevit, 'Timber for the tabernacle: text, tradition, and realia', *Eretz-Israel* 23 (1992): 137*–43*.

29 Samuel E. Balentine, *The Torah's Vision of Worship* (OBT; Minneapolis, MN: Fortress Press, 1999), 137.

30 Frank Moore Cross Jr, 'The tabernacle: a study from an archaeological and historical approach', *BA* 10 (1947): 45–68.

subsequent scholars have studied additional tent shrines in search of parallels for the tabernacle. The most comprehensive study to date is that of Michael Homan, who provides a survey and analysis of all the parallels that have been proposed for the tabernacle.[31]

Early studies, in the late nineteenth and early twentieth centuries, focused primarily on bedouin and pre-Islamic tent shrines, including the *qubba*, *'utfah* and *mahmal*. The *qubba* was a miniature tent covered with red leather, like the tabernacle, that was mounted on the back of a camel and used as a palladium and oracular device, and as the leader of a procession. The *'utfah* and the *mahmal* were derivatives of the *qubba*. The *'utfah* is a palladium made up of a wooden frame placed on the back of a camel, adorned with ostrich feathers and sometimes covered with a tent. Sacrifices are made in front of it, and the blood is sprinkled on its corners. It serves as an oracular device and also incites enthusiasm in the soldiers before a battle. The *mahmal* is like the *'utfah* but larger, with an elaborately decorated tent containing Islamic religious texts. While it is sometimes used as a palladium, it more often serves as a palanquin for tribal leaders on the hajj to Mecca. Homan notes that, while these 'are more austere than the Tabernacle, they point to the long history of Near Eastern tent shrines, and show that for pastoral societies where tents provide an important means of shelter, tents often find representations in the religion'.[32]

The strongest literary parallel is found in the Ras Shamra tablets, in which the chief god of the pantheon, El, is said to have dwelt in a tent, which is specifically called a tabernacle (*mishkan*).[33] It had multiple rooms and was stocked with elaborate furnishings cast from gold and silver, along with a throne and footstool. Its furnishings, like those of the tabernacle of the LORD, were manufactured by a specially appointed craftsman. The other gods of El's divine council were also said to dwell in tents, to which they would return after divine assemblies. Homan also surveys portable tent shrines found in Phoenician and Carthaginian literature, as well as pictorial evidence from Phoenicia, Syria and Judea.[34]

The strongest parallels are found in Egypt. Among these are the historical and material records of the funerary cult, in which tents played an important role. The deceased were prepared for burial in a tent, and Egyptian

---

31 Michael M. Homan, *To Your Tents, O Israel! The terminology, function, form, and symbolism of tents in the Hebrew Bible and the Ancient Near East* (CHANE 12; Leiden: Brill, 2002), 89–128.

32 Homan, *To Your Tents*, 93.

33 Cf. also Richard J. Clifford, 'The tent of El and the Israelite tent of meeting', *CBQ* 33 (1971): 221–7.

34 Homan, *To Your Tents*, 99–105.

nobles were sometimes buried with tents.[35] One shrine of particular interest is that of Tutankhamun, where a linen tent and wooden frame were found among four nested catafalques that housed his sarcophagus.[36] These were overlaid with gold foil, which the Egyptians were highly skilled in working.[37] The tent was made of several panels of cloth decorated with gilt bronze rosettes, which were sewn together and positioned so that the seam ran parallel to the entrance, similar to the design of the tabernacle (26.1–14). It lay between the outer two gold-plated catafalques and, since the exterior shrine did not have a roof, it served as the outermost ceiling. The tent had a wooden frame that included seven crossbars to support the fabric, and a front-hinged panel to provide access. It measured 4.32 by 2.93 metres (14 ft 2 in. x 9 ft 7 in.) and was 2.78 metres (9 ft 1 in.) high. While additional Egyptian tent shrines have been found, Homan concludes that 'this wooden frame, as well as the more elaborate gold-plated catafalques, provide some of the best parallels to the craftsmanship involved in creating the Tabernacle'.[38]

The most noteworthy parallel is the military camp of Ramesses II at Qadesh, which had been noted as early as 1913 but never fully explored. There are four reliefs with accompanying inscriptions that depict a 2:1 rectangular camp, with its entrance in the centre of the short, eastern wall. The rectangular shape is significant, since military camps were more typically elliptical.[39] A 3:1 long-room tent is inside the camp, with its entrance situated precisely in its centre. The long-room tent is made up of a 2:1 reception tent leading to the square throne tent of the pharaoh. Furthermore, the height of the tent matches with its width. In order to have an audience with the pharaoh, one would have entered Ramesses II's camp through the eastern entrance, crossed the courtyard, passed through the reception tent and, finally, entered Pharaoh's chamber, where his golden throne was flanked by falcon wings, in the same way that the ark of the covenant was flanked by winged cherubim.[40] While there are still other analogues, the military tent and camp of Ramesses II at Qadesh provide the clearest parallel to the tabernacle (see Fig. 1).[41]

---

35 The tent may have been included among the deceased's burial goods to serve as the covering for a funeral bark, a boat that would bear him or her into the underworld.

36 A catafalque is a decorated wooden framework used to house or support a coffin.

37 Cf. Yvonne J. Markowitz and Peter Lacovara, 'Gold', *OEAE* 2:34–8.

38 Homan, *To Your Tents*, 108.

39 Homan, *To Your Tents*, 114.

40 In Egyptian art, east is on the left, while west is on the right.

41 Additional parallels from Mesopotamia and the Negev are surveyed in Homan, *To Your Tents*, 116–20.

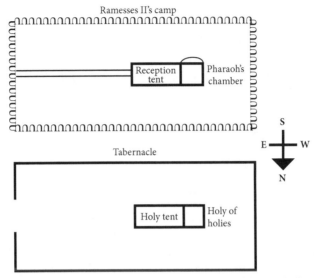

Figure 1 Comparison of Ramesses II's military tent (Abu Simbel) with the
tabernacle
(Courtesy of Michael M. Homan)

The importance of this parallel cannot be overstated. 'Here is a tent shrine for the living Egyptian god from the same time and area in which the events in [Exodus] purport to take place.'[42] In the light of these parallels, a Late Bronze Age II (1550–1250 BC) Israelite tent sanctuary influenced by Egyptian style and techniques would not be unusual at all, but might even be expected.

There have also been several proposed Near Eastern parallels for the ark of the covenant, which was the centrepiece of the tabernacle.[43] It has some similarities to a divine palanquin, which was a litter used for the transport of a statue of a god. However, divine palanquins were not laminated with gold foil, did not have boxes or lids, did not contain relics, were not carried with the use of poles, had no restrictions on who could touch them and do not appear to have been carried into battle. The ark has also been compared to the bedouin 'utfa, which was discussed above, in relation to the tabernacle. The 'utfa, however, was carried on the back of a camel, had no box, lid or poles, was not

---

42 Homan, *To Your Tents*, 114.

43 As reviewed in Scott B. Noegel, 'The Egyptian origin of the ark of the covenant', in *Israel's Exodus in Transdisciplinary Perspective: Text, archaeology, culture, and geoscience*, ed. Thomas E. Levy, Thomas Schneider and William H. C. Propp (New York, NY: Springer, 2015), 225–6.

overlaid in gold, had no cherubim and had no restrictions on human contact. Furthermore, while some were inscribed with spells and verses from the Qur'an, they do not appear to have served as reliquaries or as the throne or footstool of Allah.

Scott Noegel has recently proposed that the Egyptian sacred bark provides a 'more compelling and complete parallel' for the ark.[44] The bark was a sacred ritual object used to transport mummies or gods. It resembled a boat, but was probably never actually placed in the water. Instead it was loaded on to a barge, carried by hand, dragged on a sledge or pulled in a wagon. When it was used to transport a mummy, the sarcophagus, into which a copy of the Book of the Dead was often placed, was carried in a catafalque that was laminated with gold foil. When it was used to transport a god, it was fitted with a *naos*, laminated with gold, in which the divine image would be seated on a throne.[45] The *naos* was veiled with a canopy of wood or cloth. Barks were often decorated with cherubim, and were carried on poles by priests, who performed purification rituals before taking up the bark. A sacred bark could also be consulted for an oracle. Noegel does not suggest that the ark was actually a bark, but that the bark provided a model which the Israelites adapted for their own purposes. He explains that

> it still represented a throne and a footstool and so it still served as a symbol of the divine presence. It continued to be a sacred object that one could consult for oracles, and its maintenance continued to be the exclusive privilege of the priests.[46]

In addition to the tent and its ark, the furniture of the tabernacle locates it in a Late Bronze Age II Egyptian context.[47] In her 1974 monograph on the tabernacle menorah, Carol Meyers shows that, 'On every level, the details of its fabricature and form point to it as a manifestation of a material culture that can be located in time at the end of the Late Bronze Age.'[48] The table for the bread of the Presence (25.23–30) finds analogues in Egyptian tomb iconography, where a table for the deceased was set with loaves, often numbering 12.

---

44   Noegel, 'Egyptian origin of the ark', 226.

45   A *naos* is the inner chamber of a sanctuary.

46   Noegel, 'Egyptian origin of the ark', 230.

47   The following examples are derived from Homan, *To Your Tents*, 129–31.

48   Carol L. Meyers, *The Tabernacle Menorah: A synthetic study of a symbol from the biblical cult* (Piscataway, NJ: Gorgias Press, 2003), 182.

Much of the tabernacle's terminology is derived from Egyptian.[49] The hollow horned altar that stood in the courtyard, which Wellhausen viewed as a 'perfectly absurd construction',[50] finds a parallel in a model of a Middle Kingdom granary and butchery, where a hollow horned altar was located. Several of the rituals associated with the tabernacle are also paralleled in Late Bronze Age texts. For example, the practice of anointing priests with oil and blood has analogues in Late Bronze Age cuneiform texts from Emar, in Syria. Also, the role of priests in guarding and maintaining the tabernacle is similar to the maintenance of Hittite temples. The revelation of the tabernacle's design also mirrors building accounts of Ancient Near Eastern temples, in which the king would be given a model of the temple by the deity before he began construction. Similarly, the LORD gave Moses an exact 'pattern' on which to construct the tabernacle (25.9, 40).[51]

Cumulatively, these parallels are tremendously important in that they locate the tabernacle in Late Bronze Age II Egypt, which is where the Old Testament places its construction. In his 1947 article, Cross argued that P 'in no way represent[ed] pious fraud', but that he used 500-year-old sources that described the tent David built when he brought the ark of the covenant to Jerusalem (2 Sam. 6.17).[52] Homan goes further than Cross, and proposes that P based his description of the tabernacle on Egyptian prototypes, but that he did it unknowingly by using historical records in his possession that either pictorially or verbally described an earlier tent-shrine.[53] Kitchen goes all the way and asserts that the cumulative evidence points clearly to an origin for the tabernacle and its furnishings in Late Bronze Age Egypt.[54]

Theology of the tabernacle

The primary purpose of the author of Exodus, however, was not to consciously compose a literary account that would mirror Egyptian parallels. Instead, the author(s)' point was to make specific theological claims about what the LORD was doing in and through the tabernacle and its appurtenances. While there are many theological themes that could be highlighted, we will focus on three: new creation, the Divine Presence and the Divine Warrior.

---

49   Homan, *To Your Tents*, 115, n. 116.

50   Wellhausen, *Prolegomena*, 37.

51   Cf. Victor Hurowitz, 'The Priestly account of building the tabernacle', *JAOS* 105.1 (1985): 21–30.

52   Cross, 'The tabernacle', 217, 221–3.

53   Homan, *To Your Tents*, 114.

54   Kenneth A. Kitchen, 'The tabernacle – a Bronze Age artifact', *Eretz-Israel* 24 (1993): 119*–29*.

The tabernacle as part of a new creation

Several scholars have pointed out that there are parallels between the tabernacle texts and the creation story.[55] The LORD's seven speeches to Moses in Exodus 25—31 echo the seven days of creation. He points out that, just as the 'spirit of God' took the initiative at creation (Gen. 1.2, footnote translation), so would it be used to endow Bezalel for the building of the tabernacle (Exod. 31.3). The focus on the intricacies of the tabernacle's design and manufacture mirrors the elaborate description of creation in Genesis 1. Just as God rested after creating the world (Gen. 2.2), so the Israelites would have to rest after building the tabernacle (Exod. 31.12-17). In the same way that God surveyed the creation, declared it 'good'[56] and pronounced a blessing (Gen. 2.3), so Moses surveyed the completed tabernacle, pronounced that the Israelites had made it in accordance with God's 'pattern' and blessed them (Exod. 39.43). The completed tabernacle was dedicated on New Year's Day (Exod. 40.2, 17), which celebrated the first day of creation. These parallels were surely not accidental, but intentional. The author of Exodus intended to say that, through the Israelites' building of the tabernacle, God would create a new world for them.[57]

The tabernacle as the place of Divine Presence

If God was going to create a new world for the Israelites through the building of the tabernacle, what kind of world would it be? The world of God's original creation had been one in which God was present with humankind in unfettered relationship, illustrated through the use of anthropomorphism in the early chapters of Genesis.[58] As a result of the Fall (Gen. 3), however, humankind was driven away from the presence of God, who could not dwell in the midst of a sinful people.[59] If the building of the tabernacle would create a new world, it would be one in which the LORD would once again dwell. This purpose is reflected in the very term 'tabernacle' (*mishkan*), which means

---

55 Joseph Blenkinsopp, 'The structure of P', *CBQ* 38 (1976): 275–92; P. J. Kearney, 'Creation and liturgy: the P redaction of Ex. 25–40', *ZAW* 89 (1977): 375–87; Gordon J. Wenham, 'Sanctuary symbolism in the garden of Eden story', in *Proceedings of the Ninth World Congress of Jewish Studies*, ed. David Assaf (Jerusalem: World Union of Jewish Studies, 1986), 19–24.

56 Gen. 1.4, 10, 12, 18, 21, 25, 31.

57 Terence E. Fretheim, *Exodus* (Interpretation; Louisville, KY: John Knox Press, 1991), 269–70.

58 The author of Gen. 2 uses anthropomorphic language to convey the idea that God is present in the garden. God is one who 'formed man' (2.7), 'planted a garden' (2.8), 'put' man in the garden (2.15), commanded Adam (2.16–17), 'made' a woman and 'brought her' to the man (2.22), 'called' to Adam (2.9), spoke to Adam and Eve (2.10–19), and 'made' garments of skin for them and 'clothed' them (2.21).

59 For a brief discussion of the Fall, see Walter Brueggemann, *Reverberations of Faith: A theological handbook of Old Testament themes* (Louisville, KY: Westminster John Knox Press, 2002), 79–80.

'dwelling place' and is derived from the verb 'to dwell' (*shakan*).[60] Its innermost sanctum, the holy of holies, housed the ark of the covenant, which not only contained the tablets of the covenant but also served as the symbolic presence of the LORD. He was enthroned upon its cherubim,[61] and the ark itself was his footstool.[62] The tabernacle compound, therefore, with the ark of the covenant in its inner sanctum, represented the LORD's very dwelling. It was a recapitulation of Eden, where the LORD had first dwelled among his people.[63]

When the tabernacle and all is appurtenances were completed, the 'cloud' of the LORD's presence 'covered' the tent of meeting, 'and the glory of the LORD filled the tabernacle' (Exod. 40.34). The cloud and the glory were so encompassing of the tabernacle that Moses could not enter it (40.34–35). The LORD guided Israel by the cloud of his presence, which he would take up to signal that it was time to depart, or leave in place to signal that the Israelites should remain encamped (40.36–37). The book of Exodus concludes with the observation that 'the cloud of the LORD was on the tabernacle by day, and fire was in the cloud by night, before the eyes of all the house of Israel at each stage of their journey' (40.38). The visibility of the cloud 'before the eyes' of all Israel emphasizes that he was fully present in the midst of the people, right before their very eyes.

This conclusion is the fruition of the ideal of the Sinai covenant. In its 'blessings' section (Lev. 26.1–13),[64] the LORD promised that, if the Israelites did not make idols, observed the Sabbath, and followed the LORD's statutes and commandments, then they would experience rich blessings in the promised land (Lev. 26.1–10). This section culminates with the promise of the most profound blessing of all:

> I will place my dwelling in your midst, and I shall not abhor you. And I will walk among you, and will be your God, and you shall be my people. I am the LORD your God who brought you out of the land of Egypt, to be their slaves no more; I have broken the bars of your yoke and made you walk erect.
> (Lev. 26.11–13)

---

60 The tabernacle was also referred to as a 'sanctuary' (*miqdash*) and as the 'tent of meeting' (*'ohel mo'ed*).

61 E.g. Pss. 80.1; 99.1.

62 E.g. 1 Chron. 28.2; Pss. 99.5; 132.7.

63 For a detailed study of the symbolism of the tabernacle and its correspondence with the LORD's first 'temple', in the garden of Eden, see G. K. Beale, *The Temple and the Church's Mission: A biblical theology of the dwelling place of God* (NSBT 17; Downers Grove, IL: InterVarsity Press, 2004), 29–80.

64 For the format of the Sinai covenant, refer back to Chapter 7.

The Hebrew word translated as 'dwelling' in the foregoing passage is literally 'tabernacle'. In addition to placing his tabernacle in the midst of the Israelites, however, the LORD would also 'walk among' them, a clear allusion to the garden of Eden.[65] Clearly, the author believed the Sinai covenant would lead to the restoration of Edenic conditions.

The tabernacle as the LORD's war tent

Despite the fact that the LORD had taken up residence among his people, they were not in an Eden, but in a hostile wilderness. In this threatening environment, the LORD's identity as a warrior God took on great importance. The LORD had liberated Israel from bondage in Egypt as a warrior god,[66] and now the tabernacle would function as his war tent. In Chapter 6 we discussed a number of 'holy war' themes that shaped the Exodus narrative, and a number of these support the identification of the tabernacle as the LORD's war tent. The Israelites are also continually referred to in the exodus narratives as the LORD's 'company', a term with militaristic overtones.[67] In addition, Homan points out that the way that the LORD led them with a pillar of cloud by day and of fire by night (13.21) may have been similar to the way that Alexander the Great used a smoke signal by day and a fire signal by night to alert his troops that it was time to take up camp.[68] He also notes that implements of the Israelite camp like trumpets and standards, as well as the way the camp was taken down and transported, corresponded with Ancient Near Eastern military practices.[69] The close correspondence of the tabernacle with Ramesses' camp heightens its identification as a war camp.[70]

Some have argued that the very idea of holy war was an invention of Deuteronomic theologians, and is a literary and theological fiction. Even Wellhausen, however, saw that war was essential to the early history of Israel. He wrote that 'highwater marks of [Ancient Israel's] history were indicated by the wars it recorded', and that 'the [Israelite] camp was, so to speak, at once the cradle in which the nation was nursed and the smithy in which it was welded into unity; it was also the primitive sanctuary'.[71] And even von Rad, who believed

---

65 G. Geoffrey Harper, 'I Will Walk Among You': The rhetorical function of allusion to Genesis 1–3 in the book of Leviticus (BBRSup 21; University Park, PA: Eisenbrauns, 2018), 194–5.

66 See Chapter 6, above, for the ways that holy war shapes much of the Exodus narrative.

67 Cf. Exod. 6.26; 7.4; 12.17, 41, 51.

68 Homan, To Your Tents, 115.

69 Homan, To Your Tents, 115.

70 Homan, To Your Tents, 115.

71 Wellhausen, Prolegomena, 433.

that the schema of holy war was preserved in late Deuteronomic texts, acknowledged that 'the time of the great military deeds of [the LORD] is the time of the wandering in the desert and the Conquest, while the time of the judges . . . is insignificant in comparison'.[72] In his classic study of *The Divine Warrior in Early Israel*, Patrick Miller demonstrates that the journey of the Israelites through the wilderness is also redolent with holy war themes, both in prose texts as well as in very early poetic material.[73] He writes that:

> From Sinai, Israel and her God proceeded to Canaan, engaging enemies and adversaries along the way. The ancient poetry sees the march through the wilderness as a military endeavor. That picture is reinforced by the prose narratives (for example, Num 14.39ff.; Ex 17.8ff.) but especially by the P account in the early chapters of Numbers where the people of Israel are described as a force in military formation, each tribe being rallied around its standard. The encampment is a battle camp. The census of the men is for military purposes.[74]

Indeed, enthroned in his war tent, the LORD would lead the Israelites through the desert, defending them from hostile forces, until they arrived at the mountain of his own possession, his sanctuary, where he would take up his throne as their king (Exod. 15.17–18).

Conclusions

One of the main ideas of the entire Bible is that God wants to be in relationship with humankind.[75] God created a good world in which he dwelled in the midst of his people (Gen. 2). The author(s) of Genesis described Eden using the cosmic symbolism of temples in order to convey the idea that there was no separation between heaven and earth and that God's dwelling was in the midst of humankind.[76] God walked among his people and, somehow, they experienced his complete and unrestricted presence. When humans rebelled,

---

72 Gerhard von Rad, *Holy War in Ancient Israel* (repr.; Eugene, OR: Wipf & Stock, 2000), 131.

73 Patrick D. Miller, *The Divine Warrior in Early Israel* (repr.; Atlanta, GA: Society of Biblical Literature, 2006), 160.

74 Miller, *Divine Warrior*, 161.

75 This can be seen through God's redemptive acts in the Old Testament, which are for the purpose of reconciling humankind to God. Cf. Christoph Barth, *God With Us: A theological introduction to the Old Testament*, ed. Geoffrey W. Bromiley (Grand Rapids, MI: Eerdmans, 1991), 5–6.

76 Beale, *The Temple and the Church's Mission*, 29–80.

however, those Edenic conditions were broken and they were driven from the presence of God (Gen. 3.24). From that point forward, the rest of the Bible is one long story of God seeking to redeem human beings so that he might re-establish his presence among them. God launched a programme of redemption with Abraham, through whose descendants he promised to bless all humankind (Gen. 12.1–3). However, by the end of the book of Genesis, these descendants had migrated to Egypt in the course of a famine (Gen. 46—47) and, at the beginning of the book of Exodus, readers learn that they had ultimately been enslaved there (Exod. 1.8–11).

This leads us to the book of Exodus, which Mark Scarlata calls 'the most developed account of the Divine Presence in the entire Old Testament'.[77] He explains that 'the entire story of Exodus in its final form is about the movement of God's Divine Presence from heaven to earth so that he might abide with his people'.[78] Indeed, the arc of the story dramatically illustrates that movement. In the book of Exodus, God liberated the Israelites from slavery in Egypt, redeemed them through the Sea, and led them to Mt Sinai where he entered into a covenant relationship with them. As part of the covenant stipulations, he commanded them to 'make me a sanctuary, so that I may dwell among them' (Exod. 25.8). Much of the rest of the book of Exodus is devoted to the details of this sanctuary, attesting to its importance, and it reaches a dramatic conclusion when 'the cloud covered the tent of meeting, and the glory of the Lord filled the tabernacle . . . before the eyes of all the house of Israel' (Exod. 40.34–38). The book that began with the Israelites enslaved, and Pharaoh on his throne, ends with Israel liberated and the Lord enthroned in his tabernacle in the midst of his people.

---

77 Mark Scarlata, *The Abiding Presence: A theological commentary on Exodus* (London: SCM Press, 2018), 5.
78 Scarlata, *Abiding Presence*, 185.

9

The gospel of Israel in Exodus

The last chapter examined the tabernacle texts (Exod. 25—31; 35—40), in which God gave Moses instructions for the design and building of the tabernacle and its sacred furniture (25.1—27.21). Instead of moving on to the actual building of the tabernacle, however, the Israelites built a golden calf. They made sacrifices to it, followed by eating, drinking and revelry. In the same way that the exodus and crossing of the sea are seen as the foundational acts of salvation in the Old Testament, the golden calf incident is viewed as an archetypal act of rebellion. In the context of Israel's rebellion, however, the LORD reveals what may be the most comprehensive articulation of his character in the entire Old Testament. Known as the 'Thirteen Attributes' or 'the Divine Attribute Formula', this expression of God's qualities is repeated and echoed in later Scripture and in Jewish and Christian liturgy. In this chapter, we will review the narrative of the golden calf episode and its meaning, examine God's response to it, and then consider the revelation of God's gracious character and a portion of its reception history.

Sin and restoration at Sinai

When Moses went up the mountain to receive the instructions for the tabernacle, he was absent from the Israelite camp for 'forty days and forty nights' (Exod. 24.18). During his prolonged absence, Aaron was left in charge (24.14, 18). The people went to him and said, 'Come, make gods for us, who shall go before us; as for this Moses, the man who brought us up out of the land of Egypt, we do not know what has become of him' (32.1). They expressed their demand with some contempt for 'this Moses, the man who brought us up out of the land of Egypt', as if the LORD had nothing to do with it.[1] Their call to Aaron to fashion 'gods' was actually a command or a threat. When the text says that the people gathered 'around' him (32.1), the Hebrew should probably be understood to mean that they gathered 'against' him. Their demands

---

1 William Johnstone, *Exodus 20–40* (SHBC; Macon, GA: Smyth & Helwys, 2014), 350.

were made with hostility; they told him to 'come' and 'make', both of which are imperatives, punctuated with an exclamation point. While the Israelites may have been afraid that Moses had deserted them, or that some tragedy had befallen him, the text seems to portray their actions as hostile and obstinate, as a spiteful rebellion.

Aaron acquiesced and told the people to give him their gold earrings, which he collected and formed into a mould (Exod. 32.2–4). He cast an image of a calf and, when the people saw it, they said, 'These are your gods, O Israel, who brought you up out of the land of Egypt!' (32.4). When Aaron saw this, he built an altar in front of the image and announced that there would be a festival to the LORD on the following day. At the festival, he made burnt offerings and sacrifices of well-being. The people ate, drank and rose up to 'revel' (32.6).

The LORD told Moses to go down from the mountain immediately, because the people had 'acted perversely' and

> turn[ed] aside from the way that I commanded them; they have cast for themselves an image of a calf, and have worshipped it and sacrificed to it, and said, 'These are your gods, O Israel, who brought you up out of the land of Egypt!'
> (Exod. 32.7–8)

The LORD went on to say that he had seen how 'stiff-necked' the people were, and he told Moses to leave him alone so that his wrath could 'burn hot' against them and that he might 'consume them', after which he would begin his programme of redemption all over again and build a great nation from Moses' descendants (32.9–10).

Moses protested, however, and gave a series of reasons why God should not go through with his intended destruction of Israel. First, he argued that God had gone to a lot of trouble to liberate them from the Egyptians and bring them this far (32.11). Second, the Egyptians would misinterpret God's destruction of Israel as the act of a capricious and wicked God (32.12). Third, he reminded God of the covenant promises he had made to Israel's ancestors (32.13). As a result of Moses' prayer of protest, the LORD 'changed his mind about the disaster that he planned to bring on his people' (32.14).[2]

2　This may seem to contradict the principle of God's unchangeability, as expressed in 1 Sam. 15.29: 'the Glory of Israel will not recant or change his mind; for he is not a mortal, that he should change his mind.' However, God may change his method of responding to a person or group based on some change they have made (see Jer. 18.7–10).

Moses, accompanied by his young assistant, Joshua, headed back down the mountain, carrying the two tablets of the covenant in his hands (32.15). There was so much noise coming from the camp that Joshua thought a war had broken out, but soon realized it was the sounds of revelry (32.17–18). When they got close enough for Moses to see 'the calf and the dancing', Moses became furious, 'threw the tablets from his hands and broke them at the foot of the mountain', and then 'took the calf that they had made, burned it with fire, ground it to powder, scattered it on the water, and made the Israelites drink it' (32.19–20). Moses confronted Aaron, whom he had placed in charge, but he tried to shift the blame on the people. He said that, after he had collected the gold, he 'threw it into the fire, and out came this calf!' (32.24).

Moses stood at the entrance to the Israelite camp and issued a summons that anyone who remained on the LORD's side should rally to him, and 'all the sons of Levi' gathered around him (32.25–26). He told them to strap on their swords and go through the camp, putting to death all those who had participated in the golden calf rebellion. The text states that 'about three thousand of the people fell on that day' (32.28).[3] After the carnage, Moses ascended the mountain again, in hopes that he might 'make atonement' for Israel's sin (32.30). He told the LORD that, if he would not forgive their sin, then he could just go ahead and blot the name of Moses out of his book of life as well (32.32). The LORD assured Moses that his angel would go with the Israelites, but that, 'when the day comes for punishment, I will punish them for their sin' (32.34). In the end, the LORD sent a plague upon the people 'because they made the calf' (32.35).

The LORD told Moses that, when the Israelites left for Canaan, he would send an angel with them, but would not accompany them himself lest he 'consume' them on the way, because they were a 'stiff-necked people' (33.2–3). God told Moses to relay this to the people, who were to take off their ornaments and wait for the LORD to decide what he would do to them (33.5). The people mourned when they heard these words, but they took off their ornaments and waited on the LORD (33.4, 6).

Moses interceded on behalf of the Israelites yet again, and told the LORD that, if his presence would not go with them, then it was pointless for the Israelites to move out from Sinai at all. If he did not go with them, they would be just like any other nation on earth and would not, in fact, have found favour in God's sight (33.12–16). He also made a special appeal to the LORD that, if he had found favour with him, he would show Moses his ways, so that he

---

3 See the discussion of 'The number of Israelites who left Egypt' in Chapter 3.

might know him (33.13). The LORD answered that he would 'do the very thing that you have asked; for you have found favour in my sight, and I know you by name' (33.17). Again, Moses prayed that the LORD would reveal his glory to him (33.18). The LORD replied that he would pass before him and proclaim his name to him but that, since no one could see God's face and live, he would hide Moses in the cleft of a rock before he did so. Even then, the LORD explained that Moses would only see his 'back', but not his face (33.19–23). In order to prepare for this divine encounter, Moses was to prepare two new tablets of stone, just like the ones he had broken in the wake of the golden calf incident, and ascend Mt Sinai alone early the next morning (34.1–3).

Early the next morning, Moses climbed the mountain alone, just as the LORD had instructed. And then, Moses experienced another theophany, similar to the one that had occurred when Israel first gathered around the mountain to enter into a covenant with the LORD (19.18). In this case, the LORD passed before Moses and revealed himself as a God primarily characterized by grace and mercy (34.5–7). Moses immediately prostrated himself in worship and asked whether, if he found favour in the LORD's sight, he would go with Israel. He confessed the people's stubbornness, and asked the LORD to 'pardon' their 'iniquity' and 'sin', and take them for his inheritance (34.8–9).

The LORD announced that he would renew the covenant with Israel, and that people everywhere would see the marvels that he would perform on their behalf. He reaffirmed his promise to lead the Israelites to the land of Canaan, whose inhabitants he would 'drive out' before them (34.10–11). The LORD then presented the stipulations of the covenant (34.12–26), which are essentially a summary of the Ten Commandments (20.1–17) and the Book of the Covenant (20.22—23.19). Moses remained with the LORD for 40 days and 40 nights, during which time he neither ate nor drank, and 'he wrote on the tablets the words of the covenant, the ten commandments' (34.27–28).

Moses came back down the mountain with the two new tablets of the commandments, and he 'did not know that the skin of his face shone because he had been talking with God' (34.29).[4] When Aaron, as well as the people of Israel, saw this, 'they were afraid to come near him' (34.30). Moses summoned the people, however, and they came to him. He told them everything that the LORD had said to him on the mountain (34.31–32). Afterwards, he put a veil over his face, which he wore whenever he addressed the people. Whenever he went in to speak with the LORD, though, he would take it off (34.33–35). While the appearance of Moses' face has been disputed, what is clear is that Moses'

---

4 Jerome translated this as 'the skin of his face was horned'. For discussion, see Chapter 5.

transformed appearance was probably intended to identify him more closely with God (Exod. 7.1). In the wake of the golden calf episode, with its prob-
able Egyptian connotations, the transformation of the appearance of Moses'
face may have been intended to reaffirm his equality or superiority to Pharaoh.

With the golden calf episode behind them and with the covenant renewed,
the Israelites could proceed with the building of the tabernacle. At the outset, however, there is a restatement of the Sabbath regulations (35.1–3), which
also appear just before the golden calf episode (31.12–17). Daniel Timmer suggests that the framing of the golden calf episode with the Sabbath command
is the key to understanding it.[5] If the Israelites were to be a people among
whom the LORD could dwell, they would have to maintain their relationship
with him. Since the Sabbath was designed for this very purpose, its importance
was paramount. If Israel was to move forward, its people must always do so
by going backwards, returning to the seventh day of creation, in which they
would find constant renewal (31.17).

The tabernacle project resumed with the collection of an offering of materials to be used in the task and the appointment of overseers for the work (35.4–
7). The tabernacle was built, and the recounting of the process (36.8—39.43)
is a nearly verbatim repetition of the instructions for its construction (Exod.
26—31), except that the order is altered and the verb tenses are in the past.
When Moses saw that the people had built it just as the LORD had instructed
them, he blessed them (39.43). Moses set up the tabernacle (40.1–33) 'on the
first day of the first month' (40.1), which was New Year's Day, of the second
year after the exodus from Egypt.

When he had finished, the LORD took up residence in the tabernacle in
a magnificent theophany that brings the book of Exodus to its conclusion
(40.34–38). The presence of God in the tabernacle was so intense that no one –
not even Moses – could enter it. The establishment of the priesthood and the
sacrificial cult would provide a system for priestly leaders to enter the sanctuary and mediate between the people of Israel and God.[6] In the meantime,
however, God's programme of redemption had not been thwarted by the
people's rebellion in the golden calf episode. He had not abandoned them, but
had fully re-established his presence in their midst.

In concluding, however, the author(s) stress a key point about the
re-establishment of God's presence. Although he had taken up residence in

---

5 Cf. Daniel C. Timmer, *Creation, Tabernacle, and Sabbath: The Sabbath frame of Exodus 31:12–17;
   35:1–3 in exegetical and theological perspective* (Göttingen: Vandenhoeck & Ruprecht, 2009).

6 Cf. Patrick D. Miller, *The Religion of Ancient Israel* (LAI; Louisville, KY: Westminster John Knox
   Press, 2000), 106–30, 62–74.

the tabernacle, the point was not that he would dwell in a fixed location in the Sinai desert. Instead, the point was that he had taken up residence in the midst of his people and that, since the tabernacle was a portable shrine, he could accompany them on their journey through the wilderness. The presence of God was not dictated by the location of the tabernacle, but vice versa.[7]

> Whenever the cloud was taken up from the tabernacle, the Israelites would set out on each stage of their journey; but if the cloud was not taken up, then they did not set out until the day that it was taken up. (Exod. 40.36–37)[8]

Israel would not direct the time and direction of the journey, but would move out at God's behest. He would lead the people to his 'holy abode' (15.13), to the land of Canaan (15.15), where he would plant them on the mountain of his own possession, taking up his throne there to 'reign for ever and ever' (15.17–18).

Rebellion and renewal

The golden calf episode raises a number of questions. What was it intended to represent and why was it so serious? Why did Moses shatter the two tablets of the commandments? Why did he grind the golden calf into powder, mix it in water and make the people drink it? And how could it have been just to put 3,000 people to death in the wake of this incident?

There is disagreement about what the golden calf was intended to represent. Many interpreters point to the fact that the calf was associated with the Canaanite gods El and Baal. More specifically, Bailey proposes that it may have been intended to represent the moon god, Sin, which the ancestors had brought from Haran.[9] Cornelis Houtman suggests that it had a broader meaning, and was 'to be regarded as [a] symbol of undiminished vitality . . . a symbol of fertility', and 'on account of its strength was evidently also regarded as a reliable guide and protector'.[10] Long ago, Albright made the argument that the Israelites were not worshipping other gods at all, and that the golden calf was intended to represent the LORD and his physical presence with the

---

7   Gerhard von Rad, *Old Testament Theology*, Vol. 1: *The Theology of Israel's Historical Traditions*, trans. D. M. G. Stalker (New York, NY: Harper & Row, 1962), 278.

8   This modus operandi is repeated in Num. 9.15–23.

9   L. R. Bailey, 'The golden calf', *HUCA* 42 (1971): 97–115.

10 Cornelis Houtman, *Exodus*, Vol. 3 (HCOT; Leuven: Peeters, 2000), 639.

Israelites.[11] This latter view may be the predominant view today.[12] Building on this interpretation, Friedman suggests that Aaron had intended the calf to be a representation of the LORD, but that the people associated it with pagan gods. Aaron became afraid, and tried to redirect the worship back to God by building an altar in front of it and declaring that a festival to the LORD would be held there the following day (Exod. 32.5).[13]

The tendency to try to exonerate either Aaron or the Ancient Israelites of direct idol worship is unwarranted, however, since the Old Testament is very clear that the ancestors came from pagan cultures. After the conquest, when Joshua led the Israelites in a covenant renewal ceremony, he told the Israelites that, 'Long ago your ancestors – Terah and his sons Abraham and Nahor – lived beyond the Euphrates and served other gods' (Josh. 24.2). And, even after all they had been through – including the Sinai covenant, the receiving of the law, the wandering in the wilderness and the conquest – it appears that the Israelites had never completely relinquished those 'other gods', but had kept many of them in their families. As they went about renewing the covenant, Joshua urged the people to put away the Mesopotamian and Egyptian 'gods' they had brought with them to the promised land (Josh. 24.14). It should not be surprising that they would have brought Egyptian idols with them, since they had just spent 430 years as slaves in Egypt (Exod. 12.40), where they had 'served' the gods of that nation (Josh. 24.14).[14] Joshua's call for the Israelites to 'put away' those gods implies that they were still worshipping them. The numerous bull, cow and calf divinities were among the most important of all of Egypt's gods, and the golden calf could have represented any one of them.[15]

The nature of the 'festival to the LORD' (Exod. 32.5) that was held the next day is also unclear. The text states that the people made 'burnt-offerings' and 'sacrifices of well-being' (32.6), both of which were part of the sacrificial system outlined in Leviticus 1.3—6.7. The burnt offering, in which the sacrifice was burned entirely on the altar, had an expiatory or atoning function (Lev.

---

11 W. F. Albright, *From the Stone Age to Christianity* (2nd edn; Baltimore, MD: Johns Hopkins University Press, 1946), 299–301.

12 It is espoused, for example, by: David Noel Freedman, *The Nine Commandments: Uncovering the hidden pattern of crime and punishment in the Hebrew Bible* (New York, NY: Doubleday, 2000), 38–41; R. W. L. Moberly, *At the Mountain of God: Story and theology in Exodus 32–34* (JSOTSup 22; Sheffield: JSOT Press, 1983), 45–8; Nahum M. Sarna, *Exodus* (JPS Torah Commentary; Philadelphia, PA: Jewish Publication Society, 1991), 155; Nahum M. Sarna, *Exploring Exodus: The origins of biblical Israel* (New York, NY: Schocken, 1996), 218.

13 Richard Elliott Friedman, *Commentary on the Torah with a New English Translation* (San Francisco, CA: HarperSanFrancisco, 2001), 280.

14 When used with reference to a deity or deities, the Hebrew word 'serve' means 'worship'.

15 See Chapter 6 for a discussion of Egypt's bovine deities.

1.1–17).[16] The sacrifice of well-being, in which the meat of the sacrificial animal was consumed by priests and other participants, celebrated communion with God and was made on celebratory occasions (Lev. 3.1–17; 7.11–21).[17] The fact that the people 'sat down to eat and drink' (Exod. 32.6) was an ordinary feature of the sacrifice of well-being, which was probably somewhat festive, like an outdoor barbecue. After they ate and drank, however, 'they rose up to revel' (32.6), which could also be translated as 'play'.[18] Clearly, the revelry included singing and dancing (32.18–19), but it is not clear what else. Based on the usage of the word in other contexts, their revelry may have also involved bloodshed[19] or sexual play,[20] or both. Some translations have envisaged the revelry as an orgy of drinking and sex,[21] although this is uncertain. What is clear, however, is that it evoked Moses' anger, and he viewed it as part of their betrayal of the LORD (32.19, 25).

When Moses saw the golden calf and the revelry, he became furious and threw down the tablets of the Ten Commandments, where they shattered at the foot of the mountain (32.19). His smashing of the tablets has been understood by interpreters in a variety of ways, from a simple tantrum[22] to a symbolic act in which he broke the tablets to symbolize the way the people had broken the commandments. Building on medieval Jewish interpretation, Cassuto suggests that, when Moses saw that the people had violated the commandments, he broke the tablets in order to annul the covenant.[23] In a recent study, Michael Donahou makes an interesting comparison of Moses' breaking of the tablets to the Egyptian execration ritual, in which someone would curse his or her enemies through ritual breaking. In this case, Moses' action was far more than simply a symbol of a broken covenant. Instead, by throwing and breaking the tablets, Moses released a curse upon the Israelites 'and magically render[ed] them unable to defend themselves from the attack of the Levites' that would follow (32.25–29).[24] I would prefer to understand Moses' action as a pro-

---

16 It could also be made on joyous occasions, like the fulfilment of a vow or as a freewill-offering (Lev. 22.17–19). For more discussion, cf. Miller, *Religion of Ancient Israel*, 107–9.

17 Miller, *Religion of Ancient Israel*, 112–13.

18 As in the ASV, ESV, KJV, NASB, RSV, etc.

19 See 2 Sam. 2.14 in the ASV, KJV, RSV, etc., in which case it clearly refers to 'sword-play'.

20 See Gen. 26.8–9 in the YLT.

21 E.g. EXB, GW, GNT, TLB, NOG, NCV.

22 E.g. William H. C. Propp, *Exodus 19–40: A new translation with introduction and commentary* (AB 2A; New York, NY: Doubleday, 2006), 558.

23 Umberto Cassuto, *A Commentary on the Book of Exodus* (repr.; Jerusalem: Magnes Press, 1997), 419.

24 Michael S. Donahou, *A Comparison of the Egyptian Execration Ritual to Exodus 32:19 and Jeremiah 19* (PHSC 8; Piscataway, NJ: Gorgias Press, 2010), 198.

phetic gesture or sign-act in which, by breaking the tablets, he announced Israel's impending judgement.[25]

After having broken the tablets, Moses took the calf, burned it down and ground it into powder, which he scattered into their drinking water and made the Israelites drink it (32.20).[26] Many commentators have compared Moses' making the Israelites drink the water with the ashes of the golden calf to the ordeal of the suspected adulteress (Num. 5.11–31). In the case of a suspected adulteress in which there was no proof, a husband could bring his wife to the sanctuary, where the priest would have her drink a potion consisting of sacred water, to which dust from the sanctuary floor and the letters of a curse had been added. If she was guilty, she would experience physical symptoms but, if she showed no symptoms, she would be pronounced innocent.[27] This is not an exact parallel since, in the case of the suspected adulteress, drinking the water brought about the punishment, whereas in Exodus 32 the punishment was carried out by the Levites (Exod. 32.26–28). The parallel may lie in the water's role in determining guilt or innocence. Although this is somewhat speculative, it may have been that drinking the water with the ashes of the golden calf somehow identified those who had participated in its worship.[28]

What happened next has troubled some Bible readers. Moses summoned those who had remained faithful to the LORD, and the Levites rallied to him. He then sent them among the Israelites, and they put 'three thousand' of them to death (32.26–29). This incident has been viewed as an 'indiscriminate'[29] slaughter and a 'huge blood bath'.[30] In fact, only a small percentage of the Israelites were killed. If the numbers of Exodus are read literally, then there were 600,000 Israelites in total, and 3,000 would only amount to 0.5 per cent (Exod. 12.37).[31] Alternative approaches to understanding the Hebrew term for 'thousand' (*'eleph*) may indicate that far fewer were killed, possibly somewhere

---

25 Similar to the way that Jeremiah broke an earthenware jug in front of the elders and senior priests and announced, 'Thus says the LORD of hosts: So will I break this people and this city, as one breaks a potter's vessel' (Jer. 19.11); cf. K. G. Friebel, 'Sign-acts', in *Dictionary of the Old Testament Prophets*, ed. Mark J. Boda and J. Gordon McConville (Downers Grove, IL: IVP Academic, 2012), 707–13.

26 Propp suggests that the golden calf may have been 'metallic' or 'metal-plated', as in Isa. 30.22, which would have made it 'susceptible to burning, grinding, and sprinkling'. Propp, *Exodus 19–40*, 559.

27 For a discussion of this judicial ordeal, see 'Excursus 8', in Jacob Milgrom, *Numbers* (JPS Torah Commentary; Philadelphia, PA: Jewish Publication Society, 1990), 346–8.

28 Alternatively, see Propp, *Exodus 19–40*, 560.

29 Propp, *Exodus 19–40*, 563.

30 Houtman, *Exodus 3*:668.

31 See also Num. 1.46 and 26.51.

between 18 and 60.[32] In either case, Martin Noth points out that the text does not explain the grounds on which these were killed.[33] It may be that those put to death were those who had either organized or participated in the golden calf rebellion, who had been singled out somehow in the ordeal of drinking the water sprinkled with its ashes.

The reactions of God and his prophet, Moses, were very strong. God was furious, and he urged Moses to leave him alone so that he could unleash his anger against Israel (32.10). The LORD vowed that he would punish the people and, in fact, unleashed a plague among them (32.34–35). He insisted that, when the Israelites moved out from Sinai, he would not go up among them, because he might consume them (33.3). Was God's reaction evidence of his injustice and capriciousness? Moses broke the tablets of the Ten Commandments, melted the golden calf, ground it into powder, mixed it in water and made the Israelites drink it and, finally, put those who organized and participated in its worship to death. Was Moses simply throwing a tantrum?

Such an assessment fails to understand the seriousness of the golden calf episode. As discussed in Chapter 7, the Sinai covenant was patterned after Ancient Near Eastern suzerain–vassal covenants, with the LORD in the position of suzerain and Israel as his vassal. The LORD had redeemed the Israelites in the exodus in order that they might be his people. In the covenant ceremony, they had sworn to be loyal to him as their suzerain. And yet, at the very moment when God was handing the tablets of the law to Moses for deposit, they were at the foot of the mountain making the golden calf. As Thomas Dozeman points out, 'The golden calf signifies the Israelites' rejection of the covenant.'[34] And, according to the terms of the covenant, the LORD would have been within his rights to make reprisal against Israel. Garrett observes that 'the golden calf episode, no less than the crossing of the [sea], is an archetypal event' that 'demonstrates Israel's proclivity toward apostasy in the one crucial area of idolatry. This episode is thus the paradigm for Israel's greatest failing, the sin that would dominate the nation until the exile.'[35] In post-biblical Jewish literature, the golden calf episode is viewed as 'the nearest equivalent to the concept of original sin'.[36]

---

32   See the discussion of 'The number of Israelites who left Egypt' in Chapter 3.

33   Martin Noth, *Exodus: A commentary* (Philadelphia, PA: Westminster Press, 1962), 250.

34   Thomas B. Dozeman, *Exodus* (ECC; Grand Rapids, MI: Eerdmans, 2009), 686.

35   Duane A. Garrett, *A Commentary on Exodus* (KEL; Grand Rapids, MI: Kregel Academic, 2014), 615.

36   M. Aberback and L. Smolar, 'The golden calf episode in postbiblical literature', *HUCA* 39 (1968): 91–116.

What is remarkable is that, in the wake of the golden calf incident, God did not destroy the Israelites but forgave their sin and renewed his covenant with them. He did this on the basis of his own nature and character, which he revealed to Moses in one of the most important theophanies of the Old Testament.

The Lord's revelation to Moses

In the wake of the golden calf incident, Moses made a threefold petition to God for his presence and for a deeper knowledge of his ways (Exod. 33.12–14, 15–17, 18–23). In response, God instructed Moses to position himself at a certain place, with the promise that he would show Moses all his 'goodness' and proclaim the divine name before him (33.19). Once Moses had stationed himself in the prescribed location, the text reports that the Lord descended in a cloud, stood with Moses and proclaimed the divine name, 'The Lord' (34.5). Then, the text reports that:

> The Lord passed before him, and proclaimed,
>> 'The Lord, the Lord,
>> a God merciful and gracious,
>> slow to anger,
>> and abounding in steadfast love and faithfulness,
>> keeping steadfast love for the thousandth generation,
>> forgiving iniquity and transgression and sin,
>> yet by no means clearing the guilty,
>> but visiting the iniquity of the parents
>> upon the children
>> and the children's children,
>> to the third and the fourth generation.'
>
> (Exod. 34.6–7)

This proclamation became foundational for Ancient Israel's conception of God and, later, for Jewish and Christian theology.[37] In Jewish tradition, the passage has come to be known as the 'Thirteen Attributes'.[38] In the academic literature,

---

37 Pieces of the formula first occur in the Ten Commandments, in connection with the prohibition of idolatry (Exod. 20.4–6; Deut. 5.8–10), although there the promise of mercy is preceded by the threat of judgement.

38 This name for Exod. 34.6–7 first appears in *b. Rosh HaShanah* 17b. Cf. also Moses Maimonides, *The Guide of the Perplexed*, trans. Shlomo Pines, 2 vols (Chicago, IL: University of Chicago Press, 1963), 1:124.

it is often referred to as the 'Divine Attribute Formula', which is the terminology we will use here. The Divine Attribute Formula presents an inventory of divine qualities that emphasizes God's love and mercy, while not discounting his justice. The characteristics that are emphasized are all clearly intended to create the cumulative impression that the LORD is a loving and gracious God. He is 'merciful' (*raḥum*), 'gracious' (*ḥanun*), 'slow to anger' (*'erekh 'apaim*), and abounding in 'steadfast love' (*ḥesed*) and 'faithfulness' (*'emet*).

The LORD's graciousness and loving-kindness compel him to forgiveness, and verse 7 lists three kinds of sins that he forgives. The first of these is 'iniquity' (*'avon*), which has to do with turning aside from a straight path. The second is 'transgression' (*pesha'*), which is an expression of rebellion. The third is 'sin' (*ḥata'*), which is often understood as an action that 'misses the mark', although this suggests that it refers to accidental actions. The Hebrew word, however, can also refer to intentional sin. While some have tried to distinguish between these three varieties of sin, it may be that the author's intention was not to distinguish between them, but 'to mention various synonyms in order to cover the entire range of wrongdoing'.[39] In other words, the LORD's graciousness and loving-kindness are so expansive that there is virtually no sin that is out of their reach.

This does not mean, however, that he ignores 'the guilty' (34.7). This may seem to contradict the foregoing statements about God's readiness to forgive, but it is simply the other side of God's graciousness and loving-kindness. It could be understood in one of at least two ways. First, it could be referring to the unrepentant guilty who defiantly continue in sin. Such individuals should not think that God will simply ignore their sin because he is gracious and merciful. To do so, in fact, would be unjust. Second, it could be that this reflects an intentional paradox in the proclamation: '[the LORD] forgives iniquity, and yet he also punishes it, even to the fourth generation'.[40] In other words, 'punishment is not excluded even where he has resolved to forgive', as illustrated in the fact that he still brought a plague upon the Israelites (32.35), even after he had resolved not to destroy them (32.14).[41] In either case, the pronouncement clearly indicates that God's grace and mercy must be held in balance

---

39 Cassuto, *Commentary on the Book of Exodus*, 440.

40 Walter Houston, 'Exodus', in *The Oxford Bible Commentary*, ed. John Barton and John Muddiman (Oxford: Oxford University Press, 2001), 89.

41 Houston ('Exodus', 89) points out that what Moses had pleaded against in 32.5–9 was the LORD's complete destruction of his people and the total withdrawal of his presence from them, not that God would withhold any and all punishment.

with his justice and punishment. In some cases, the LORD may visit 'the iniquity of the parents upon the children and the children's children, to the third and the fourth generation' (34.7). This does not mean that he will punish later generations who may be innocent,[42] but rather that 'the punishment can be very severe, with repercussions on generations yet unborn'.[43]

The Divine Attribute Formula concludes with a contrast between the LORD's judgement and love. While his judgement may extend to the third or fourth generation, his 'steadfast love' (*ḥesed*) extends to the thousandth generation (34.7). This contrast serves to emphasize that the God of Israel is, above all else, gracious, loving, forgiving and merciful, even to sinners. Alexander observes that this formula first appears in the prohibition against making and worshipping idols in the Ten Commandments (20.5–6). He writes, 'The link between the two passages is hardly coincidental, given that the events of ch. 34 occur in response to the Israelites' worship of the golden bull.'[44]

This revelation of the LORD's gracious and compassionate character was good news for Israel, and provided the basis for Moses' petition for divine pardon on the people's behalf (34.9). The whole sordid affair of the golden calf thus came to an end when, on the basis of his own gracious nature and character, the LORD forgave the Israelites and renewed his covenant with them (34.10).

The Divine Attribute Formula in Old Testament and apocryphal prayers

Later rabbis viewed the Divine Attribute Formula as a direct divine revelation of the order of prayer. Rabbi Johanan taught that God said to Moses, 'Whenever Israel sin[s], let them carry out this service before Me, and I will forgive them.'[45] In other words, when the people of Israel sinned, they should pray the words of Exodus 34.6–7. Likewise, Christian interpreters have viewed this passage as paramount. Moberly, for example, refers to it as 'the fullest statement about the divine nature in the whole Bible'.[46] Similarly, Patrick states that the gracious disposition of the LORD revealed here is the 'hallmark' of the LORD's

---

42 For this potential problem, see the discussion in Ezek. 18.

43 Garrett, *Commentary on Exodus*, 653.

44 T. Desmond Alexander, *Exodus* (AOT 2; London: Apollos, 2017), 647.

45 From *b. Rosh HaShanah* 17b; cited in Isidore Epstein, ed., *The Babylonian Talmud: Seder Mo'ed*, 18 vols (London: Soncino Press, 1938), 4:68.

46 R. W. L. Moberly, *Old Testament Theology: Reading the Hebrew Bible as Christian Scripture* (Grand Rapids, MI: Baker Academic, 2013), 192.

identity; the 'predicate of his being'; the '"center" of the divine personality which conditions and circumscribes all [other] depictions'.[47] Although Exodus 34.6-7 is cited numerous times throughout the rest of the Old Testament, in the rest of this chapter we will focus on its usage in prayers and, finally, its integration into Jewish and Christian liturgy.

Torah

The Divine Attribute Formula resurfaces in the Pentateuch in the book of Numbers. After the establishment of the Sinai covenant, the Israelites marched to the brink of Canaan, and Moses sent out spies to reconnoitre the land and bring back a report. When the spies returned, they claimed that the land of Canaan was full of walled cities inhabited by giants, and this dissuaded the Israelites from believing they could take the land. The people were filled with panic and, once more, the LORD considered striking them with pestilence and disinheriting them (Num. 14.12). However, Moses pleaded with the LORD once again, first on the basis of the LORD's own reputation and, second, on the basis of the Divine Attribute Formula. Using an exact quotation of Exodus 34.6-7, Moses asked God to forgive the people of Israel because it was in his very nature to do so (Num. 14.18).

Prophets

The Divine Attribute Formula is appropriated in several of the Minor Prophets,[48] but it is only used in prayer in the book of Jonah. The book of Jonah portrays a prophet who served during the reign of King Jeroboam II (793–753 BC), after Assyria had been forced out of Damascus and Jeroboam was able to rebuild Israel without interference. In the meantime, the LORD sent Jonah to preach to the Ninevites, who promptly repented and were spared (Jonah 3.5–10), an outcome that infuriated the prophet. After their repentance, Jonah prayed to God in anger and said:

> O LORD! Is this not what I said while I was still in my own country? That is why I fled to Tarshish at the beginning; for I knew that you are a gracious God and merciful, slow to anger, and abounding in steadfast love, and ready to relent from punishing.
> (Jonah 4.2)

---

47   Dale Patrick, *The Rendering of God in the Old Testament* (Minneapolis, MN: Fortress Press, 1981), 39.
48   It is echoed in Joel 2.13 and alluded to in Mic. 7.18–20.

Many readers have the false impression that Jonah was angry because he had a misconception of God's character. Jonah's use of the Divine Attribute Formula, however, shows that this was not the case. Jonah fled from God because he understood God's character so clearly.[49] He simply disapproved of these divine attributes, and actually misused the Divine Attribute Formula as part of his complaint against God.[50]

Writings

In the Writings, the Divine Attribute Formula is cited in a number of prayers. It is frequently cited in the Psalms, which contain the sung prayers of Israel.[51] We note especially Psalm 103, a psalm of thanksgiving for God's goodness and forgiving love, because it is essentially an extended commentary on Exodus 34.6–7. Psalm 103.8 quotes Exodus 34.6 verbatim. As a whole, this psalm notes the many aspects of God's mercy and emphasizes his readiness to forgive sinners.[52] The LORD's merciful nature is demonstrated in the exodus events, which provide the theme for Psalm 103.

After the destruction of the Temple, prayer grew in importance as the Judeans sought ways to make offerings to God and seek atonement for sin other than through the sacrificial system. Already during the Second Temple period, prayer paralleled and complemented sacrifice. Prayer eventually became something of a substitute for sacrifice,[53] and came to be viewed as a form of cultic service or worship (an Avodah)[54] long before AD 70.[55] David Flusser has shown that many Second Temple prayers fit the pattern

---

49 See the comments of T. Desmond Alexander in David W. Baker, Bruce Waltke and T. Desmond Alexander, *Obadiah, Jonah and Micah* (Downers Grove, IL: InterVarsity Press, 1988), 127.

50 T. B. Dozeman, 'Inner-biblical interpretation of Yahweh's gracious and compassionate character', *JBL* 108 (1989): 217. A similar use occurred about a century later, after Assyria had come to oppress Israel. At that time, the book of Nahum records a prophetic oracle against its capital, Nineveh, in which the prophet Nahum called upon God to avenge his people. Nahum proclaimed. 'A jealous and avenging God is the LORD, the LORD is avenging and wrathful; the LORD takes vengeance on his adversaries and rages against his enemies. The LORD is slow to anger but great in power, and the LORD will by no means clear the guilty' (Nahum 1.2–3). At the beginning of v. 3, Nahum's statement that 'The LORD is slow to anger but great in power' is a direct alteration of Exod. 34.6, which states that the LORD is 'slow to anger, and abounding in steadfast love and faithfulness'. Like Jonah, Nahum altered the Divine Attribute Formula to emphasize the power of Israel's God, who will come to avenge his oppressed people.

51 E.g. Pss. 86.5, 15; 103.8; 145.8.

52 Rolf A. Jacobson, 'Psalm 103', in Nancy deClaissé-Walford, Rolf. A Jacobson and Beth LaNeel Tanner, *The Book of Psalms* (NICOT; Grand Rapids, MI: Eerdmans, 2014), 759–68.

53 Esther G. Chazon, 'Prayers from Qumran and their historical implications', *Dead Sea Discoveries* 1 (1994): 265–84.

54 From the Hebrew verb *'avad*, 'to work' or 'to serve'.

55 Joseph Heinemann, *Prayer in the Talmud: Forms and patterns*, trans. Richard Sarason (Studia Judaica 9; New York, NY: de Gruyter, 1977), 15.

of the Tahanun, a prayer for grace that is said as part of morning and afternoon prayers on weekdays. Its elements include: (1) a supplication to God for help; (2) a review of past divine saving deeds; and (3) repentance and a prayer for forgiveness.[56] One of the most significant of these is in Nehemiah 9, in which Ezra quotes and alludes to the Divine Attribute Formula repeatedly. The Israelites were gathered 'with fasting and in sackcloth, and with earth on their heads' to confess their sins and worship the LORD (Neh. 9.1–5). Ezra then uttered a prayer in which he recited God's providential care in creation (Neh. 9.6), the election of Abraham (Neh. 9.7–8), the exodus from Egypt (Neh. 9.9–11), the wilderness wanderings (Neh. 9.12–21) and Israel's life in the promised land (Neh. 9.22–31). Ezra said that, immediately after this foundational saving event occurred, the Israelites 'stiffened their necks and determined to return to their slavery in Egypt', but that the LORD did not forsake them. He explained God's persistent faithfulness to his people by appealing to the Divine Attribute Formula: 'But you are a God ready to forgive, gracious and merciful, slow to anger and abounding in steadfast love, and you did not forsake them' (Neh. 9.17).

After having rehearsed the whole story of God's dealings with Israel, Ezra alluded to the Divine Attribute Formula once again, noting that 'in your great mercies you did not make an end of them or forsake them, for you are a gracious and merciful God' (Neh. 9.31). Ezra's prayer attests to his belief that the whole history of God's dealings with his people demonstrates his tendency to be gracious and show mercy.[57] And it was on the basis of that belief that he appealed to God for forgiveness when the people had married foreign wives and generally forsaken God's law.[58]

Exodus 34.6–7 also shaped several prayers in the Apocrypha, Pseudepigrapha and Dead Sea Scrolls,[59] but the fullest use of the Divine Attribute Formula may be found in 2 Esdras in the context of a dialogue between Ezra and the angel Uriel about the fate of sinners on the day of judgement (2 Esd. 3—10). Throughout the conversation, Ezra sympathized with sinners, and he asked Uriel to reveal to him that, in the end, God would show grace and extend forgiveness to sinners, since they make up the brunt of the earth's population.

---

56 David Flusser, 'Psalms, hymns and prayers', in *The Literature of the Jewish People in the Period of the Second Temple*, Vol. 2: *Jewish Writings of the Second Temple Period*, ed. M. E. Stone (Assen: Van Gorcum, 1984), 570–1.

57 Cf. D. N. Freedman, 'The Chronicler's purpose', *CBQ* 23 (1961): 440.

58 For a discussion of the intermarriage crisis, cf. Joseph Blenkinsopp, *Judaism: The First Phase: The place of Ezra and Nehemiah in the origins of Judaism* (Grand Rapids, MI: Eerdmans, 2009), 63–71.

59 These include: the Prayer of Manasseh and 2 Esdras in the Apocrypha; the lament in *Joseph and Aseneth* in the Pseudepigrapha; and 1QH 10.14–35 and 4Q504 in the Dead Sea Scrolls.

The angel argued that sinners should not be shown mercy, since they had all the opportunity in the world to repent. If they did not, they would only have themselves to blame.

Ezra refused to accept the idea that mercy would not inform God's dealings with sinful humankind, and he responded to Uriel by making the case that God would deal mercifully with sinners at the judgement. In order to make his case, he quoted from Exodus 34.6–7, embellishing it with the language of Psalm 103 in order to strengthen his argument (2 Esd. 7.132–140).[60] Ezra argued that God would find a way to save some sinners; otherwise, the number of those saved on the day of judgement would be too small.

Ezra also used the Divine Attribute Formula in a beautiful prayer, in which he made the point that it is precisely because of how God had dealt with sinners throughout human history that he had come to be called merciful. He explained that:

> It is because of us sinners that you are called merciful. For if you have desired to have pity on us, who have no works of righteousness, then you will be called merciful. For the righteous, who have many works laid up with you, shall receive their reward in consequence of their own deeds. But what are mortals, that you are angry with them; or what is a corruptible race, that you are so bitter against it? For in truth there is no one among those who have been born who has not acted wickedly; among those who have existed there is no one who has not done wrong. For in this, O LORD, your righteousness and goodness will be declared, when you are merciful to those who have no store of good works.
> (2 Esd. 8.31–36)

It is specifically when God shows mercy to those who have not accumulated any good works for themselves that his merciful nature is established.

The appropriation of the Divine Attribute Formula in liturgy

As Jewish and Christian liturgies developed, they incorporated scriptural traditions, and quotations of and allusions to the Divine Attribute Formula are frequent. Benno Jacob points out that the Thirteen Divine Attributes have

---

60 Jacob M. Myers, *I and II Esdras* (AB 42; New York, NY: Doubleday, 1974), 257–8.

been a leitmotif of Jewish penitential prayers, which Jews have used 'to plead to [God] with complete contrition, ardor, and zeal'.[61] Leon Liebreich points out that the Tahanun that occurs after the Amidah[62] on weekdays includes a petition that alludes to the Divine Attribute Formula: 'Merciful and gracious One, I have sinned before thee; O LORD, who is full of compassion, have mercy on me and accept my supplications.'[63]

The *Zohar*'s most famous passage, the *Berickh shemeih*,[64] a prayer that was incorporated into the Torah service for Sabbath morning under the influence of sixteenth-century rabbi Isaac Luria, alludes to the Divine Attribute Formula. It reads:

> You are the one who nourishes all and sustains all; You are ruler of all, You rule over kings, and kingdom is Yours. I am a servant of the blessed Holy One, before whom I bow. Not in a human do I put my trust, nor in a son of God, but only in the God of heaven, who is God of truth and acts abundantly in goodness and truth. In Him do I trust, and to His holy and glorious name I utter praises. May it be Your will to fulfill the desires of my heart – and the heart of all Your people Israel – for good, for life, and for peace.[65]

The clause 'and acts abundantly in goodness and truth' derives from the rendering of Exodus 34.6 in *Targum Onqelos*.[66] The Thirteen Attributes of God are also recited on festival days when the Torah is brought out of the Torah Ark.[67]

Christian liturgy is heavily indebted to Jewish liturgy,[68] and a number of early prayers included in the *Apostolic Constitutions* are thought to be of Jewish

---

61   Benno Jacob, *The Second Book of the Bible: Exodus*, trans. Walter Jacob (Hoboken, NJ: Ktav, 1992), 985.

62   The Amidah ('the standing prayer'), also known as the Shemonah Esreh, is the central prayer of the Jewish liturgy.

63   Leon J. Liebreich, 'The impact of Nehemiah 9:5–37 on the liturgy of the synagogue', *HUCA* 32 (1961): 227–37.

64   The title means 'blessed is his name'.

65   Daniel C. Matt, *The Zohar: Pritzker edition*, Vol. 6 (Stanford, CA: Stanford University Press, 2011), 175.

66   Israel Drazin, *Targum Onkelos to Exodus: An English translation of the text with analysis and commentary* (Jersey City, NJ: Ktav, 1990), 312.

67   Raphael Posner, Uri Kaploun and Shalom Cohen, eds, *Jewish Liturgy: Prayer and synagogue service through the ages* (New York, NY and Jerusalem: Leon Amiel and Keter, 1975), 143.

68   Cf. Paul F. Bradshaw, *The Search for the Origins of Christian Worship: Sources and methods for the study of early liturgy* (2nd edn; New York, NY: Oxford University Press, 2002); Andrew B. McGowan, *Ancient Christian Worship: Early Christian practices in social, historical, and theological perspectives* (Grand Rapids, MI: Baker Academic, 2014); Frank Senn, *Christian Liturgy: Catholic and Evangelical* (Minneapolis, MN: Fortress Press, 1997).

origin and contain rich allusions to the Old Testament.[69] Of particular relevance are *Hellenistic Synagogal Prayer* 12, a long hymn of praise to God that includes a review of history from creation to the conquest, and *Hellenistic Synagogal Prayer* 2, which specifically quotes the Divine Attribute Formula (2:3).

In contemporary liturgies of the Church, worshippers appeal to the mercy of God in prayers of confession, and they are assured of his mercy in proclamations of absolution or forgiveness that often echo Exodus 34.6–7. In the Book of Common Prayer, for example, the confession of sin itself is made to a 'most merciful God', and it is followed by a proclamation of his mercy.[70]

Conclusions

In this chapter, we have considered how Exodus 34.6–7 was good news for Ancient Israel. The passage comes in the wake of the golden calf episode, which is sandwiched between the instructions for the building of the tabernacle (Exod. 25—31) and the record of its actual construction (Exod. 35—40). Its location is vitally important, in that it 'constitutes a retrospective systematic theological reflection on the narrative beginning in Exodus 32'.[71] The golden calf episode, which literally occurred while the LORD was outlining the terms for their covenant relationship, addresses 'a fundamental theological question: What stance does God take to the sin of the people of God . . .?'[72] God's own revelation that he is compassionate, gracious, committed, steadfast and forgiving, but that he does not clear those who persist in sin rather than repenting of it, was good news for Ancient Israel. It was good news because the Israelites struggled with sin throughout their history, and it is good news for God's people today.

God's self-revelation in Exodus 34.6–7, which came to be known as the Divine Attribute Formula, came to function in Ancient Israel as a paradigm for prayer. It often served as the starting point for intercessory prayers.[73] Israel

69 Cf. James H. Charlesworth, 'A prolegomenon to a new study of the Jewish background of the hymns and prayers in the New Testament', *JJS* 33 (1982): 283–5; David Fiensy, *Prayers Alleged to Be Jewish: An examination of the Constitutiones Apostolorum* (BJS; Chico, CA: Scholars Press, 1985).

70 *The Book of Common Prayer* (New York, NY: The Church Hymnal Corporation, 1979), 360. For a discussion of the general confession, cf. Marion J. Hatchett, *Commentary on the American Prayer Book* (New York, NY: HarperSanFrancisco, 1979), 341–4.

71 John Goldingay, *Old Testament Theology*, Vol. 1: *Israel's Gospel* (Downers Grove, IL: InterVarsity Press, 2003), 37.

72 Goldingay, *Israel's Gospel*, 408.

73 Dozeman, *Exodus*, 738–9. The fact that the words of Exod. 34.6–7 were known to all leads Propp to ask whether these verses may have been 'Yahweh's revelation of a chant that Israel can use in future

appealed to God's gracious character by echoing, quoting from or alluding to the Divine Attribute Formula. In appropriating it, the Ancient Israelites would often reinterpret it in the light of their current circumstances and needs. Even today, thousands of years after these attributes were first proclaimed to Ancient Israel, they are good news.

---

crises to remind God of his transgenerational mercy' (William H. C. Propp, *Exodus 19–40: A new translation with introduction and commentary* (AB 2A; New York, NY: Doubleday, 2006), 610).

10
Secondary characters in Exodus

There is no such thing as a story without characters. Stories are populated by characters who are either the subjects or objects of action in the narrative, and each of whom has a greater or lesser degree of importance in relation to others in the story. Some are the 'main' characters, while others are supporting or secondary characters. Main characters tend to be more complex, while secondary characters are usually less developed. Typically, writers will limit the number of main characters in a story in order to avoid confusion. If a story has too many characters, it becomes cluttered and confusing, with constant repetition of names in order to clarify who is acting upon whom, to whom the various pronouns are referring, and so on. Limiting the number of primary actors, and including some secondary characters, makes for a clearer narrative that readers can easily follow. In his recent study of Old Testament narrative, Jerome Walsh explains the differences between these kinds of characters. Main characters 'will regularly do more, speak more, undergo more, or change more than secondary characters'.[1] He outlines the various techniques narrators use to indicate their importance, including naming them first or more often, keeping them in the foreground, having them speak in a variety of situations with a variety of people. Secondary characters are also important, but only secondarily so, since they function as supporting actors for the main characters. They may serve as a foil, provide a contrast to, or highlight one of the main characters in some way. Walsh writes that:

> Though secondary characters can often present interesting features in their own right, if they were as complex and intriguing as main characters, readers would be distracted and the effect of the story would be diluted. If everybody is important, nobody is important.[2]

---

1 Jerome T. Walsh, *Old Testament Narrative: A guide to interpretation* (Louisville, KY: Westminster John Knox Press, 2010), 24.
2 Walsh, *Old Testament Narrative*, 24.

Up to this point, our study has focused on the main characters in the book of Exodus. There are, however, a number of secondary characters who play important roles in the story. In this chapter, we will study five of these, including the Hebrew midwives, Aaron, Miriam, Jethro and Joshua, and consider their importance to the larger Exodus narrative.

The Hebrew midwives

The book of Exodus begins by recounting the migration of the Israelites to Egypt during the ancestral period (Exod. 1.1–7). Initially, there were only 70 people in all, but they were 'fruitful and prolific' and 'they multiplied and grew exceedingly strong, so that the land was filled with them' (1.7). Eventually, a pharaoh arose who had no memory of Joseph, and he became concerned because the Hebrews were so numerous. He worried that they might 'increase and, in the event of war, join our enemies and fight against us and escape from the land' (1.10–11). He enslaved them to build the supply cities of Pithom and Ramesses, 'but the more they were oppressed, the more they multiplied and spread, so that the Egyptians came to dread the Israelites' (1.12). The Egyptians increased their workload and treated them ruthlessly (1.13–14). Finally, Pharaoh commanded the Hebrew midwives Shiphrah and Puah to allow female Hebrews to be born, but to kill the boys (1.15–16). These midwives, however, 'feared God' and 'did not do as the king of Egypt commanded them, but they let the boys live' (1.17). As a result, the Hebrews continued to multiply (1.20). Pharaoh summoned the midwives and demanded to know why they had allowed baby boys to be born (1.18). The midwives claimed that the Hebrew women were more vigorous than Egyptian women and that they would simply give birth before a midwife arrived (1.19). As a result, God 'dealt well with the midwives; and the people multiplied and became very strong. And because [they] feared God, he gave them families' (1.20–21).

While the text gives virtually no details about these two midwives, they played a crucial role in the early history of Israel. Mayer Gruber notes that 'Exod 1:1–2, in its highly schematic survey of Hebrew history from the descent of Jacob into Egypt until the birth of Moses, mentions by name only the midwives Shiphrah and Puah'.[3] She also suggests that 'the Talmudic at-

---

3 Mayer I. Gruber, 'Puah', in *Women in Scripture: A dictionary of named and unnamed women in the Hebrew Bible, the apocryphal/deuterocanonical books, and the New Testament*, ed. Carol Meyers (Grand Rapids, MI: Eerdmans, 2000), 138.

tribution of the redemption from Egypt to the merit of the virtuous wom-
en of that generation' was probably a reference to them.[4] Certainly, these
women were heroes. Without their daring disobedience of Pharaoh's edict,
surely many of the baby boys of the exodus generation would not have sur-
vived. But who were these midwives? Were they Hebrews or Egyptians? How
could they have serviced the entire population of Hebrews, especially if there
were 600,000 of them? And, last but not least, how can they be viewed as
heroes for lying?

The identity of the midwives is not entirely clear. The Hebrew text could
be read to say that they were 'Hebrew midwives' or that they were 'midwives
to the Hebrews'. If the first translation is correct, that would mean they were
Hebrews, but if the second, then they may have been Egyptian (or some other ethnicity). The NRSV's translation of Exodus 1.15, which renders them as
Hebrews, is probably correct, since the names Shiphrah and Puah are Semitic.[5] The interpretative conundrum of how two midwives could have provided for the entire Hebrew population is a chimera, since the text does not actually say that they were the only midwives. Instead, the text says that there
were many midwives but that, for some reason, these two were singled out
(1.15). It may be that they were representatives or leaders of a guild of Hebrew
midwives.[6] Since they are secondary characters in the narrative, it may be
that they are what Walsh calls 'group characters' who act as representatives
for the whole. 'The two midwives are not fleshed out, but are, so to speak,
the face of the group.'[7]

In any case, they did not obey Pharaoh's instructions to kill all Hebrew
male babies, because they 'feared God' (1.17). When Pharaoh confronted them
about it, they lied, and God rewarded them because of it (1.21). Lying is certainly viewed as unethical in the Old Testament, and some interpreters have
argued that the midwives' deception cannot be excused.[8] However, their lie
to Pharaoh must be understood through the lens of their identity as Hebrews

---

4 Gruber, 'Puah', 138.

5 Albright reports the occurrence of the name 'Shiphrah' in an eighteenth-century BC list of Egyptian
   slaves, and the name 'Puah' may be derived from the Ugaritic word for 'girl' (pgt). Cf. W. F. Albright,
   'Northwest-Semitic names in a list of Egyptian slaves from the eighteenth century', *JAOS* 74 (1954):
   222–33. Having a Semitic name, however, is not definitive. Hagar, for example, was an Egyptian who
   had a Semitic name.

6 Cf. Carol Meyers, 'Guilds and gatherings: women's groups in Ancient Israel', in *Realia Dei: Essays in
   archaeology and biblical interpretation in honor of Edward F. Campbell, Jr. at his retirement*, ed. Prescott
   H. Williams Jr and Theodore Hiebert (Atlanta, GA: Scholars Press, 1999), 161–70.

7 Walsh, *Old Testament Narrative*, 25.

8 E.g. Walter C. Kaiser Jr, *Toward Old Testament Ethics* (Grand Rapids, MI: Academie, 1983), 270–4.

enslaved in a foreign and oppressive empire. Like the legendary tricksters and underdogs of other cultures, the midwives, through their deception, subverted the pharaoh's attempt to squelch the Hebrew population.[9] Additionally, their lie must also be seen in relation to their loyalty to the LORD. As Hebrews, they were *dis*loyal to Pharaoh and the Egyptians, but they were *true* to the LORD and his people. Because of their courage, ingenuity, and loyalty to God and his people, 'the people multiplied and became very strong' (1.21).

Aaron

Aaron was Moses' older brother and a descendant of Levi (Exod. 4.14). Up until recently, the etymology of the Hebrew name Aharon has been unclear. Recently, however, Michael Homan has made a compelling case that it may be an Egyptianized form of the Semitic word for tent (*ohel*) with an adjectival suffix (*on*) that yields the name Aharon, which would mean something like 'tent-man'.[10] The Bible includes two genealogies that list Moses, Aaron and Miriam as siblings.[11] Aaron would have grown up in Goshen as a slave, while Moses, since he had been adopted by Pharaoh's daughter (Exod. 1.10), presumably grew up in the palace.[12] When Moses fled from Egypt, at the age of about 40 (Acts 7.23), Aaron continued living in Goshen, where he remained throughout Moses' 40-year sojourn in Midian. Aaron, therefore, spent much of his life as a slave.

When God called Moses to return to Egypt to confront Pharaoh, Moses raised a series of objections over two chapters that culminated in a focus on his mouth.[13] After his initial return to Egypt in which he failed to secure release for the Hebrews, he objected that, 'The Israelites have not listened to me; how then shall Pharaoh listen to me, poor speaker that I am?' (6.12). A few verses later, he repeated the argument and asked God, 'Since I am a poor speaker, why would Pharaoh listen to me?' (6.30). One of the ways that the LORD responded to Moses' objections was by appointing Aaron to be his spokesman (4.14–16; 7.1–2), and Aaron served in this capacity throughout the time of the

---

9   For this folklore theme, see the study of Susan Niditch, *A Prelude to Biblical Folklore: Underdogs and tricksters* (Champaign, IL: University of Illinois Press, 2000).

10   Michael M. Homan, *To Your Tents, O Israel! The terminology, function, form, and symbolism of tents in the Hebrew Bible and the Ancient Near East* (CHANE 12; Leiden: Brill, 2002), 121–3.

11   These appear in Num. 26.59 and 1 Chron. 6.3.

12   Moses' earliest years, however, may have been spent in his mother's home. See the discussion in Chapter 4.

13   See Chapter 6 for a full discussion of these.

plagues and, according to the Pentateuchal narratives, the period of the exodus and the wilderness wandering.[14] Aaron's role is explained using the metaphor of a prophet as one who speaks for God (4.14–16).

Aaron also served as an assistant for Moses, and the text often refers to them together as 'Moses and Aaron' (chs 5—12). In Pharaoh's court, he also seems to have functioned in a way similar to that of Pharaoh's lector-priests.[15] On the way from Egypt to Mt Sinai, Aaron and Hur supported Moses' hands while Joshua led the Israelites in fighting the Amalekites in the valley below (17.8–13). At Sinai, Aaron joined the elders in seeing God and eating and drinking during the covenant ratification ceremony (24.1–11). Even after having had such a close encounter with the Lord himself, Aaron allowed himself to be pressured by the people into building a golden calf (32.1–4). The purpose of the golden calf is debated and, while some have argued that it may have been intended to represent the Lord or serve as the throne for his invisible presence, it may have represented a myriad of bovine deities the Israelites had known in Egypt.[16] Regardless, the making and worship of the golden calf was viewed as an egregious sin and as a betrayal of Israel's covenant commitment to the Lord. Only Moses and his impassioned intercession spared Aaron.

In the midst of the texts about building and equipping the tabernacle, the Lord instructed that Aaron and his four sons be presented to the Lord for service as priests (28.1). Detailed instructions were given about the design of the priestly vestments (28.4–43) which, as many commentators have pointed out, point to both the glory and beauty of the priestly ministry. Eugene Merrill writes that

> the worship of [the Lord] thus had transcendent, even frightening, forms but it was also invested with aesthetic attraction, [and] all of the items of apparel are rich in symbolism, suggesting that the priest in his very appearance was a metaphor of divine-human mediation.[17]

---

14 Cf. Alan Millard, 'Moses, the tongue-tied singer!' in 'Did I Not Bring Israel Out of Egypt?' Biblical, archaeological, and Egyptological perspectives on the exodus narratives, ed. James K. Hoffmeier, Alan R. Millard and Gary A. Rendsburg (Winona Lake, IN: Eisenbrauns, 2016), 133–42.

15 In Exod. 7.8–12, 19–20, 22; 8.5–7; 8.16–18 Aaron is specifically named as the one who competed with Pharaoh's lector-priests in performing signs and wonders. Lector-priests were known for performing miraculous feats. Cf. Denise M. Doxey, 'Priesthood', OEAE 3:69.

16 See the discussion in Chapter 9.

17 Eugene H. Merrill, 'Aaron', in Dictionary of the Old Testament: Pentateuch, ed. T. Desmond Alexander and David W. Baker (Downers Grove, IL: InterVarsity Press, 2003), 2.

The ordination of Aaron and his sons to the priesthood was to include a series of sacrifices and rituals (29.1–34). Once the covenant had been renewed (34.10–28), following the golden calf incident (32.1–35), the priestly vestments were made according to the instructions the LORD had given (39.1–31). When the rites of ordination were carried out, Aaron and his sons were brought forward and washed in water in preparation for the ceremony (Lev. 8.6). Moses then put the priestly vestments on Aaron and anointed him as priest, and then dressed his sons as well (Lev. 8.7–13). He carried out the rest of the rites of ordination (Lev. 8.14–36), and Aaron began his priestly ministry (Lev. 9). His descendants were set aside for priestly service (Num. 3.5–10), and they were given the authority to pronounce a special blessing over the people (Num. 6.22–27).

While Aaron is an important figure in the book of Exodus because of his role as Moses' spokesperson and assistant, the identification of him and his sons as priests was vital. Priests would play a key role in maintaining the covenant, its law and, indeed, the entire religious system of Ancient Israel. Their role was vital for the very survival and well-being of the nation.[18]

As Patrick Miller observes:

> Throughout Israel's history, the priest and the priestly community exercised a fundamental role in maintaining the order of life in the community and stood at the center of religious practice, whether carried out in a family setting or at local or state levels.[19]

The naming of Aaron as the first priest, therefore, completed the triad of the Sinai covenant, which included the covenant, the law and the priesthood.[20]

Miriam

Miriam was Moses' and Aaron's sister, and was known as a prophetess (Exod. 15.20). The name Miriam is probably Egyptian, and a number of possible meanings have been proposed, including 'love', 'beloved', 'heart desires' or

---

18 Cf. Joseph Blenkinsopp, *Sage, Priest, Prophet: Religious and intellectual leadership in Ancient Israel* (LAI; Louisville, KY: Westminster John Knox Press, 1995), 80–3.

19 Patrick D. Miller, *The Religion of Ancient Israel* (LAI; London and Louisville, KY: SPCK and Westminster John Knox Press, 2000), 162.

20 For detailed studies, see: Merrill, 'Aaron', 1–3; Richard D. Nelson, 'Aaron', *NIDB* 1:3–4; Nahum M. Sarna, 'Aaron', *EncJud* 2:4–7; John R. Spencer, 'Aaron', *ABD* 1:1–6; Gordon J. Wenham, 'Aaron', *NIDOTTE* 4:346–8.

'Beloved of [followed by the name of a deity]'.[21] The Bible includes two genealogies that list Moses, Aaron and Miriam as the children of Amram and Jochebed, who were Hebrew slaves in Egypt (Num. 26.59; 1 Chron. 6.3). Although her name is not yet mentioned, Miriam appears in the birth story of Moses (Exod. 2.1–10). After Moses' birth, Jochebed had tried to hide him for three months (2.2). When it became impossible to hide him any longer, she built a papyrus basket sealed with pitch, hid the baby in it and 'placed it among the reeds on the bank of the river' (2.3). Miriam 'stood at a distance, to see what would happen to him' (2.4). She was surely standing guard over the baby until he was discovered.[22] Pharaoh's daughter noticed the basket when she went down to bathe in the Nile and her attendants retrieved it. When she opened it, she saw the crying child and took pity on him (2.5–6). Miriam came forward and offered to find a Hebrew woman to act as a nursemaid, to which the princess agreed. Miriam went and called Moses' Levite mother, whom Pharaoh's daughter then hired to nurse the child (2.7). 'When the child grew up', Jochebed brought him back to the princess (2.10), which may not have been until he was somewhere between three and five years old. If this was the case, it would mean that Moses was exposed to Hebrew thought, culture and religion during his early childhood years.[23]

Miriam first appears by name after the account of the crossing of the sea. The text refers to her as 'the prophet Miriam', and she is the first Hebrew woman to bear the title.[24] She led the Hebrew women in singing, dancing and playing drums (15.20–21), and it is often assumed that her singing was either some or all of Miriam's prophetic activity. What she sang, however, was certainly longer than what has been preserved in 15.21. A fragment of a manuscript discovered at Qumran contains at least seven additional lines of further material after Exodus 15.21 and before verses 22–26.[25] These supplementary lines appear to contain an expanded version of the Song of Miriam, but they are too fragmentary to provide even a partial reconstruction of her song. They repeat some of the elements from the Song of Moses and, since the first line of

---

21 James K. Hoffmeier, 'Egyptian religious influences on the early Hebrews', in *'Did I Not Bring Israel Out of Egypt?'* (ed. Hoffmeier, Millard and Rendsburg), 19.

22 Elaine James, 'Miriam and her interpreters', in *Women's Bible Commentary*, ed. Carol A. Newsome, Sharon A. Ringe and J. E. Lapsley (3rd edn; Louisville, KY: Westminster John Knox Press, 2012), 67.

23 See 'The early life and call of Moses' in Chapter 4.

24 Later OT prophetesses include Deborah (Judg. 4.4); Huldah (2 Kings 22.14); Noadiah (Neh. 6.14); and Isaiah's wife (Isa. 8.3).

25 Cf. Emanuel Tov and Sidnie White, 'Reworked Pentateuch', in *Qumran Cave 4*, Vol. 8: *Parabiblical Texts*, Part 1, ed. Harold Attridge et al. (DJD 13; Oxford: Clarendon Press, 1995), 187–351. For a recent study, see Ariel Feldman, 'The Song of Miriam (4Q365 6a ii + 6c 1–7) revisited', *JBL* 132.4 (2013): 905–11.

Miriam's song very nearly repeats the first line of that of Moses, many have concluded that she was either repeating or responding antiphonally to the Song of Moses to the women. It seems more likely that Exodus 15.21 contains only the opening line of the song, which itself has not been preserved.[26]

Regardless of the extent of Miriam's song, the more pertinent question here is: does it define her prophetic activity? Some have suggested that it does, since many of the prophetic speeches in the Major Prophets are recorded in poetry.[27] However, the ministries of earlier prophets like Samuel, Elijah and Elisha are not associated with poetry, but are largely recounted in narrative.[28] Prophetic activity included far more than prophetic speech.[29] In any case, there is nothing in the contents of Miriam's song that seems especially prophetic. Furthermore, the song is a classic example of a victory song and is not prophetic speech at all.[30] It appears that Miriam's song cannot help us to understand her role as a prophetess.

There is one text – Numbers 12 – that directly addresses the nature of Miriam's prophetic role. In it, Miriam and Aaron claimed that the LORD spoke through them as well as through Moses (Num. 12.2). In response to their assertion, the LORD explained that the way he spoke to prophets was different from the way he communicated with Moses. While he spoke to prophets in dreams and visions, he spoke with Moses 'face to face – clearly, not in riddles; and he beholds the form of the LORD' (Num. 12.8). After the LORD had departed, he punished Miriam with leprosy (12.10). This story is not about the insufficiency of Miriam, but about the uniqueness of Moses. It does not deny Miriam's prophetic authority, but places it – along with all other prophetic activity – below that of Moses.

But why was she singled out for punishment? Feminist interpreters have noted that the author of the book of Exodus was likely influenced by the patriarchal values of his day. This is evident in the fact that Miriam remains nameless throughout the story of Moses' birth and childhood (Exod. 2.1–10),

---

26 Frank Moore Cross Jr, *Canaanite Myth and Hebrew Epic: Essays in the history of the religion of Israel* (Cambridge, MA: Harvard University Press, 1973), 123–4.

27 See the discussion of 'Poetry in the prophetic books', in J. A. Cook, 'Hebrew language', in *Dictionary of the Old Testament Prophets*, ed. Mark J. Boda and J. Gordon McConville (Downers Grove, IL: IVP Academic, 2012), 307–18.

28 There are, however, a few prophetic pronouncements in the Former Prophets that are recorded as poetry (e.g. 1 Sam. 15.22–23).

29 For the wide-ranging function of prophets in Ancient Israel, see Blenkinsopp, *Sage, Priest, Prophet*, 115–65.

30 Cf. Lawrence Boadt, *Reading the Old Testament: An introduction* (2nd edn; New York, NY: Paulist Press, 2012), 247.

even though she played an instrumental role. Angeline Song suggests that the author had a 'pro-Moses focalization' and 'deliberately put [Miriam] out of sight'.[31] Feminist interpreters likewise tend to view Miriam's treatment in Numbers 12 as unfair. Phyllis Trible, for example, writes that God's punishment 'undercuts her in gender and point of view'.[32] Similarly, Naomi Graetz writes that God was 'incensed' and 'disgraced her in front of the people'.[33] In a recent study, however, Esther Hamori suggests that Miriam was singled out for punishment because she was known as a prophet while Aaron was not.[34] She notes that, in Numbers 12.1, when the text states that 'Miriam and Aaron spoke against Moses', the Hebrew pronoun is actually feminine singular and should be translated 'she spoke'. She suggests that, while Aaron was implicated, 'this story focuses on a claim that is in some sense specific to Miriam'.[35] Miriam challenged the notion that Moses had exclusive access to the LORD and, while he did not disagree with her, he insisted that Moses had superior access to him. Miriam was punished, but only temporarily. The traditions behind the book of Numbers clearly acknowledged Miriam's role as a prophet of the LORD, 'whose authority is diminished only in comparison to the unsurpassed authority of Moses'.[36]

Feminist interpreters are correct that Miriam's role is diminished in the text. However, even though none of her prophetic words or deeds were recorded, her importance reverberates in later biblical, Jewish and Christian tradition. When she died, the wells in the desert were said to have dried up (Num. 20.2). The association of Miriam with songs, drums and dance echoes in the Psalter.[37] When Micah recalled the exodus, he named Moses, Aaron and Miriam as having shared leadership (Mic. 6.8). Jeremiah alluded to her in his eschatological vision (Jer. 31.4). In the world of Hellenistic Judaism, many women bore the name Mary, the Greek equivalent to the Hebrew Miriam. And, in the New Testament, Mary's song echoes that of Miriam (Luke 1.46–55). All of

---

31 Angeline M. G. Song, 'Imaging Moses and Miriam re-imaged: through the empathic looking glass of a Singaporean Peranakan woman', in *Exodus and Deuteronomy*, ed. Athalya Brenner and Gale A. Yee (TatC; Minneapolis, MN: Fortress Press, 2012), 180.

32 Phyllis Trible, 'Bringing Miriam out of the shadows', *BRev* 5.1 (1989): 22.

33 Naomi Graetz, 'Miriam and me', in *Exodus and Deuteronomy* (ed. Brenner and Yee), 165–6.

34 Esther J. Hamori, *Women's Divination in Biblical Literature: Prophecy, necromancy, and other arts of knowledge* (New Haven, CT: Yale University Press, 2015), 61–81.

35 Hamori, *Women's Divination*, 78.

36 Hamori, *Women's Divination*, 80.

37 Cf. Pss. 68.25; 81.2; 150.4.

the traditions about Miriam, whether positive or negative, 'testify to her prominence, power, and prestige in early Israel'.[38]

Jethro

While main characters are fleshed out, secondary characters typically are not, which means that there are sometimes many anomalies associated with them.[39] Jethro is a case in point. When Moses fled Egypt, he went to the land of Midian, where he fought for a shepherdess and gained the favour of her father Jethro, who was a 'priest of Midian'. Moses dwelled with Jethro, tended his sheep and married Zipporah, one of his daughters (Exod. 2.11–22). The text does not name the religion in which Jethro served as a priest. While tending Jethro's flocks, Moses had a theophany, in which the LORD revealed himself to him. The LORD commissioned Moses to deliver the enslaved Israelites from Egypt (3.1–22). Moses asked his father-in-law for permission to return to his kindred in Egypt and, with his blessing, he and Zipporah, along with their sons, set out for Egypt (4.18–20).

After the exodus and once the Israelites had arrived at Mt Sinai, Jethro visited him there (18.1–6). Aside from the fact that he brought Moses' wife and children to him, his visit was important for at least two reasons. First, Jethro either acknowledged or reaffirmed his faith in the supremacy of Israel's God. When Jethro arrived, Moses told him what the LORD had done at the Sea and in the wilderness, and Jethro was so deeply impressed that he said, 'Now I know that the LORD is greater than all gods' (Exod. 18.11). Jethro brought a burnt offering and other sacrifices to God, and Moses, Aaron and all the elders of Israel came and ate bread 'with Moses' father-in-law in the presence of God' (18.12). Based on this passage, some scholars credit the origin of Mosaic religion to Jethro. In their view, Moses learned what he knew about the LORD from Jethro, who had already been a priest of the LORD. Moses, in turn, introduced this tribal god of the Midianites to Israel.[40] On the other hand, the text does not say that Jethro was a 'priest of the LORD', and he never mentioned the LORD until after Moses' report. Furthermore, Jethro was also called 'Reuel', a theophoric name that means 'friend of god', which is based on the Hebrew

38 Phyllis Trible, 'Miriam 1', in *Women in Scripture* (ed. Meyers), 128.

39 Walsh, *Old Testament Narrative*, 27–8.

40 E.g. André Lemaire, *The Birth of Monotheism: The rise and disappearance of Yahwism*, trans. André Lemaire and Jack Meinhardt (Washington, DC: Biblical Archaeology Society, 2007), 19–28; Thomas Römer, *The Invention of God*, trans. Raymond Geuss (Cambridge, MA: Harvard University Press, 2015), 51–70.

'el ('god' or 'God') rather than *yah* (an abbreviation of the Tetragrammaton). Hoffmeier concludes that, 'Based on the biblical evidence, it appears that Jethro learned of [the LORD] through Moses.'[41]

It is difficult to be definitive on this issue. If it is true, as I argue in Chapter 4, that the name of the LORD was known among the Hebrews as early as the time of Abraham, if not before, then it would not be surprising if the Midianites knew about the Hebrew God. The Midianites were descendants of Abraham by Keturah (Gen. 25.2, 4; 1 Chron. 1.32, 33) and, if he already knew and worshipped the LORD, then it would not be unreasonable to suppose that they did too. However, this does not necessarily mean that Moses first learned about the LORD through Jethro for, as I also suggest in Chapter 4, Moses apparently lived with his mother during his early childhood. If the Hebrews knew and worshipped the LORD during Egyptian bondage, then she may very well have sought to inculcate that faith in him during those formative years. Moses himself, therefore, may have already known about the LORD from his childhood. Again, there are many anomalies associated with Jethro.

In any case, Jethro's visit was important for another reason, which was that he assisted Moses in setting up an administrative and judicial system for Israel. Jethro observed that Moses 'sat as judge for the people, while the people stood around him from morning until evening' (Exod. 18.13). The administrative demands upon Moses were so great that he was preoccupied the entire day. When Jethro, with the authority of his status as father-in-law and priest of Midian, asked him why he undertook this work alone, Moses explained that the people came to him 'to inquire of God' (18.15), which suggests that, in each case, he consulted the LORD in order to reach the proper verdict.[42] Jethro told Moses that what he was doing was 'not good', that he would wear himself out and that he could not do it alone (18.17–18). He urged him to teach the people 'the statutes and instructions and make known to them the way they are to go and the things they are to do' (18.20), so that they themselves could share in the responsibility for the creation of a just society. He also recommended that Moses identify 'able men' who feared God, were trustworthy and hated dishonest gain, and appoint them over the people 'as officers over thousands, hundreds, fifties, and tens' (18.21).[43] While the people would continue to bring

---

41 James K. Hoffmeier, *Ancient Israel in Sinai: The evidence for the authenticity of the wilderness tradition* (New York, NY: Oxford University Press, 2005), 238.

42 E.g. Num. 15.32–36; 27.1–11; 36.1–12.

43 Various suggestions have been proposed for the origin of the structure of Israel's judiciary. Noth, for example, assumes that it was derived from the organization of the levy, while Hyatt suggests that it was based on the structure of Israel's military. Cf. J. P. Hyatt, *Commentary on Exodus* (NCB;

the most important cases to Moses, they could present the minor cases to these officers.[44] The establishment of such a judicial system would relieve Moses of having to bear the entire burden for administering justice among the Israelites and, instead, equip the people themselves to share it (18.22). Jethro predicts that the implementation of the model he proposed was that Moses would be able to endure as the people's leader, while the people would be able to live together in peace (18.23). Moses implemented his advice and appointed lower judges over groups of thousands, hundreds, fifties and tens, and the text concludes with a description of the system's effective operation and Jethro's departure (18.24–27). The establishment of an Israelite judiciary was a vitally important step in Israel's preparation to become a nation.[45]

Joshua

The character Joshua is rarely in the foreground in the book of Exodus and may therefore be easily missed. He is not introduced until after the crossing of the Sea, when the Amalekites attacked the Israelites while they were encamped at Rephidim. Moses told Joshua to take some men and go out and fight with the Amalekites, while he stood at the top of the hill with his staff in his hand (Exod. 17.8–9). Joshua did so and, as long as Moses held his staff aloft, Israel prevailed, whereas, when he lowered it, Amalek would begin to prevail. Aaron and Hur supported Moses' hands so that he could continue to hold up his staff, and Joshua defeated the Amalekites (17.10–16). Afterwards, God instructed Moses to make a record of the event in 'a book'[46] and 'recite it in the hearing of Joshua' (17.14). Since the LORD would be at war with Amalek 'from generation to generation' (17.16), this important battle had a permanent significance and needed to be remembered. Apparently, the LORD wanted it impressed upon Joshua so that he could recount it to a following generation.

From that point on, in the rest of the book of Exodus and the Pentateuch, Joshua appears as Moses' aide. While Moses' held the exalted title 'servant of

---

London: Marshall, Morgan & Scott, 1971), 194; Martin Noth, *Exodus: A commentary* (Philadelphia, PA: Westminster Press, 1962), 150.

44 This system was temporary and, after Israel's settlement, elders would try cases on the village level (e.g. Ruth 4.1–2; 1 Sam. 16.4; Jer. 26). Cf. H. Reviv, *The Elders in Ancient Israel: A study of a biblical institution* (Jerusalem: Magnes Press, 1989).

45 Umberto Cassuto, *A Commentary on the Book of Exodus* (repr.; Jerusalem: Magnes Press, 1997), 211–12.

46 The Hebrew word *sepher*, which the NRSV renders as 'book', refers to anything written down, and could refer to a text or a tablet.

the LORD',[47] Joshua is referred to as his 'assistant'. [48] He would work with Moses as his protégé, in preparation for the day when he would assume the leadership of God's people.

When God instructed Moses to ascend Mt Sinai to receive the law, Moses took Joshua with him (24.13). The narrative of 32.17–18 'makes it plain that we are to assume that he alone accompanied Moses during at least some of the additional climb up Sinai'.[49] Apparently, Joshua was with Moses when he entered the cloud of God's glory that had settled on Mt Sinai and remained in it for 40 days and nights (24.15–18). His close encounter with God would have surely had a transformative effect on his conception of, relationship with, and commitment to the LORD.

Another arena in which Joshua was involved with Moses was at the 'tent of meeting' where, before the erection of the tabernacle, Moses would go to consult with the LORD (33.7–11).[50] When Moses would go into the tent, 'the pillar of cloud would descend and stand at the entrance of the tent, and the LORD would speak with Moses' (33.9). His encounters with the LORD in this tent are described as having been 'face to face, as one speaks to a friend' (33.11), a description obviously intended to convey the idea that Moses had a uniquely intimate relationship with the LORD. When Moses would leave and return to the camp, sometimes Joshua would remain in the tent, in the presence of God (33.11). These intimate encounters with the LORD prepared Joshua spiritually to assume the leadership of Israel after Moses' death (Josh. 1).

Conclusions

In this chapter, we have considered several of the secondary characters in the book of Exodus, including the Hebrew midwives, Aaron, Miriam, Jethro and Joshua. While each of them is important, they serve primarily as supporting actors whose primary purpose is either to contribute to the portrayal of the main characters or to support the goals of the narrative in some way. The

---

47 E.g. Exod. 14.31; Deut. 34.5; Josh. 1.1, 2, 7, 13, 15, etc.

48 His status as 'assistant' or 'minister' is mentioned four times in the OT, including: Exod. 24.13; 33.11; Num. 11.28; and Josh. 1.1.

49 John I. Durham, *Exodus* (WBC 3; Waco, TX: Word, 1987), 346.

50 The nature of this 'tent of meeting' is somewhat confusing, since the same terminology is used for the tabernacle (e.g. Exod. 27.21; 28.43; 29.30; 30.26). This appears to have been a smaller tent that Moses used for private consultation with the LORD. For a review of interpretive approaches, cf. Duane A. Garrett, *A Commentary on Exodus* (KEL; Grand Rapids, MI: Kregel Academic, 2014), 643–6; William H. C. Propp, *Exodus 19–40: A new translation with introduction and commentary* (AB 2A; New York, NY: Doubleday, 2006), 599.

Hebrew midwives served as a foil to Pharaoh and helped the people of Israel to multiply and grow strong. Aaron provided support to Moses as his spokesman and assistant and, later, served as Israel's first chief priest. Miriam helped to ensure the infant Moses' survival and adoption into the pharaonic household and, later, served the Israelites as a prophetess. Although the nature of her prophetic work is not entirely clear, she served with Moses and Aaron as a leader during the exodus and wilderness wandering. Jethro listened to Moses' account of the exodus and the LORD's triumph over Pharaoh and his armies at the sea, and affirmed his supremacy over all other gods. He also advised Moses about how to set up a judiciary, which was an important step in preparing Israel to become a nation. Joshua is in Moses' shadow throughout the book of Exodus, serving as the leader of the army and also as Moses' assistant. These roles, however, served to prepare Joshua to take centre stage as Israel's leader after the death of Moses. Each of these characters, while secondary, plays a key role in supporting the goals of the narrative of Exodus.

11

Echoes of Exodus in the Old Testament

Reception history is 'an approach to biblical study interested in the "after-life" of biblical texts: how they have been received and appropriated by diverse readers across time and in a variety of media'.[1] It seeks to follow the journey of the text down through the centuries, with a view to discovering its application and impact. In undertaking this task, it goes beyond a focus on professional interpreters, and is 'open to a wide range of interpreters' and 'to broader dimensions of reception', including in art, literature, music, political thought and worship, to name a few.[2] These interpreters were not focused on the kinds of questions that concern contemporary critical scholars, such as those of sources, origins or background. And, as they sought to apply the text for their own audiences, they did not always limit themselves to authorial intention, or necessarily to the meaning assigned to the text by its first readers. In the next three chapters, we will consider the reception history of Exodus and its themes in the Old Testament, the New Testament, and in the arts and culture. None of these studies will be exhaustive, but will simply demonstrate the profound impact that Exodus and its themes have had on later interpreters. Discovering the meaning that previous generations of readers found in these texts may open up new avenues of understanding for contemporary readers.

Moses

Moses, the central human character in the book of Exodus, features prominently in the subsequent books of the Pentateuch. After the exodus from Egypt, he led the Israelite slaves through 40 years of wilderness wandering until they reached the eastern boundary of the promised land. There, on the Moabite plains, he renewed the covenant with a new generation of Israelites and

---

1 Christopher Rowland and Ian Boxall, 'Reception criticism and theory', *OEBI* 2:206–15.
2 Rowland and Boxall, 'Reception criticism and theory', 207.

presented them with its law. He gave a written copy of it to the priests, whom he instructed to read it to the people every seven years, so that each new generation could learn it (Deut. 31.9–13). He pronounced final blessings upon the people (Deut. 33), and then the LORD led him up Mt Nebo, where he showed him the land. Moses was allowed to see it from a distance, but not to enter it (Deut. 34.4–5). Before he died, Moses laid hands on Joshua and appointed him as his successor (Num. 27.12–23). After his death, God assured Joshua that he would be with him, just as he had been with Moses (Josh. 1.5; 3.7) and, throughout the book of Joshua, Moses' leadership is mirrored in his.[3]

There are few references to Moses the man outside of the Pentateuch, but his memory looms large with reference to the law and to the 'new Moses' prophecy. Throughout the rest of the Old Testament, most references to Moses are in connection with the 'book of the law of Moses' or 'the law' that he commanded the Israelites to follow.[4] Psalm 90, although its composition and context are disputed, bears a superscription that identifies it with Moses.[5] In the Major Prophets, Isaiah points to 'the days of old, of Moses his servant' (Isa. 63.11), to remind the Israelites of God's mercy, whereas Jeremiah tells the Judeans that they had persisted in sin so long that, even if Moses appealed on their behalf, God would no longer forgive them (Jer. 15.1). In the Minor Prophets, Micah mentions Moses, along with Aaron and Miriam, as a leader of Israel during the period of the exodus and wilderness wandering (Mic. 6.4), and Malachi concludes with an appeal to his readers, from God himself, to 'remember the teaching of my servant Moses, the statutes and ordinances that I commanded him at Horeb for all Israel' (Mal. 4.4), in order to avoid judgement on the coming Day of the LORD.[6]

The 'new Moses' prophecy, which states that the LORD would one day raise up a prophet like Moses from among God's people whom they should heed (Deut. 18.15–22), has also kept Moses' legacy alive throughout the ages. The Israelites had already had a number of negative experiences with prophets (e.g. Balaam), and they knew that such prophets could not be trusted. The new Moses prophecy, therefore, did not predict merely the rise of the prophetic office, but of a prophet 'like Moses', that is, a prophet who would actually speak on

---

3 Hélène Dallaire and Denise Morris, 'Joshua and Israel's exodus from the desert wilderness', in *Reverberations of the Exodus in Scripture*, ed. R. Michael Fox (Eugene, OR: Pickwick, 2014), 18–34.

4 E.g. Josh. 1.7; 23.6; 2 Kings 14.6; 21.8; 23.25; Ezra 3.2; 7.6; Neh. 1.7; 8.1; 13.1; 2 Chron. 25.4; 34.14; 35.12.

5 Cf. Allen P. Ross, *A Commentary on the Psalms*, 3 vols (KEL; Grand Rapids, MI: Kregel Academic, 2011–16), 3:24–7.

6 For Moses in post-biblical Judaism, see Dennis T. Olson, 'Moses', *NIDB* 4:151.

behalf of God and whose words could be trusted. Some ancient Jewish interpreters understood this to mean that Moses was a type of the coming Messiah.[7] Rabbi Berekia (c. AD 350), for example, said in the name of Rabbi Isaac, 'As the first redeemer (Moses) was, so shall the latter redeemer be.'[8] The messianic interpretation of the new Moses prophecy kept it alive and relevant in Ancient Israel, in Judaism and in emergent Christianity.

Circumcision

Circumcision was not instituted during the period of the exodus but, according to the Pentateuch, had been practised by the Hebrews since the time of the ancestors. It was originally instituted as the sign of the covenant God made with Abraham, and probably symbolized the idea that Abraham and his descendants' procreation was to be disciplined for covenant purposes.[9] Circumcision was to be a perpetual ordinance for Abraham and his descendants (Gen. 17.10–14). Whether it was practised consistently among the Hebrews during the oppression in Egypt, however, is unknown. When Pharaoh's daughter opened the basket in which Moses had been placed and exclaimed that he must be a Hebrew (Exod. 2.6), early Jewish interpreters supposed that she must have observed that he was circumcised.[10] Propp suggests that 'the plain sense' of the text is preferable, in which case she would have concluded that 'any abandoned child must be Hebrew'.[11] When Moses was first returning to Egypt, along with his wife Zipporah and his son Gershom, the LORD tried to kill Gershom because he was not circumcised (Exod. 4.24).[12] This would indicate that, as a Hebrew, Moses should have already

7 Howard M. Teeple, *The Mosaic Eschatological Prophet* (JBLMS 10; Philadelphia, PA: Society of Biblical Literature, 1957), ch. 3.

8 *Eccl. Rab.* 1.9§1. Cited in A. Cohen, *Midrash Rabbah: Ecclesiastes* (London and New York, NY: Soncino Press, 1983), 33.

9 Cf. John Goldingay, 'The significance of circumcision', *JSOT* 88 (2000): 3–18; Meredith Kline, *By Oath Consigned: A reinterpretation of the covenant signs of circumcision and baptism* (Grand Rapids, MI: Eerdmans, 1975).

10 E.g. *Exod. Rab.* 1.24. My thanks to Dr Rebecca Abts Wright, C. K. Benedict Professor of Old Testament at the School of Theology at the University of the South, who first directed me to this source.

11 William H. C. Propp, *Exodus 1–18: A new translation with introduction and commentary* (AB 2; New York, NY: Doubleday, 1999), 151.

12 It is usually assumed that Moses is the subject of the LORD's attack, as in Helmut Utzschneider and Wolfgang Oswald, *Exodus 1–15* (IECOT; Stuttgart: Kohlhammer, 2015), 139. In the original circumcision ordinance, however, it is the uncircumcised who are to be 'cut off' from God's people (Gen. 17.14). For this and other reasons, it seems that the central figure of this episode is not Moses, but rather Gershom, his eldest son. Cf. John D. Currid, *Exodus*, Vol. 1: *Chapters 1–18* (Darlington: Evangelical Press, 2000), 115–17.

circumcised Gershom on the eighth day after his birth, in accordance with Hebrew tradition (Gen. 17.12).

Regardless of whether circumcision was known and practised during the oppression, the Passover instructions in Exodus 12 include the strict requirement that any male who ate the Passover meal, including slaves and foreigners, must be circumcised (Exod. 12.43–49). The association of circumcision with Passover reappears in the book of Joshua. After the Israelites had crossed the River Jordan, the LORD instructed Joshua to make flint knives and 'circumcise the Israelites a second time' (Josh. 5.2). The narrator explains that, while the males of the exodus generation had been circumcised, they failed to circumcise the sons born to them on the wilderness journey (Josh. 5.4–7).

Circumcision came to be viewed as an ethnic marker in Ancient Israel. It marked the Israelites as members of the covenant community, while the uncircumcised were outsiders, or Gentiles.[13] At times, the term 'uncircumcised' was even used as a term of derision for non-Israelites.[14] The Israelites themselves, however, could be 'uncircumcised', metaphorically, in their hearts. The idea that the Israelites could be circumcised on the outside but uncircumcised on the inside makes it clear that circumcision was meant to be more than an ethnic marker. It was meant to be a symbol of commitment to the covenant.[15] As such, it came to be used with reference to the heart.[16] Already in the second generation after the exodus, Moses urged God's people to circumcise the foreskin of their hearts and quit being stubborn (Deut. 10.16). Many years later, Jeremiah urged the wayward Judeans to circumcise themselves to the LORD, and to remove the foreskin of their hearts, lest his wrath consume them for their evil doings (Jer. 4.4).[17] Even if the worst of the covenant curses were to be realized and the Israelites were to be exiled from the promised land, however, the LORD himself would bring them back and circumcise their hearts, as well as the hearts of their descendants, so that they could fully love the LORD and therefore live (Deut. 30.6). In the end, physical circumcision was an outward and visible sign of God's inward and invisible grace.

---

13 For references to non-Israelites as the 'uncircumcised', cf. eg. Judg. 14.3; 15.18; 2 Sam. 1.20; Ezek. 28.10; 31.18; 32.19, 21, 24–32.

14 E.g. Gen. 34.14; 1 Sam. 14.6; 17.26, 36; 31.4; 1 Chron. 10.4; Isa. 52.1.

15 See n. 9 above.

16 Werner E. Lemke, 'Circumcision of the heart: the journey of a biblical metaphor', in *God So Near: Essays on Old Testament theology in honor of Patrick Miller*, ed. N. Bowen and Brent Strawn (Winona Lake, IN: Eisenbrauns, 2003), 299–319.

17 For additional figurative allusions to being 'uncircumcised', see: Exod. 6.30; Lev. 19.23; 26.41; Jer. 9.25–26; Ezek. 44.7, 9.

Passover

The first Passover had triggered the exodus and led to the Israelites' freedom and their becoming a nation (Exod. 12), and instructions were given about its perpetual celebration as an annual festival commemorating the LORD's redemption (12.24–27).[18] Whether the Israelites celebrated the Passover during the wilderness wanderings is unknown. The book of Joshua reports that, when they entered the land of Canaan, the Israelites celebrated the Passover in the evening on the fourteenth day of the month (Josh. 5.10–12).

It is not clear how consistently the Passover was observed after that, since there are few scriptural references to it. According to the author(s) of the Deuteronomistic History,[19] the kingdoms of Israel and Judah were unfaithful to the LORD. By the seventh century BC, the kingdom of Israel had long been destroyed by the Assyrians and Judah was in a downward spiral of apostasy. King Josiah (reigned 640–609 BC) instituted reforms based on a copy of the 'book of the law' that was found during renovation of the First Temple. During the reform, he ordered that the people keep the Passover, and the author of Kings observes that 'no such Passover had been kept since the days of the judges who judged Israel, even during all the days of the kings of Israel and of the kings of Judah' (2 Kings 23.22). Some have supposed that this means the Israelites had not observed the Passover at all since the time of the judges. However, the author notes that what was unique about this Passover was that it was celebrated 'in Jerusalem' (2 Kings 23.23). It may be that this was the first time it was celebrated as a pilgrimage festival in Jerusalem. When it was celebrated prior to that time, it would have been on the local level.[20]

The Chronicler reports that there had been a Passover at the First Temple in the days of King Hezekiah (reigned 729–686 BC) (2 Chron. 30). This must not have been a regular practice, however, because neither the priests nor the people expected it. The priests had not sanctified themselves and the people had not assembled. For these reasons, Hezekiah announced that it would be held in the second month of the year (2 Chron. 30.2–3).[21]

The book of Ezra reports that, when the exiles returned from Persia, they celebrated the Passover (Ezra 6.19–22). They celebrated it in the first month,

---

18   See Chapter 4.

19   The Deuteronomic History is a hypothetical historical work comprised of the books of Deuteronomy, Joshua, Judges, Samuel and Kings, constituting a single account of Ancient Israel's national history.

20   The instructions in Exod. 12.1–28 envisage a family celebration, whereas those in Deut. 16.1–8 seem to prescribe a corporate celebration.

21   It was supposed to be observed in the first month (Exod. 12.1–3).

in accordance with the original Passover prescriptions (Exod. 12.1–3). There is a contrast with the Passovers of Hezekiah and Josiah in that, on this occasion, the priests were completely prepared (Ezra 6.20). There is also a concern with 'separation . . . from the pollutions of the nations of the land' (Ezra 6.21). These details reflect new developments in the practice of Sabbath observance in the Second Temple period, including the slaughter of the Passover lambs by the Levites and the emphasis on ritual purity among both the officials and the laity, neither of which was required by the instructions for the Passover in the Pentateuch.[22] These emphases may reflect a time 'when Judaism was taking on increasingly the character of a religious community and one which felt the consequent threat of defilement from contacts with those who were "outsiders," even though they might be living close to or among them'.[23] These emphases reflect the efforts of the returnees to adapt to their new situation as a Persian province. And, even though they celebrated the Passover with great joy (Ezra 6.22), they now celebrated it as vassals of Persia. In former times, the focus of the Passover had been on remembering the past but, from this point on, it would have a future orientation that included a longing for the restoration of Israel's independence.

The covenant

The Sinai covenant was paramount for early Israel's identity and was the foundation of its legal status as a nation. After Moses renewed the covenant with the second generation of Israelites after the exodus, he proclaimed to them that, 'This very day you have become the people of the LORD your God' (Deut. 27.9).[24] The contents of the covenant renewal were recorded in the book of Deuteronomy, which can be understood as Ancient Israel's constitution.[25] When the exilic author(s) of the books of 1–2 Kings set out to write the national history of Israel, his primary purpose was not to write laudatory political biography, but to answer the question of why the Israelites ended up in exile.[26]

---

22 J. B. Segal, *The Hebrew Passover from the Earliest Times to A.D. 70* (London: Oxford University Press, 1963), 12, 226.

23 H. G. M. Williamson, *Ezra, Nehemiah* (WBC 16; Waco, TX: Word, 1985), 85.

24 The Hebrew word translated here as 'people' (*'am*) refers to a unified people, such as a religious group or a nation.

25 S. Dean McBride Jr, 'Polity of the covenant people: the book of Deuteronomy', in *Constituting the Community: Studies on the polity of Ancient Israel in honor of S. Dean McBride, Jr.*, ed. John T. Strong and Steven S. Tuell (Winona Lake, IN: Eisenbrauns, 2005), 17–33.

26 The books of 1–2 Kings must have been completed after 561 BC, since that is the date of the last recorded historical event (2 Kings 25.27–30). The author does not reference Cyrus or the edict of

In order to answer this question, the author(s) analysed each of Israel's and Judah's kings with respect to the ruler's covenant faithfulness. His survey of the history of the monarchy reveals that Israel was destroyed by the Assyrians and Judah conquered and carried into exile by the Babylonians because of their persistent violation of their covenant with God. If the Israelites ever hoped to be restored, they must repent of their sin, turn back to the Lord and live in covenant faithfulness.

Contrary to popular conceptions of Ancient Israel's prophets as prognosticators of a distant and unknown future, their main focus was actually on the covenant. Most of the material in both the Major and Minor Prophets addresses the covenant disobedience of Israel and Judah and their impending judgement in exile. The prophets have sometimes been referred to as the Lord's prosecuting attorneys, warning the people of the consequences of covenant violation.[27]

The prophets accused the people of Israel of having persisted in sin, urged them to repent immediately and warned that if they did not, they would be sent into exile. Their announcement of impending exile was not the prediction of an unknown future, but simply an announcement of the culmination of the covenant curses of Deuteronomy 28.15–68.

The prophets marshalled three kinds of evidence to validate their charge that Israel had violated the covenant, including: (1) idolatry; (2) social injustice; and (3) religious ritualism. Idolatry was, of course, a violation of the first and second commandments. Idolatry was the 'original sin' to which Israel perpetually returned. The Israelites built a golden calf at the very inception of the nation (Exod. 32) and, after the division of the kingdom, they installed golden calves in the northern sanctuaries in Bethel and Dan (1 Kings 12.25–33). Both the northern and southern kingdoms essentially created a pantheon, worshipping Baal, Asherah and others alongside the Lord. They maintained the ritual of worshipping the Lord in the Temple while also sacrificing to regional gods and participating in their festivals.[28] The most comprehensive account of this syncretistic idolatry is found in Ezekiel 8.5–18, where the spirit of God took Ezekiel on a tour of the Jerusalem Temple. There, he saw an idol at the north

---

539 BC, which brought the exile to an end (2 Chron. 36.22–23). Therefore, the book(s) must have been completed sometime during the last couple of decades of the exile.

27   The idea of the prophets as 'prosecuting attorneys' is based on their use of 'legal procedure' or trial speeches. Cf. Claus Westermann, *Basic Forms of Prophetic Speech*, trans. H. White (Louisville, KY: Westminster John Knox Press, 1991), 169–76.

28   See the essays in Francesca Stavrakopoulou and John Barton, eds, *Religious Diversity in Ancient Israel and Judah* (London: T&T Clark, 2010).

gate, carvings of idols and unclean animals on the temple walls, women burning incense to the Babylonian vegetation god Tammuz, and the elders inside the Temple with their backs to the presence of the LORD, facing east and bowing to the sun.[29] These 'great abominations' would drive the LORD 'far from [his] sanctuary' (Ezek. 8.6). And, indeed, in a dramatic vision, Ezekiel saw the glory of the LORD move away from the threshold of the Temple, out to the eastern gate, and then depart out over the horizon.[30] God would not dwell among a rebellious people.

Idolatry was not merely a legal violation of the covenant, but an interpersonal breach. The central formula of the Sinai covenant was the LORD's commitment that 'I will walk among you, and will be your God, and you shall be my people' (Lev. 26.12). Idolatry was a rejection of this relationship. Several of the prophets emphasized the emotional hurt that God felt at this rejection. For God, idolatry was not just a legal issue, but a relational issue. To make this point, several of the prophets use the case of a husband betrayed by an unfaithful wife as a metaphor for the LORD's betrayal by his people.[31] Hosea, Joel and Amos develop the theme of warnings about God's impending divorce from Israel because of her unfaithfulness. The Book of the Twelve denounces Judah for marrying prohibited women (Mal. 2.10–15), a metaphor for abandoning God.[32]

Similarly, the concern for social justice was not the result of an obsession with technical violations of the covenant. Instead, it was relational. The covenant required proper relationships among members of the covenant community.[33] The LORD was concerned with justice for all, especially the weak and powerless. This concern is manifested in requirements for the fair treatment of workers (Deut. 24.14–15), justice in the court system (Deut. 19.15–21), and special care for widows, orphans and foreigners, who were especially vulnerable.[34] As Israel's relationship with the LORD deteriorated, however, so did the people's ethics. Hosea illustrates the correlation between a relationship with God and social ethics. He said that because there is 'no knowledge of God in

---

29 For a detailed discussion of the 'abominations' in the Temple, see Daniel I. Block, *The Book of Ezekiel: Chapters 1-24* (Grand Rapids, MI: Eerdmans, 1997), 283–300.

30 The progression appears in Ezek. 9.3; 10.15a; 11.22–23.

31 Cf. esp. Isa. 54.1–8; 62.1–5; Jer. 2.1–3.5; Ezek. 16; 23; Hos. 1—3.

32 The interpretation of this pericope in Malachi is disputed. For a discussion, see Ralph L. Smith, *Micah-Malachi* (WBC 32; Waco, TX: Word, 1984), 318–25.

33 As outlined in the Ten Commandments.

34 Widows, orphans and strangers represented the most vulnerable members of society, and the law made frequent mention of the need to protect them. Cf. Exod. 22.21–24; Lev. 19.34; 25.35; Deut. 10.18; 14.28–29; 15.7–11; 24.17–18; 26.12; 27.19; 31.12.

the land', 'swearing, lying, and murder, and stealing and adultery break out', and 'bloodshed follows bloodshed' (Hos. 4.1–2). The deterioration of ethics was considered so serious as to invalidate sacrifice. Isaiah, for example, proclaimed that, because of the nation's social injustices, the LORD would hide his eyes and not listen when people made their sacrifices (Isa. 1.10–17). Similarly, Micah exclaimed that justice was more important to God than the ritual of sacrifice (Mic. 6.7–8).

The prophets' third piece of evidence that Israel had violated the covenant was ritualism. Ritualism is not the use of ritual per se, but the belief that the process of carrying out rituals is the extent of the religion. The Ancient Israelites forgot that ritual was merely the means to their relationship with the LORD, not the substitute for it. They had come to believe that proper ritual would cover over serious covenant violations like social injustice and idolatry. The prophets declared that this was hypocritical and not what God wanted at all. According to Isaiah, for example, the LORD expressed his weariness with Judah's continual fulfilment of religious obligations accompanied by an evil lifestyle. The people's 'solemn assemblies with iniquity' were nothing more than a trampling of his courts and a burden to the LORD that he was weary of bearing (Isa. 1.11–15). What the LORD really wanted was an inward purity manifested in outward action. The LORD called upon Judah, saying: 'Wash yourselves; make yourselves clean; remove the evil of your doings from before my eyes; cease to do evil, learn to do good; seek justice, rescue the oppressed, defend the orphan, plead for the widow' (Isa. 1.16–17). In an oft-cited passage, Micah powerfully makes the point:

'With what shall I come before the LORD, and bow myself before God on high? Shall I come before him with burnt-offerings, with calves a year old? Will the LORD be pleased with thousands of rams, with ten thousands of rivers of oil? Shall I give my firstborn for my transgression, the fruit of my body for the sin of my soul?' He has told you, O mortal, what is good; and what does the LORD require of you but to do justice, and to love kindness, and to walk humbly with your God?
(Mic. 6.6–8)

The second main point of the prophetic message was that if God's people would not repent, then they would go into exile. Much of the prophetic material outlines the terrible judgement that would befall them in exile. As noted above, this was not the prediction of a distant, unknown future, but an announcement of the culmination of the covenant curses of Deuteronomy 28.15–68.

The third and final point of the prophetic message was that, even if God's people were to go into exile, there would still be hope beyond that for a glorious, future restoration in which God would make a 'new covenant' with his people. The term itself actually only occurs in Jeremiah 31.31, where the prophet emphasizes its discontinuity with its Mosaic predecessor. Even though the LORD was Israel's husband, who 'took them by the hand to bring them out of the land of Egypt' (Jer. 31.32), the Israelites still broke the Mosaic covenant. In the new covenant, the LORD promises:

> I will put my law within them, and I will write it on their hearts; and I will be their God, and they shall be my people. No longer shall they teach one another, or say to each other, 'Know the LORD', for they shall all know me, from the least of them to the greatest, says the LORD; for I will forgive their iniquity, and remember their sin no more.
> (Jer. 32.33–34)

In the new covenant era, the law will be written on the hearts of God's people, which will prevent them from falling into sin and enable their obedience.[35] This does not mean that, in the new covenant era, people will earn their salvation. Instead, it will be the LORD who forgives their iniquity, and keeping the law will simply be a natural by-product of their deep relationship with the LORD, whom they will know intimately.

Ezekiel does not use the term 'new covenant', but the book contains the same kind of new covenant theology as Jeremiah. The LORD announced that, when the exiles returned, he would 'give them one heart, and put a new spirit within them' (Ezek. 11.19). He would 'remove the heart of stone from their flesh and give them a heart of flesh, so that they may follow my statutes and keep my ordinances and obey them' (Ezek. 11.19–20). Later, the LORD repeated and elaborated upon these promises. He would bring the exiles back from the nations to which they had been exiled and sprinkle clean water on them, cleansing them from all their uncleanness and idolatry (Ezek. 36.24–25). Furthermore, he would remove their heart of stone and give them a new heart 'of flesh', along with his very own spirit, which would enable them to follow his statues and ordinances (Ezek. 36.26–27). The culmination of the LORD's restorative acts would be Israel's re-establishment in the land he had given to their ancestors, where he would be their God and they would be his people

---

35 Gerald L. Keown, Pamela J. Scalise and Thomas G. Smothers, *Jeremiah 26–52* (WBC 27; Dallas, TX: Word, 1995), 134.

(Ezek. 36.28). Although the term is not expressly used, these things equate to a new covenant which the LORD would establish with this restored and transformed people. Daniel Block concludes that 'Jeremiah and Ezekiel obviously have the same covenant renewal in mind, but what Jeremiah attributes to the divine Torah, Ezekiel ascribes to the infusion of the divine [spirit]'.[36] In both cases, Jeremiah and Ezekiel envisage the new covenant as stemming from the LORD's extraordinary grace, since Israel's sin would have justified his complete rejection of the nation. Instead, the LORD would perform a dramatic new exodus by which he would redeem and restore his people as 'a priestly kingdom and a holy nation' (Exod. 19.6).

The Ten Commandments

Since the Ten Commandments were the stipulations of the Mosaic covenant, they are naturally a prominent theme throughout the Old Testament. They are repeated (Deut. 5.1–21) and elaborated upon in the book of Deuteronomy (5.6—26.19). As noted above, the main focus of the books of 1–2 Kings is on the historical outcome of Israel's persistent rebellion against its suzerain and its continued violation of the terms of its covenant with him. The people's continued rebellion is summarized in the repeated refrain that they had abandoned the LORD and gone after other gods, and that they had embraced the customs of the native inhabitants of the land.[37] The second book of Kings contains a lengthy indictment of both Israel and Judah, which attributes the downfall of both kingdoms to the abandonment of the covenant and the rejection of the commandments. With regard to Israel, its people 'sinned against the LORD their God, who had brought them up out of the land of Egypt from under the hand of Pharaoh king of Egypt' by worshipping other gods and adopting the customs of the nations around them (2 Kings 17.7–8). They 'despised his statutes, and his covenant' and 'they rejected all the commandments of the LORD their God and made for themselves cast images of two calves' (2 Kings 17.15, 16). Likewise, the inhabitants of Judah also 'did not keep the commandments of the LORD their God' (2 Kings 17.19), but went after other gods and embraced the customs of the nations around them. In the end, Israel and Judah abandoned both the covenant and all its commandments. This was a rejection of their very identity and it led to their demise as nations.

---

36 Daniel I. Block, *The Book of Ezekiel: Chapters 25–48* (Grand Rapids, MI: Eerdmans, 1998), 356–7.
37 Cf. 2 Kings 17.7–8, 35–40; 22.17.

In the poetic books, the commandments are a frequent theme in the Psalms. Two of the psalms, Psalms 19 and 119, are Torah psalms, a subcategory of instructional psalms.[38] They are essentially hymns to the law. Both of them use a host of synonyms for the law to weave a tapestry of praise for God's instructions. The author of Psalm 19 waxes eloquent on the beauty of the law:

The law of the LORD is perfect,
　　reviving the soul;
the decrees of the LORD are sure,
　　making wise the simple;
the precepts of the LORD are right,
　　rejoicing the heart;
the commandment of the LORD is clear,
　　enlightening the eyes;
the fear of the LORD is pure,
　　enduring for ever;
the ordinances of the LORD are true
　　and righteous altogether.
More to be desired are they than gold,
　　even much fine gold;
sweeter also than honey,
　　and drippings of the honeycomb.
(Ps. 19.7–10)

Likewise, the author of Psalm 119, the longest psalm in the entire Psalter at 176 verses, uses a seemingly endless variety of synonyms for law in his paean to God's instructions. He begins by exclaiming that those who walk in the law of the LORD are 'happy' (Ps. 119.1). He treasures God's 'word' in his heart so that he might not sin against him (119.11). He asks that the LORD would open his eyes so that he might behold 'wondrous things' in it (119.18). The LORD's commandments enlarge his understanding (119.32) and bring him 'delight' (119.35). He finds his delight in God's laws because he loves them (119.47, 97). If one wonders why the author of this hymn would feel such passion for God's law, he provides the answer in 119.45, in which he explains, 'I shall walk at liberty, for I have sought your precepts.' This author did not think of the law as hemming him in at all, but as liberating him by exposing evil directions

---

38　Nancy deClaissé-Walford, Rolf A. Jacobson and Beth LaNeel Tanner, *The Book of Psalms* (NICOT; Grand Rapids, MI: Eerdmans, 2014), 20.

(119.101) and false ways (119.104) that might lead him astray. Such positive views of the law and its commandments fly in the face of conceptions of Old Testament law as repressive.[39]

The commandments also feature in the wisdom literature, despite the notion that was widely held in the nineteenth and early twentieth centuries that wisdom was disconnected from Israel's history, cult and covenant.[40] It is true that there are few allusions in the wisdom literature to Israel's history, but there is evidence that Ancient Israel's sages were deeply influenced by the ideology of the covenant and its commandments.[41] In one study, Michael Fishbane has demonstrated a number of verbal allusions to Deuteronomy's account of the Ten Commandments in Proverbs 6.20–35.[42] These include references to the fifth (Prov. 6.20), seventh (6.32), eighth (6.30–31) and tenth (6.25, 29) commandments. The entire book of Proverbs is replete with praise of the law in general and references to the Ten Commandments in particular. For example, the sages advise that those who are wise 'will heed [the] commandments, but a babbling fool will come to ruin' (Prov. 10.8), and that 'Those who despise the word bring destruction on themselves, but those who respect the commandment will be rewarded' (13.13). Several proverbs allude to the ninth commandment in denouncing false witnesses[43] and emphasizing the importance of honesty (e.g. 24.26). The sages teach that 'those who keep the commandment will live', whereas 'those who are heedless of their ways will die' (19.16). They often allude to the fifth command, to honour one's father and mother, which they viewed as essential for a stable and healthy society.[44] They also understood that coveting, prohibited in the tenth commandment, was the foundation of wickedness and therefore urged God's people to be on their guard against it.[45] Numerous proverbs praise the law in general and teach that those who followed the commandments would flourish. The world view of the sages was clearly shaped by the commandments.

---

39 See Chapter 2 for how a negative view of law contributed to the development of source criticism.

40 Cf. Brevard S. Childs, *Biblical Theology of the Old and New Testaments* (Minneapolis, MN: Fortress Press, 1993), 187.

41 See the insightful study of C. Marvin Pate, J. Scot Duvall, J. Daniel Hays, E. Randolph Richards, W. Dennis Tucker Jr and Preben Vang, *The Story of Israel: A biblical theology* (Downers Grove, IL: InterVarsity Press, 2004), 71–87.

42 Michael Fishbane, 'Torah and tradition', in *Tradition and Theology in the Old Testament*, ed. D. A. Knight (Philadelphia, PA: Fortress Press, 1977), 275–300.

43 E.g. Prov. 19.5, 9; 24.28; 25.18.

44 E.g. Prov. 20.20; 21.28; 23.17, 22, 24–25; 30.17.

45 E.g. Prov. 21.26; 24.1; 27.4.

The Major Prophets frequently refer to Israel's violation of the Ten Commandments in order to substantiate their charge that Israel had broken the covenant God had made with it. The first four commands, which focus on the relationship with God, are most frequently cited. In the eighth century BC, Isaiah charged that the land was 'filled with idols' (Isa. 2.8) that the Israelites worshipped (Isa. 2.20). Jeremiah, too, charged the people with breaking the first commandment by worshipping 'images' and 'foreign idols' (Jer. 8.19), and he insisted that only strict obedience to the covenant and to the Ten Commandments would prevent the LORD's destruction of Judah and Jerusalem.[46] God took Ezekiel on a tour of the Temple (Ezek. 8—10), during which he revealed to the prophet that these violations were not just individual but also national.

The Sabbath was also paramount for maintaining the religious life of Israel. Isaiah praised and encouraged those who kept it,[47] and rebuked those who profaned it.[48] Jeremiah urged the people to hallow the Sabbath day and warned them of the consequences that would come if they continued to disregard it (Jer. 17.19–27). Ezekiel said that Israel's neglect and profanation of the Sabbath was symptomatic of a pattern of rebellion that had reoccurred since the days of the wilderness wandering (Ezek. 20.13).[49] In Ezekiel's vision of restoration, he anticipated that Israel would once again worship on the Sabbath, when they would bring their sacrifices and offerings (Ezek. 46.3–12).

The prophets also point to Israel's violation of the last six commandments in their indictments of Israel. The prophets metaphorically point to the breaking of the sixth commandment when they exclaim that the people's hands are full of blood, that they have committed bloody crimes or that they have defiled the land with blood.[50] The seventh commandment, the prohibition of adultery, is cited frequently in the prophets. The prophets used adultery as a metaphor for Israel's unfaithfulness to God.[51] It was apparently also a problem in Israelite society. In his famous Temple Sermon, Jeremiah listed it among the sins of which the Israelites were guilty (Jer. 7.9). Later, in a letter to the exiles in Babylon, he wrote that adultery was one of the sins for which they were being punished (Jer. 29.23). In the Major Prophets, the last three commandments – stealing, bearing false witness and coveting – are the least frequently

---

46 Cf. Jer. 11.3–5; 17.24–27.
47 E.g. Isa. 56.2, 4, 6–7.
48 E.g. Isa. 56.6; 58.13.
49 Cf. also Ezek. 20.16, 21, 24; 22.6, 8; 23.38.
50 E.g. Isa. 1.15; 5.7; 59.3, 7; Jer. 19.4; 22.17; Ezek. 7.23; 9.9; 22.1–31.
51 E.g. Jer. 3.9; 5.7; Ezek. 23.37, 43.

mentioned. Jeremiah mentions stealing in his Temple Sermon (Jer. 7.9). In Isaiah, it is most frequently the leaders who are charged with lying.[52] Jeremiah does accuse the people of deceiving their neighbours (Jer. 9.5), but he, too, levels his harshest accusations of deceitfulness against Israel's leadership, the scribes and the prophets.[53]

References to the Ten Commandments are not as frequent in the Minor Prophets. Although these prophets did remind the people of their obligation to keep the commandments, they mainly condemned them for breaking the covenant. When Israel was redeemed and restored as 'a priestly kingdom and a holy nation' (Exod. 19.6), its people would keep the LORD's commandments.

The tabernacle

The book of Exodus ascribes tremendous importance to the tabernacle and its appurtenances. It represented God's presence with his people, which was the focal point of all God's laws and regulations at Sinai. While the book of Exodus records the planning and construction of the tabernacle, Leviticus explains the purpose of its features and gives instructions for its services. The altar of burnt offering and a bronze basin were situated in the courtyard. The altar was where people would bring their sacrifices (Exod. 27.1–8). Once a priest had approved an animal for sacrifice, the worshipper would solemnly lay his or her hands on the animal's head, and that person's sins would symbolically be transferred to it (Lev. 1.4). The animal would be slaughtered and its blood would be dashed against all sides of the altar, while the parts of the animal would be burned on its surface (Lev. 1.5–9).

Just as the giving of the tabernacle instructions had been followed by the golden calf episode (Exod. 32), so the inauguration of the priesthood in Leviticus 9 is followed by a story of priestly malfeasance. Aaron's sons, Nadab and Abihu, offered 'unholy fire' before the LORD and were punished with death as a result (Lev. 10.1–2).

The tabernacle's inner sanctum, the holy of holies, which housed the ark of the covenant, was a restricted zone. If anyone came inside, behind the curtain that divided the holy place from the most holy place, and looked upon the ark, he or she would die, because the LORD appeared in the cloud upon the mercy seat (Lev. 16.2). Only one person, the high priest, was allowed inside, and only then once a year, on the Day of Atonement. On that day, after purifying

---

52 Cf. Isa. 9.15; 28.15.
53 E.g. Jer. 8.8; 14.14; 23.14; 23.25–26, 32; 27.10, 14–16; 29.9, 21, 31.

himself, the high priest would sacrifice a bull to make atonement for himself and his house. He would bring a special incense to apply to the fire that was inside the curtain, which would produce a cloud of smoke that would prevent him from looking upon the mercy seat and being stricken with death (Lev. 16.13). At the same time, he would take some of the blood of the bull and sprinkle its blood on the mercy seat seven times to make atonement for himself and his family. This procedure would be repeated with a goat in order to make atonement for the people. The high priest would also make atonement for the sanctuary itself, as well as the altar of burnt offering. He would then go out to the people and place his hands on the head of another goat, symbolically transferring the sins of all Israel upon it. This goat would 'bear on itself all their iniquities to a barren region', and be 'set free in the wilderness' (Lev. 16.22). The Day of Atonement ritual symbolically purified the high priest, the people and the tabernacle so that God and the people could live together in the same space.

The book of Numbers explains the organization of camping and marching during the wilderness period. The Israelite camp was not a regular nomadic camp. Instead, the tribes were arranged around the tabernacle, which was situated at the centre of the tribes. The tribe of Judah had the most warriors and so guarded the entrance to the tabernacle, which was on its eastern side (Lev. 2).

On the whole, the tabernacle expressed a great theological irony. By its very form, it communicated God's desire to live among his people. At the same time, however, the increasing restriction of access from its exterior to its interior, as well as the elaborate systems of sacrifice and mediation even for those approved to enter it, communicates the persistent effects of sin, which result in separation from God. The tabernacle in the midst of the camp did symbolize the dwelling of God among the people, but its restricted access and associated rituals also meant that the average Israelite – and even the average priest – would never stand in his presence. The high priest was the only one who was ever allowed inside the holy of holies, and that was only once a year and under the threat of death (Lev. 16.2). Although God was once again with humankind, humankind was still separated from God.

The tabernacle and its ceremonies also had important didactic functions. Everything about it, including the structure itself as well as its rituals, taught Israel what sin and forgiveness were all about. The tabernacle illustrated the concrete realities of designated precincts, the workings of mediation through a priesthood, the link between sacrifice and atonement, and the removal of sin.

The tabernacle served as a portable sanctuary throughout the wilderness period and until the building of the First Temple. When the Israelites entered

Canaan, they presumably set up the tabernacle at Gilgal, where they made camp (Josh. 4.19). After that, it may have been relocated to Mt Ebal (Josh. 8.30–35). At some point, it was moved to Shiloh (Josh. 18.1), where it remained throughout the period of the judges (1 Sam. 2.22). After the destruction of Shiloh,[54] the tabernacle was eventually set up at the high place of Gibeon (1 Chron. 21.29). When David expressed his desire to build a temple for God, the LORD answered him through Nathan in a prophetic oracle:

> Are you the one to build me a house to live in? I have not lived in a house since the day I brought up the people of Israel from Egypt to this day, but I have been moving about in a tent and a tabernacle. Wherever I have moved about among all the people of Israel, did I ever speak a word with any of the tribal leaders of Israel, whom I commanded to shepherd my people Israel, saying, 'Why have you not built me a house of cedar?' (2 Sam. 7.5–7)

When Solomon later built the Temple, he brought the tent of meeting to Jerusalem (1 Kings 8.4=2 Chron. 5.5). After that, the tabernacle is not mentioned again in the book of Kings, although there are some references to it in Chronicles that suggest that its rituals may have continued to operate as part of the services of the Temple.[55] Richard Elliott Friedman has proposed that either the tabernacle was erected inside the Temple or that its fabrics and boards were stored in the temple treasury.[56] The authors of 1–2 Kings and Chronicles both understood that the locus of God's presence had shifted to the First Temple, and that the priestly ministries that had once been carried out in the portable sanctuary were now conducted in its permanent location in Jerusalem, where the LORD caused his name to dwell (1 Kings 8.1–53).

The ark of the covenant

Although the ark of the covenant was the central piece of furniture inside the tabernacle, it has a life of its own in the biblical traditions. It symbolized the presence of the LORD, which meant that, wherever the ark was, the LORD was there also. The ark led the people throughout the period of the wilderness

---

54 The destruction of Shiloh is not reported in the historical books, but is referred to in Jer. 7.12, 14; 26.6, 9.

55 Cf., e.g., 1 Chron. 16.33; 23.32; 2 Chron. 24.6; 29.5–7.

56 Richard Elliott Friedman, 'Tabernacle', ABD 6:292–300.

wanderings and its movements directed those of the Israelites themselves. A fragment of an ancient poem preserved in the wilderness narrative points to its use as a war palladium:

Whenever the ark set out, Moses would say,

'Arise, O Lord, let your enemies be scattered,
    and your foes flee before you.'

And whenever it came to rest, he would say,

'Return, O Lord of the ten thousand thousands of Israel.'
(Num. 10.35–36)

When the Israelites crossed the River Jordan into Canaan, the ark was carried by priests at the front of the march (Josh. 3.14), which symbolized the idea that God was leading the advance. Likewise, at the taking of Jericho, the priests carried the ark in a procession around the city once a day for six days and, on the seventh day, they processed around it seven times (Josh. 6.1–15).

The Ark Narrative of 1 Samuel 4—6 recounts a battle between the Israelites and the Philistines in which the ark was captured. According to the text, the Israelites had sustained heavy casualties in battle against the Philistines (1 Sam. 4.1–2). They returned with the ark, in the hopes that it might turn the tide (4.3–11), but the Philistines captured it and installed it in the temple of Dagon at Ashdod, one of the cities of the Philistine pentapolis (5.2). It seemed as if not only the Israelites had been defeated, but also their God. The next morning, however, the Philistines observed that the statue of Dagon had fallen in front of the ark (5.3–4). They stood it back up but, when they returned to the temple the next morning, the statue of Dagon had fallen again and, this time, it was dismembered. They were terrified, and sent it to Gath. However, after it had arrived there, a plague of tumours broke out among its Philistine inhabitants, and they became panicked (5.9). They sent it to Ekron, but the plague of tumours broke out there as well, and its residents were too frightened to keep the ark. The Philistines called a leadership summit and decided to return the ark to the Israelites (5.11). They loaded it on to a cart laden with offerings of gold and sent it to the Israelites at Beth-shemesh (6.1–12). On the surface, it had appeared that the Lord had been defeated and carried into captivity at Ashdod. In reality, however, he was actually invading Philistine territory. In Ashdod, he had vanquished Dagon in his own temple, and then he had marched through three of the cities of the Philistine pentapolis, where he smote one after another. In the end, he returned to Israel loaded with tribute and plunder from Philistine cities.[57]

The inhabitants of Beth-shemesh rejoiced to see the ark and made burnt offerings and sacrifices. However, the descendants of the otherwise unknown Jeconiah were ambivalent, and the LORD therefore struck down 70 of them. As a result, the people of Beth-shemesh sent the ark to Kiriath-jearim, where it was placed in the custody of Abinadab, and there it remained for the next 20 years (6.19—7.2).

Eventually, David brought the ark to Jerusalem in a great procession, in which 'David and all the house of Israel were dancing before the LORD with all their might, with songs and lyres and harps and tambourines and castanets and cymbals' (2 Sam. 6.5). At one point, a man named Uzzah 'reached out his hand to the ark of God and took hold of it, for the oxen shook it', and the LORD struck him down (6.6-7). David was angry that the LORD had struck Uzzah down, and he became 'afraid of the LORD that day' (6.9). He was 'unwilling to take the ark of the LORD into his care in the city of David' and, instead, left it in the house of a Gittite, where it remained for the next three months (6.10–11). When David received word that the man's household had been blessed because of the presence of the ark, he decided again to bring it all the way to Jerusalem. This time, however, he conducted the journey with great care and, 'when those who bore the ark of the LORD had gone six paces, he sacrificed an ox and a fatling' (6.13).[58] 'David danced before the LORD with all his might', and 'all the house of Israel brought up the ark of the LORD with shouting, and with the sound of the trumpet' (6.14–15). It was installed in a tent that David had prepared for it (6.17), but was apparently carried into battle from time to time as a war palladium (2 Sam. 11.11). After Solomon completed the Temple, it was brought in procession and installed in the holy of holies (1 Kings 8.1–12).

The Chronicler recounts that Josiah, in the course of his reforms, instructed that the ark be put in the Temple, and that it no longer needed to be carried on the Levites' shoulders (2 Chron. 35.3). It is not clear why the ark would have had to be reinstalled in the Temple, although it has been suggested that it may have been removed from the inner sanctum during the reign of Manasseh and housed in temporary shelters. In any case, according to tradition, the

---

57   For a discussion of the Ark Narrative, see David Toshio Tsumura, *The First Book of Samuel* (NICOT; Grand Rapids, MI: Eerdmans, 2007), 184–229.

58   It is not clear whether he made one offering six paces after they had set out, or whether the offering was repeated after every six paces.

ark disappeared around the end of the seventh century or the beginning of the sixth. It was probably destroyed along with the Temple in 586 BC.[59]

The last mention of the ark in the canon is in Jeremiah, who says that, in the latter days, the Israelites 'shall no longer say, "The ark of the covenant of the LORD." It shall not come to mind, or be remembered, or missed; nor shall another one be made' (Jer. 3.16). The reason was that, in the eschatological age, 'the ark would no longer have a function', since 'Jerusalem itself would become God's throne on earth'.[60]

The priesthood

In Moses' final blessing upon Israel, his blessing upon the Levites summarizes their job description in Ancient Israel. Their responsibilities included divination, instruction and sacrifice (Deut. 33.8–11). They were entrusted with the Urim and the Thummim, which were devices like dice used to determine the will of God. They were also tasked with the teaching of *tôrâ*, including the law and its ordinances. The third duty mentioned in the blessing of Moses is sacrifice. The Levitical legislation includes various tasks that priests would undertake when making sacrifices, including presenting the sacrifice on the altar, burning it and dealing with the blood of an animal sacrifice (Lev. 1—7). According to the Priestly legislation of the Pentateuch, the Levites were dedicated to serve Aaron and his descendants as assistants to the high priest (Num. 3.5–10).[61]

The role of the Levites expanded to cover a wide variety of tasks. They were in charge of the work in the Temple, served as officers and judges, functioned as gatekeepers, and were responsible for the musical praise of the LORD (1 Chron. 23.1–6).[62] Their service was organized into weekly rotations in 24 courses (1 Chron. 24.4). They were also in charge of the temple treasuries and the treasuries of the dedicated gifts (1 Chron. 26.20; 2 Chron. 8.15), and served as scribes

---

59 Cf. John Day, 'Whatever happened to the ark of the covenant?', in *Temple and Worship in Biblical Israel*, ed. John Day (London: T&T Clark, 2005), 250–70.

60 Peter C. Craigie, Page H. Kelley and Joel F. Drinkard Jr, *Jeremiah 1–25* (WBC 26; Dallas, TX: Word, 1991), 61.

61 This distinction is viewed by some as a demotion that originated in the post-exilic period, but it may have been a distinction that was already present in earlier periods. For an overview of the discussion, see Patrick D. Miller, *The Religion of Ancient Israel* (LAI; London and Louisville, KY: SPCK and Westminster John Knox Press, 2000), 171–4.

62 Cf. also 2 Chron. 5.12–14; 7.6.

and teachers, and administrators and judges (1 Chron. 26.29; 34.13).[63] In addition, the Levites were responsible for collecting the temple tax (2 Chron. 24.4-7; 34.9), contributions, tithes and dedicated things (2 Chron. 31.11-16). Many of the priestly roles became moot with the destruction of the Temple. The priestly roles were restored, however, after the exile.[64]

In both the Major and Minor Prophets, the priests of Israel and Judah are often viewed negatively. In the eighth century BC, Hosea lamented that Israel's priests, who were supposed to be the people's spiritual leaders, had themselves become idolatrous (Hos. 10.5-6). When Amos indicted the sanctuaries of Israel for their corruption, Amaziah priest of Bethel rebuked him and told him to go back to Judah (Amos 7.12). In his proclamation of the coming judgement of Judah, Zephaniah announced that God would 'cut off . . . the name of the idolatrous priests' (Zeph. 1.4). In the wake of the Babylonian invasion of Jerusalem in 597 BC, the court prophets claimed that the threat from Babylon would not last long, while Jeremiah said that they were lying and that Judah would remain under its control for some time (Jer. 27.16-22). The text implies the complicity of the priests, who heard both prophecies but provided no direction.[65] When Jerusalem fell to the Babylonians in 586 BC, Judah's priests were viewed as culpable for its demise (Lam. 4.13, 16). Ezekiel, a priest who was among those deported to Babylon in 597 BC, was taken by God on a visionary tour of the Jerusalem Temple, during which he witnessed how its priests had allowed the worship of foreign gods in its precincts (Ezek. 8).

Some of the prophets envisioned a renewal of the priesthood. In Ezekiel's vision of the New Temple, for example, he imagined the reinstallation of the Levites (Ezek. 44.9-14) and the Zadokites (44.15-16) to temple service. In this new era, the priests would live up to the original expectations of the priesthood. They would teach the people the difference between the holy and the common and between the unclean and the clean, arbitrate in disputes, keep the laws and statutes regarding festivals, and keep the Sabbath holy (Ezek. 44.23-24). Interestingly, Ezekiel's vision of the New Temple does not mention a high priest or a holy of holies, nor does he envisage a Day of Atonement when the high priest would enter the holy of holies in order to make atonement. In the closing verses of Isaiah, the prophet envisaged a great ingathering of Diaspora Jews and proselytes from among the nations who would

---

63 For a detailed discussion of the work of the Levites, see Joseph Blenkinsopp, *Sage, Priest, Prophet: Religious and intellectual leadership in Ancient Israel* (LAI; Louisville, KY: Westminster John Knox Press, 1995), 94-8.

64 Cf. Neh. 12.1-26; Hag. 2.10-19; Zech. 3; 6.9-15.

65 Cf. Jer. 27.16; 28.1, 5.

return to Jerusalem (Isa. 66.18–21). From among these, Isaiah claimed, the LORD would 'take some of them as priests and as Levites' (Isa. 66.21).[66] In this vision, he imagined that the Temple would no longer be 'a place where privileged priests perform sacrifices', but 'will have truly become "a house of prayer for all nations"'.[67]

Zechariah contains a vision of the cleansing of the priests (Zech. 3.1–10). In it, the LORD told the prophet that he was ultimately going to bring his servant, 'the Branch', to minister to his people (3.8). With the arrival of the Branch, he would 'remove the guilt of this land in a single day', and 'you shall invite each other to come under your vine and fig tree' (3.9–10). The Branch is a title for the Messiah, whose coming is clearly anticipated in this fourth vision. In his subsequent prophecy of the coronation of the Branch, however, Zechariah seems to anticipate two figures. The prophet proclaims that 'he shall build the temple of the LORD' and also that 'he shall bear royal honour, and shall sit and rule on his throne', with 'a priest by his throne, with peaceful understanding between the two of them' (6.12–13). The Qumran sectarians took such passages to mean that there would be two messianic figures in the new age, one a priestly messiah from the line of Aaron and the other a royal messiah from the line of David.[68]

The exodus itself

The exodus events themselves, especially the departure from Egypt and the crossing of the Sea, represent the foundational act of salvation in the Old Testament and are rehearsed, reflected upon and alluded to in every part of the canon. In the Pentateuch, Israel's exodus deliverance is often cited as the motive for observing the commands of the law. It provided the basis for observance of the Ten Commandments (Exod. 20.2) in general and the Sabbath command in particular (Deut. 5.15). The prohibition against mistreating aliens living among the Israelites was predicated on the fact that they themselves had been aliens in the land of Egypt (Exod. 22.21; 23.9). In the blessings and curses associated with the Sinai covenant, the blessings were assured on the basis of what the LORD had already done in leading the Israelites out of Egypt (Lev. 26.13). At the end of the wilderness wandering, when the Israelites asked the

---

66　The term 'Levites' is used here for those who perform cultic functions, rather than as a tribal designation.

67　John D. W. Watts, *Isaiah 34–66* (WBC 25; Waco, TX: Word, 1987), 365.

68　James VanderKam and Peter Flint, *The Meaning of the Dead Sea Scrolls: Their significance for understanding the Bible, Judaism, Jesus, and Christianity* (New York, NY: HarperSanFrancisco, 2002), 265–7.

Edomites for peaceful passage through their territory, they appealed to what God had done for them in the exodus (Num. 20.14–17). Later, when Balak summoned Balaam to curse Israel, in an attempt to prevent its people crossing through Moab, the prophet affirmed that God had brought them out of Egypt and confirmed his blessing upon them (Num. 23.18–24, esp. 22).

While the Israelites were camped on the Moabite plains, on the brink of the promised land, Moses led the people in a covenant renewal, as recorded in the book of Deuteronomy. The book shares the same basic outline and structure of the second-millennium covenants of the Ancient Near East.[69] It begins with a preamble, which introduces the LORD as Israel's suzerain (Deut. 1.1–5). This is followed by a historical prologue that reviews how God liberated the Israelites in the exodus and brought them through the wilderness to the brink of the promised land (Deut. 1.6–3.29). The longest part of the book contains the covenant stipulations, which are an expansion of the Ten Commandments (chs 4—26). The next several chapters detail the curses and blessings connected with the covenant (chs 27—30). The final chapters provide for succession, and include an invocation of witnesses and provision for public reading (chs 31—34). Since the book of Deuteronomy reflects the renewal of the Sinai covenant, there are frequent references and allusions to the book of Exodus. The LORD had brought Israel 'out of the iron-smelter, out of Egypt, to become a people of his very own possession' (Deut. 4.20). The events involved in the exodus were so unique that they testified to the matchlessness of God:

> For ask now about former ages, long before your own, ever since the day that God created human beings on the earth; ask from one end of heaven to the other: has anything so great as this ever happened or has its like ever been heard of? Has any people ever heard the voice of a god speaking out of a fire, as you have heard, and lived? Or has any god ever attempted to go and take a nation for himself from the midst of another nation, by trials, by signs and wonders, by war, by a mighty hand and an outstretched arm, and by terrifying displays of power, as the LORD your God did for you in Egypt before your very eyes? To you it was shown so that you would acknowledge that the LORD is God; there is no other besides him.
> (Deut. 4.32–35)

---

69 Meredith G. Kline, *The Treaty of the Great King: The covenant structure of Deuteronomy* (Grand Rapids, MI: Eerdmans, 1963); Kenneth A. Kitchen, *On the Reliability of the Old Testament* (Grand Rapids, MI: Eerdmans, 2003), 289–94.

The great salvation the Israelites had experienced in the exodus was intended to evoke their loyalty, devotion and worship,[70] and lead to the establishment of Israel as 'a priestly kingdom and a holy nation' (Exod. 19.6).[71]

The exodus reverberates throughout the historical books. Rahab told the Israelite spies that the inhabitants of Canaan had heard about what the LORD had done for Israel in the exodus and the crossing of the sea, and that their 'hearts melted, and there was no courage left in any of [them]' (Josh. 2.8–13). She confessed that the LORD was supreme and asked to assimilate among the Israelite people (Josh. 2.11–14). Likewise, the Gibeonites had heard about what God had done in the exodus and sought to enter into a covenant with Israel (Josh. 9.9–10). Near the end of his life, Joshua led the Israelites in a renewal of the covenant, in which his call for the Israelites to renew their commitment to the LORD was based on a review of his gracious acts on their behalf, especially in the exodus and the crossing of the Sea (Josh. 24.5–7). The narrator of the book of Judges lamented Israel's disobedience in the wake of what God had done in the exodus and his commitment to never break his covenant with Israel (Judg. 2.1).[72] In chastising the people for wanting a king, Samuel recited how God had rescued Israel in the exodus (1 Sam. 10.17–18). After the division of the kingdom, Jeroboam set up golden calves at Bethel and Dan to represent the God 'who brought you up out of the land of Egypt' (1 Kings 12.28), in order to try to prevent the northern tribes from reverting to the house of David. And the author of 1 Kings used the exodus as the chronological reference by which to date the construction of the First Temple (1 Kings 6.1).

In the poetic books, the exodus is 'the most frequent historical motif in the Book of Psalms'.[73] Psalm 66 recalls how the LORD 'turned the sea into dry land' so that they could pass through on solid ground (Ps. 66.6). Psalm 77 expresses awe at how the LORD made a way through the sea, and led his people Israel 'like a flock by the hand of Moses and Aaron' (Ps. 77.16–20). Psalm 78 rehearses 'the glorious deeds of the LORD, and his might, and the wonders that he has done' (Ps. 78.4), and recounts that 'in the sight of their ancestors he worked marvels in the land of Egypt, in the fields of Zoan', and 'divided the sea and let them pass through it, and made the waters stand like a heap' (78.12–13). It also mentions the pillar of cloud that led the Israelites

---

70   E.g. Deut. 8.11, 14; 26.5–11.

71   Cf. Deut. 7.6; 14.21; 26.19.

72   Cf. also Judg. 2.12; 6.8, 13.

73   Erik Haglund, *Historical Motifs in the Psalms* (ConBOT 23; Uppsala: CWK Gleerup, 1984), 102.

by day and the pillar of fire that led them by night, as well as other wonders God performed in the wilderness (78.14–16). Psalm 118, a song of victory, quotes directly from the Song of Moses (118.14). Psalm 136 celebrates God's work, both in creation and in history, and notes specifically how God 'struck Egypt through their firstborn . . . and brought Israel out from among them . . . with a strong hand and an outstretched arm, for his steadfast love endures for ever' (136.10–12).

Several of the psalms, however, lament that the Israelites forgot what the LORD had done for them in the exodus. In Psalm 78, for example, the psalmist explains that it was because the Israelites 'did not keep in mind his power, or the day when he redeemed them from the foe' (78.42), that they turned away from God and did not observe his decrees (78.56–58). In Psalm 106, the psalmist attributes the exile to the repeated sins of the people of Israel, which he attributed to their having forgotten the 'wonderful works' the LORD had done on their behalf, the 'steadfast love' he had shown them in Egypt (Ps. 106.7) and his 'awesome deeds by the Red Sea' (106.22).[74]

The exodus was an important theme to the prophets, who frequently used it as a symbol for the return from exile. The pioneer of this method was Isaiah, who gave great prominence to the exodus, so much so that 'all the other events in Israel's history recede into the background'.[75] He used the exodus to encourage the exilic Jews in Babylon, but he transformed it. In his reworked exodus, a new, anonymous servant, the Messiah, would bring Israel back from exile.[76] This return would not simply be a return to the conditions of covenant blessing outlined in Deuteronomy 28.1–14. Instead, it would be comprised of a multi-ethnic group mixed together with the remnant of restored Israelites streaming to Jerusalem to worship the LORD (Isa. 66.18–24). Jeremiah, who had seen the destruction of Jerusalem first-hand and witnessed the deportation of thousands of his fellow citizens, also imagined a future exodus that would surpass the old. He prophesied that a day would come when people would no longer say, 'As the LORD lives who brought the people of Israel up out of the land of Egypt', but would instead say, 'As the LORD lives who brought the people of Israel up out of the land of the north and out of all the lands where he had driven them', because he would bring them back to the land that he

---

74 For further discussion of Exodus and the Psalms, see Daniel J. Estes, "'The Psalms, the exodus, and Israel's worship', in *Reverberations* (ed. Fox), 35–50.

75 Claus Westermann, *Isaiah 40–66* (OTL; Philadelphia, PA: Westminster Press, 1969), 22.

76 John I. Durham, 'Isaiah 40–55: a new creation, a new exodus, a new messiah', in *The Yahweh/Baal Confrontation and Other Studies in Biblical Literature and Archaeology: Essays in honour of Emmett Willard Harnick* (SBEC 35; Lewiston, NY: Edwin Mellen Press, 1995), 47–56.

had given to their ancestors (Jer. 16.14–15).[77] In the same way that the first exodus had laid the foundation for God's covenant with Israel, so the second exodus would lay the foundation for a new covenant (Jer. 31.31–32). It would go far beyond its predecessor, however, in that God would put his law within his people and write it on their hearts (Jer. 31.32–34). Several of the so-called Minor Prophets share this same eschatological view of the exodus. Hosea, for example, looked forward to a time when God would renew his relationship with Israel in the desert, 'as at the time when she came out of the land of Egypt' (Hos. 2.14–15).[78] Similarly, in Amos, the re-establishment of the Davidic dynasty is predicated on a new exodus (Amos 9:11–15).

The story of the return of the Judean exiles is told in the books of Ezra and Nehemiah and in the prophetic books of Haggai and Zechariah. Ezra records the return from exile during the reign of Cyrus, the first king of the Persian Empire. He initiated the building of the Second Temple and instituted a number of religious reforms, and Nehemiah led the people in repairing the city wall. Many scholars have interpreted the narrative of Ezra-Nehemiah as a new exodus. Ezra and Nehemiah both, however, viewed the conditions of the returnees negatively, as 'slavery' (Ezra 9.8; Neh. 9.17). Even though the exiles had returned to the promised land, the fullness of the prophetic expectations about the new exodus had not been realized. The Israelites continued to violate the commandments.[79] The Davidic throne had not and could not be reinstated, because Israel was still subject to the Persians. And the nations were certainly not streaming to Zion. Nehemiah summarized the Judeans' miserable situation:

> Here we are, slaves to this day – slaves in the land that you gave to our ancestors to enjoy its fruit and its good gifts. Its rich yield goes to the kings whom you have set over us because of our sins; they have power also over our bodies and over our livestock at their pleasure, and we are in great distress.
> (Neh. 9.36–37)

Joshua Williams argues that 'Ezra-Nehemiah presents the return from exile as an anticipated, but ultimately unsuccessful attempt to fulfil the prophetic

---

77   This prophecy is repeated verbatim in Jer. 23.7–8.

78   Cf. Hos. 2.14–20; 11.1, 11; 13.14.

79   See Ezra's penitential prayer (Ezra 9.1–15) and the national confession of the Jews (Neh. 9.1–37), both of which lament the continued violation of the covenant stipulations even after the return.

expectations of a second exodus'.[80] The book ends with the community engaged in the same behaviours that had ensnared it before (Neh. 13.4–31),[81] and the promise of a new exodus forestalled until some future time.

Likewise, neither of the post-exilic prophets Haggai and Zechariah viewed the return to Judea as so great that no one would ever mention the exodus from Egypt again (Jer. 16.14–15). In Haggai, when the returnees rebuilt the Temple, the LORD told them he was with them (Hag. 2.4), but there is no account of his having filled the Second Temple with his presence as he did the First Temple (1 Kings 8.10–13). Instead, the LORD told the people that his restoration of the glory of the Temple would happen 'in a little while', when he would 'shake all the nations' so that they would stream into Jerusalem bringing their treasures with them to offer at the Temple (Hag. 2.6–7). At that time, the LORD would also 'overthrow the throne of kingdoms' and 'destroy the strength of the kingdoms of the nations' (Hag. 2.21–22). These expectations are clearly eschatological.[82] Similarly, Zechariah put great stress on the need to complete the Temple and proclaimed that it would be a sign that the LORD had returned to dwell in the midst of his people.[83] However, he too indicted the returnees for their persistent sin and deferred his expectation of the LORD's return to Zion to the future (Zech. 8.1–8). When the true restoration took place, it would not be a simple return to the blessings of Deuteronomy 28 (Zech. 8.11–12). Instead, it would be an amazing new exodus that would include 'many peoples and strong nations' who would 'come to seek the LORD of hosts in Jerusalem' (Zech. 8.20–23; 10.8–12).[84]

In the Second Temple period, it appears that most Jews believed that Israel's exile was still in progress. When the LORD inaugurated a new exodus that would lead to the restoration of Israel's fortunes and his acknowledgement by the nations, then the exile would truly be at an end.[85] Until then, the longing for a new exodus remained a future hope.

---

80 Joshua E. Williams, 'Promise and failure: second exodus in Ezra-Nehemiah', in *Reverberations* (ed. Fox), 74.

81 In Neh. 13.4–31, the Jews repeated the failures of Neh. 10.28–39.

82 Cf. the discussion in Smith, *Micah-Malachi*, 157–8.

83 Cf. Zech. 1.17; 2.10–12; 4.9–10; 6.12; 8.8.

84 Smith, *Micah-Malachi*, 238–41.

85 For a fuller discussion of this theme, see N. T. Wright, *The New Testament and the People of God* (Christian Origins and the Question of God 1; London and Minneapolis, MN: SPCK and Fortress Press, 1992), 268–72. For recent interaction with Wright's thesis of Israel's continuing exile, see the essays in James M. Scott, *Exile: A conversation with N. T. Wright* (Downers Grove, IL: IVP Academic, 2017).

Conclusions

In this chapter, we have explored how Exodus and its themes were appropriated by the authors of other Old Testament books. These authors did not limit themselves to studying the text's original meaning, but sought out its implications for their own day. As the kingdoms of Israel and Judah deteriorated spiritually and faced the prospect of exile, Exodus and its themes took on new meaning. Moses became the prototype of a future prophet to whom the people would listen and be obedient. Circumcision became an operation that the LORD would carry out upon his stubborn people's hearts. Passover became a festival that looked forward to the time when he would once again liberate his people. In that day, the LORD, in his extraordinary grace, would make a new covenant with his people, who would be enabled to follow his statutes and ordinances. The LORD would once again dwell in the midst of the people, and a priestly messiah would mediate his presence. In all these ways and more, the subjects and themes of Exodus took on a future orientation. In the next chapter, we will see how the authors of the New Testament traced out its meaning in their own day.

12
Echoes of Exodus in the New Testament

As I noted in an earlier chapter, Martin Noth identified the exodus as the kernel of the entire Pentateuch.[1] As such, it had a tremendous influence on the writing of the New Testament. It is not surprising that Jesus and virtually all the authors of the New Testament drew heavily upon it. As a source of quotations, it ranks second only behind Deuteronomy. While they often quoted the book of Exodus, however, sometimes their citations were more subtle, and readers must be sensitive to evocation and influence, subtle citation, allusion, echoes and reminiscences of Exodus in the New Testament.[2] In this chapter, we will consider the reception of Exodus and its themes in the Gospels, Acts, the epistles of Paul, Hebrews and the General Epistles, and Revelation. We will not consider authorial, source- or form-critical issues, but will focus solely on tracing out some of the main lines of reception in these works.

Exodus and its themes in the Gospels

Traditionally, the nature and purpose of the Gospels have been understood in christological terms, with a focus on their systematic theological interpretation of the person and work of Jesus. In 1975, Meredith Kline charted the direction for a radical shift when he proposed that the origins of the gospel genre could be found in the Old Testament, specifically, in the book of Exodus.[3] This approach defines the nature and purpose of the Gospels in covenantal terms. It identifies the underlying theme of the Gospels as that of their Exodus counterpart: the inauguration of the covenant. Jesus' suffering, death and resurrection, as they are presented in the Gospels, have a covenantal orientation.

---

1 Martin Noth, *A History of Pentateuchal Traditions*, trans. Bernhard W. Anderson (Englewood Cliffs, NJ: Prentice-Hall, 1972), 46–62.

2 For a definition of terms and a study of their usage as they relate to Exodus, see Bryan D. Estelle, *Echoes of Exodus: Tracing a biblical motif* (Downers Grove, IL: IVP Academic, 2018), 19–60.

3 Meredith Kline, *The Structure of Biblical Authority* (2nd edn; Eugene, OR: Wipf & Stock, 1997), 172–203.

Their authors appropriate the exodus–Sinai experiences to tell the story of Jesus, and they use explicitly covenantal terminology in their accounts of his suffering, death and resurrection. Kline compares the canonical function of the Gospels to that of the two tablets of the Sinai covenant. In the same way that the two tablets provided documentary attestation for the Sinai covenant, the Synoptic Gospels provided documentary attestation for the new covenant.[4] If his proposal is correct, then it should come as no surprise that the Synoptic Gospels and John are replete with allusions to the book of Exodus, which is indeed the case.

Matthew

Matthew clearly intended to portray Jesus as a 'new Moses', as Dale Allison demonstrates in his comprehensive study, *The New Moses: A Matthean typology*.[5] In his account of Jesus' birth and infancy (Matt. 1.18—2.23), for example, Matthew plainly borrows language from the narrative of Moses' birth in Exodus[6] and specifically quotes a biblical text that has to do with the deliverance from Egypt.[7] In his account of the Transfiguration (Matt. 17.1-8), Matthew sought to parallel what occurred when Moses descended Sinai with the tablets of the law (Exod. 34.29-35).[8] Having established these parallels, Matthew presents the Sermon on the Mount (Matt. 5—7) as the new covenant Torah delivered by the new Moses.[9] At the Last Supper, he has Jesus explain that the new covenant would be ratified by his own blood (Matt. 26.28), just as the Sinai covenant had been ratified by sacrifice (Exod. 24.8).[10] Allison concludes that:

> If it is true that Jesus was, for Matthew, the hermeneutical key to unlocking the religious meaning of the Jewish Bible, it is also true that the Jewish Bible was for him the hermeneutical key to unlocking the religious meaning of Jesus.[11]

---

4 Kline, *Structure of Biblical Authority*, 197.

5 The most comprehensive study of Jesus as a new Moses is Dale C. Allison Jr, *The New Moses: A Matthean typology* (Minneapolis, MN: Fortress Press), 1993.

6 In Matt. 2.19, Matthew borrows the language of Exod. 4.19-20.

7 In Matt. 2.15, Matthew expressly quotes from Hos. 11.1. For discussion, see Allison, *New Moses*, 140-65.

8 Allison, *New Moses*, 243-8.

9 Allison, *New Moses*, 172-94.

10 Allison, *New Moses*, 256-61.

11 Allison, *New Moses*, 289.

If Matthew wrote his Gospel after the fall of Jerusalem, then he was writing in a time when Christianity was fast becoming a Gentile religion. In those changing times, Allison suggests that he intentionally wrote a book that 'would demonstrate that the Messiah himself followed in the footsteps of the lawgiver, and that therefore to abandon Moses is to abandon Jesus'.[12]

Mark

Numerous scholars have observed that Isaiah had a major influence on Mark's Gospel. In his volume on *Isaiah's New Exodus in Mark*, Rikki Watts, in particular, makes the case that Isaiah's 'new exodus' theme is the hermeneutical key not only to Mark's structure, but also to his understanding of the nature and character of Jesus as the Messiah.[13] He explains that, 'In keeping with the role of the opening sentence in literary antiquity, Mark's sole explicit editorial citation of the OT should be expected to convey the main concerns of his prologue and, therefore, his Gospel.'[14] At the outset, Mark cites Isaiah 40.3, which announces the LORD's coming to initiate the new exodus, and this provides the overall conceptual framework for his Gospel. He argues that Isaiah's new exodus schema involves three stages, including: (1) the LORD's deliverance of his exiled people from the power of the nations and their idols; (2) the journey along the 'Way' in which the LORD would lead his people from their captivity among the nations; and (3) their arrival in Jerusalem, where the LORD would be enthroned in a gloriously restored Zion. While 'this appears to be reflected in the simplicity of Mark's basic literary outline, which comprises "Jesus' ministry in Galilee and Beyond" (1:16 – 8:21/26), the "Way" (8:22/27 – 10:45/52) and "Jerusalem" (10:46/11:1 – 16:8)', the correlation is not direct.[15] For Mark, God's plan involved the 'necessary' (8.31) suffering and death of Isaiah's Servant (Isa. 53).[16]

In addition to the new exodus theme, Mark's Gospel also contains numerous allusions to the book of Exodus itself. For example, the Sadducees, in a rare encounter with Jesus, presented him with a dilemma based on the law of levirate marriage (Mark 12.18–27). In their hypothetical scenario, a woman's husband died and, in order to fulfil the obligations of levirate marriage, his seven brothers each married her, in turn, but they all died too. Their question was,

---

12 Allison, *New Moses*, 290.

13 Rikki E. Watts, *Isaiah's New Exodus* (Grand Rapids, MI: Baker Academic, 1997).

14 Watts, *Isaiah's New Exodus*, 90.

15 Watts, *Isaiah's New Exodus*, 135.

16 Watts, *Isaiah's New Exodus*, 221–302.

when the resurrection came, whose wife would she be? (Mark 12.23). Jesus answered, in part, with a quote from the book of Exodus. He asked:

> Have you not read in the book of Moses, in the story about the bush, how God said to him, 'I am the God of Abraham, the God of Isaac, and the God of Jacob'? He is God not of the dead, but of the living; you are quite wrong. (Mark 12.26–27)

In this case, Jesus used the story of the burning bush (Exod. 3.1–6) to argue for the resurrection from the dead.

Another example of Mark's use of Exodus themes comes in his account of the Last Supper. In the course of this last meal with his disciples, Jesus declared that the cup he shared with them was 'my blood of the covenant . . . poured out for many' (Mark 14.24–25). He was alluding to Moses' use of blood in the making of the covenant at Sinai. As part of the ratification ceremony, burnt offerings and offerings of well-being were made, and Moses took some of the blood of these offerings and 'dashed it on the people, and said, "See the blood of the covenant that the LORD has made with you in accordance with all these words"' (Exod. 24.8). In the same way that the LORD established the Sinai covenant with Israel by blood, so did Jesus inaugurate the new covenant.

Luke

Luke portrays Jesus as the prophet like Moses and as the Son of God. Long ago, Hans Conzelmann introduced the idea that Luke divided salvation history into three periods, including: (1) the period of Old Testament promise or prophecy; (2) the period of the historical life of Jesus; and (3) the period of the Church, which would be concluded with the Parousia.[17] This provides Luke with a prophetic structure that he utilizes both in his Gospel and in the book of Acts. In Luke, he portrays Jesus as the prophet like Moses (Deut. 18.15–22) and uses Moses to reveal the basic prophetic pattern.[18] Luke Timothy Johnson explains that 'in the section of Stephen's speech (Acts 7) devoted to Moses, Luke structures the account to make it correspond precisely with the story of Jesus as Luke himself tells it'.[19] The effect is to make Moses a prototype of Jesus, and to portray Jesus as the prophet like Moses.

---

17   Hans Conzelmann, *The Theology of St. Luke*, trans. Geoffrey Buswell (New York, NY: Harper & Row, 1960), 16–17.

18   Luke Timothy Johnson, *The Acts of the Apostles* (SP 5; Collegeville, MN: Liturgical Press, 1992), 13.

19   Johnson, Acts of the Apostles, 13.

Another key theme in Luke that connects back to Exodus is the wilderness temptation (Luke 4.1–13). In the first of the temptations, the devil challenged him, saying, 'If you are the Son of God . . .' (Luke 4.3). Reginald Fuller identifies this as a christological narrative that is concerned with what it means to be the 'son of God'. Israel was God's firstborn son (Exod. 4.22) whom, after the exodus, the LORD let into the wilderness by a pillar of cloud by day and a pillar of fire by night (Exod. 13.21–22). In the wilderness, however, the Israelites 'complained' (Exod. 15.24), lamented that they had ever left Egypt (15.2–3) and quarrelled with Moses (17.2). Later, they 'complained in the hearing of the LORD about their misfortunes' (Num. 11.1), and they grumbled about the manna that God provided (Num. 11.6). They objected that they did not have meat (Num. 11.4–6) but, when the LORD sent it, they did not appreciate it (Num. 11.33). In the end, Israel – God's son – rebelled in the wilderness and forfeited the promise (Num. 14.1–23). In Luke's account, however, when Jesus was led into the wilderness by the Spirit (Luke 4.1) and tested for 40 days, he obeyed. 'Where Israel disobeyed, Jesus, the true Israel, obeyed God.'[20]

A very important link to Exodus themes is found in Jesus' inaugural sermon (Luke 4.16–30). This is another christological narrative and may be one of the most important passages in the entire Gospel of Luke.[21] In it, Luke uses Jesus' inaugural sermon to set forth the whole programme of Luke-Acts. He tells how, at the beginning of his ministry, Jesus attended the synagogue in Nazareth and, when he stood up to read the Scripture, was handed the scroll of Isaiah. Luke recounts that:

He unrolled the scroll and found the place where it was written:

'The Spirit of the LORD is upon me,
   because he has anointed me
      to bring good news to the poor.
He has sent me to proclaim release to the captives
   and recovery of sight to the blind,
      to let the oppressed go free,
to proclaim the year of the LORD's favour.'
(Luke 4.18–19)

---

20   Reginald H. Fuller, 'The Gospel of Luke' (unpublished lectures, June–July 1997).
21   Fuller, 'Gospel of Luke'.

After he had finished the reading and handed the scroll back to the attendant, he sat down and announced that, 'Today this scripture has been fulfilled in your hearing' (Luke 4.21). Even though Jesus did not read directly from Exodus, he read from Isaiah 61.1–2, which is a new exodus text.[22] This is a christological narrative, in which Jesus articulated his own vision of what it meant for him to be the Messiah. According to Luke, he understood it to mean that he was the eschatological herald of the new exodus.

Another significant link with Exodus in the book of Luke is found in its account of the Transfiguration (Luke 9.28–36). This is another christological narrative that reveals something about the nature and character of Jesus as the Christ. Luke says that the Transfiguration occurred 'about eight days' (Luke 9.28) after the foregoing teaching, but Mark reads 'after six days'. Mark's emphasis on the fact that six days had elapsed is probably intended to parallel Moses' ascent of Mt Sinai after the cloud of God's glory had covered it for six days. At that time, Moses ascended the mountain and 'entered the cloud' of God's glory, where he remained for 40 days and 40 nights (Exod. 24.15–18). Jesus took Peter, James and John up on to a mountain to pray. While he was praying he was transfigured, and they saw Moses and Elijah talking with him. In the same way that Moses had been in the cloud of God's glory on the mountain, Moses and Elijah were with Jesus in glory. They were in the very presence of God.[23] What is unique about Luke's account of the Transfiguration is that he tells us that the three of them were 'speaking of his departure, which he was about to accomplish at Jerusalem' (Luke 9.31). The Greek word translated as 'departure' is *exodos* which, in this case, refers to Jesus' journey to Jerusalem, which would culminate in his death. Joseph Fitzmyer points out that the real significance of Luke's description of the 'glory' here is the way he connects it to Jesus' upcoming exodus. In the same way that the LORD's glory was related to that experience of Israel, so it would now be experienced in Jesus' death in Jerusalem.[24]

In addition to the theme of Jesus as a new Moses, Luke's Gospel also contains a number of more subtle allusions to the book of Exodus. For example, in a confrontation with the Jerusalem scribes, when they accused Jesus of being empowered by Satan, Jesus replied, 'If it is by the finger of God that I cast

---

22   Cf. the discussion in Estelle, *Echoes of Exodus*, 244–9.

23   The Transfiguration is usually paralleled with Moses' descent from the mountain with the two tablets of the law, when 'his face shone because he had been talking with God' (Exod. 34.29). See, however, the discussion of 'Moses as a divine figure' in Chapter 5.

24   Joseph A. Fitzmyer, *The Gospel According to Luke (I–IX)* (AB 28; New York, NY: Doubleday, 1970), 794–5.

out the demons, then the kingdom of God has come to you' (Luke 11.20). In the parallel accounts, Matthew has 'Spirit of God' (12.28) and Mark does not include this saying of Jesus at all (Mark 3.20–30). Luke includes this specific wording in order to make an allusion to the confession of Pharaoh's magicians after the third plague (Exod. 8.19).[25]

John

Long ago, Jacob Enz argued that the book of Exodus served as a literary type for the Gospel of John in its entirety.[26] There are indeed numerous ways that the Gospel of John interacts with and builds upon the book of Exodus. Several of these feature in John's prologue, establishing themes that will be prominent throughout the Gospel. At the outset, John compares the Word (Logos) with Moses (John 1.1–18). Moses asked to see God's 'glory' (Exod. 33.18), but he answered that 'you cannot see my face; for no one shall see me and live' (33.20). Instead, the LORD showed him his back (33.21–23). The Word, on the other hand, was 'facing' God from the beginning of time (John 1.1).[27] Whereas Moses was not allowed to see God, the Word was with God, face to face, and, John asserts, was in fact God.

The prologue reaches its climax with the incarnation of the Word in Jesus Christ (John 1.14–18). John writes that 'the Word became flesh and lived among us' (John 1.14). The Greek word translated here as 'lived' is literally 'encamped', in the sense of pitching a tent, and was clearly chosen in order to allude to the tabernacle. John goes on to say that, 'We have seen his glory' (v. 14), recalling the glory of the LORD filling the tabernacle (Exod. 40.34). The fact that John intended to allude to the tenting of God with the people of Israel in the exodus 'is evident in the close association of the phrase "encamped among us" with the "glory" (*doxa*) of the Word'.[28] The prologue concludes by returning to the allusion to Exodus 33.20, that no one could see God, and then announcing that 'It is God the only Son, who is close to the Father's heart, who has made him known' (John 1.18).

The body of the Gospel of John can then be broken into two halves, each of which can be understood through the lens of Exodus. The first half, the Book

---

25   For a discussion of the textual differences between the accounts of Matthew and Luke, see Craig A. Evans, 'Exodus in the New Testament: patterns of revelation and redemption', in *The Book of Exodus: Composition, reception, and interpretation*, ed. Thomas B. Dozeman, Craig A. Evans and Joel N. Lohr (Leiden: Brill, 2014), 440–5.

26   Jacob J. Enz, 'The book of Exodus as a literary type for the Gospel of John', *JBL* 76.3 (1957): 208–15.

27   John 1.1 uses the preposition *pros* with the accusative, which means 'to', 'towards' or 'facing'. Cf. J. Ramsey Michaels, *The Gospel of John* (NICNT; Grand Rapids, MI: Eerdmans, 2010), 47, n. 6.

28   Michaels, *Gospel of John*, 79.

of Signs (1.19—12.5), echoes the signs in Exodus that culminated in the deliverance at the Sea. In John, there are seven selected signs that establish that Jesus is the Messiah of God, including: (1) changing water to wine (2.1–11); (2) cleansing the Temple (2.13–22); (3) healing an official's son (4.46–54); (4) healing a lame man (5.1–15); (5) feeding the multitude (6.1–15); (6) healing a blind man (9.1–41); and (7) the raising of Lazarus (11.1–44). The second half of the Gospel of John, the Book of the Passion (13.1—20.31), recounts how the Messiah was exalted through his suffering. Just as Israel saw the signs the LORD had performed in the exodus and came to fear him and to believe in his servant Moses (Exod. 14.31), John's hope was that, when people read his account of the signs Jesus had performed, they would 'come to believe that Jesus is the Messiah, the Son of God, and that through believing you may have life in his name' (John 20.31).

Among the many additional parallels with Exodus in the Gospel of John, the 'I am' sayings, Jesus' farewell discourse and John's characterization of Jesus as the Passover lamb stand out. John recounts seven 'I am' sayings, in which Jesus appropriated the Tetragrammaton that was revealed to Moses in the burning bush (Exod. 3.14–15). These include: (1) 'I am the bread of life' (John 6.35, 48, 51); (2) 'I am the light of the world' (John 8.12; 9.5); (3) 'I am the gate' (John 10.7, 9); (4) 'I am the good shepherd' (John 10.11, 14); (5) 'I am the resurrection and the life' (John 11.25); (6) 'I am the way, and the truth, and the life' (John 14.6); and (7) 'I am the true vine' (John 15.1). These important pronouncements express the idea that God's saving powers were present in Jesus but, even more than that, they indicate that he himself manifested the divine name.[29] In Robert Wilkinson's major study of the Tetragrammaton, he concludes that what John intended to express with the 'I am' sayings is that 'what commenced at the Burning Bush was accomplished in him', in 'Christ as the Tetragrammaton'.[30]

John's account of Jesus' farewell discourse (John 13—17) recalls Moses' farewell to Israel in the book of Deuteronomy. Kline notes that, in each case, 'it is the hour of covenant ratification', and that both include 'similar elements like election of the covenant servants, the Lord-servant relationship, the giving of commandments, the covenant witnesses, and the appointment of a successor for the departing mediator'.[31] In the end, both Moses (Deut. 33) and

---

29   Robert J. Wilkinson, *Tetragrammaton: Western Christians and the Hebrew name of God from the beginnings to the seventeenth century* (SHCT 179; Leiden: Brill, 2015), 108.

30   Wilkinson, *Tetragrammaton*, 108.

31   Kline, *Structure of Biblical Authority*, 193.

Jesus (John 17) bestow a final blessing upon their followers in which they express their highest aspirations for them, and then take their leave from the site of a mountaintop.

Finally, in John's account of Jesus' death on the cross, he characterizes Jesus as the Passover lamb. While Jesus was on the cross, the Jewish leadership asked Pilate to have the legs of the crucified broken so that they would die quickly and thus not violate the approaching Sabbath (John 19.31). The soldiers went around breaking the legs of those who had been crucified but, when they reached Jesus, they thought he might already be dead, so they pierced his side in order to check (John 19.33–34). John interpreted this through the lens of the Passover instructions, which stipulated that none of the bones of the Passover lamb should be broken (John 19.36; Exod. 12.5–10, 46).[32]

Exodus in the Acts of the Apostles

In the book of Acts, Luke continues to develop the new exodus themes that he introduced in his Gospel. One of these themes is the early Christian community as the New Temple. This theme mirrors the building of the tabernacle in Exodus. There, after defeating Pharaoh and his forces, Moses led the Israelites to Mt Sinai, where they entered into a covenant relationship with God and, once this was ratified, he built the tabernacle so that the LORD could once again dwell in the midst of the people (Exod. 25.8). After its completion, the tabernacle was filled with God's glory, visibly present in the form of a great cloud (Exod. 40.34–35). Luke's story of the 'prophet like Moses' follows the same pattern. After Jesus had defeated the forces of Satan and sealed the new covenant with the people, he erected the sanctuary. Luke had already recorded the raising up of the Temple of the new covenant in his Gospel's resurrection account, in the sense that Jesus himself was that Temple.[33] However, the further antitypical parallel to the building of the tabernacle is in the Pentecost event (Acts 2).[34] Similar to the way that a cloud covered the tabernacle when the LORD's glory filled it (Exod. 40.34), 'tongues, as of fire' rested upon each of the apostles who had gathered in Jerusalem (Acts 2.3). In biblical and early Judaic texts, tongues of fire are indicative of a theophany from a heavenly sanctuary, which leads Gregory Beale to suggest that the descent of the Holy Spirit

---

32 For a recent study of John's use of the book of Exodus, see Thomas N. Willoughby, '"The Word became flesh and tabernacled among us": a primer for the exodus in John's Gospel', in *Reverberations of the Exodus in Scripture*, ed. R. Michael Fox (Eugene, OR: Pickwick, 2014), 121–38.

33 Jesus specifically referred to himself as the Temple in John 2.21.

34 Kline, *Structure of Biblical Authority*, 194.

at Pentecost may 'be conceived as the descent of God's tabernacling presence from his heavenly temple'.[35] For Luke, the locus of God's indwelling presence had moved into the early Christian community, which had itself become the New Temple.[36]

Another important theme in Acts, carried over from Luke's Gospel, is salvation history. Throughout Luke-Acts, Luke intended to narrate the continued unfolding of God's programme of redemption in the life of Jesus and the early Church. One of the clearest ways he does this is through the speeches in Acts, especially those made in Jewish contexts. In Peter's Pentecost speech, the very first Christian sermon, he applied the terms *Kyrios* and 'Messiah' to the risen Christ (Acts 2.36). These two christological titles are very significant. *Kyrios*, which means 'Lord', was used by Palestinian Jews in the last pre-Christian centuries as a substitute for the Tetragrammaton.[37] By applying it to Jesus, Peter claimed that the risen Jesus was equal to the LORD.[38] The term 'Messiah', while not derived from Exodus, was certainly connected with the idea of the new exodus.[39] In his speech in Solomon's Portico, Peter specifically proclaimed that Jesus was the 'prophet like Moses' (Acts 3.22–23). In Stephen's speech before the Sanhedrin (Acts 7.2–53), he recounted the stories of Abraham, Joseph and Moses, each of whom was rejected by Israel but ultimately vindicated by God. In this speech, therefore, Stephen used Moses as 'another type of Jesus, the rejected one'.[40] In Paul's address in the synagogue at Pisidian Antioch (Acts 13.16–41), his first major address in Acts, he likewise surveyed the history of Israel, but with only a brief mention of the period of Egyptian bondage (13.17). His point, however, is 'the continuity between Israel and the church'.[41] The same God who delivered Israel from bondage in Egypt had now 'brought to Israel a Saviour, Jesus, as he promised' (13.23). The work of this Saviour, however, has fulfilled that of Moses, since 'everyone who believes

---

35 G. K. Beale, *The Temple and the Church's Mission: A biblical theology of the dwelling place of God* (NSBT 17; Downers Grove, IL and Leicester: InterVarsity Press and Apollos, 2004), 206.

36 The idea that the New Temple would be comprised of a community was not new, but was held by a number of counter-temple movements in the period of Second Temple Judaism. For an introduction and survey of such movements, see Nicholas Perrin, *Jesus the Temple* (London and Grand Rapids, MI: SPCK and Baker Academic, 2010), 17–45.

37 Wilkinson, *Tetragrammaton*, 91–103.

38 Joseph A. Fitzmyer, *The Acts of the Apostles* (AB 31; New York, NY: Doubleday, 1997), 260.

39 See Chapter 11.

40 Fitzmyer, *Acts of the Apostles*, 375.

41 Hans Conzelmann, *Acts of the Apostles: A commentary on the Acts of the Apostles* (Hermeneia; Philadelphia, PA: Fortress Press, 1987), 103.

[in him] is set free from all those sins from which you could not be freed by the law of Moses' (13.39).

Another major theme in the book of Acts is the mission to the Gentiles, which also has roots in new exodus theology. Before his Ascension, Luke records Jesus as having said, 'But you will receive power when the Holy Spirit has come upon you; and you will be my witnesses in Jerusalem, in all Judea and Samaria, and to the ends of the earth' (Acts 1.8). Dennis Johnson identifies several allusions to Isaiah in this passage, in which the Spirit of God is poured out upon God's people, they are called upon to be his witnesses, and their witness is to extend to the ends of the earth, calling upon pagan nations to abandon their idols and turn to the LORD for salvation.[42] This reflects the emphases in Jesus' inaugural sermon and in the Gospel of Luke as a whole. Estelle concludes that, 'The continuity between Luke and Acts demonstrates that the Isaianic new exodus is coming into its own: salvation is now for all those who will receive the life-giving word of the Messiah, Jew and Gentile alike.'[43]

Exodus in the epistles of Paul and the Pastoral Epistles

As a devout Jew and a Pharisee, Paul was deeply influenced by the Torah, and themes and stories from Exodus play a significant part in some of his most important theological discussions. Romans, Paul's magnum opus, is replete with Exodus allusions. One of his major concerns, for example, was the issue of the 'righteousness of God' (*dikaiosynē theou*), a phrase connected with 'God's being in the right, his action of making people right before him, *and* the resultant status of those made right'.[44] Paul understood the righteousness of God as coming through Jesus Christ, 'whom God put forward as a sacrifice of atonement by his blood' (Rom. 3.25). The Greek word translated as 'atonement' in the NRSV (*hilastērion*) is elsewhere used for the 'mercy seat', the space between the wings of the cherubim on the top of the ark of the covenant where the high priest would sprinkle the sacrificial blood in order to secure atonement (Lev. 16.14). Douglas Moo concludes that, 'By referring to Christ as this "mercy seat," then, Paul would be inviting us to view Christ as the

---

42   Johnson identifies allusions in Acts 1.8 to Isa. 32.15; 43.10, 12; 44.8; 49.6; 45.22. Cf. Dennis E. Johnson, *The Message of Acts in the History of Redemption* (Phillipsburg, NJ: P&R, 1997), 35–6.

43   Estelle, *Echoes of Exodus*, 262.

44   Douglas J. Moo, *The Epistle to the Romans* (NICNT; Grand Rapids, MI: Eerdmans, 1996), 72.

New Covenant equivalent, or antitype, to this Old Covenant "place of atonement," and, derivatively, to the ritual of atonement itself.[45]

Another important concern that Paul dealt with in several of his letters was the issue of whether and how to include Gentiles in the Church, which was initially entirely Jewish. In order to address this issue, Paul turned to the story of the rise and fall of Pharaoh during the period of the exodus. Paul quotes Scripture as saying to Pharaoh, 'I have raised you up for the very purpose of showing my power in you, so that my name may be proclaimed in all the earth' (Rom. 9.17).[46] For Paul, Pharaoh's eminence was not an end in and of itself, but it was so that God could demonstrate his own greatness by vanquishing him. Paul concluded, 'So then he has mercy on whomsoever he chooses, and he hardens the heart of whomsoever he chooses' (Rom. 9.18). His point is that God had the prerogative to broaden the Church to include Gentiles.

Another theme from Exodus that Paul interacts with in Romans is the law. In a sweeping assertion, he claims that Christ is 'the end of the law so that there may be righteousness for everyone who believes' (Rom. 10.4). Many commentators argue that Paul was not claiming that the law came to an end or ceased with Christ, but that Christ was the goal and culmination (*telos*) of the law because he provided righteousness for those who believed in him.[47] Richard Longenecker insists, however, that while the concepts of 'purpose', 'goal' and 'fulfilment' may legitimately be seen in Paul's use of 'end' (*telos*) in Romans 10.4:

> the feature the apostle highlights is 'termination,' 'end,' or 'cessation' of the Mosaic law in any positive or custodial fashion in this new age of salvation history, which is characterized by the Lordship of Christ and the ministry of God's Holy Spirit.[48]

N. T. Wright helpfully negotiates the balance between these views, explaining that:

> The Torah is neither abolished as though it were bad or demonic, nor affirmed in the sense in which the Jews took it. It was a good thing, given deliberately by God for a specific task and a particular period of time. When the task is done and the time is up, the Torah reaches its goal,

---

45   Moo, *Epistle to the Romans*, 232.

46   Paul draws upon Exod. 9.16 as a supporting text.

47   Robert Jewett, *Romans: A commentary* (Hermeneia; Minneapolis, MN: Fortress Press, 2006), 619.

48   Richard N. Longenecker, *The Epistle to the Romans* (NIGTC; Grand Rapids, MI: Eerdmans, 2016), 850.

which is also the conclusion of its intended reign, not because it was a bad thing to be abolished but because it was a good thing whose job is done.[49]

The idea that the Torah had a temporary function and that it would be replaced by new Torah was not unique to Paul, but was original to the Old Testament and current to Jewish tradition in Paul's day. As Charles Quarles has demonstrated in a recent study, the Pentateuch itself foretold the coming of a prophet like Moses who would deliver new divine commandments, and Jews of the Second Temple era and the rabbinic period expected that this figure would mediate a new covenant and teach a new Torah.[50] Paul believed that Jesus was the prophet like Moses and that he had both fulfilled the Mosaic Torah and delivered a new one.

Paul made frequent allusion to Exodus in his letters to the church at Corinth. In his first letter, in order to address the issue of divisions in the Corinthian church, he drew on the idea of the church as a counter-temple movement. He rhetorically asked his readers, 'Do you not know that you are God's temple and that God's Spirit dwells in you?' (1 Cor. 3.16). In this case, Paul was speaking to the church as a collective, and so the second-person pronoun 'you' is in the plural. His argument 'presupposes that the temple has already been established in Christ and, simultaneously, that it is presently constituted by the believing community'.[51] Paul severely criticized the Corinthians for tolerating a case of incest in the congregation (1 Cor. 5.1–8). He warned them that 'a little yeast leavens the whole batch' and urged them to remove the old yeast (1 Cor. 5.6–7). The removal of yeast led Paul to think of the preparations for Passover (Exod. 12.15) and thus the Passover lamb, and he exclaimed, 'For our paschal lamb, Christ, has been sacrificed' (1 Cor. 5.7). A little later, Paul fuses baptismal and eucharistic imagery together with the exodus story in order to invite the Corinthians to interpret their own situation in terms of how God dealt with the Israelites during the exodus generation (1 Cor. 10.1–5). He referred to the Ancient Israelites as 'our ancestors' (1 Cor. 10.1), shaping a new identity for the Corinthians. They had been 'baptized' into Moses when they crossed the sea (1 Cor. 10.2; Exod. 14.21–22) and experienced the miraculous provision of water (Exod. 17.1–7), and yet still sinned by building the golden calf (Exod. 32.6, 19).

49   N. T. Wright, *The Climax of the Covenant: Christ and the law in Pauline theology* (Minneapolis, MN: Fortress Press, 1993), 241.

50   Charles L. Quarles, 'Jesus as a teacher of new covenant Torah: an examination of the Sermon on the Mount', in *Matthew as Teacher in the Gospel of Matthew*, ed. Charles L. Quarles and Charles N. Ridlehoover (LNTS; Edinburgh; T&T Clark, forthcoming).

51   Perrin, *Jesus the Temple*, 69.

Paul's point was that, if the Corinthians shared in Ancient Israel's gifts, then they were also at risk of sharing Israel's danger, that of idolatry.[52]

In his second letter to the Corinthians, Paul continued to use the book of Exodus as a tool for elucidating the Christian experience. Drawing upon the story of Moses and his veil (Exod. 34.29–35), Paul affirmed that those who are in Christ have the veil removed, so that they can fully see the divine glory which is in Christ (2 Cor. 3.7–18). Paul made the case that, whereas Moses' ministry was temporary, Christ's is permanent. He also adapts the image, so that Moses' veil became a veil over the minds of the Israelites who read the Torah without understanding that Christ was its goal. Paul concluded that, when one comes to Christ, one can find him in the Torah (2 Cor. 3.14–15). Even more, the removal of the veil allows believers ultimately to be transformed into the image of Christ themselves (2 Cor. 3.18).

In the book of Galatians, Paul was concerned with the question of whether or not Gentile Christians needed to follow the Torah. He argued that the Galatian Christians were already complete in Christ and that it was therefore unnecessary. He explained that the law had laid the foundation for the full revelation of God's plan of salvation that came in the person of Jesus Christ. It did this by serving as a 'disciplinarian' until Christ came (Gal. 3.24). Paul was referring to a pedagogue (*paidagogos*), a kind of servant who accompanied a child to school and back, carrying his books and writing materials, protected the child from assault and accidents, and taught him good manners. When the child had grown up, the pedagogue was no longer needed and was dismissed. Paul used the pedagogue as a metaphor for the law and how it worked in Israelite history. He explained that the law 'was our disciplinarian until Christ came', but 'now that faith has come, we are no longer subject to a disciplinarian, for in Christ Jesus you are all children of God through faith' (Gal. 3.24–25). In Paul's mind, 'The "coming of Christ" ended the period of the Torah, like the task of the pedagogue ends when the boy has reached the age of maturity.'[53]

While Paul argued that the period of the Torah had ended, he explained that there was a 'law of Christ' to which Christians were subject (Gal. 6.2). Long ago, C. H. Dodd proposed that this is probably a reference to the Sermon on the Mount, and many interpreters have held to this view.[54] James Dunn suggests that 'it means that law (Torah) as interpreted by the love command in

52   Carla Swafford Works, *The Church in the Wilderness: Paul's use of exodus traditions in 1 Corinthians* (WUNT 2/379; Tübingen: Mohr Siebeck, 2014), 42–88.

53   Hans Dieter Betz, *Galatians: A commentary on Paul's letter to the churches in Galatia* (Hermeneia; Philadelphia, PA: Fortress Press, 1979), 178.

54   C. H. Dodd, *The Gospel and the Law of Christ* (London and New York, NY: Longmans Green, 1947).

the light of the Jesus-tradition and the Christ-event'.[55] Hans Dieter Betz suggests that Paul appropriated the concept of Torah from his opponents in order to say that Christ fulfilled it, but that it must not have been an important concept for Paul or he would have introduced it earlier in his letter.[56] The idea of law, however, is not antithetical to messianism at all. In fact, as Quarles points out, 'Some rabbis argued that in the messianic age, God's people would receive a new Torah',[57] and that 'This Torah could even be described specifically as the "Torah of the Messiah"' (*Midr. Eccl.* 11.8).[58] Paul's expression 'the law of Christ' is equivalent to that of 'the Torah of the Messiah'. Jesus was the Messiah who was bringing a new Torah. In his epistles, Paul mentions nine times that Christians are 'under the law' of Christ. He said that there are laws to keep (1 Cor. 7.19) and these laws cover what the law of Moses intended. Paul integrated some of the Mosaic laws into the New Testament.[59] Quarles is surely correct that Christ was the bringer of a 'new' or 'messianic' Torah.[60]

In the book of Ephesians, David Starling proposes that Paul used a new exodus hermeneutical framework that he established in the first three chapters and reinforced in the exhortations of the final chapter.[61] The opening doxology (Eph. 1.3–14), which takes the form of a *berakah*,[62] recalls the election of the people of Israel (Eph. 1.4/Deut. 4.37–38), their adoption as God's son (Eph. 1.5/Exod. 4.22–23), their redemption in the exodus (Eph. 1.7/Exod. 6.6; 15.13), the revelation at Sinai (Eph. 1.9/Ezek. 20.11; Neh. 9.14) and the inheritance that they would receive at the end of their journey (Eph. 1.11/Exod. 15.17).[63] In Paul's account of the readers' salvation in Ephesians 2.11–22, he suggests that he intended for his readers to 'understand their salvation in Christ as a participation in the fulfillment of second exodus promises originally given to exiled Israel'.[64] And, finally, he suggests that the armour Paul urges his readers

---

55 J. D. G. Dunn, *The Epistle to the Galatians* (BNTC; London: A&C Black, 1993), 323.

56 Betz, *Galatians*, 300–1.

57 *Lev. Rab.* 13.3; *Tg. Isa.* 12.3; *Tg. Ket.* on Songs 5.10; *Midr. Eccl.* 2.1; *Yal.* on Isa. 26.2.

58 Quarles, 'Jesus as a teacher of new covenant Torah', n.p.

59 E.g. 1 Cor. 9.20–21; Gal. 6.2; Col. 3.20; etc.

60 For the idea that the Messiah would bring a 'new' or 'messianic' Torah, see: W. D. Davies, *Paul and Rabbinic Judaism* (London: SPCK, 1955), 69–74, 142–5, 174–6; W. D. Davies, *Torah in the Messianic Age and/or the Age to Come* (SBLMS 7; Philadelphia, PA: Society of Biblical Literature, 1952), 91ff.

61 David Starling, 'Ephesians and the hermeneutics of the new exodus', in *Reverberations* (ed. Fox), 139–59.

62 A *berakah* is a blessing, derived from the Old Testament and from synagogue worship, that follows a formalized pattern.

63 Starling, 'Ephesians', 142.

64 Starling, 'Ephesians', 147.

to put on in Ephesians 6.4–17 'is laced with intertextual references to the language and imagery of Isaiah', and that Paul intended his readers to

> see themselves as participating in the conflict and triumph of God himself, the Divine Warrior of Isaiah 59 who intervenes to save and whose arm brings him victory – an image that is itself an echo of the language and imagery of Exod 15.[65]

If Starling is right, it may be that Paul intended for his readers to understand the story of Christ as a typological echo of the original exodus and a fulfilment of the Old Testament hope for a new exodus.

This would certainly be consistent with Paul's approach in Colossians, where Paul clearly used exodus typology to describe the Christian experience of salvation. He wrote that, 'He has rescued us from the power of darkness and transferred us into the kingdom of his beloved Son, in whom we have redemption, the forgiveness of sins' (Col. 1.13–14). Paul directly echoes the language of Exodus, which recounts that, when God called Moses to go confront Pharaoh, he assured him that he would 'redeem' Israel (Exod. 6.6) and, after the crossing of the sea, it reports that 'the LORD saved Israel that day from the Egyptians; and Israel saw the Egyptians dead on the seashore' (Exod. 14.30). Christian salvation mirrors the exodus in that 'God ransoms us by Christ's entrance into enemy territory to recapture the captives and take them into freedom – transporting them from enemy territory back home'.[66]

There are few references to Exodus in the Pastoral Epistles, although their author was clearly very familiar with the book, as well as traditions associated with it. The author of 2 Timothy uses 'Jannes and Jambres', the magicians who 'opposed Moses' (2 Tim. 3.8), as types for the kinds of godless people who would oppose the truth in the last days. The magicians were unnamed in the book of Exodus, but the author of 2 Timothy obviously knew of Jewish traditions in which these names were preserved.[67] In the letter to Titus, when the author urged his protégé to teach sound doctrine, he based his appeal on the exodus. Titus should be faithful to Jesus Christ, because 'he it is who gave himself for us that he might redeem us from all iniquity and purify for himself a people of his own who are zealous for good deeds' (Titus 2.14). The

---

65 Starling, 'Ephesians', 149.

66 Scot McKnight, *The Letter to the Colossians* (NICNT; Grand Rapids, MI: Eerdmans, 2018), 125.

67 Cf. Martin Dibelius and Hans Conzelmann, *The Pastoral Epistles: A commentary on the Pastoral Epistles* (Hermeneia; Philadelphia, PA: Fortress Press, 1972), 117.

author's wording was primarily influenced by the LORD's declaration that Israel would 'be my treasured possession out of all the peoples' (Exod. 19.5).[68] Clearly, Exodus and its associated traditions shaped the thinking of the author of the Pastoral Epistles.

Exodus in Hebrews and the General Epistles

Even though there are only two or three direct quotes from the book of Exodus in the letter to the Hebrews, 'no book of the Jewish Scriptures surpasses Exodus's presence in its fabric'.[69] The letter to the Hebrews is a sermon, probably written by an early Christian pastor between about AD 50 and 90, about how Jesus was the consummation and fulfilment of all God's previous saving work.[70] The pastor began his sermon by saying that, 'Long ago God spoke to our ancestors in many and various ways by the prophets, but in these last days he has spoken to us by a Son' (Heb. 1.1–2). He went on to present Jesus as the realization of God's programme of salvation. He compared and contrasted Moses and Christ (3.1–18), and understood Jesus as the eschatological high priest (4.14—5.10). The pastor also compared Jesus' priesthood with that of Melchizedek and argued that Jesus had attained perfection in his priesthood, since his single sacrifice was efficacious for all time (7.1–28). He insisted that Jesus' high-priestly ministry is continuing, since he is now seated 'at the right hand of the throne of the Majesty in the heavens', where he continues to minister in the heavenly sanctuary (8.1–13). The pastor proclaimed that Christ's sacrifice was so effective that it cleanses and sanctifies the people of God so that they themselves can enter God's presence (10.39). In his famous 'hall of faith' passage (11.1—12.3), which explores the meaning of faith through telling the stories of many of Israel's ancestors, he held up Moses as a paragon of faith (11.23–28). This history of the faithful people of God reaches its consummation in Jesus, 'the pioneer and perfecter of our faith' (12.2). Finally, the pastor concluded that God's revelation on Sinai has been fulfilled in Christ, who has mediated a new covenant (12.18–28). The letter to the Hebrews is unique in the New Testament in its lengthy and detailed exploration of how Jesus was the fulfilment of the covenant, the law, the priesthood, the

---

68 Dibelius and Conzelmann, *Pastoral Epistles*, 143.

69 Radu Gheorghita, 'περὶ τῆς ἐξόδου . . . ἐμνημόνευσεν, "he spoke about the exodus"': echoes of Exodus in Hebrews', in *Reverberations* (ed. Fox), 161.

70 For a detailed discussion of the authorship and date of the book, as well as its identification as a 'Christian synagogue homily', see Gareth Lee Cockerill, *The Epistle to the Hebrews* (NICNT; Grand Rapids, MI: Eerdmans, 2012), 2–16.

tabernacle and the sacrifices, all of which make their entry on to the biblical stage in the book of Exodus.[71]

The General Epistles are likewise steeped in the theology of Exodus, but contain only a few direct references. In James, there is a clear understanding of the Sermon on the Mount as the new covenant Torah. This is made clear by a number of verbal parallels between Matthew 5—6 and the epistle of James.[72] James refers to the 'royal law' (Jas. 2.8) and the 'law of liberty' (Jas. 1.25; 2.12), clear allusions to the law associated with Leviticus 19.18, 'you shall love your neighbour as yourself', which Jesus expanded upon in Matthew 5.43–48. James also identifies Jesus as the lawgiver (Jas. 4.12) and also as the one divine judge (Jas. 4.12; 5.8–9).

Peter understood the Church through the lens of the cultic institutions of Exodus and the Isaianic new exodus. He urged members of the believing community to allow themselves to be built into a 'spiritual house' or temple built of 'living stones' (1 Pet. 2.4–5). Peter drew upon the prophetic imagery of Isaiah, who proclaimed that Zion would ultimately be re-established with a new 'foundation stone, a tested stone, a precious cornerstone, a sure foundation' (Isa. 28.16).[73] Those who belonged to this community would themselves comprise 'a holy priesthood' that would offer 'spiritual sacrifices acceptable to God through Jesus Christ' (1 Pet. 2.5). Peter identifies the Church as 'a chosen race, a royal priesthood, a holy nation, God's own people' (1 Pet. 2.9), all of which are terms originally used to describe Israel's identity as a covenant community (Exod. 19.6).

The epistles of John contain a number of allusions to Exodus and its themes. In a clear allusion to the 'teaching of Moses' (*sepher Moshe*), John referred to Jesus' teaching as the 'teaching of Christ' (2 John 9). Like Paul, John understood Jesus as the bringer of a 'new' or 'messianic' Torah. John stressed the need to follow his 'commandments' (1 John 2.3). This may be a reference to the love commandment, which Jesus enjoined upon his disciples at the Last Supper (John 13.34) and which is mentioned several times by John in his epistles.[74] John mentions other commandments, too, by which he may have meant to refer to Jesus' ethical teachings in the Sermon on the Mount.[75] He concluded his first epistle with an allusion to the second commandment's prohibition

---

71 For a detailed study of these five elements, see Gheorghita, 'περὶ τῆς ἐξόδου . . . ἐμνημόνευσεν', 160–86.

72 Quarles, 'Jesus as a teacher of new covenant torah', forthcoming.

73 See also 1 Cor. 3.16–17; 2 Cor. 6.16; Eph. 2.20–22; 1 Tim. 3.15; Heb. 3.6.

74 Cf. 1 John 2.7–8; 3.11–24; 4.7–21; 2 John 5–6.

75 Cf. 1 John 5.2–5; 2 John 6.

of idols (1 John 5.21). John did not just understand Jesus as a teacher of Torah, however, but he also understood his messianic role sacrificially. Specifically, he viewed Jesus' death as an 'atoning sacrifice' (1 John 2.2; 4.10).[76]

Jude saw the Old Testament as a lens through which to correctly view the present. In urging his readers to faithfulness, he used the punishment of the exodus generation as an example of how God punishes rebellious people (Jude 1.5).

Exodus in Revelation

The eschatological exodus is one of the major themes of the book of Revelation. While the theme appears in many parts of both the Old and New Testaments, Richard Bauckham argues that the idea is most fully developed in the book of Revelation.[77] The central image in John's portrayal of the new exodus is Jesus as the lamb (Rev. 5.6, 9–10). John's portrayal is clearly meant to identify Jesus with the lamb sacrificed at Passover, because he explains that Christ, by being 'slaughtered', 'ransomed for God saints from every tribe and language and people and nation' by his blood, and 'made them to be a kingdom and priests serving our God' (Rev. 5.6, 9–10). John's words unmistakably echo those of the Sinai covenant (Exod. 19.5–6), by which God made the Israelites his own people. He also referred to Jesus' saving work as 'ransoming' those whom God would save, using one of the Old Testament's favourite words for the exodus.[78] Bauckham suggests that the two witnesses in Revelation 11.1–14 are, at least in part, modelled on Moses and the plagues of Egypt. He also identifies the 'sea of glass' by which the Christian martyrs stand, victorious in heaven (Rev. 15.2–4), as a 'heavenly Red Sea, through which they have passed', and their song as a variation on the Song of Moses (Exod. 15). He understands the plagues that befall their enemies (Rev. 15.1, 5—16.21) as having been modelled on the plagues of Egypt, and the final judgement in the series (16.18) as modelled on the Sinai theophany. Bauckham concludes that:

> John's use of the new exodus imagery shows that for him the decisive eschatological event has already occurred: the new Passover Lamb has

---

76 See Paul A. Rainbow, *Johannine Theology: The Gospels, the epistles, and the Apocalypse* (Downers Grove, IL: IVP Academic, 2014), 207–8.

77 Richard Bauckham, *The Theology of the Book of Revelation* (Cambridge: Cambridge University Press, 1993), 71–2.

78 The exodus from Egypt is often referred to as a ransoming of the Israelites from slavery (e.g. Deut. 7.8; 13.5).

been slaughtered and he has ransomed a people for God. The goal of the new exodus is still to be attained, when Christ's people will reign with him as priests on earth (20:4–6; 22:3–5), attaining their theocratic independence in the promised land.[79]

One of the most significant aspects of John's revelation is his portrayal of the new heavens and the new earth (21.1—22.5). He saw 'the holy city, the new Jerusalem, coming down out of heaven from God, prepared as a bride adorned for her husband' (21.2). And then a voice from heaven pronounced, 'See, the home of God is among mortals. He will dwell with them; they will be his peoples, and God himself will be with them' (21.3). The words that the NRSV translates here as 'home' and 'dwell' could also be rendered as 'tabernacle'. This represents the realization of the ultimate goal of creation, that God would dwell in the midst of humankind and that humans would be in relationship with God. After humankind was driven out of the garden of Eden, cherubim with a flaming sword were placed at its eastern entrance (Gen. 3.24). There was now a rift between humans and God; they no longer had unfettered access to God. From that point forward, the biblical drama becomes a story of God seeking to re-establish his presence among human beings. He established his presence first at the tabernacle, then at the Temple and then in Jesus Christ (John 1.14). After the Ascension of Jesus, his presence took up residence in the believing community itself (Acts 2.1–4).[80] When John writes that God re-establishes his tabernacle in the world, he is saying that God has finally come to fully re-establish his presence in the midst of humankind. Mounce stresses that the metaphor of the tabernacle is not meant to suggest a temporary dwelling, but that, 'From this point on God remains with his people throughout eternity.'[81] John's vision is of the fulfilment of the eschatological exodus, when the enthronement of God in the midst of the people will ultimately be realized.[82]

Conclusions

In this chapter, we have seen that the book of Exodus and its themes and institutions shaped the theology of the New Testament authors. Ancient Israel's identity as God's 'firstborn son' (Exod. 4.22) provided the background for their

---

79   Bauckham, *Theology of the Book of Revelation*, 72.

80   Cf. also 1 Cor. 3.16–17, and the discussion of Pauline theology, above.

81   Robert H. Mounce, *The Book of Revelation* (NICNT; Grand Rapids, MI: Eerdmans, 1990), 372.

82   At the original exodus, the Song of Moses envisaged a procession to the holy city, where the LORD would be enthroned in his sanctuary (Exod. 15.18).

understanding of Jesus as God's Son. Their experience of salvation from the last plague in Egypt through the Passover served as the basis for their understanding of Jesus as the 'Lamb of God who takes away the sin of the world' (John 1.29). The exodus and Sinai covenant served as the model for the birth of the Church at Pentecost and the basis of its identity as the new covenant community. The establishment of a 'kingdom of priests' also served as the basis for a ministry to the nations in fulfilment of the original Abrahamic promises (Gen. 12.1–3).[83] Even while the authors of the New Testament believed that the new exodus had occurred in and through the work of Jesus Christ, they continued to use the original exodus in the same way that it was used in later periods of Old Testament history, 'as a paradigmatic teaching for present and future generations'.[84] The exodus provided the basis for their challenge to Christian communities to live lives worthy of their calling (e.g. 1 Cor. 10.1–21; 1 Pet. 2.9–10). And, in the end, it provides the model for an exodus still to come.[85]

---

83 Terence E. Fretheim, '"Because the whole earth is mine": theme and narrative in Exodus', *Int* 50.3 (1996), 229–39.

84 Michael Fishbane, 'The "exodus" motif/the paradigm of historical renewal', in *Text and Texture: A literary reading of selected texts*, ed. Michael Fishbane (Oxford: Oneworld, 1998), 121.

85 For a detailed summary of the impact of Exodus and its themes upon the New Testament, see Robin Routledge, 'The exodus and biblical theology', in *Reverberations* (ed. Fox), 187–209.

13

Echoes of Exodus in Western culture

As we have seen in the last two chapters, the book of Exodus had a major impact on the Old and New Testaments. Its influence, however, has gone far beyond the pages of the Bible. The book of Exodus has contributed to the formation of Western culture itself. Studying the Bible is 'a garden of delights' that allows us 'to expand the discipline of biblical studies to embrace a much wider world of biblical interpretation'.[1] In this chapter, we will expand our approach to include the reception history of Exodus in art, architecture, cinema, music and politics in order to explore its impact and appropriation in these fields.

Art

Throughout the ages, the people and events of Exodus have provided subject matter for many of the great artists of history. One of the most famous artworks inspired by Exodus is *Moses* by Michelangelo (1475–1564). Michelangelo lived and worked during the High Renaissance, a period between about 1495 and 1527 when Rome came to artistic pre-eminence. During this period, a series of powerful and ambitious popes created a papal state in Italy with Rome as its capital. These popes lived in the opulent splendour of secular princes, and they sought to embellish the city with great works of art. They commissioned artists from all over Italy to make great works of art, and thus made Italy at this time the artistic capital of Europe. Michelangelo saw himself first and foremost as a sculptor, a calling which he viewed as superior to painting, since he thought that the sculptor shared, to an extent, the divine power to create a human being. It was not that the artist was an actual creator, but that he or she rendered subjects that were found in the natural

---

1 Emma England and William John Lyons, 'Explorations in the reception of the Bible', in *Reception History and Biblical Studies: Theory and practice*, ed. Emma England and William John Lyons (LHB/OTS 615; London: Bloomsbury, 2015), 3.

world, which had been conceived by the divine mind and were therefore beautiful. The Renaissance theory of art, therefore, was to imitate the divine revelation hidden within nature, and the human form was typically glorified. Michelangelo was commissioned to design and sculpt the tomb of Julius II, and its sculpture of Moses captures the spirit of the entire project, which he completed in about 1513–15. The leader of Ancient Israel is rendered as a titan, carved in marble and measuring 2.5 metres (8 ft 4 in.) in height. Horns adorn his head, his muscles are tensed and his veins are swollen. He is seated, with the tablets of the law under one arm and with his other hand gripping the coils of his beard, which hang down to his waist. While his body appears relaxed, as if he may have been resting after having received the tablets of the law, it also seems as if he is about to move into action. His head is turned towards his left shoulder and, although he is seated, it is as if he is about to rise to his feet. He is lifting his right leg in front, while his left knee is bent below him, and both heels are off the ground, so that it appears he is pushing off with the balls of his feet. Gardner suggests that Michelangelo may have intended to portray Moses at the very moment when he heard the Israelites worshipping the golden calf at the foot of Mt Sinai. Michelangelo's rendering of Moses with a glorious physique, as well as his close attention to his personality and psychic state, are typical of the High Renaissance.[2]

In the Late Renaissance, there was a movement called 'Mannerism' that lasted from about 1520 to the end of the sixteenth century. The Mannerists carried the style of the artists of the High Renaissance even further, so that their forms appear exaggerated, distorted and even bizarre. During this period, Rosso Fiorentino (1494–1540) painted *Moses Defending the Daughters of Jethro*, which he portrayed as a titanic struggle. Moses and the other figures in this painting have the powerful musculature of Michelangelo's figures, but they are portrayed in violent athletic poses. While these pieces both draw on Exodus for their subject matter, they also reflect the humanistic values of the ages in which the artists lived and worked.

An entirely different use of Exodus themes can be found in Surrealism (*c*.1924–45), an artistic movement inspired by Sigmund Freud's theories of dreams and the unconscious. Surrealists created dreamlike imagery by juxtaposing unbelievable forms with incredible landscapes. Marc Chagall (1887–1985), who has been described as the quintessential Jewish artist of the twentieth century, was born in an obscure Russian village but went on

---

2   For discussion, see Fred S. Kleiner, *Gardner's Art through the Ages: A global history*, Vol. 2 (16th edn; Spartanburg, SC: Cengage Learning, 2018), 469–70.

to study and work in Paris, Berlin and New York. He often used the artistic theories and practices of the times to explore themes connected with the Jewish people. He spent more than ten years working on *Exodus* (1952–66), which portrays the seminal salvation event of Jewish history. The painting features a vast crowd of shtetl Jews streaming from the background to the foreground, led by Moses, standing at the bottom right, holding the Ten Commandments.[3] The crowd apparently represents both the Ancient Israelites on their way to the promised land and also shtetl Jews migrating to Israel throughout the Second World War up to the establishment of the State of Israel in 1948. The entire scene is presided over by Christ with his arms outstretched on the cross as if embracing the crowd. Interestingly, although Moses is painted in white, the crowd is made up of dark and muted colours, while the crucified Christ is strikingly yellow, which draws the viewers' eye to him as the central figure. The depiction of both the exodus and the crucifixion in this painting seem to suggest the importance of faith in a world beset by wars and pogroms, while the unexpected juxtaposition of Jewish and Christian images may imply a hope that divided humankind might somehow become one.

The biblical exodus continues to provide a lens for understanding other peoples' struggle for freedom. In 2002, Swiss artist Alain Foer produced a piece of computer-generated art entitled *Crossing the Red Sea*, which consists of a single line made up primarily of black men walking towards the viewer.[4] The marchers, most of whom are wearing placards hanging around their necks that read 'I AM A MAN', are walking from the centre background to the right foreground. Their march is taking place through a line of military vehicles on one side and a line of soldiers with bayonet-tipped weapons on the other. Scott Langston observes that 'the viewer's position virtually places him or her with the soldiers', so that he or she 'is challenged either to join the march for justice, or to take a place with those bearing weapons. There is no neutrality in this exodus.'[5]

The common factor in these four selections is that each of them reflects its milieu. Michelangelo's *Moses* and Fiorentino's *Moses Defending the Daughters of Jethro* both reflect the humanistic values of the High Renaissance and the Late Renaissance. Chagall's *Exodus* mirrors the hope and idealism of the

---

3 Ingo F. Walther, *Marc Chagall (1887–1985): Painting as poetry* (Düsseldorf: Benedikt Taschen, 1987), 80–3.

4 For a reproduction of the image, see Scott M. Langston, *Exodus through the Centuries* (Blackwell Bible Commentaries; Malden, MA: Blackwell, 2006), 158, pl. 13.

5 Langston, *Exodus through the Centuries*, 159.

post-war years. And Foer's *Crossing the Red Sea* echoes the longing for freedom of those oppressed by apartheid in South Africa. In each case, the artist did not restrict himself to the original meaning of Exodus, but adapted and shaped its message for his own time and circumstances. The art of these individuals reflected their own culture, rather than that of the author of Exodus.

Architecture

The tabernacle, to which so much of the book of Exodus is devoted, has had a major influence on the religious architecture of both Judaism and Christianity. In Judaism, the synagogue shares the basic design of the tabernacle. The origins of the synagogue are obscure, and have been sought in Babylon, Egypt and Israel, but may never be known. What is clear is that, by the Roman and Byzantine periods, it had become the religious, cultural and social centre of the Jewish community. More than a hundred have been excavated in Israel, and the Talmud reports that over 480 synagogues were located in Jerusalem alone at the time of the Jewish revolt. There were three main architectural types: (1) the broadhouse, a rectangular building with a niche built in its broad side, facing Jerusalem, and with its benches also positioned so that the congregation too would face the holy city; (2) the 'Galilean-type' basilica, which was rectangular, built with ashlar stones and paved with flagstones, and had entrances on the short side that faced Jerusalem but did not contain a fixed niche; and (3) longhouse basilicas, which were apsidal basilicas with an apse facing Jerusalem. There have been different opinions about the origin of these various designs but, until recently, the consensus has generally been that 'there is no evident uniformity among any of these synagogues regarding entrances, orientation, benches, main prayer hall, bema, or setting'.[6]

Recent research, however, has demonstrated that ancient synagogues share common features and appear to have been designed and built according to a shared pattern. According to the book of Exodus, that pattern was revealed from heaven (Exod. 25.8, 9, 40), and was followed first in the design and construction of the tabernacle and, subsequently, the First Temple.[7] In a recent monograph, John Wilkinson demonstrates that the synagogue

---

6   John McRay, *Archaeology and the New Testament* (Grand Rapids, MI: Baker, 1991), 72.

7   For the source-critical discussion about whether the tabernacle preceded the Temple or vice versa, see Chapter 8.

continued to follow this traditional design.[8] Just like the tabernacle and the Temple before it, the synagogue design was based on an imitation of the heavenly temple. The identification of the synagogue with the Temple continued to develop throughout antiquity and the medieval period.[9] By the third century AD, the cabinet that housed the Torah scroll had come to be called the Torah Ark, reminiscent of the ark of the covenant, and its curtain was called the *paroket*, which recalled the curtain in the Temple and the tabernacle before it.[10]

Like the synagogue, the earliest origins of Christian meetings places are unknown. Since Christianity was not a legal religion in the time of the early empire, Christians could not corporately own property and there was therefore no such thing as ecclesiastical architecture. New Testament references to early Christian worship indicate that it took place primarily in homes.[11] After Constantine (d. 337) had embraced and legalized Christianity, churches began to be built.[12] One of the first Christian church buildings was Old St Peter's in Rome, which was believed to be built over the place where Peter had been buried. It was a rectangular building oriented towards the east and was entered through a gateway building that led into an open, colonnaded court called an atrium, which led into an entrance hall called a narthex. Beyond the narthex was the body of the church, which consisted of the nave and low side aisles. At the end of the nave was a transverse aisle, or transept. At the end of the building, in the centre of the far wall of the transept, was the apse, a semicircular niche where the altar was located.

There has been much debate about the origins of the Christian basilica. It has conventionally been thought of as an adaptation of Roman public buildings of the same name, which served as law courts and commercial exchanges, with some features possibly derived from the Roman house and the chapels of the catacombs.[13] According to ancient documents, however, church design, like that of the synagogue, depended on the design of the heavenly temple.[14]

---

8 John Wilkinson, *From Synagogue to Church: The Traditional Design: Its beginning, its definition, its end* (London: Routledge, 2002).

9 Steven Fine and John David Brolley, 'Synagogue', *NIDB* 5:417–18.

10 See the entries on 'Ark', 'Parokhet' and 'Synagogue', in Ellen Frankel and Betsy Platkin Teutsch, *The Encyclopedia of Jewish Symbols* (Northvale, NJ: Jason Aronson, 1992), 12–13, 126, 167–8.

11 Wayne Meeks, *The First Urban Christians: The social world of the apostle Paul* (New Haven, CT: Yale University Press, 1983), 75–7.

12 The Edict of Milan, which gave the Church freedom of worship, was published in AD 312.

13 E.g. F. L. Cross and E. A. Livingstone, 'Basilica', in *The Oxford Dictionary of the Christian Church* (Oxford: Oxford University Press, 1983), 141.

14 Wilkinson, *From Synagogue to Church*, 1.

Churches were laid out according to the same rules, and the same proportions were used in the church building as in the synagogue. This conventional layout of both synagogues and churches starts from the earliest synagogue whose plan we can measure, and it continues, without exception, to churches that were built in AD 800. Wilkinson calls this layout 'the traditional design' and explains that it was intended to facilitate the imitation of the Temple in heaven.[15] In the same way that the tabernacle and the Temple had been the location of God's presence in Ancient Israel, so the Church was intended to be the locus of God's presence for the new Christian community.[16] Like their ancestors before them, when Jews and Christians gather in synagogues and churches for worship today, therefore, they are entering into structures built according to the 'pattern' of the heavenly Temple (Exod. 25.9).

Cinema

Films based on the book of Exodus face a number of challenges, two of which are how to tell one of the most important stories in Western culture and how to portray one of the most complex characters ever presented in literature. In addition to the challenges inherent in the subject matter, Michael Homan points out that there are also challenges associated with the audiences who will view the films and the producers who make them. Audiences who will watch a Bible film do not want to be surprised. He explains, 'They have preconceived ideas and want them reaffirmed, much the same as did theater audiences attending the religious dramas of ancient Greece', and so 'Moses is most often depicted in movies by duplicating safe and familiar images, such as Michelangelo's statue of Moses'.[17] As for the producers, they typically use the film to engage in 'heavy-handed moralizing of contemporary issues'.[18] In other words, the producer adapts the ancient story of the exodus so that it speaks to present-day problems. Since the advent of cinema, there have been five feature-length movies made about the exodus, of which we will consider three.

---

15 Wilkinson, *From Synagogue to Church*, 1–13.

16 Bert Daelemans discusses the relationship between the tabernacle, the Temple and the ecclesia. Cf. Bert Daelemans, *Spiritus Loci: A theological method for contemporary church architecture* (SRA 9; Leiden: Brill, 2015), 20–8.

17 Michael M. Homan, 'The Good Book and the bad movies: Moses and the failure of biblical cinema', in *Milk and Honey: Essays on Ancient Israel and the Bible in appreciation of the Judaic Studies program at the University of California, San Diego*, ed. Sara Malena and David Miano (Winona Lake, IN: Eisenbrauns, 2007), 89–90.

18 Homan, 'The Good Book and the bad movies', 91.

Cecil B. DeMille's 1956 version of *The Ten Commandments* is the most famous 'Bible epic'. It starred Charlton Heston as Moses and Yul Brynner as Ramesses, and used the story of the exodus primarily to address the issue of slavery. The film begins with an introduction, in which DeMille himself states that the theme of the production is the evils of slavery. At the end of the film, Moses tells the Israelites to 'go [and] proclaim liberty throughout all the land, and to all the inhabitants thereof'. Bruce Babington and Peter Evans observe that, in the final scene, where Moses is shown standing on the mountaintop holding his staff up with his right hand, he looks a lot like the Statue of Liberty.[19] Homan points to an exchange between Joshua and Moses to suggest that the film endorsed Martin Luther King's non-violent approach in the civil rights movement.[20] Joshua wanted to launch an insurrection against the Egyptians, but Moses insisted that God would deliver them by a shepherd's staff rather than a sword. The film also contained undertones of women's liberation, as well as subtle hints of its Christian character.

In 1999, DreamWorks released *The Prince of Egypt*, starring Val Kilmer as both Moses and God, and Ralph Fiennes as Ramesses. This was the first feature-length animated version of the exodus story, and the animation allowed not only for beautiful imagery, but also for some creative solutions to difficult problems that had stymied live versions, such as how to depict God. Like *The Ten Commandments*, *The Prince of Egypt* is also primarily about slavery, which is made explicit in Moses' insistence that, 'No kingdom should be built on the backs of slaves.' It also enhances the role of women, although it alters the biblical story in order to do so. In the film, Moses is accompanied by Zipporah rather than Aaron, who is reduced to a simpering weakling. The ten plagues are not a battle between the gods, but are about Egypt's 'contempt for life'. Interestingly, it is acceptable for the death plague to be levelled at Egypt because of its 'contempt for life', but not so that the Egyptians might know that the LORD is God. These alterations to the storyline are the result of the influence of modern culture, in which conflict over the superiority of the deity would not be considered acceptable, whereas conflict on behalf of the oppressed would be found agreeable. Homan observes that essentially 'all violence is removed from the story', and that 'even God "gets off the hook"' since he is 'forced to carry out the killing of the Egyptian firstborn because Ramesses himself ordered all Israelites dead'.[21]

---

19 Bruce Babington and Peter William Evans, *Biblical Epics: Sacred narrative in the Hollywood cinema* (Manchester: Manchester University Press, 1993), 10.

20 Homan, 'The Good Book and the bad movies', 102.

21 Homan, 'The Good Book and the bad movies', 111.

The most recent Exodus film is Ridley Scott's 2014 *Exodus: Gods and Kings*, starring Christian Bale as Moses and Joel Edgerton as Ramesses. This film is a return to the 'Bible epic' genre, and yet it breaks with previous Exodus movies in a number of important ways. It faced hostility before it was even released, due to Christian Bale's characterization of Moses as 'schizophrenic' and 'barbaric'.[22] It is also certainly 'the most violent Exodus ever filmed', and it 'reflects [Scott's] remaking of Moses as a kind of General Maximus [the hero of the 2000 film *Gladiator*]' as well as 'the evolution of violence in the American cinema since the biblical films of the fifties'.[23] Michelle Fletcher has also noted that the film has a strong resemblance to disaster films, which typically address contemporary audience concerns, such as overconfidence in technology, millennial fears and post-9/11 anxieties.[24]

Additional innovations in *Exodus: Gods and Kings* have to do with Scott's portrayal of God and of miracles. He portrays Moses' encounters with the divine as conversations with an 11-year-old boy, played by British actor Isaac Andrews. It is unclear, however, whether the boy is an angel, God himself or only a figment of Moses' imagination. In the end, while *Exodus: Gods and Kings* is a film in which God plays a central role, it is ultimately non-committal about whether or not he even exists.[25] Another question that arises from the portrayal of the divine as an 11-year-old child has to do with the nature and character of God, whether the film intends to portray God as innocent and benevolent or impudent and impulsive.[26] With regard to the miracles of Exodus, Scott portrays them as natural occurrences. Cheryl Exum suggests that this strategy is inevitable in any modern version of the biblical story, since 'it is more intelligible to modern audiences in terms of our attitudes and values and assumptions about the way the world works and the way people behave'.[27]

In these examples, although the films are based on the Bible, they are also artistic statements, reflections of popular culture and expressions of reception history.

---

22 David Tollerton, '"Hmmm . . . but LOVED the plagues": on engaging with Ridley Scott's epic and its audiences', in *Biblical Reception 4: A New Hollywood Moses: On the spectacle and reception of Exodus: Gods and Kings*, ed. David Tollerton (London: Bloomsbury, 2017), 4.

23 David Shepherd, '"See this great sight"': Ridley Scott's *Exodus: Gods and Kings* and the evolution of biblical spectacle in the cinema', in *Biblical Reception 4*, ed. David Tollerton (London: Bloomsbury, 2017), 79–80.

24 Michelle Fletcher, 'Once upon an apocalypse: exodus, disaster, and a long, long time ago?' Pp. 91–112 in *Biblical Reception 4* ed. Tollerton), 91–112.

25 Matthew A. Collins, 'Depicting the divine: the ambiguity of Exodus 3 in *Exodus: Gods and Kings*', in *Biblical Reception 4* (ed. Tollerton), 34.

26 Collins, 'Depicting the divine', 35–7.

27 J. Cheryl Exum, 'Exodus: male gods and kings', in *Biblical Reception 4* (ed. Tollerton), 46.

Music

The impact of Exodus on music has been far reaching, with musical treatments ranging from antiquity to modern times.[28] In the eighteenth century, the exodus appeared most frequently in oratorios and musical dramas about Moses. The most important musical treatment of God's saving deeds in the exodus, according to Jan Assmann, is George Frideric Handel's oratorio *Israel in Egypt* (1738).[29] In October of that year, he had finished the score of *Saul*, 'a work of epochal significance not just in the life of its composer but in the history of music itself'.[30] *Saul* is a dramatic oratorio, which was a completely new form of musical theatre. It was 'a unique masterpiece that became acknowledged as the unsurpassed model for the new genre', and it 'set the course for the following decades of his composing career'.[31] Handel began work on *Israel in Egypt* only four days after completing *Saul*, and completed it in just one month, between 1 October and 1 November.

Israel in Egypt is composed entirely of selected passages from the Old Testament, mainly from Exodus and the Psalms. Handel originally composed it in three parts, the first of which consisted of a lament over the death of Joseph. The opening performance was poorly received, probably because London audiences were not used to such extended choral arrangements, and probably also because Part 1, which was a dirge, was about half an hour long. Handel quickly revised the work by removing the opening 'Lamentations' section and adding Italian-style arias like the ones that contemporary audiences were used to and enjoyed. In its revised form, *Israel in Egypt* was a great success. Today, many performances of the work use the original three-part version. In Part 1, which is set long before the events in Exodus, the Israelites mourn the death of Joseph, who had risen to high office in Egypt after having been sold into slavery by his brothers. Part 2 presents the narrative of the exodus. It begins with an announcement that a new pharaoh has come to the throne who does not remember Joseph, and proceeds with God's call to Moses to lead his people out of bondage. The ten plagues are recounted, after which Pharaoh finally agrees to let the Israelites go. After they leave, however, he changes his mind and pursues them. The waters of the Red Sea are miraculously parted so that the Israelites

---

28 Cf. the indexes in Siobhán Dowling Long and John F. A. Sawyer, *The Bible in Music: A dictionary of songs, works, and more* (Lanham, MD: Rowman & Littlefield, 2015).

29 Jan Assmann, *The Invention of Religion: Faith and covenant in the book of Exodus*, trans. Robert Savage (Princeton, NJ: Princeton University Press, 2018), 176.

30 Assmann, *Invention of Religion*, 174.

31 Assmann, *Invention of Religion*, 174.

can safely cross, but they return and engulf the Egyptians. In Part 3, the Israelites celebrate their deliverance with a series of joyful choruses. This piece concludes with a soprano solo and chorus proclaiming that 'the Lord shall reign for ever and ever' and 'the horse and his rider hath he thrown into the sea'.

Assmann calls attention to the circumstances in which Handel composed *Israel in Egypt*. He points out that the oratorio's protagonist is the people of Israel and that, since the Puritan Revolution, England had traced its descent from Ancient Israel and the people of the exodus. He notes that in 1738, England had not yet achieved any victories in its war with Spain, and he suggests that Handel used the exodus to appeal to the people of England in the same way that the biblical prophets used it to appeal to Ancient Israel and Judah. He wanted them to 'take courage from the example of Israel's delivery from Egypt and England's own delivery from the Spanish armada in 1588'.[32]

In churches, music had been entirely in the hands of the choir since about the eighth century, and it was not until the sixteenth century that hymns were sung by the entire congregation. Martin Luther was instrumental in this process, and his first spiritual song, which he wrote in 1523, triggered the writing of hymns throughout Germany and in other countries, ushering in a golden age of hymn writing. In the ensuing centuries, scores of hymns were written, and many echoed the book of Exodus. In 1779, for example, John Newton wrote 'Glorious Things of Thee Are Spoken', which is about the universal Church and its story. The first two verses contain a vision of the new city of God (Heb. 12.22), and then the third verse looks back upon the early journey of the Israelites after the exodus, with reference to the pillar of cloud by day and of fire by night, as well as the provision of the manna in the wilderness (Exod. 13.21; 16.31). It reads:

> Round each habitation hov'ring,
> See the cloud and fire appear,
> For a glory and a cov'ring,
> Showing that the Lord is near;
> Thus deriving from our banner
> Light by night and shade by day,
> Safe they feed upon the manna
> Which He gives them when they pray.[33]

---

32   Assmann, *Invention of Religion*, 178.

33   John Newton, 'Glorious Things of Thee Are Spoken', *The United Methodist Hymnal* (Nashville, TN: The United Methodist Publishing House, 1989), no. 731.

This verse in particular draws upon Exodus to remind worshippers of God's presence, protection and provision.

In 1859, John Mason Neale published a translation of a hymn originally written in Greek by the last of the church fathers, John of Damascus (d. 749), in which he used the exodus as a paradigm for the salvation of Christ. The first verse extols God for the salvation he brought about in the exodus:

> Come, ye faithful, raise the strain
> Of triumphant gladness;
> God hath brought forth Israel
> Into joy from sadness;
> Loosed from Pharaoh's bitter yoke
> Jacob's sons and daughters,
> Led them with unmoistened foot
> Through the Red Sea waters.[34]

This verse calls attention to the biblical claim that the Israelites crossed the Red Sea on dry ground (Exod. 14.21–22), which heightened the miracle. Not only did the Israelites cross the Red Sea, but they did not even get their feet wet. The subsequent verses build on this miraculous display of God's power to extol the majesty of what he later did in Christ.

Exodus continues to provide inspiration for hymn writers up to the present time. In 1979, for example, Father Jan Michael Joncas (b. 1951), a liturgical theologian and composer of contemporary Catholic music, published 'On Eagle's Wings', a devotional hymn based on Psalm 91, Exodus 19.4 and Matthew 13. The song as a whole praises God for his providential protection, and the lines based on Exodus 19.4 apply God's miraculous protection in the exodus to the worshipper:

> And He will raise you up on eagles' wings
> Bear you on the breath of dawn
> Make you to shine like the sun
> And hold you in the palm of God's hand.[35]

---

34 John of Damascus, 'Come, Ye Faithful, Raise the Strain', trans. John Mason Neale, *United Methodist Hymnal*, no. 315.

35 Michael Joncas, 'On Eagle's Wings', *United Methodist Hymnal*, no. 143.

The hymn is widely used as a contemplative hymn at Catholic masses and in mainline Protestant and Evangelical services as well. It was sung at many of the funerals of victims of the September 11, 2001 terrorist attack on the Twin Towers, and was performed during the 2007 funeral mass for Luciano Pavarotti in Modena, Italy. Through this hymn, the message of God's provision in the exodus continues to be shared with contemporary audiences.

Politics

The Old Testament had a tremendous influence on the thought of America's founders. It was cited more often than any other book during the founding era, even more than the French political philosopher Montesquieu or the Roman statesmen Cato or Plutarch.[36] The American political tradition is deeply indebted to the Old Testament. Of all the portions of the Old Testament canon, the Pentateuch was most important and, of the Pentateuchal books, Exodus and Deuteronomy were cited the most. These books contained three key features that shaped early American political thought, including: (1) the idea of election, that God had chosen the people of America to advance his plan to redeem the world; (2) the narrative of the exodus; and (3) the idea of covenant. These three elements contributed to the self-understanding of most of the founders, even those who were not theists.

Modern Western political thought, however, can be traced back long before the founding of America. It owes much of its emphasis on religious liberty to the Protestant Reformation. Reformation thinkers such as Martin Luther and John Calvin believed that liberty of conscience is a hallmark of Christ's spiritual government, while civil government remains part of God's providential design for humanity to facilitate a functional and just society. The interplay of these two governments in Reformation theology has helped shape the modern idea of self-government.[37] The Protestant Reformation led to a great war in England between the Reformers and the Church of England. One sect of the reformers in England was called the Puritans, who thought of themselves as the elect people of God, like the Ancient Israelites, chosen to further God's plan for the world. When the *Mayflower* set out across the Atlantic to the New World, about half of its passengers were Protestant

---

36 Donald Lutz, 'The relative influence of European writers on late eighteenth-century American political thought', *American Political Science Review* 78 (1984): 189–97.

37 See, e.g., Matthew J. Tuininga, *Calvin's Political Theology and the Public Engagement of the Church: Christ's two kingdoms* (Cambridge: Cambridge University Press, 2017); John Witte Jr, *God's Joust, God's Justice: Law and religion in the Western tradition* (Grand Rapids, MI: Eerdmans, 2006), 1–62.

dissenters. William Bradford, a pilgrim aboard the *Mayflower* and the leader of the first colony, viewed their journey as a re-enactment of the exodus. They drafted the Mayflower Compact (1620) as a covenant that would commit them and their descendants to God's mission for the founding of the colonies. The ideas enshrined in it would develop into the concept of American exceptionalism, which is the idea that the United States has a unique role to play on the world stage. Another important Puritan leader was John Winthrop (1587–1649) who, in order to contribute to the colonizing of the New World, helped to establish the Massachusetts Bay Colony and became its governor. The influential American Puritan minister, Cotton Mather, wrote a biography of Winthrop in which he compared him to Moses.[38] This biography was part of a larger work, entitled *Magnalia Christi Americana*, or The Great Works of Christ in America, in which he portrayed the history of the United States as a re-enactment of the history of Ancient Israel. Mather's preaching and writing was a major contributor to the development of the mythology of America as a new Israel.

As the colonies were established, their laws were shaped by those of Exodus. For example, the legal code originally entitled 'Abstract of the laws of New England', written by John Cotton (1585–1682), cited the Ten Commandments as perpetual laws. Cotton also devoted a paragraph to explaining why the Ten Commandments remained binding. John Winthrop referred to Cotton's laws as 'Moses his judicials'. In another example, the New Haven Legal Code (1656) was based on 'Moses his judicials' and contained numerous biblical citations, including several from the book of Exodus.

Another major Puritan was Jonathan Edwards (1703–58), America's most important early theologian. In 'Some thoughts concerning the present revival of religion in New England' (1742), he explained that the work of God in the latter days would begin in America. His *Miscellanies* (1722), which are made up of personal notebooks in which he wrote on all kinds of topics, make it clear that he understood America to be the new Israel.

Exodus and its themes continued to play a significant role during the Revolutionary period. Thomas Paine (1737–1809) drew heavily on the Hebraic republican tradition in his pro-Revolutionary pamphlets *Common Sense* (1776) and the seventh issue of *The American Crisis* (1776–83), in which he argued for individual liberties, the illegitimacy of monarchy, and government

---

38 Cotton Mather, *Magnalia Christi Americana*, Books 1 and 2, ed. Kenneth B. Murdock (Cambridge, MA: Harvard University Press, 1977), 213–28.

by the people and for the people.[39] After the Declaration of Independence was adopted on 4 July 1776, and a committee was formed to design a national seal, Thomas Jefferson and Benjamin Franklin both drew on the book of Exodus in their proposals for its design. Jefferson proposed an image of the Israelites in the wilderness being led by a cloud by day and a pillar of fire by night (Exod. 13.18–22), while Franklin suggested an image of Moses at the Red Sea raising his staff, with the sea overwhelming Pharaoh, who is seated in an open chariot with a crown on his head and a sword in his hand (Exod. 14.21–29). Franklin's proposal also included rays from a pillar of fire in the clouds reaching down to Moses, in order to convey the idea that he was following God's direction. In one of the most popular sermons of the Revolutionary period, 'The Church's flight from the wilderness' (1776), Samuel Sherwood identified Americans as God's chosen people, who were inheriting their country in fulfilment of God's promises to Israel in Exodus 19.3–6.

In the early Republic, Exodus was frequently cited as providing the basis for many American ideals. For example, when Thomas Jefferson (1743–1826) drafted the Virginia Statute of Religious Freedom (1777), he appears to have based it, in part, on Exodus 23.2, which teaches that people must be at liberty to make their own decisions and not be influenced or forced by others, especially by those in positions of power. In his address on 'The perpetuation of our political institutions' to the Young Men's Lyceum of Springfield, Illinois (27 January 1838), Abraham Lincoln (1809–65) clearly echoed the covenant ratification ceremony of Exodus 24.1–8 when he called upon his listeners to swear to remember and uphold American law. He urged:

> Let every American, every lover of liberty, every well wisher to his posterity, swear by the blood of the Revolution, never to violate in the least particular, the laws of the country; and never to tolerate their violation by others.

He went on to insist that reverence for America's laws should be

> taught in schools, in seminaries, and in colleges; let it be written in Primers, spelling books, and in Almanacs; let it be preached from the pulpit, proclaimed in legislative halls, and enforced in courts of justice.

---

39 Cf. Nathan Perl-Rosenthal, 'The "divine right of republics": Hebraic republicanism and the debate over kingless government in Revolutionary America', *The William and Mary Quarterly*, 3rd series, 66.3 (2009): 535–64.

And, in short, let it become the political religion of the nation; and let the old and the young, the rich and the poor, the grave and the gay, of all sexes and tongues, and colors and conditions, sacrifice unceasingly upon its altars.[40]

In the same way that the covenant and its laws had bound the Ancient Israelite people into a nation, Lincoln believed that America's laws would provide the glue for its national fabric.

In the era of slavery, abolitionism and the American Civil War, Exodus and its themes continued to play a significant role. Albert Raboteau explains that the story of the exodus held special meaning for slaves themselves:

The story of Exodus contradicted the claim made by defenders of slavery that God intended Africans to be slaves. On the contrary, Exodus proved that slavery was against God's will and that slavery would end someday. The where and the how remained hidden in divine providence, but the promise of deliverance was certain. Moreover, the notion that blacks were inferior to whites was disproved by Exodus, which taught the slaves that they, like the Israelites of old, were a special people, chosen by God for deliverance.[41]

These sentiments were explained by a slave named Polly to her mistress:

We poor creatures have need to believe in God, for if God Almighty will not be good to us some day, why were we born? When I heard of his delivering his people from bondage I know it means the poor African.[42]

On 2 March 1807, the US Congress passed a federal law prohibiting the importation of new slaves into the United States. The law took effect on 1 January 1808 and, on that very day, the Revd Absalom Jones, America's first black priest, preached a Thanksgiving sermon commemorating its passage. In his sermon, Jones compared the enslavement of the Ancient Israelites with that

---

40 Abraham Lincoln, 'The perpetuation of our political institutions: address before the Young Men's Lyceum of Springfield, Illinois (January 27, 1838)', in *The Collected Works of Abraham Lincoln*, ed. Roy P. Basler, 9 vols (New Brunswick, NJ: Rutgers University Press, 1953), <http://abrahamlincolnonline.org/lincoln/speeches/lyceum.htm>.

41 Albert J. Raboteau, *Canaan Land: A religious history of African Americans* (New York, NY: Oxford University Press, 2001), 44.

42 Cf. Raboteau, *Canaan Land*, 44.

of African Americans. He proclaimed that, just as God had 'come down to deliver' the Ancient Israelites from the Egyptians (Exod. 3.8), so he had 'come down' to deliver Africans from their modern-day enslavement. Throughout his sermon, he repeated the Exodus refrain, proclaiming that God 'came down into the United States'; he 'came down into the British Parliament'; and he 'came down into the Congress of the United States'.[43] Despite the passage of this federal law, however, Africans who were already enslaved in America remained so.

In the continuing debate over slavery, both those for and against it sought to draft the Bible in their cause. However, it was very easy for pro-slavery interpreters to use Scripture to justify slavery, since it was an institution that was practised in both the Old and New Testaments, and there are no explicit condemnations of it. For example, Dr M. J. Raphall, a New York rabbi, presented a sermon entitled 'The Bible view of slavery' (1861), in which he made extensive use of Scripture to justify slavery. Among many other texts, he used passages from Exodus 20, 21 and 22 to argue that, while slaves were human persons who should be treated with dignity, slavery as an institution was legal and just. There were also abolitionists who made good use of Scripture in arguing against slavery, such as Dr Benjamin Rush (1746–1813), an early abolitionist, who had argued that slavery was immoral and went against Christianity. In 'An address to the inhabitants of the British settlements in America upon slave keeping' (1773), he alluded to a number of texts from the Pentateuch, including Exodus 21 and 34, in order to argue that slaveholding in Ancient Israel was for specific and limited purposes and that, with the advent of Christianity, it was no longer permissible. In the antebellum South, however, anti-slavery literature has generally been characterized as biblically weak.[44]

Recently, Jack Davidson has restored a previously unpublished manuscript of Eli Caruthers, a Presbyterian minister in Greensboro, North Carolina, in the 1860s, entitled 'American slavery and the immediate duty of southern slaveholders'. The 400-page book was based on Exodus 10.3, in which God commanded the pharaoh of the Israelite oppression to 'Let my people go that they may serve me' (KJV).[45] Caruthers' argument was that God's command to Pharaoh to let his people go was based on creation, and that

---

43 See the excerpt in Raboteau, *Canaan Land*, 40–1.

44 Cf. the criticisms in Mark Noll, *America's God: From Jonathan Edwards to Abraham Lincoln* (Oxford: Oxford University Press, 2002), 413–17.

45 The manuscript has recently been published. Cf. Jack R. Davidson, *American Slavery and the Immediate Duty of Southern Slaveholders: A transcription of Eli Washington Caruthers's unpublished manuscript against slavery* (Eugene, OR: Pickwick, 2018), 15–16.

if the creator has made humanity 'of one blood' then 'for one to compel others to serve him all their life without compensation, and to entail that compulsory service upon his unborn posterity, is unjust, inhumane and criminal before high heaven'.[46]

On these principles, Caruthers argued that Exodus 10.3 'applies to all situations of similar circumstances in the created order'.[47] He compared American slaveholders to the pharaoh of the Israelite oppression, who were committing crimes against God through their slaveholding. Davidson summarizes Caruthers' argument that, 'Slavery violates God's ongoing relationship with creation because it interprets perceived differences between ethnic groups for the purpose of exploitation, undermining the unity and equality of humanity established at creation.'[48] Since, in Caruthers' thinking, the claim of the Exodus text applies to all nations, then the enslaved Africans in God's eyes were just as much 'my people' as were the Ancient Israelites and deserved to be completely liberated from their slavery. He concludes that 'the enslavement of Africans, or any nation, is a violation of the Exodus text and in defiance of the creator's claim'.[49] Jack Davidson explains that 'Caruthers's manuscript is unusual for a nineteenth-century document of southern origin because it presents a scripturally based argument against slavery'.[50] When it was discovered in 1898, the eminent American historian John Spencer Bassett (1867–1928) proclaimed that 'it is doubtful if a stronger or clearer anti-slavery argument was ever made on this continent'.[51] The rediscovery of Caruthers' manuscript provides some correction for the common misconception that those who defended Scripture in antebellum America were always pro-slavery, while those who were anti-slavery were those who championed the Enlightenment or the Declaration of Independence. In the light of Caruthers' manuscript, this view is obviously a stereotype.

In any case, the experience of African Americans in this period was vastly different from that of the Puritans, who identified America with the promised land and themselves with the chosen people. African Americans did not

---

46 Jack R. Davidson, *Still Letting My People Go: An analysis of Eli Washington Caruthers's manuscript against American slavery and its universal application of Exodus 10:3* (Eugene, OR: Pickwick, 2018).

47 Davidson, *Still Letting My People Go*, 16–17.

48 Davidson, *Still Letting My People Go*, 18.

49 Davidson, *Still Letting My People Go*, 32.

50 Davidson, *Still Letting My People Go*, 2.

51 John Spencer Bassett, *Antislavery Leaders of North Carolina* (Baltimore, MD: Johns Hopkins University Press, 1898), 60. Cited in Davidson, *Still Letting My People Go*, 2.

conceive of America this way, nor did they see themselves as a chosen people. For them, America was a place of bondage. During the period of slavery and abolitionism, singing was one of the ways that slaves sought to cope with their bondage. In their singing, 'black people "Africanized" Christianity in America as they sought to find meaning in the turn of events that made them involuntary residents in a strange and hostile land'.[52] Naturally, because of their experience of bondage, the story of the exodus particularly resonated with them and is featured in many of their hymns. One of the most important African spirituals is 'O Mary, Don't You Weep', a 'slave song' that originated before the civil war. In it, Mary of Bethany weeps over the death of her brother Lazarus (John 11.32–33) and is consoled with a reminder that God defeated Pharaoh at the Red Sea. The chorus reads:

> O Mary, don't you weep, don't you mourn,
> O Mary, don't you weep, don't you mourn;
> Pharaoh's army got drown-ded,
> O Mary, don't you weep.[53]

Another song that was important during this period was 'Go Down, Moses', which is based on God's call to Moses to go to Pharaoh and command him to let God's people go, so that they might serve him (Exod. 4.21–23; 5.1–3):

> When Israel was in Egypt's land,
> let my people go;
> oppressed so hard they could not stand,
> let my people go.
>
> Refrain:
> Go down, Moses,
> way down in Egypt's land;
> tell old Pharaoh
> to let my people go!
>
> 'Thus saith the Lord,' bold Moses said,
> let my people go;

---

52 C. Eric Lincoln and Lawrence H. Mamiya, *The Black Church in the African American Experience* (Durham, NC and London: Duke University Press, 1990), 348.

53 Unknown, 'O Mary, Don't You Weep', *United Methodist Hymnal*, no. 134.

'if not, I'll smite your firstborn dead,'
let my people go.

No more shall they in bondage toil,
let my people go;
let them come out with Egypt's spoil,
let my people go.

We need not always weep and mourn,
let my people go;
and wear those slavery chains forlorn,
let my people go.

Come, Moses, you will not get lost,
let my people go;
stretch out your rod and come across,
let my people go.[54]

Harriet Tubman, who began her Underground Railroad work in 1850, is said to have sung this song to signal slaves that she was in the area in order to help them escape. She herself was referred to as 'Moses', since she led escaped slaves to freedom.

During the civil war, leaders of both the Union and the Confederacy appealed to Scripture to support their cause. One of the most famous preachers of the day was Henry Ward Beecher (1813–87), pastor of Plymouth Church in Brooklyn. At the outset of the civil war, during the battle of Fort Sumter, Beecher preached a sermon entitled 'The battle set in array' (1861), in which he urged his audience to support the Union's cause. For his sermon text, he used Exodus 14.15, in which the LORD said to Moses, 'Why do you cry out to me? Tell the Israelites to go forward.' The Israelites had been liberated from Egypt in the exodus but, once the pharaoh and his army had begun to pursue them, they regretted having left Egypt and wanted to return to slavery (Exod. 14.10–12). It was at this point that the LORD told Moses to tell the Israelites that they ought to go forward. Similarly, Beecher's audience should make a stalwart commitment to fight to preserve the union.

Early in the civil war, Oliver Wendell Holmes Jr (1841–1935), who went on to become one of the most famous justices of the US Supreme Court, joined

54 Unknown, 'Go Down, Moses', *United Methodist Hymnal*, no. 448.

the Union army. At the beginning of his service, he wrote a poem entitled 'Canaan' (1862) in which he waxed eloquent about the justness of the northern cause. In the fourth stanza, he referred to the Song of Moses (Exod. 15.1–18):

What song is this you're singing?
The same that Israel sung
When Moses led the mighty choir,
And Miriam's timbrel rung!
To Canaan! To Canaan!
The priests and maidens cried:
To Canaan! To Canaan!
The people's voice replied.
To Canaan, to Canaan,
The Lord has led us forth,
To thunder through the adder dens
The anthems of the North.

At the height of the war, on Thursday, 19 November 1863, Abraham Lincoln delivered the Gettysburg Address at the dedication of the Soldiers' National Cemetery in Gettysburg, Pennsylvania. Four and a half months earlier, the Union armies had defeated Confederate troops at the battle of Gettysburg, a conflict that left about 3,155 dead and 14,529 wounded. Although his remarks were very brief, with only 271 words, Lincoln's Gettysburg Address has come to be viewed as one of the most powerful and influential articulations of American national purpose. He began by referring back to the signing of the Declaration of Independence, 'Four score and seven years ago', when the founders had 'brought forth on this continent a new nation, conceived in Liberty, and dedicated to the proposition that all men are created equal'. He described the civil war as a test that would determine 'whether that nation, or any nation so conceived and so dedicated, can long endure'. He ended by saying that those who had fought and died on the battlefield at Gettysburg had done so in order 'that this nation, under God, shall have a new birth of freedom – and that government of the people, by the people, for the people, shall not perish from the earth'. Although Lincoln did not specifically refer to the book of Exodus in his address, his references to individual freedom and the right to self-government and representative government certainly echo Pentateuchal instructions about representative government (Exod. 18) and limitations on the executive branch (Deut. 17.14–20).[55]

---

55 For the establishment of the early Israelite judiciary, see the discussion of 'Jethro' in Chapter 10.

After the civil war, the book of Exodus and its themes resonated most prominently in the African American community, and especially in the civil rights movement. The songs, sermons and speeches of the civil rights movement often portrayed the struggle of black Americans as parallel to that of the Ancient Israelites, who longed to escape the bondage of Egypt and enter a promised land of freedom. Among the songs of the civil rights movement, 'Come and Go with Me to That Land', for example, clearly evoked the exodus and applied it to the struggle of African Americans. Its verses sang about a land where there were no Jim Crow laws, no burning churches, but instead singing and freedom. It was a land where there would be no Chief Pritchett, African Americans would be free, all would be well, there would be peace, and there would be no more weeping, crying or bowing. The chorus invited everyone to join in the journey to that land.[56] A similar hymn, entitled 'I'm on My Way to the Freedom Land', emphasized the determination to reach the promised land of freedom.[57] Another example was a hymn entitled 'Been Down in the South', which praised God for freedom after having experienced life in the southern states.[58] The ninth verse exclaims, 'The only thing that we did wrong [was that we] stayed in the wilderness a day too long.' This song clearly draws on exodus imagery, with the South representing Egypt, and staying in the wilderness too long is a reference to the wilderness wanderings, when the Ancient Israelites failed to come out of the wilderness and enter the promised land. These songs, and others like them, provided essential fuel that sustained the civil rights movement. 'The freedom songs', Lincoln and Mamiya explain, 'did not passively lament the black condition; they made God active in human history day by day with social agitation.'[59] Many of them did this by appropriating the exodus and applying it to the contemporary struggle for freedom.

Since Emancipation (1863), African Americans have read the story of the exodus as the story of their own deliverance from bondage, and it rose to the forefront especially during the civil rights movement. The greatest leader of the civil rights movement was Martin Luther King Jr, who

adopted a series of biblical personae, masks, that captured the several roles he understood himself to be playing in American life. These roles

---

56 Guy and Candie Carawan, eds, *Sing for Freedom: The story of the civil rights movement through its songs* (Montgomery, AL: NewSouth Books, 2007), 55.

57 Carawan, *Sing for Freedom*, 62–3.

58 Carawan, *Sing for Freedom*, 80–1.

59 Lincoln and Mamiya, *Black Church*, 373.

coincided . . . with the most profound expectations that America, 'the nation with a soul of a church,' lays upon its public servants.[60]

Richard Lischer explains that King 'not only wore these masks but also spent his life in an effort to live into them', and 'They became his truest self'.[61] One of these roles was that of the 'prophet like Moses' (Deut. 18.15–18), which shaped not only King's preaching, but his very identity. Like Moses, King sought to mediate a religious covenant with the American people. Like the prophets, he perceived the true nature of the evil around him, proclaimed it to the people and urged them to change course. Like the prophets, he debunked the nation's false religiosity. And, like the prophets, he engaged in symbolic actions that were powerful signs of what God was doing in the world. 'A festive parade of thousands along a state highway', for example, 'symbolized the Exodus from Egypt'.[62] King's use of Exodus and its themes was not limited to his preaching and speaking, but shaped his whole approach to leadership in the civil rights movement.

King certainly did appeal to exodus imagery in his speaking. Ironically, however, as the historian James Smylie has observed, he rarely alluded to the Exodus narrative in his formal writings.[63] This was probably because he understood that his messages were addressed to the whole nation, and so he sought 'to identify the Movement with mainstream Western values, thereby creating a symbolic consensus between white and black people of good will'.[64] Lischer also points out that, even when the exodus and associated themes are not mentioned, many of King's sermons and addresses 'either presuppose an Exodus framework or make allusions to the narrative'.[65] Lischer lists a number of King's sermons that work from an Exodus framework, including 'A Christian movement in a revolutionary age', 'The birth of a new nation', 'Desirability of being maladjusted', 'The meaning of hope' and his finale, 'I see the promised land'.[66]

Several of King's sermons and writings, however, did draw directly on imagery from the book of Exodus. For example, in 'The death of evil upon the

---

60 Cf. Richard Lischer, *The Preacher King: Martin Luther King, Jr. and the word that moved America* (New York, NY: Oxford University Press, 1995), 172–3.

61 Lischer, *Preacher King*, 173.

62 Lischer, *Preacher King*, 197.

63 Cf. James H. Smylie, 'On Jesus, pharaohs, and the chosen people: Martin Luther King as biblical interpreter and humanist', *Int* 24 (January 1970): 74–91.

64 Lischer, *Preacher King*, 180.

65 Lischer, *Preacher King*, 211.

66 Lischer, *Preacher King*, 211.

seashore', he used Exodus 14.30, in which the Israelites are said to have seen the Egyptians lying dead upon the seashore, as a sermon text. In this sermon, King used the defeat of the Egyptians at the Red Sea as an illustration of the truth that evil would ultimately fall before God.[67] In his 1958 book, *Stride Toward Freedom*, which became the handbook of the civil rights movement, King used Exodus 16.1–3 to address the ordeals of emancipation. This passage recounts how, once the Israelites had left Mt Sinai and gone out into the wilderness, they complained against Moses and Aaron. They lamented:

> If only we had died by the hand of the LORD in the land of Egypt, when we sat by the fleshpots and ate our fill of bread; for you have brought us out into this wilderness to kill this whole assembly with hunger. (Exod. 16.3)

King explained that slaves can 'become accustomed to being slaves' and that they 'do not always welcome their deliverers'. Sometimes, slaves 'prefer the "fleshpots of Egypt" to the ordeals of emancipation'.[68] He compared the apathy of some of the Israelites of the exodus generation to that of some African Americans to the civil rights movement, but replied that returning to Egypt was 'not the way out', and 'to accept passively an unjust system is to cooperate with that system'.[69] In the same way that Moses urged the beleaguered Israelites to 'go forward' (Exod. 14.15), King encouraged all African Americans to take their part in the struggle for freedom. King used a modified version of this illustration in 'A tough mind and a tender heart', when he said that there were 'softminded individuals among us [who] feel that the only way to deal with oppression is by adjusting to it. They acquiesce and resign themselves to segregation.'[70] In this sermon, he called 'softminded acquiescence' 'cowardly' and argued that 'we cannot win the respect of the white people of the South or elsewhere if we are willing to trade the future of our children for our personal safety and comfort'. Furthermore, he insisted, 'we must learn that passively to accept an unjust system is to co-operate with that system, and thereby to become a participant in its evil'.[71]

---

67 Martin Luther King Jr, 'The death of evil upon the seashore', *Strength to Love* (Philadelphia, PA: Fortress Press, 1981; repr. Cleveland, OH: Collins & World, 1977), 77–86.

68 Martin Luther King Jr, '*Stride Toward Freedom* (1958)', in *A Testament of Hope: The essential writings of Martin Luther King, Jr.*, ed. James M. Washington (New York, NY: HarperCollins, 1986), 482.

69 King, '*Stride Toward Freedom* (1958)', 482.

70 Martin Luther King Jr, 'A tough mind and a tender heart', *Strength to Love*, 18.

71 King, 'A tough mind and a tender heart', 18.

In King's final sermon, 'I see the promised land', which he delivered at the Mason Temple in Memphis, Tennessee, on 3 April 1968, he alluded to the exodus at both the beginning and the end of the sermon. He began by noting that, if he could travel anywhere, he would go 'across the Red Sea, through the wilderness on toward the promised land' but, as he reached his conclusion, he expressed uncertainty about what lay ahead. He alluded to the end of Moses' journey, when the LORD took him to the top of Mt Nebo and allowed him to look over into the promised land, even though he would never enter it (Deut. 1.1–8). He said:

> I don't know what will happen now. We've got some difficult days ahead. But it doesn't matter with me now. Because I've been to the mountaintop. And I don't mind. Like anybody, I would like to live a long life. Longevity has its place. But I'm not concerned about that now. I just want to do God's will. And He's allowed me to go up to the mountain. And I've looked over. And I've seen the promised land. I may not get there with you. But I want you to know tonight, that we, as a people, will get to the promised land. And I'm happy, tonight. I'm not worried about anything. I'm not fearing any man. Mine eyes have seen the glory of the coming of the LORD.[72]

King must have sensed that, like Moses, his journey was coming to an end. And yet he felt that, like Moses, he had been given an assurance that his people would reach the 'promised land'. He concluded with a quote from 'The Battle Hymn of the Republic' (1861), whose author had seen 'the glory of the coming of the Lord', an allusion both to Old Testament prophetic proclamations of the coming Day of the LORD and also to New Testament expectation of its apocalyptic fulfilment.[73] King's final sermon leaves contemporary readers with the longing for the final consummation of the new exodus, in which God's justice and righteousness will be fully realized.

A survey of the reception of Exodus and its themes in the political realm would not be complete without mention of federal, state and local monuments throughout the USA. The Washington Monument, located on the National Mall in Washington, DC, was completed in 1884 and commemorates George Washington. He had served as the commander-in-chief of the Continental

---

72 Martin Luther King Jr, 'I see the promised land', in *A Testament of Hope* (ed. Washington), 286.
73 Julia Ward Howe, 'The Battle Hymn of the Republic', *United Methodist Hymnal*, no. 717. For some of the scriptural allusions, cf. Jer. 25.20–31; Mal. 4.1–4; Rev. 14.14–19.

Army during the Revolutionary War and was the first president of the United States. The monument, which stands at about 170 metres (555 ft) high and, at the time of its completion, was the world's tallest man-made structure, is in the shape of an obelisk, which evokes Ancient Egypt. While the choice of an obelisk may have reflected nineteenth-century 'Egyptomania', it also recalled the might of Ancient Egypt, Ancient Israel's enslavement there, and the person of Moses and his leadership in the exodus.[74] On the east side of the entrance to the Supreme Court, there is a group of marble sculptures of great lawgivers that includes Moses, Confucius and Solon. The inscription in the architrave reads, 'Justice the Guardian of Liberty'.[75]

Additional monuments that feature themes from Exodus are the memorials to the Ten Commandments that have been the subject of controversy in recent years. By the late nineteenth century, the Ten Commandments had become a widely accepted element of American culture, as documented by Jenna Weissman Joselit in her book, *Set in Stone: America's embrace of the Ten Commandments*.[76] She describes the rise of interest in the Ten Commandments during the aftermath of the Second World War, which prompted Americans in Austin, Texas; Denver, Colorado; Wallace, Idaho; Cedar Rapids, Iowa; Redondo Beach, California, as well as in other cities, to want monuments to the Ten Commandments erected in their communities. The Ten Commandments were viewed positively as providing America with a pedigree, a source of spiritual guidance, and evidence of American exceptionalism. Eventually, Ten Commandments monuments stood in the public squares of more than a hundred American cities. In twenty-first century America, however, as society grew more secular:

> they symbolized a looming cultural divide between those eager to blur the line between church and state and those just as eager to keep it intact, between those who promoted religion everywhere and those who preferred to have it privatized.[77]

---

74 Cf. James P. Irvine, *Concerning Washington and His Monument* (Washington, DC: A. Downing, 1875). More recently, see John Steele Gordon, *Washington's Monument and the Fascinating History of the Obelisks* (New York, NY: Bloomsbury, 2016).

75 Cf. the 'Building Features' section of the Supreme Court website, at: <https://supremecourt.gov/about/buildingfeatures.aspx>.

76 Jenna Weissman Joselit, *Set in Stone: America's embrace of the Ten Commandments* (Oxford: Oxford University Press, 2017).

77 Joselit, *Set in Stone*, 48.

In 2002, an injunction was sought, and won, to have the Ten Commandments monument removed from the grounds of the Texas state capitol on the grounds that it violated the First Amendment of the US Constitution. This case set in motion a series of lawsuits that have resulted in the removal of Ten Commandments monuments from public grounds. Many of these monuments have been relocated to private grounds, where they continue to serve as visible reminders of the enduring influence of the Ten Commandments.

Conclusions

In this chapter, we have surveyed the reception history of Exodus down through the ages, but we have only scratched the surface. We have encountered the limitations identified by England and Lyons as inherent within reception-historical study, which include the vast quantity of fields in which the text has made an impact on its journey of more than two millennia down through history.[78] This means that students and scholars are forced to study a diversity of material that lies outside the areas in which they have received training, including those we have considered in this chapter, but also additional fields like media, popular culture, philosophy and economics. Obviously, no one can be an expert in every field. England and Lyons suggest that the future may 'require replacing some of the methods in scholarly training, and undertaking more disciplinary cross-fertilization and collaborative work'.[79] Certainly, it would take a legion of scholars trained in a multitude of fields to trace out the impact the book of Exodus has had over more than two millennia. Even so, the task can never be completed, because the reception history of the book of Exodus is a continuing process. Whenever and wherever the book of Exodus is read, preached, sung or appropriated in other ways, it is 'living and active' (Heb. 4.12) and continues to proclaim that the LORD is the God who seeks to save human beings and establish his presence in their midst.

---

78   England and Lyons, 'Explorations in the reception of the Bible', 6.
79   England and Lyons, 'Explorations in the reception of the Bible', 6.

Bibliography

Aberback, M., and L. Smolar. 'The golden calf episode in postbiblical literature.' *HUCA* 39 (1968): 91–116.

Adrom, Faried, and Matthias Müller. 'The Tetragrammaton in Egyptian sources – facts and fiction.' Pp. 93–113 in *The Origins of Yahwism*. BZAW 484. Ed. Jürgen van Oorschot and Markus Witte. Berlin: de Gruyter, 2017.

Ahlström, Gösta. *Who Were the Israelites?* Winona Lake, IN: Eisenbrauns, 1986.

Albrektson, Bertil. *History and the Gods: An essay on the idea of historical events as divine manifestations in the Ancient Near East and in Israel.* CB/OTS 1. Winona Lake, IN: Eisenbrauns, 2011.

Albright, W. F. *From the Stone Age to Christianity.* 2nd edn. Baltimore, MD: Johns Hopkins University Press, 1946.

——. 'Northwest-Semitic names in a list of Egyptian slaves from the eighteenth century.' *JAOS* 74 (1954): 222–33.

Aldred, Cyril. *The Egyptians.* Rev. edn. London: Thames & Hudson, 1984.

Alexander, T. Desmond. *Exodus.* AOT 2. London: Apollos, 2017.

Aling, Charles F. 'The biblical city of Ramses.' *JETS* 25.2 (1982): 129–38.

——. *Egypt and Bible History.* Grand Rapids, MI: Baker, 1981.

Allam, S. 'Slaves.' *OEAE* 3:293–6.

Allison, Dale C., Jr. *The New Moses: A Matthean typology.* Minneapolis, MN: Fortress Press, 1993.

Alter, Robert. *The Art of Biblical Narrative.* New York, NY: Basic, 1981.

Alter, Robert, and Frank Kermode, eds. *The Literary Guide to the Bible.* Cambridge, MA: Belknap Press, 1987.

Amit, Yairah. *Reading Biblical Narratives: Literary criticism and the Hebrew Bible.* Minneapolis, MN: Augsburg Fortress, 2001.

Archer, G. L. *A Survey of Old Testament Introduction* (rev. edn; Chicago, IL: Moody, 1994).

Arnold, Clinton E. *Ephesians.* ECNT. Grand Rapids, MI: Zondervan, 2010.

Assmann, Jan. 'Amun.' Pp. 28–32 in *Dictionary of Deities and Demons in the Bible.* Ed. Karel van der Toorn, Bob Becking and Pieter W. van der Horst. 2nd edn. Leiden: Brill, 1999.

——. 'Exodus and memory.' Pp. 3–15 in *Israel's Exodus in Transdisciplinary Perspective: Text, archaeology, culture, and geoscience.* Ed. Thomas E. Levy, Thomas Schneider and William H. C. Propp. New York, NY: Springer, 2015.

——. *From Akhenaten to Moses: Ancient Egypt and religious change.* Cairo: American University in Cairo Press, 2014.

——. *The Invention of Religion: Faith and covenant in the book of Exodus.* Trans. Robert Savage. Princeton, NJ: Princeton University Press, 2018.

____. 'Re.' Pp. 689–92 in *Dictionary of Deities and Demons in the Bible.* Ed. Karel van der Toorn, Bob Becking and Pieter W. van der Horst. 2nd edn. Leiden: Brill, 1999.

Babcock, Bryan C. *Sacred Ritual: A study of the West Semitic ritual calendars in Leviticus 23 and the Akkadian text Emar 446.* BBRSup 9. Winona Lake, IN: Eisenbrauns, 2014.

Babington, Bruce, and Peter William Evans. *Biblical Epics: Sacred narrative in the Hollywood cinema.* Manchester: Manchester University Press, 1993.

Baden, Joel S. *The Book of Exodus: A biography.* LGRB. Princeton, NJ and Oxford: Princeton University Press, 2019.

——. *The Composition of the Pentateuch: Renewing the Documentary Hypothesis.* New Haven, CT and London: Yale University Press, 2012.

Bailey, L. R. 'The golden calf.' *HUCA* 42 (1971): 97–115.

Baker, David L. *The Decalogue: Living as the people of God.* Downers Grove, IL: IVP Academic, 2017.

——. 'Last but not least: the tenth commandment.' *HBT* 27 (2005): 3–24.

Baker, David W. 'God, Names of.' Pp. 359–68 in *Dictionary of the Old Testament: Pentateuch.* Ed. T. Desmond Alexander and David W. Baker. Downers Grove, IL: InterVarsity Press, 2003.

——, Bruce Waltke and T. Desmond Alexander. *Obadiah, Jonah and Micah.* Downers Grove, IL: InterVarsity Press, 1988.

Balentine, Samuel E. *The Torah's Vision of Worship.* OBT. Minneapolis, MN: Fortress Press, 1999.

Balogh, Amy L. *Moses among the Idols: Mediators of the divine in the Ancient Near East.* Lanham, MD: Lexington/Fortress Academic, 2018.

Baltzer, K. *The Covenant Formulary in Old Testament, Jewish, and Early Christian Writings.* Trans. D. E. Green. Philadelphia, PA: Fortress Press, 1971.

Bandstra, Barry L. *Reading the Old Testament: Introduction to the Hebrew Bible.* 4th edn. Belmont, CA: Wadsworth, 2008.

Barr, James. *The Semiotics of Biblical Language.* London: SCM Press, 1983.

Barth, Christoph. *God With Us: A theological introduction to the Old Testament.* Ed. Geoffrey W. Bromiley. Grand Rapids, MI: Eerdmans, 1991.

Bassett, John Spencer. *Antislavery Leaders of North Carolina*. Baltimore, MD: Johns Hopkins University Press, 1898.

Batto, Bernard F. 'Mythic dimensions of the exodus tradition.' Pp. 187–95 in *Israel's Exodus in Transdisciplinary Perspective: Text, archaeology, culture, and geoscience*. Ed. Thomas E. Levy, Thomas Schneider and William H. C. Propp. New York, NY: Springer, 2015.

Bauckham, Richard. *The Theology of the Book of Revelation*. Cambridge: Cambridge University Press, 1993.

Beale, G. K. *The Temple and the Church's Mission: A biblical theology of the dwelling place of God*. NSBT 17. Downers Grove, IL and Leicester: InterVarsity Press and Apollos, 2004.

Beckman, Gary M. *Hittite Diplomatic Texts*. 2nd edn. Atlanta, GA: Scholars Press, 1999.

Beitzel, Barry J. *The New Moody Atlas of the Bible*. Chicago, IL: Moody, 2009.

Beking, Bob. 'More than one god? Three models for construing the relations between YHWH and the other gods.' Pp. 60–76 in *Divine Doppelgängers: YHWH's ancient look-alikes*. Ed. Collin Cornell. University Park, PA: Eisenbrauns, 2020.

Berlin, Adele. *Poetics and Interpretation of Biblical Narrative*. Winona Lake, IN: Eisenbrauns, 1994.

Berman, Joshua A. *Ani Maamin: Biblical criticism, historical truth and the Thirteen Principles of Faith*. Jerusalem: Maggid, 2020.

——. *Inconsistency in the Torah: Ancient literary convention and the limits of source criticism*. Oxford: Oxford University Press, 2017.

——. 'The Kadesh inscriptions of Ramesses II and the Exodus sea account (Exodus 13:17–15:19.' Pp. 93–112 in *'Did I Not Bring Israel Out of Egypt?' Biblical, archaeological, and Egyptological perspectives on the exodus narratives*. Ed. James K. Hoffmeier, Alan R. Millard and Gary A. Rendsburg. BBRSup 13. Winona Lake, IN: Eisenbrauns, 2016.

Betz, Hans Dieter. *Galatians: A commentary on Paul's letter to the churches in Galatia*. Hermeneia. Philadelphia, PA: Fortress Press, 1979.

Bietak, Manfred. 'Comments on the "exodus."' Pp. 163–70 in *Egypt, Israel, Sinai: Archaeological and historical relationships in the biblical period*. Ed. Anson F. Rainey. Tel Aviv: Tel Aviv University, 1987.

——. 'On the historicity of the exodus: what Egyptology today can contribute to assessing the biblical account of the sojourn in Egypt.' Pp. 17–37 in *Israel's Exodus in Transdisciplinary Perspective: Text, archaeology, culture, and geoscience*. Ed. Thomas E. Levy, Thomas Schneider and William H. C. Propp. New York, NY: Springer, 2015.

——, and E. Czerny, eds. *Tell El-Dab'a I: Tell El-Dab'a and Qantir, the site and its connections with Avaris and Piramesse*. Vienna: Austrian Academy of Sciences Press, 2001.

Bleiberg, Edward. 'Storage.' *OEAE* 3:327–29.

Blenkinsopp, Joseph. *Judaism: The First Phase: The place of Ezra and Nehemiah in the origins of Judaism*. Grand Rapids, MI: Eerdmans, 2009.

——. 'The Midianite-Kenite Hypothesis revisited and the origins of Judah.' *JSOT* 33.2 (2008): 131–53.

——. *The Pentateuch: An introduction to the first five books of the Bible*. New York, NY: Doubleday, 1992.

——. *Sage, Priest, Prophet: Religious and intellectual leadership in Ancient Israel*. LAI. Louisville, KY: Westminster John Knox Press, 1995.

——. 'The structure of P.' *CBQ* 38 (1976): 275–92.

Block, Daniel I. *The Book of Ezekiel: Chapters 1–24*. Grand Rapids, MI: Eerdmans, 1997.

——. *The Book of Ezekiel: Chapters 25–48*. Grand Rapids, MI: Eerdmans, 1998.

——. *The Gods of the Nations: Studies in Ancient Near Eastern national theology*. 2nd edn. ETS Studies. Grand Rapids, MI: Baker, 2000.

Boadt, Lawrence. *Reading the Old Testament: An introduction*. 2nd edn. New York, NY: Paulist Press, 2012.

Boling, Robert G. *Judges: A new translation with introduction and commentary*. AB 6A. New York, NY: Doubleday, 1975.

Bonhême, Marie-Ange. 'Kingship.' Trans. Elizabeth Schwaiger. *OEAE* 2:238–45.

The Book of Common Prayer. New York, NY: The Church Hymnal Corporation, 1979.

Booysen, Rian. *Thera and the Exodus: The exodus explained in terms of natural phenomena and the human response to it*. Winchester: O-Books, 2012.

Bowie, Andrew. *Introduction to German Philosophy: From Kant to Habermas*. Cambridge: Polity Press, 2003.

Bradshaw, Paul F. *The Search for the Origins of Christian Worship: Sources and methods for the study of early liturgy*. 2nd edn. New York, NY: Oxford University Press, 2002.

Breasted, James Henry, ed. *Ancient Records of Egypt*. 5 vols. Chicago, IL: University of Chicago Press, 1906.

Brewer, Douglas J. 'Cattle.' *OEAE* 1:242–4.

Broderick, Herbert R. *Moses the Egyptian in the Illustrated Old English Hexateuch*. Notre Dame, IN: University of Notre Dame Press, 2017.

Brueggemann, Walter. 'The book of Exodus.' *NIDB* 1:676–981.

———. *Reverberations of Faith: A theological handbook of Old Testament themes.* Louisville, KY: Westminster John Knox Press, 2002.

Budge, E. A. *From Fetish to God in Ancient Egypt.* New York, NY: Benjamin Blom, 1972.

Butzer, Karl W. 'Nile.' *OEAE* 2:550.

Carawan, Guy and Candie, eds. *Sing for Freedom: The story of the civil rights movement through its songs.* Montgomery, AL: NewSouth Books, 2007.

Cassuto, Umberto. *A Commentary on the Book of Exodus.* Reprint. Jerusalem: Magnes Press, 1967.

———. *The Documentary Hypothesis and the Composition of the Pentateuch.* Jerusalem and New York, NY: Shalem Press, 2006.

Chang, C., and H. A. Koster. 'Beyond bones: toward an archaeology of pastoralism.' *Advances in Archaeological Method and Theory* 9 (1986): 97–148.

Charles, R. H. *The Book of Jubilees.* Jerusalem: Makor, 1972.

Charlesworth, James H. 'A prolegomenon to a new study of the Jewish background of the hymns and prayers in the New Testament.' *JJS* 33 (1982): 265–85.

Chazon, Esther G. 'Prayers from Qumran and their historical implications.' *Dead Sea Discoveries* 1 (1994): 265–84.

Childs, Brevard S. *Biblical Theology in Crisis.* Philadelphia, PA: Westminster Press, 1970.

———. *Biblical Theology of the Old and New Testaments.* Minneapolis, MN: Fortress Press, 1993.

———. *The Book of Exodus: A critical, theological commentary.* Philadelphia, PA: Westminster Press, 1974.

———. *Introduction to the Old Testament as Scripture.* Philadelphia, PA: Fortress Press, 1979.

Clifford, Richard J. 'The tent of El and the Israelite tent of meeting.' *CBQ* 33 (1971): 221–7.

Coats, George W. *Exodus 1–18.* FOTL 2A. Grand Rapids, MI: Eerdmans, 1999.

———. *Moses: Heroic man, man of God.* JSOTSup 57. Sheffield: Sheffield Academic Press, 1988.

———. *The Moses Tradition.* JSOTSup 161. Sheffield: Sheffield Academic Press, 1993.

———, ed. *Saga, Legend, Tale, Novella, Fable: Narrative forms in Old Testament literature.* JSOTSup 35. Sheffield: JSOT Press, 1985.

Cockerill, Gareth Lee. *The Epistle to the Hebrews.* NICNT. Grand Rapids, MI: Eerdmans, 2012.

Cohen, A. *Midrash Rabbah: Ecclesiastes*. London and New York, NY: Soncino Press, 1983.

Collins, C. John. *Reading Genesis Well: Navigating history, poetry, science, and truth in Genesis 1–11*. Grand Rapids, MI: Zondervan, 2018.

Collins, John J. *Introduction to the Hebrew Bible*. 3rd edn. Minneapolis, MN: Fortress Press, 2018.

Collins, Matthew A. 'Depicting the divine: the ambiguity of Exodus 3 in *Exodus: Gods and Kings*.' Pp. 9–39 in *Biblical Reception 4: A New Hollywood Moses: On the spectacle and reception of Exodus: Gods and Kings*. Ed. David Tollerton. London: Bloomsbury, 2017.

Conzelmann, Hans. *Acts of the Apostles: A commentary on the Acts of the Apostles*. Hermeneia. Philadelphia, PA: Fortress Press, 1987.

——. *The Theology of St. Luke*. Trans. Geoffrey Buswell. New York, NY: Harper & Row, 1960.

Coogan, Michael D. *The Old Testament: A historical and literary introduction to the Hebrew Bible*. 4th edn. Oxford: Oxford University Press, 2017.

——. *The Ten Commandments: A short history of an ancient text*. New Haven, CT: Yale University Press, 2014.

Cook, J. A. 'Hebrew language.' Pp. 307–18 in *Dictionary of the Old Testament Prophets*. Ed. Mark J. Boda and J. Gordon McConville. Downers Grove, IL: IVP Academic, 2012.

Cotter, Wendy. 'Miracle.' *NIDB* 4:99–106.

Craigie, Peter C., Page H. Kelley and Joel F. Drinkard Jr. *Jeremiah 1–25*. WBC 26. Dallas, TX: Word, 1991.

Cross, F. L., and E. A. Livingstone. 'Basilica.' P. 141 in *The Oxford Dictionary of the Christian Church*. Oxford: Oxford University Press, 1983.

Cross, Frank Moore, Jr. *Canaanite Myth and Hebrew Epic*. Cambridge, MA: Harvard University Press, 1973.

——. 'The priestly tabernacle in the light of recent research.' Pp. 169–80 in *Temples and High Places in Biblical Times*. Ed. Abraham Biran. Jerusalem: Hebrew Union College, 1981.

——. 'The tabernacle: a study from an archaeological and historical approach.' *BA* 10 (1947): 45–68.

Cross, Frank Moore, Jr, and David Noel Freedman. 'The Song of Miriam.' *JNES* 14 (1955): 237–50.

——. *Studies in Ancient Yahwistic Poetry*. SBLDS. Missoula, MT: Scholars Press, 1975. Reprint: Grand Rapids, MI; Eerdmans, 1995.

Currid, John D. *Ancient Egypt and the Old Testament*. Grand Rapids, MI: Baker, 1997.

——. *Exodus*, Vol. 1: *Chapters 1–18*. Darlington: Evangelical Press, 2000.

Daelemans, Bert. *Spiritus Loci: A theological method for contemporary church architecture*. SRA 9. Leiden: Brill, 2015.

Dallaire, Hélène, and Denise Morris. 'Joshua and Israel's exodus from the desert wilderness.' Pp. 18–34 in *Reverberations of the Exodus in Scripture*. Ed. R. Michael Fox. Eugene, OR: Pickwick, 2014.

Dalley, Stephanie. 'Gods from north-eastern and north-western Arabia in cuneiform texts from the First Sealand Dynasty, and a cuneiform inscription from Tell en-Naṣbeh, *c*.1500 BC.' *Arab. Arch. Epig.* 24.2 (2013): 177–85.

Davidson, Jack R. *American Slavery and the Immediate Duty of Southern Slaveholders: A transcription of Eli Washington Caruthers's unpublished manuscript against slavery*. Eugene, OR: Pickwick, 2018.

——. *Still Letting My People Go: An analysis of Eli Washington Caruthers's manuscript against American Slavery and its universal application of Exodus 10:3*. Eugene, OR: Pickwick, 2018.

Davies, W. D. *Paul and Rabbinic Judaism*. London: SPCK, 1955.

——. *Torah in the Messianic Age and/or the Age to Come*. SBLMS 7. Philadelphia, PA: Society of Biblical Literature, 1952.

Davis, John J. *Moses and the Gods of Egypt*. 2nd edn. Grand Rapids, MI: Baker, 1986.

Davis, Thomas W. 'Exodus on the ground: the elusive signature of nomads in Sinai.' Pp. 223–39 in *'Did I Not Bring Israel Out of Egypt?' Biblical, archaeological, and Egyptological perspectives on the exodus narratives*. Ed. James K. Hoffmeier, Alan R. Millard and Gary A. Rendsburg. Winona Lake, IN: Eisenbrauns, 2016.

Day, John. 'Whatever happened to the ark of the covenant?' Pp. 250–70 in *Temple and Worship in Biblical Israel*. Ed. John Day. London: T&T Clark, 2005.

deClaissé-Walford, Nancy, Rolf. A Jacobson and Beth LaNeel Tanner. *The Book of Psalms*. NICOT. Grand Rapids, MI: Eerdmans, 2014.

DeRouchie, Jason. 'Counting the ten: an investigation into the numbering of the Decalogue.' Pp. 93–125 in *For Our Good Always: Studies on the message and influence of Deuteronomy in honor of Daniel I. Block*. Ed. Jason S. DeRouchie, Jason Gile and Kenneth J. Turner. Winona Lake, IN: Eisenbrauns.

Dever, William G. 'The exodus and the Bible: what was known; what was remembered; what was forgotten?' Pp. 399–408 in *Israel's Exodus in Transdisciplinary Perspective: Text, archaeology, culture, and geoscience*. Ed.

Thomas E. Levy, Thomas Schneider and William H. C. Propp. New York, NY: Springer, 2015.

———. 'Is there any archaeological evidence for the exodus?' Pp. 67–86 in *Exodus: The Egyptian evidence*. Ed. E. S. Frerichs and L. H. Lesko. Winona Lake, IN: Eisenbrauns, 1997.

———. *What Did the Biblical Writers Know and When Did They Know It? What archaeology can tell us about the reality of Ancient Israel*. Grand Rapids, MI: Eerdmans, 2002.

———. *Who Were the Early Israelites and Where Did They Come From?* Grand Rapids, MI: Eerdmans, 2003.

Dibelius, Martin, and Hans Conzelmann. *The Pastoral Epistles: A commentary on the Pastoral Epistles*. Hermeneia. Philadelphia, PA: Fortress Press, 1972.

Dodd, C. H. *The Gospel and the Law of Christ*. London and New York, NY: Longmans Green, 1947.

Donahou, Michael S. *A Comparison of the Egyptian Execration Ritual to Exodus 32:19 and Jeremiah 19*. PHSC 8. Piscataway, NJ: Gorgias Press, 2010.

Douglas, Mary. *Purity and Danger: An analysis of the concepts of pollution and taboo*. New York, NY: Frederick A. Praeger, 1966.

Doxey, Denise M. 'Priesthood.' *OEAE* 3:68–73.

Dozeman, Thomas B. *Commentary on Exodus*. ECC. Grand Rapids, MI: Eerdmans, 2009.

———. *God at War: Power in the exodus tradition*. New York, NY: Oxford University Press, 1996.

———. 'Inner-biblical interpretation of Yahweh's gracious and compassionate character.' *JBL* 108 (1989): 207–23.

———. *The Pentateuch: Introducing the Torah*. Minneapolis, MN: Fortress Press, 2017.

———, ed., *Methods for Exodus* (MBI; Cambridge: Cambridge University Press, 2010).

Dozeman, Thomas B., Craig A. Evans and Joel N. Lohr, eds. *The Book of Exodus: Composition, reception, and interpretation*. Leiden: Brill, 2014.

Drazin, Israel. *Targum Onkelos to Exodus: An English translation of the text with analysis and commentary*. Jersey City, NJ: Ktav, 1990.

Driver, Godfrey Rolles. 'Affirmation by exclamatory negation.' *JANES* 5 (1973): 107–14.

Driver, S. R. *The Book of Exodus*. Cambridge Bible for Schools and Colleges. Cambridge: Cambridge University Press, 1911.

———. *An Introduction to the Literature of the Old Testament*. Reprint. Cleveland, OH and New York, NY: Meridian, 1956 [1897].

Dunand, Françoise, and Christiane Zivie-Coche. *Gods and Men in Egypt: 3000 BCE to 395 CE*. Ithaca, NY: Cornell University Press, 2004.

Dunn, J. D. G. *The Epistle to the Galatians*. BNTC. London: A&C Black, 1993.

Durham, John I. *Exodus*. WBC 3. Waco, TX: Word, 1987.

———. 'Isaiah 40–55: a new creation, a new exodus, a new messiah.' Pp. 47–56 in *The Yahweh/Baal Confrontation and Other Studies in Biblical Literature and Archaeology: Essays in honour of Emmett Willard Harnick*. SBEC 35. Lewiston, NY: Edwin Mellen Press, 1995.

Eissfeldt, Otto. *The Old Testament: An introduction*. 3rd edn. New York, NY: Harper & Row, 1966.

Ellis, Peter. *The Yahwist: The Bible's first theologian*. Notre Dame, IN: Fides, 1968.

England, Emma, and William John Lyons. 'Explorations in the reception of the Bible.' Pp. 3–13 in *Reception History and Biblical Studies: Theory and practice*. Ed. Emma England and William John Lyons. LBH/OTS 615. London: Bloomsbury, 2015.

Enns, Peter. *Inspiration and Incarnation: Evangelicals and the problem of the Old Testament*. Grand Rapids, MI: Baker, 2005.

Enz, Jacob J. 'The book of Exodus as a literary type for the Gospel of John.' *JBL* 76.3 (1957): 208–15.

Epstein, Isidore, ed. *The Babylonian Talmud: Seder Mo'ed*. 18 vols. London: Soncino Press, 1938.

Estelle, Bryan D. *Echoes of Exodus: Tracing a biblical motif*. Downers Grove, IL: IVP Academic, 2018.

Estes, Daniel J. 'The Psalms, the exodus, and Israel's worship.' Pp. 35–50 in *Reverberations of the Exodus in Scripture*. Ed. R. Michael Fox. Eugene, OR: Pickwick, 2014.

Evans, Craig A. 'Exodus in the New Testament: patterns of revelation and redemption.' Pp. 440–64 in *The Book of Exodus: Composition, reception, and interpretation*. Ed. Thomas B. Dozeman, Craig A. Evans and Joel N. Lohr. Leiden: Brill, 2014.

Exum, J. Cheryl. 'Exodus: male gods and kings.' Pp. 40–56 in *Biblical Reception 4: A New Hollywood Moses: On the spectacle and reception of Exodus: Gods and Kings*. Ed. David Tollerton. London: Bloomsbury, 2017.

Fee, Gordon D. *The First Epistle to the Corinthians*. NICNT. Grand Rapids, MI: Eerdmans, 1987.

Feldman, Ariel. 'The Song of Miriam (4Q365 6a ii + 6c 1–7) revisited.' *JBL* 132.4 (2013): 905–11.

Feldman, Louis H. *Philo's Portrayal of Moses in the Context of Ancient Judaism*. Notre Dame, IN: University of Notre Dame Press, 2007.

Fiensy, David. *Prayers Alleged to Be Jewish: An examination of the Constitutiones Apostolorum.* BJS. Chico, CA: Scholars Press, 1985.

Fine, Steven, and John David Brolley. 'Synagogue.' *NIDB* 5:416–27.

Finegan, J. *Let My People Go: A journey through Exodus.* New York, NY: Harper & Row, 1963.

Finkelstein, Israel. *Living on the Fringe: The archaeology and history of the Negev, Sinai and neighbouring regions in the Bronze and Iron Ages.* Reprint. Sheffield: Sheffield Academic Press, 2001.

Finkelstein, Israel, and Neil Asher Silberman. *The Bible Unearthed: Archaeology's new vision of Ancient Israel and the origins of its sacred texts.* New York, NY: Free Press, 2001.

Fischer, David Hackett. *Historians' Fallacies: Toward a logic of historical thought.* New York, NY: Harper & Row, 1970.

Fischer-Elfert, Hans-W. 'Education.' *OEAE* 1:438–42.

Fishbane, Michael. *Biblical Interpretation in Ancient Israel.* Oxford: Clarendon Press, 1985.

——. 'The "exodus" motif/the paradigm of historical renewal.' Pp. 121–40 in *Text and Texture: A literary reading of selected texts.* Ed. Michael Fishbane. Oxford: Oneworld, 1998.

——. 'Torah and tradition.' Pp. 275–300 in *Tradition and Theology in the Old Testament.* Ed. D. A. Knight. Philadelphia, PA: Fortress Press, 1977.

Fitzmyer, Joseph A. *The Acts of the Apostles: A new translation with introduction and commentary.* AB 31. New York, NY: Doubleday, 1998.

——. *The Gospel According to Luke (I–IX).* AB 28. New York, NY: Doubleday, 1970.

Fleming, Daniel E. *Time at Emar: The cultic calendar and the rituals from the diviner's house.* Winona Lake, IN: Eisenbrauns, 2000.

Flesher, Paul V. M. 'Bread of the Presence.' *ABD* 1:780–1.

Fletcher, Michelle. 'Once upon an apocalypse: exodus, disaster, and a long, long time ago?', in *Biblical Reception 4: A New Hollywood Moses: On the spectacle and reception of Exodus: Gods and Kings.* Ed. David Tollerton. London: Bloomsbury, 2017.

Flusser, David. 'Psalms, hymns and prayers.' Pp. 551–77 in *The Literature of the Jewish People in the Period of the Second Temple and the Talmud,* Vol. 2: *Jewish Writings of the Second Temple Period.* Ed. M. E. Stone. Assen: Van Gorcum, 1984.

Fokkelman, J. P. 'Exodus.' Pp. 56–65 in *The Literary Guide to the Bible.* Ed. Robert Alter and Frank Kermode. Cambridge, MA: Belknap Press, 1987.

Foster, John L. 'The *Hymn to Aten*: Akhenaten worships the sole god.' *CANE* 3:1751–61.

Fox, Everett. *Genesis and Exodus: A new English rendition with commentary and notes*. New York, NY: Schocken, 1990.

Frandsen, Paul John. 'Taboo.' *OEAE* 3:345–6.

Frankel, Ellen, and Betsy Platkin Teutsch. *The Encyclopedia of Jewish Symbols*. Northvale, NJ: Jason Aronson, 1992.

Frankfort, Henri. *Ancient Egyptian Religion: An interpretation*. Mineola, NY: Dover, 2011.

Freedman, David Noel. 'The Chronicler's purpose.' *CBQ* 23 (1961): 436–42.

———. 'Early Israelite history in the light of early Israelite poetry.' Pp. 3–23 in *Unity and Diversity: Essays in history, literature, and religion of the Ancient Near East*. Ed. Hans Goedicke and J. J. M. Roberts. Baltimore, MD: Johns Hopkins University Press, 1975.

———. *The Nine Commandments: Uncovering the hidden pattern of crime and punishment in the Hebrew Bible*. New York, NY: Doubleday, 2000.

Fretheim, Terence E. '"Because the whole earth is mine": theme and narrative in Exodus.' *Int* 50.3 (1996): 229–39.

———. *Exodus*. Interpretation: A Bible commentary for teaching and preaching. Louisville, KY: John Knox Press, 1991.

———. 'The plagues as ecological signs of historical disaster.' *JBL* 110 (1991): 385–96.

Friebel, K. G. 'Sign-acts.' Pp. 707–13 in *Dictionary of the Old Testament Prophets*. Ed. Mark J. Boda and J. Gordon McConville. Downers Grove, IL: IVP Academic, 2012.

Friedman, Richard Elliott. *The Bible with Sources Revealed: A new view into the five books of Moses*. New York, NY: HarperSanFrancisco, 2003.

———. *Commentary on the Torah with a New English Translation*. San Francisco, CA: HarperSanFrancisco, 2001.

———. *The Exodus: How it happened and why it matters*. New York, NY: HarperOne, 2017.

———. 'Tabernacle.' *ABD* 6:292–300.

Gager, John G. *Moses in Greco-Roman Paganism*. Nashville, TN: Abingdon Press, 1972.

Gane, Roy E. *Old Testament Law for Christians: Original context and enduring application*. Grand Rapids, MI: Baker Academic, 2017.

Gardiner, Alan H. 'Adoption extraordinary.' *JEA* 26 (1941): 23–9.

———. 'The delta residence of the Ramessides pt. I', *JEA* 5 (1918): 127–271.

Garfinkel, Yosef, and Ganor, Saar. *Khirbet Qeiyafa*, Vol. 1: *Excavation Report, 2007–2008*. Jerusalem: Israel Exploration Society, 2009.

Garrett, Duane A. *A Commentary on Exodus*. KEL. Grand Rapids, MI: Kregel Academic, 2014.

Garstang, John. *Joshua and Judges*. London: Constable, 1931.

Geraty, Lawrence T. 'Exodus dates and theories.' Pp. 55–64 in *Israel's Exodus in Transdisciplinary Perspective: Text, archaeology, culture, and geoscience*. Ed. Thomas E. Levy, Thomas Schneider and William H. C. Propp. New York, NY: Springer, 2015.

Gerdmar, Anders. *The Roots of Theological Anti-Semitism: German biblical interpretation and the Jews, from Herder to Kittel and Bultmann*. Leiden: Brill, 2009.

Gerstenberger, Eberhard. 'Covenant and commandment.' *JBL* 84 (1965): 38–51.

Gheorghita, Radu. 'περὶ τῆς ἐξόδου . . . ἐμνημόνευσεν, "*he spoke about the exodus*": echoes of *Exodus* in Hebrews.' Pp. 160–86 in *Reverberations of the Exodus in Scripture*. Ed. R. Michael Fox. Eugene, OR: Pickwick, 2014.

Ginzberg, Louis. *The Legends of the Jews*. 6 vols. Philadelphia, PA: Jewish Publication Society, 1928.

Goedicke, H. 'The chronology of the Thera/Santorin explosion.' Pp. 57–62 in *High, Middle, or Low? Acts of the Second International Colloquium on Absolute Chronology, Schloß Haindorf/Lanlois, 12–15 August 1990*. Ägypten und Levante 3. Vienna: Austrian Academy of Sciences Press, 1992.

———. *The Speos Artemidos Inscription of Hatshepsut and Related Discussions*. Oakville, CT: Halgo, 2004.

———. 'The Tetragrammaton in Egyptian?' *Society for the Study of Egyptian Antiquities* 24 (1994): 24–7.

Goldingay, John. *Old Testament Theology*, Vol. 1: *Israel's Gospel*. Downers Grove, IL: InterVarsity Press, 2003.

———. 'The significance of circumcision.' *JSOT* 88 (2000): 3–18.

Goodfriend, Elaine Adler. 'Adultery.' *ABD* 1:82–6.

Gordon, John Steele. *Washington's Monument and the Fascinating History of the Obelisks*. New York, NY: Bloomsbury, 2016.

Gottwald, Norman K. *The Hebrew Bible: A socio-literary introduction*. Minneapolis, MN: Fortress Press, 2002.

Graetz, Naomi. 'Miriam and me.' Pp. 157–68 in *Exodus and Deuteronomy*. Ed. Athalya Brenner and Gale A. Yee. TatC. Minneapolis, MN: Fortress Press, 2012.

Greenberg, Moshe. *Understanding Exodus: A holistic commentary on Exodus 1–11*. 2nd edn. Eugene, OR: Cascade, 2013.

Griffiths, J. Gwyn. 'The Egyptian derivation of the name Moses.' *JNES* 12 (1953): 225–31.

Gruber, Mayer I. 'Puah.' Pp. 137–8 in *Women in Scripture: A dictionary of named and unnamed women in the Hebrew Bible, the apocryphal/deuterocanonical books, and the New Testament.* Ed. Carol Meyers. Grand Rapids, MI: Eerdmans, 2000.

Habachi, L. 'Khatana-Qantir: importance.' *ASAE* 52 (1954): 443–559.

Habel, Norman. 'The form and significance of the call narratives.' *ZAW* 77 (1965): 297–323.

——'"Yahweh, maker of heaven and earth": a study in tradition criticism.' *JBL* 91 (1972): 321–7.

Haglund, Erik. *Historical Motifs in the Psalms.* ConBOT 23. Uppsala: CWK Gleerup, 1984.

Hallo, William W. 'Cult statue and divine image: a preliminary study.' Pp. 1–17 in *Scripture in Context II.* Ed. W. Hallo, J. C. Moyer and L. G. Perdue. Winona Lake, IN: Eisenbrauns, 1983.

Halpern, Baruch. 'The exodus from Egypt: myth or reality?' Pp. 86–113 in *The Rise of Ancient Israel.* Ed. Hershel Shanks. Washington, DC: Biblical Archaeology Society, 1992.

Hamilton, Victor P. *Handbook on the Pentateuch.* 2nd edn. Grand Rapids, MI: Baker, 2005.

Hamori, Esther J. *Women's Divination in Biblical Literature: Prophecy, necromancy, and other arts of knowledge.* New Haven, CT: Yale University Press, 2015.

Hansen, Nicole B. 'Snakes.' *OEAE* 3:296–9.

Haran, Menahem. 'Shiloh and Jerusalem: the origin of the Priestly tradition in the Pentateuch.' *JBL* 81 (1962): 14–24.

Harper, G. Geoffrey. *'I Will Walk Among You': The rhetorical function of allusion to Genesis 1–3 in the book of Leviticus.* BBRSup 21. University Park, PA: Eisenbrauns, 2018.

Harrelson, Walter J., ed. *The New Interpreter's Study Bible: New Revised Standard Version with the Apocrypha.* Nashville, TN: Abingdon Press, 2003.

Harris, Mark. 'The Thera theories: science and the modern reception history of the exodus.' Pp. 91–9 in *Israel's Exodus in Transdisciplinary Perspective: Text, archaeology, culture, and geoscience.* Ed. Thomas E. Levy, Thomas Schneider and William H. C. Propp. New York, NY: Springer, 2015.

Hartenstein, Friedhelm. 'The beginnings of YHWH and "longing for the origin"': a historico-hermeneutical query.' Pp. 283–307 in *The Origins of Yahwism.* BZAW 484. Ed. Jürgen van Oorschot and Markus Witte. Berlin: de Gruyter, 2017.

Hasel, Gerhard F. 'Biblical theology movement.' Pp. 163–6 in *Evangelical Dictionary of Theology.* Ed. W. A. Elwell. 2nd edn. Grand Rapids, MI: Baker, 2001.

Hatchett, Marion J. *Commentary on the American Prayer Book.* New York, NY: HarperSanFrancisco, 1979.

Hawkins, Ralph K. 'Cattle.' *EBR* 4:1069.

——. 'The forty-thousand men of Joshua 4:13.' Pp. 150–8 in *Hebrew and Beyond: Studies in honor of Rodney E. Cloud.* Ed. David Musgrave. Montgomery, AL: Amridge University Press, 2016.

——. *How Israel Became a People.* Nashville, TN: Abingdon Press, 2013.

——. *The Iron Age I Structure on Mt. Ebal: Excavation and interpretation.* Winona Lake, IN: Eisenbrauns, 2012.

——. 'Zoan', *NIDB* 5:990.

Heinemann, Joseph. *Prayer in the Talmud: Forms and patterns.* Trans. Richard Sarason. Studia Judaica 9. New York, NY: de Gruyter, 1977.

Helyer, Larry R. 'Abraham's eight crises: the bumpy road to fulfilling God's promise of an heir.' Pp. 41–52 in *Abraham and Family: New insights into the patriarchal narratives.* Ed. Hershel Shanks. Washington, DC: Biblical Archaeology Society, 2000.

Hendel, Ronald. 'The exodus as cultural memory: Egyptian bondage and the Song of the Sea.' Pp. 65–77 in *Israel's Exodus in Transdisciplinary Perspective: Text, archaeology, culture, and geoscience.* Ed. Thomas E. Levy, Thomas Schneider and William H. C. Propp. New York, NY: Springer, 2015.

Herrmann, W. 'El.' Pp. 274–80 in *Dictionary of Deities and Demons in the Bible.* Ed. Karel van der Toorn, Bob Becking and Pieter W. van der Horst. 2nd edn. Leiden: Brill, 1999.

Heschel, Abraham Joshua. *The Sabbath: Its meaning for modern man.* New York, NY: Farrar, Straus & Young, 1952.

Hess, Richard S. 'The divine name Yahweh in Late Bronze Age sources?' *UF* 23 (1991): 181–8.

——. *Israelite Religions: An archaeological and biblical survey.* Grand Rapids, MI: Baker Academic, 2007.

——. *The Old Testament: A historical, theological, and critical introduction.* Grand Rapids, MI: Baker Academic, 2016.

——. 'Onomastics of the exodus generation in the book of Exodus.' Pp. 37–48 in *'Did I Not Bring Israel Out of Egypt?' Biblical, archaeological, and Egyptological perspectives on the exodus narratives.* Ed. James K. Hoffmeier, Alan R. Millard and Gary A. Rendsburg. BBRSup 13. Winona Lake, IN: Eisenbrauns, 2016.

Hillers, Delbert R. *Covenant: The history of a biblical idea.* Baltimore, MD: Johns Hopkins University Press, 1969.

——. *Treaty Curses and the Old Testament Prophets*. Biblica et Orientalia 16. Rome: Pontifical Biblical Institute, 1964.

Hoffmeier, James K. *Akhenaten and the Origins of Monotheism*. Oxford: Oxford University Press, 2015.

——. *Ancient Israel in Sinai: The evidence for the authenticity of the wilderness tradition*. New York, NY: Oxford University Press, 2005.

——. 'The arm of God versus the arm of Pharaoh in the exodus narratives.' *Bib* 67 (1986): 378–87.

——. 'Egypt, Plagues in.' *ABD* 2:374–8.

——. 'Egyptian religious influences on the early Hebrews.' Pp. 3–35 in *'Did I Not Bring Israel Out of Egypt?' Biblical, archaeological, and Egyptological perspectives on the exodus narratives*. Ed. James K. Hoffmeier, Alan R. Millard and Gary A. Rendsburg. BBRSup 13. Winona Lake, IN: Eisenbrauns, 2016.

——. *Israel in Egypt: The evidence for the authenticity of the exodus tradition*. New York, NY: Oxford University Press, 1997.

——. '"These things happened": why a historical exodus is essential for theology.' Pp. 99–134 in *Do Historical Matters Matter To Faith? A critical appraisal of modern and postmodern approaches to Scripture*. Wheaton, IL: Crossway, 2012.

——. 'What is the biblical date for the exodus? A response to Bryant Wood.' *JETS* 50.2 (2007): 225–47.

Hoffmeier, James K., and Stephen O. Moshier. '"The Ways of Horus": reconstructing Egypt's east frontier defense network and the military road to Canaan in New Kingdom times.' Pp. 34–61 in *Excavations in North Sinai: Tell el-Borg I*. Ed. James K. Hoffmeier. Winona Lake, IN: Eisenbrauns, 2014.

Holladay, William L. *A Concise Hebrew and Aramaic Lexicon of the Old Testament*. Grand Rapids, MI: Eerdmans, 1988.

Homan, Michael M. 'The Good Book and the bad movies: Moses and the failure of biblical cinema.' Pp. 87–112 in *Milk and Honey: Essays on Ancient Israel and the Bible in appreciation of the Judaic Studies program at the University of California, San Diego*. Ed. Sara Malena and David Miano. Winona Lake, IN: Eisenbrauns, 2007.

——. *To Your Tents, O Israel! The terminology, function, form, and symbolism of tents in the Hebrew Bible and the Ancient Near East*. CHANE 12. Leiden: Brill, 2002.

Hornung, Erik. 'Ancient Egyptian religious iconography.' *CANE* 3:1711–30.

——. *Conceptions of God in Ancient Egypt: The one and the many*. Trans. John Baines. Ithaca, NY: Cornell University Press, 1982.

Hort, Greta. 'The plagues of Egypt.' *ZAW* 69 (1957): 84–103.

———. 'The plagues of Egypt, II.' *ZAW* 70 (1958): 48–59.

Houston, Walter. 'Exodus.' Pp. 67–91 in *The Oxford Bible Commentary*. Ed. John Barton and John Muddiman. Oxford: Oxford University Press, 2001.

Houtman, Cornelius. *Exodus*, Vol. 1. HCOT. Leuven: Peeters, 1993.

———. *Exodus*, Vol. 3. HCOT. Leuven: Peeters, 2000.

Huffmon, H. B. 'Name.' Pp. 610–12 in *Dictionary of Deities and Demons in the Bible*. Ed. Karel van der Toorn, Bob Becking and Pieter W. van der Horst. 2nd edn. Leiden: Brill, 1999.

Hume, David. *Of Miracles*. Reprint. Chicago, IL: Open Court, 1985.

Humphreys, Colin J. *The Miracles of Exodus: A scientist's discovery of the extraordinary natural causes of the biblical stories*. New York, NY: HarperSanFrancisco, 2003.

Hurowitz, Victor (Avigdor). *I Have Built You an Exalted House: Temple building in the Bible in light of Mesopotamian and Northwest Semitic Writings*. JSOTSup 115. Sheffield: JSOT Press, 1992.

———. 'The Priestly account of building the tabernacle.' *JAOS* 105.1 (1985): 21–30.

Hyatt, J. P. *Commentary on Exodus*. NCB. London: Marshall, Morgan & Scott, 1971.

Imes, Carmen Joy. *Bearing YHWH's Name at Sinai: A reexamination of the Name Command of the Decalogue*. University Park, PA: Eisenbrauns, 2018.

Irvine, James P. *Concerning Washington and His Monument*. Washington, DC: A. Downing, 1875.

Jack, J. W. *The Date of the Exodus: In the light of external evidence*. Edinburgh: T&T Clark, 1925.

Jacob, Benno. *The Second Book of the Bible: Exodus*. Trans. Walter Jacob. Hoboken, NJ: Ktav, 1992.

Jacobovici, Simcha. *The Exodus Decoded*. Toronto: Syndicado, 2016.

James, Elaine. 'Miriam and her interpreters.' Pp. 67–69 in *Women's Bible Commentary*. Ed. Carol A. Newsome, Sharon A. Ringe and J. E. Lapsley. 3rd edn. Louisville, KY: Westminster John Knox Press, 2012.

Jewett, Robert. *Romans: A commentary*. Hermeneia. Minneapolis, MN: Fortress Press, 2006.

Johnson, Dennis E. *The Message of Acts in the History of Redemption*. Phillipsburg, NJ: P&R, 1997.

Johnson, Luke Timothy. *The Acts of the Apostles*. SP 5. Collegeville, MN: Liturgical Press, 1992.

Johnston, Gordon. 'What biblicists need to know about Hittite treaties.' Paper presented at the Annual Meeting of the Evangelical Theological Society. San Antonio, TX, 16 November 2016.

Johnstone, William. *Exodus*. OTG. Sheffield: JSOT Press, 1990.

——. *Exodus 20–40*. SHBC. Macon, GA: Smyth & Helwys, 2014.

Joselit, Jenna Weissman. *Set in Stone: America's embrace of the Ten Commandments*. Oxford: Oxford University Press, 2017.

Kaiser, Walter C., Jr. 'Exodus.' Pp. 285–497 in vol. 2 of *The Expositor's Bible Commentary*. Ed. Frank E. Gaebelein. 12 vols. Grand Rapids, MI: Zondervan, 1990.

——. *Toward Old Testament Ethics*. Grand Rapids, MI: Academie, 1983.

Kaufmann, Yehezkel. *The Religion of Israel: From its beginnings to the Babylonian exile*. Trans. Moshe Greenberg. New York, NY: Schocken, 1972.

Kearney, P. J. 'Creation and liturgy: the P redaction of Ex. 25–40.' *ZAW* 89 (1977): 375–87.

Keller, Werner. *The Bible as History*. 2nd rev. edn. New York, NY: Morrow, 1981.

Keown, Gerald L., Pamela J. Scalise and Thomas G. Smothers. *Jeremiah 26–52*. WBC 27. Dallas, TX: Word, 1995.

King, Martin Luther, Jr. 'I see the promised land (3 April 1968).' Pp. 279–86 in *A Testament of Hope: The essential writings of Martin Luther King, Jr.* Ed. James M. Washington. New York, NY: HarperCollins, 1986.

——. *Strength to Love*. Philadelphia, PA: Fortress Press, 1981. Reprinted Cleveland, OH: Collins & World, 1977.

——. 'Stride Toward Freedom (1958).' Pp. 417–90 in *A Testament of Hope: The essential writings of Martin Luther King, Jr.* Ed. James M. Washington. New York, NY: HarperCollins, 1986.

Kitchen, Kenneth A. 'Egyptians and Hebrews, from Raʿamses to Jericho.' Pp. 65–131 in *The Origin of Early Israel – Current Debate: Biblical, historical, and archaeological perspectives, Irene Levi-Sala Seminar, 1997*. Ed. Shmuel Aḥituv and Eliezer D. Oren. Beer-Sheva: Ben-Gurion University of the Negev Press, 1998.

——. 'Exodus, The.' *ABD* 2:700–8.

——. 'From the brickfields of Egypt.' *TynBul* 27 (1976): 137–47.

——. *On the Reliability of the Old Testament*. Grand Rapids, MI: Eerdmans, 2003.

——. 'The tabernacle – a Bronze Age artifact.' Pp. 119*–29* in *Eretz-Israel* 24. Ed. Shmuel Aḥituv and Baruch A. Levine. Jerusalem: Israel Exploration Society, 1993.

Kitchen, Kenneth A., and Paul J. N. Lawrence. 'Plagues of Egypt.' Pp. 1001–3 in *The New Bible Dictionary*. Ed. J. D. Douglas. Grand Rapids, MI: Eerdmans, 1962.

——. *Treaty, Law and Covenant in the Ancient Near East*, 3 vols. Wiesbaden: Harrassowitz, 2012.

Klein, Ralph W. 'Back to the future: the tabernacle in the book of Exodus.' *Int* 50 (1996): 264–76.

Kleiner, Fred S. *Gardner's Art through the Ages: A global history*, Vol. 2. 16th edn. Spartanburg, SC: Cengage Learning, 2018.

Kline, Meredith G. *By Oath Consigned: A reinterpretation of the covenant signs of circumcision and baptism.* Grand Rapids, MI: Eerdmans, 1975.

——. *The Structure of Biblical Authority.* 2nd edn. Eugene, OR: Wipf & Stock, 1997.

——. *The Treaty of the Great King: The covenant structure of Deuteronomy.* Grand Rapids, MI: Eerdmans, 1963.

Knight, Douglas A. *Law, Power, and Justice in Ancient Israel.* LAI. Louisville, KY: Westminster John Knox Press, 2011.

——. 'Village law and the Book of the Covenant.' Pp. 163–79 in *'A Wise and Discerning Mind': Essays in honor of Burke O. Long.* Ed. Saul M. Olyan and Robert C. Culley. Brown Judaic Studies 325. Providence, RI: Brown Judaic Studies, 2000.

Knight, G. A. F. *Theology as Narration.* Grand Rapids, MI: Eerdmans, 1976.

Kuhn, Thomas S. *The Structure of Scientific Revolutions.* 3rd edn. Chicago, IL: University of Chicago Press, 1996.

Labuschagen, C. J. 'The meaning of *bĕyād rāma* in the Old Testament.' Pp. 143–8 in *Von Kanaan bis Kerala: Festschrift für J. P. M. van der Ploeg.* Ed. W. E. Delsman et al. AOAT 211. Neukirchen-Vluyn: Neukirchener, 1982.

Langston, Scott M. 'Exodus in early twentieth-century America: Charles Reynolds Brown and Lawrence Langner.' Pp. 433–46 in *The Oxford Handbook on the Reception History of the Bible.* Ed. Michael Lieb, Emma Mason and Jonathan Roberts. Oxford: Oxford University Press, 2011.

——. *Exodus through the Centuries.* Blackwell Bible Commentaries. Malden, MA: Blackwell, 2006.

Laughlin, John C. H. *Archaeology and the Bible.* New York, NY: Routledge, 1999.

——. 'Idol.' *NIDB* 3:8–11.

——. 'Idolatry.' *NIDB* 3:11–14.

Leach, Bridget, and John Tait. 'Papyrus.' *OEAE* 3:22–4.

Lemaire, André. *The Birth of Monotheism: The rise and disappearance of monotheism.* Trans. André Lemaire and Jack Meinhardt. Washington, DC: Biblical Archaeology Society, 2007.

Lemche, Niels Peter. *Ancient Israel: A new history of Israelite society.* BibSem 5; Sheffield: JSOT Press, 1988.

Lemke, Werner E. 'Circumcision of the heart: the journey of a biblical metaphor.' Pp. 299–319 in *God So Near: Essays on Old Testament theology in honor of Patrick Miller*. Ed. N. Bowen and Brent Strawn. Winona Lake, IN: Eisenbrauns, 2003.

Lesko, Leonard H. 'Death and the afterlife in Ancient Egyptian thought.' *CANE* 3:1763–74.

Licht, Jacob. 'Miracle.' *EncJud* 14:305–6.

Lichtheim, Miriam. 'Sinuhe.' Pp. 77–82 in vol. 1 of *The Context of Scripture: Canonical compositions from the biblical world*. Leiden: Brill, 2003.

Liebreich, Leon J. 'The impact of Nehemiah 9:5–37 on the liturgy of the synagogue.' *HUCA* 32 (1961): 227–37.

Lincoln, Abraham. 'The perpetuation of our political institutions: address before the Young Men's Lyceum of Springfield, Illinois (January 27, 1838).' *The Collected Works of Abraham Lincoln*. Ed. Roy P. Basler. 9 vols. New Brunswick, NJ: Rutgers University Press, 1953. <http://abrahamlincolnonline.org/lincoln/speeches/lyceum.htm>.

Lincoln, C. Eric, and Lawrence H. Mamiya. *The Black Church in the African American Experience*. Durham, NC and London: Duke University Press, 1990.

Lischer, Richard. *The Preacher King: Martin Luther King, Jr. and the word that moved America*. New York, NY: Oxford University Press, 1995.

Long, Siobhán Dowling, and John F. A. Sawyer. *The Bible in Music: A dictionary of songs, works, and more*. Lanham, MD: Rowman & Littlefield, 2015.

Long, V. Philips. *The Art of Biblical History*. Foundations of Contemporary Interpretation 5. Grand Rapids, MI: Zondervan Academic, 1994.

Longenecker, Richard N. *The Epistle to the Romans*. NIGTC. Grand Rapids, MI: Eerdmans, 2016.

Lucas, E. C. 'Miracles.' Pp. 695–701 in *Dictionary of the Old Testament: Historical books*. Ed. B. T. Arnold and H. G. M. Williamson. Downers Grove, IL: InterVarsity Press, 2005.

Luft, Ulrich H. 'Religion.' *OEAE* 3:139–45.

Lutz, Donald. 'The relative influence of European writers on late eighteenth-century American political thought.' *American Political Science Review* 78 (1984): 189–97.

McBride, S. Dean, Jr. 'Polity of the covenant people: the book of Deuteronomy.' Pp. 17–33 in *Constituting the Community: Studies on the polity of Ancient Israel in honor of S. Dean McBride, Jr*. Ed. John T. Strong and Steven S. Tuell. Winona Lake, IN: Eisenbrauns, 2005.

——. 'Transcendent authority: the role of Moses in Old Testament traditions.' *Int* 44 (1990): 229–39.

McCarter, P. Kyle, Jr. *1 Samuel: A new translation with introduction and commentary*. AB 8; New York, NY: Doubleday, 1980.

———. 'The patriarchal age: Abraham, Isaac and Jacob.' Pp. 1–34 in *Ancient Israel: From Abraham to the Roman destruction of the Temple*. 3rd edn. Ed. Hershel Shanks. Washington, DC: Biblical Archaeology Society, 2011.

McCarthy, D. J. *Old Testament Covenant: A survey of current opinions*. Richmond, VA: John Knox Press, 1972.

———. *Treaty and Covenant: A study in form in the ancient oriental documents and in the Old Testament*. Analecta Biblica 21. Rome: Pontifical Biblical Institute. Reprint of 3rd edn. Winona Lake, IN: Eisenbrauns, 1981.

McGowan, Andrew B. *Ancient Christian Worship: Early Christian practices in social, historical, and theological perspectives*. Grand Rapids, MI: Baker Academic, 2014.

Machinist, Peter. 'The question of distinctiveness in Ancient Israel: an essay.' Pp. 196–212 in *'Ah, Assyria . . .': Studies in Assyrian history and Ancient Near Eastern historiography presented to Hayim Tadmor*. Scripta Hierosolymitana 33. Jerusalem: Magnes Press, 1991.

McKnight, Scot. *The Letter to the Colossians*. NICNT. Grand Rapids, MI: Eerdmans, 2018.

McRay, John. *Archaeology and the New Testament*. Grand Rapids, MI: Baker, 1991.

Maimonides, Moses. *The Guide of the Perplexed*. Trans. Shlomo Pines. 2 vols. Chicago, IL: University of Chicago Press, 1963.

Malinowski, Bronislaw. *A Scientific Theory of Culture*. Chapel Hill, NC: University of North Carolina Press, 1944.

Manning, S. W. 'Eruption of Thera/Santorini.' Pp. 457–74 in *The Oxford Handbook of the Bronze Age Aegean*. Ed. E. H. Cline. New York, NY: Oxford University Press, 2010.

———. *A Test of Time: The volcano of Thera and the chronology and history of the Aegean and east Mediterranean in the mid-second millennium BC*. Oxford: Oxbow, 1999.

Markowitz, Yvonne J., and Peter Lacovara. 'Gold.' *OEAE* 2:34–8.

Martens, Elmer. 'The oscillating fortunes of "history" within Old Testament theology.' Pp. 313–40 in *Faith, Tradition, and History: Old Testament historiography in its Near Eastern context*. Ed. A. R. Millard, J. K. Hoffmeier and D. W. Baker. Winona Lake, IN: Eisenbrauns, 1994.

Mather, Cotton. *Magnalia Christi Americana*, Books 1 and 2. Ed. Kenneth B. Murdock. Cambridge, MA: Harvard University Press, 1977.

Mathews, Danny. *Royal Motifs in the Pentateuchal Portrayal of Moses*. New York, NY: T&T Clark International, 2012.

Matt, Daniel C. *The Zohar: Pritzker edition*, Vol. 6. Stanford, CA: Stanford University Press, 2011.

Mattingly, Gerald L. 'Adultery.' Pp. 4–5 in *Dictionary of the Ancient Near East*. Ed. Piotr Bienkowski and Alan Millard. Philadelphia, PA: University of Pennsylvania Press, 2000.

———. 'Family.' Pp. 113–14 in *Dictionary of the Ancient Near East*. Ed. Piotr Bienkowski and Alan Millard. Philadelphia, PA: University of Pennsylvania Press, 2000.

Meeks, Wayne. *The First Urban Christians: The social world of the apostle Paul*. New Haven, CT: Yale University Press, 1983.

Mellinkoff, Ruth. *The Horned Moses in Medieval Art and Thought*. Berkeley, CA: University of California Press, 1970.

Mendenhall, George E. *Ancient Israel's Faith and History: An introduction to the Bible in its context*. Ed. Gary A. Herion. Louisville, KY: Westminster John Knox Press, 2001.

———. 'Covenant forms in Israelite tradition.' Pp. 209–33 in *The Cultural and Religious Creativity of Ancient Israel: The collected essays of George E. Mendenhall*. Ed. Gary A. Herion and Herbert B. Huffmon. University Park, PA: Eisenbrauns, 2018.

———. 'The suzerainty treaty structure: thirty years later.' Pp. 312–29 in *The Cultural and Religious Creativity of Ancient Israel: The collected essays of George E. Mendenhall*. Ed. Gary A. Herion and Herbert B. Huffmon. University Park, PA: Eisenbrauns, 2018.

Mendenhall, George E., and Gary A. Herion. 'Covenant.' *ABD* 1:1179–1202.

Mercer, S. A. B. *The Pyramid Texts*. 4 vols. New York, NY: Longmans, Green, 1952.

Merling, David. *The Book of Joshua: Its theme and role in archaeological discussions*. AUSDDS 23. Berrien Springs, MI: Andrews University Press, 1997.

———. 'Large numbers at the time of the exodus.' *NEASB* 44 (1999): 15–27.

Merrill, Eugene H. 'Aaron.' Pp. 1–3 in *Dictionary of the Old Testament: Pentateuch*. Ed. T. Desmond Alexander and David W. Baker. Downers Grove, IL: InterVarsity Press, 2003.

———. *Kingdom of Priests: A history of Old Testament Israel*. Rev. edn. Grand Rapids, MI: Baker, 2008.

Meyers, Carol L. 'Ephod.' *ABD* 2:550.

———. *Exodus*. Cambridge: Cambridge University Press, 2005.

———. 'Guilds and gatherings: women's groups in Ancient Israel.' Pp. 161–70 in *Realia Dei: Essays in archaeology and biblical interpretation in honor of*

Edward F. Campbell, Jr. at his retirement. Ed. Prescott H. Williams Jr and Theodore Hiebert. Atlanta, GA: Scholars Press, 1999.

——. *The Tabernacle Menorah: A synthetic study of a symbol from the biblical cult.* Piscataway, NJ: Gorgias Press, 2003.

Michaels, J. Ramsey. *The Gospel of John.* NICNT. Grand Rapids, MI: Eerdmans, 2010.

Milgrom, Jacob. *Numbers.* JPS Torah Commentary. Philadelphia, PA: Jewish Publication Society, 1990.

Millard, Alan. 'The Hebrew divine name in cuneiform and Hebrew texts.' Pp. 113–25 in *Bible et Proche-Orient: Mélanges André Lemaire III.* Ed. Josette Elayi and Jean-Marie Durand. Transeu 45. Paris: France, 2014.

——. 'Moses, the tongue-tied singer!' Pp. 133–42 in *'Did I Not Bring Israel Out of Egypt?' Biblical, archaeological, and Egyptological perspectives on the exodus narratives.* Ed. James K. Hoffmeier, Alan R. Millard and Gary A. Rendsburg. Winona Lake, IN: Eisenbrauns, 2016.

——. 'Property ownership and inheritance.' P. 235 in *Dictionary of the Ancient Near East.* Ed. Piotr Bienkowski and Alan Millard. Philadelphia, PA: University of Pennsylvania Press, 2000.

Miller, Patrick D. *The Divine Warrior in Early Israel.* Reprint. Atlanta, GA: Society of Biblical Literature, 2006.

——. *Israelite Religion and Biblical Theology: Collected essays.* JSOTSup 267. Sheffield: Sheffield Academic Press, 2000.

——. *The Religion of Ancient Israel.* LAI. London and Louisville, KY: SPCK and Westminster John Knox Press, 2000.

——. *The Ten Commandments.* Interpretation: Resources for the use of Scripture in the Church. Louisville, KY: Westminster John Knox Press, 2009.

Moberly, R. W. L. *At the Mountain of God: Story and theology in Exodus 32–34.* JSOTSup 22. Sheffield: JSOT Press, 1983.

——. *The Old Testament of the Old Testament: Patriarchal narratives and Mosaic Yahwism.* Minneapolis, MN: Fortress Press, 1992.

——. *Old Testament Theology: Reading the Hebrew Bible as Christian Scripture.* Grand Rapids, MI: Baker Academic, 2013.

Moo, Douglas J. *The Epistle to the Romans.* NICNT. Grand Rapids, MI: Eerdmans, 1996.

Moor, Johannes C. de. *The Rise of Yahwism: The roots of Israelite monotheism.* Leuven: Leuven University Press, 1990.

Moran, William L. *The Amarna Letters.* Baltimore, MD: Johns Hopkins University Press, 1992.

Mounce, Robert H. *The Book of Revelation*. NICNT. Grand Rapids, MI: Eerdmans, 1990.

Musgrave, David, ed. *Hebrew and Beyond: Studies in honor of Rodney E. Cloud*. Montgomery, AL: Amridge University Press, 2016.

Myers, Jacob M. *I and II Esdras*. AB 42. New York, NY: Doubleday, 1974.

Na'aman, Nadav. 'The "Kenite Hypothesis" in the light of the excavations at Ḥorvat 'Uza.' Pp. 171–82 in *Not Only History: Proceedings of the conference in honor of Mario Liverani*. Ed. Gilda Bartoloni and Maria Giovanna Biga with the assistance of Armando Bramanti. Winona Lake, IN: Eisenbrauns, 2016.

Nelson, Richard D. 'Aaron.' *NIDB* 1:3–4.

Niditch, Susan. *A Prelude to Biblical Folklore: Underdogs and tricksters*. Champaign, IL: University of Illinois Press, 2000.

Nielsen, Eduard. *The Ten Commandments in New Perspective: A traditio-historical approach*. SBT 2.7. London: SCM Press, 1968.

Noegel, Scott B. 'The Egyptian origin of the ark of the covenant.' Pp. 223–42 in *Israel's Exodus in Transdisciplinary Perspective: Text, archaeology, culture, and geoscience*. Ed. Thomas E. Levy, Thomas Schneider and William H. C. Propp. New York, NY: Springer, 2015.

——. 'Moses and magic: notes on the book of Exodus.' *JANES* 24 (1996): 45–59.

Nogueira, Paulo. 'Exodus in Latin America.' Pp. 447–59 in *The Oxford Handbook on the Reception History of the Bible*. Ed. Michael Lieb, Emma Mason and Jonathan Roberts. Oxford: Oxford University Press, 2011.

Noll, Mark. *America's God: From Jonathan Edwards to Abraham Lincoln*. Oxford: Oxford University Press, 2002.

Noth, Martin. *Exodus: A commentary*. Philadelphia, PA: Westminster Press, 1962.

——. *A History of Pentateuchal Traditions*. Trans. Bernhard W. Anderson. Englewood Cliffs, NJ: Prentice-Hall, 1972.

O'Connor, D., and D. P. Silverman, eds. *Ancient Egyptian Kingship*. Leiden: Brill, 1995.

Oded, Bustanay. '"The command of the god" as a reason for going to war in the Assyrian royal inscriptions.' Pp. 223–30 in *'Ah, Assyria . . .': Studies in Assyrian history and Ancient Near Eastern historiography presented to Hayim Tadmor*. Scripta Hierosolymitana 33. Ed. Mordechai Cogan and Israel Eph'al. Jerusalem: Magnes Press, 1991.

Olson, Dennis T. 'Moses.' *NIDB* 4:142–52.

Olyan, Saul M., and Robert C. Culley. *Law, Power, and Justice in Ancient Israel*. Louisville, KY: Westminster John Knox Press, 2011.

Oren, Eliezer D. 'The "Ways of Horus" in north Sinai.' Pp. 69–119 in *Egypt, Israel, Sinai: Archaeological and historical relationships in the biblical world*. Ed. Anson F. Rainey. Tel Aviv: Tel Aviv University, 1987.

Oswald, Wolfgang. 'Lawgiving at the mountain of God (Exodus 19–24).' Pp. 169–92 in *The Book of Exodus: Composition, reception, and interpretation*. Ed. Thomas B. Dozeman, Craig A. Evans and Joel N. Lohr. Leiden: Brill, 2014.

Pate, C. Marvin, J. Scot Duvall, J. Daniel Hays, E. Randolph Richards, W. Dennis Tucker Jr and Preben Vang. *The Story of Israel: A biblical theology*. Downers Grove, IL: InterVarsity Press, 2004.

Patrick, Dale. *The Rendering of God in the Old Testament*. Minneapolis, MN: Fortress Press, 1981.

Perl-Rosenthal, Nathan. 'The "divine right of republics": Hebraic republicanism and the debate over kingless government in Revolutionary America.' *The William and Mary Quarterly*, 3rd series, 66.3 (2009): 535–64.

Perrin, Nicholas. *Jesus the Temple*. London and Grand Rapids, MI: SPCK and Baker Academic, 2010.

Peterson, David L. 'Prophet, prophecy.' *NIDB* 4:622–48.

Petrie, W. M. Flinders. *Egypt and Israel*. London: SPCK, 1911.

——. *Hyksos and Israelite Cities*. London: Office of School of Archaeology University College and Bernard Quaritch, 1906.

Pfeiffer, Henrik. 'The origin of YHWH and its attestation.' Pp. 116–43 in *The Origins of Yahwism*. BZAW 484. Ed. Jürgen van Oorschot and Markus Witte. Berlin: de Gruyter, 2017.

Philo. *The Works of Philo: Complete and unabridged*. Trans. C. D. Yonge. Peabody, MA: Hendrickson, 1993.

Posner, Raphael, Uri Kaploun and Shalom Cohen, eds. *Jewish Liturgy: Prayer and synagogue service through the ages*. New York, NY and Jerusalem: Leon Amiel and Keter, 1975.

Pritchard, James B., ed. *Ancient Near Eastern Texts Relating to the Old Testament*. 3rd edn. Princeton, NJ: Princeton University Press, 1969.

Propp, William H. *Exodus 1–18: A new translation with introduction and commentary*. AB 2; New York, NY: Doubleday, 1999.

——. *Exodus 19–40: A new translation with introduction and commentary*. AB 2A; New York, NY: Doubleday, 2006.

Quarles, Charles L. 'Jesus as a teacher of new covenant Torah: an examination of the Sermon on the Mount.' In *Matthew as Teacher in the Gospel of Matthew*. Ed. Charles L. Quarles and Charles N. Ridlehoover. LNTS. Edinburgh: T&T Clark, forthcoming.

Rabinowitz, Louis Isaac. 'God, Names of: in the Talmud.' *EncJud* 7:676–7.

Raboteau, Albert J. *Canaan Land: A religious history of African Americans*. New York, NY: Oxford University Press, 2001.

Rainbow, Paul A. *Johannine Theology: The Gospels, the epistles, and the Apocalypse*. Downers Grove, IL: IVP Academic, 2014.

Rainey, Anson F., and R. Steven Notley. *The Sacred Bridge: Carta's atlas of the biblical world*. Jerusalem: Carta, 2006.

Ramsey, George W. 'Is name-giving an act of domination in Genesis 2:23 and elsewhere?' *CBQ* 50 (1988): 24–35.

Redford, Donald B. *Akhenaten: The heretic king*. Princeton, NJ: Princeton University Press, 1984.

——. *Egypt, Canaan, and Israel in Ancient Times*. Princeton, NJ: Princeton University Press, 1992.

——. 'The great going forth: the expulsion of West Semitic speakers from Egypt.' Pp. 437–45 in *Israel's Exodus in Transdisciplinary Perspective: Text, archaeology, culture, and geoscience*. Ed. Thomas E. Levy, Thomas Schneider and William H. C. Propp. New York, NY: Springer, 2015.

——. 'The literary motif of the exposed child (cf. Ex. ii 1–10).' *Numen* 14 (1967): 209–28.

——. 'The monotheism of Akhenaten', in *Aspects of Monotheism: How God is one*. Ed. Hershel Shanks. Washington, DC: Biblical Archaeology Society, 1997.

——. *The Wars of Syria and Palestine of Thutmose III*. Leiden: Brill, 2003.

Redford, Donald B., and G. Wheeler. 'Ancient Egypt's silence about the exodus.' *AUSS* 40 (2002): 257–64.

Rendsburg, Gary A. 'Moses as equal to Pharaoh.' Pp. 201–19 in *Text, Artifact, and Image: Revealing Ancient Israelite religion*. Ed. Gary M. Beckman and Theodore J. Lewis. Brown Judaic Studies 346. Providence, RI: Brown University Press, 2006.

——. 'Moses the magician.' Pp. 243–58 in *Israel's Exodus in Transdisciplinary Perspective: Text, archaeology, culture, and geoscience*. Ed. Thomas E. Levy, Thomas Schneider and William H. C. Propp. New York, NY: Springer, 2015.

Rendtorff, Rolf. *The Canonical Hebrew Bible: A theology of the Old Testament*. Trans. David E. Orton. Blandford Forum: Deo, 2005.

——. 'The concept of revelation in Ancient Israel.' Pp. 25–53 in *Revelation as History*. Ed. Wolfhart Pannenberg, in association with Rolf Rendtorff, Trutz Rendtorff and Ulrich Wilkens. Trans. David Granskou. New York, NY: Macmillan, 1968.

——. *Egypt, Canaan, and Israel in Ancient Times*. Princeton, NJ: Princeton University Press, 1992.

——. 'The monotheism of Akhenaten.' Pp. 11–26 in *Aspects of Monotheism: How God is one*. Ed. Hershel Shanks. Washington, DC: Biblical Archaeology Society, 1997.

——. *The Old Testament: An introduction*. Minneapolis, MN: Fortress Press, 1986.

——. 'What we miss by taking the Bible apart.' *BRev* 14.1 (1998): 42–4.

Reviv, H. *The Elders in Ancient Israel: A study of a biblical institution*. Jerusalem: Magnes Press, 1989.

Ritner, Robert K. 'Magic: an overview.' *OEAE* 2:321–6.

Römer, Thomas. *The Invention of God*. Trans. Raymond Geuss. Cambridge, MA: Harvard University Press, 2015.

——. 'The revelation of the divine name to Moses and the construction of a memory about the origins of the encounter between Yhwh and Israel.' Pp. 305–15 in *Israel's Exodus in Transdisciplinary Perspective: Text, archaeology, culture, and geoscience*. Ed. Thomas E. Levy, Thomas Schneider and William H. C. Propp. New York, NY: Springer, 2015.

Ross, Allen P. *A Commentary on the Psalms*. 3 vols. KEL. Grand Rapids, MI: Kregel Academic, 2011–16.

——. 'Did the patriarchs know the name of the Lord?' Pp. 323–9 in *Giving the Sense: Understanding and using Old Testament historical texts*. Ed. David M. Howard Jr and Michael A. Grisanti. Grand Rapids, MI: Kregel, 2003.

Roth, Ann Macy. 'The representation of the divine in Ancient Egypt.' Pp. 24–37 in *Text, Artifact, and Image: Revealing Ancient Israelite religion*. Ed. Gary M. Beckman and Theodore J. Lewis. BJS 346. Providence, RI: Brown Judaic Studies, 2006.

Roth, Martha T. *Law Collections from Mesopotamia and Asia Minor*. 2nd edn. Atlanta, GA: Society of Biblical Literature, 1997.

Routledge, Robin. 'The exodus and biblical theology.' Pp. 187–209 in *Reverberations of the Exodus in Scripture*. Ed. R. Michael Fox. Eugene, OR: Pickwick, 2014.

Rowland, Christopher and Ian Boxall. 'Reception criticism and theory.' *OEBI* 2:206–15.

Saidel, Benjamin A. 'The Bedouin tent: an ethno-archaeological portal to antiquity or a modern construct?' Pp. 465–86 in *The Archaeology of Mobility: Old World and New World nomadism*. Ed. Hans Barnard and Willeke Wendrich. Los Angeles, CA: Cotsen Institute of Archaeology at UCLA, 2008.

Salamon, Amos, Steve Ward, Floyd McCoy, John Hall and Thomas E. Levy. 'Inspired by a tsunami? An earth sciences perspective on the Exodus narrative.' Pp. 109–29 in *Israel's Exodus in Transdisciplinary Perspective: Text, archaeology, culture, and geoscience*. Ed. Thomas E. Levy, Thomas Schneider and William H. C. Propp. New York, NY: Springer, 2015.

Saner, Andrea D. *'Too Much to Grasp': Exodus 3:13–15 and the reality of God*. JTISup 11. Winona Lake, IN: Eisenbrauns, 2015.

Sarna, Nahum M. 'Aaron.' *EncJud* 2:4–7.

——. *Exodus*. JPS Torah Commentary. Philadelphia, PA: Jewish Publication Society, 1991.

——. *Exploring Exodus: The origins of biblical Israel*. New York, NY: Schocken, 1986.

Sarna, Nahum, and Hershel Shanks. 'Israel in Egypt: the Egyptian sojourn and the exodus.' Pp. 35–57 in *Ancient Israel: From Abraham to the Roman destruction of the Temple*. 3rd edn. Washington, DC: Biblical Archaeology Society, 2011.

Scarlata, Mark. *The Abiding Presence: A theological commentary on Exodus*. London: SCM Press, 2018.

Schneider, Thomas. 'The first documented occurrence of the god Yahweh? (Book of the Dead Princeton "Roll 5").' *JANER* 7.2 (2008): 113–20.

Scolnic, Benjamin E. 'Moses and the horns of power.' Pp. 569–79 in *Judaism: Festschrift in honor of Dr. Robert Gordis*. Ed. Eugene B. Borowitz. New York, NY: American Jewish Congress, 1991.

Scott, James M. *Exile: A conversation with N. T. Wright*. Downers Grove, IL: IVP Academic, 2017.

Segal, J. B. *The Hebrew Passover from the Earliest Times to A.D. 70*. London: Oxford University Press, 1963.

Seitz, Christopher R. *Word Without End: The Old Testament as abiding theological witness*. Grand Rapids, MI: Eerdmans, 1998.

Senn, Frank. *Christian Liturgy: Catholic and Evangelical*. Minneapolis, MN: Fortress Press, 1997.

Shafer, Byron E., ed. *Temples of Ancient Egypt*. Ithaca, NY: Cornell University Press, 1997.

Shanks, Hershel. 'The exodus and the crossing of the Red Sea, according to Hans Goedicke.' *BAR* 7.5 (1981): 42–50.

Shepherd, David. '"See this great sight": Ridley Scott's *Exodus: Gods and Kings* and the evolution of biblical spectacle in the cinema.' Pp. 75–90 in *Biblical Reception 4: A New Hollywood Moses: On the spectacle and reception of Exodus: Gods and Kings*. Ed. David Tollerton. London: Bloomsbury, 2017.

Silberman, Lou H. 'Wellhausen and Judaism.' *Semeia* 25 (1982): 75–82.

Silverman, David P. 'Divinity and deities in Ancient Egypt.' Pp. 58–87 in *Religion in Ancient Egypt: Gods, myths, and personal practice*. Ed. Byron E. Shafer. Ithaca, NY: Cornell University Press, 1991.

Simpson, William Kelly. *The Literature of Ancient Egypt: An anthology of stories, instructions, stelae, autobiographies, and poetry*. 3rd edn. New Haven, CT: Yale University Press, 2003.

Sivertsen, Barbara J. *The Parting of the Sea: How volcanoes, earthquakes, and plagues shaped the story of the exodus*. Princeton, NJ: Princeton University Press, 2009.

Ska, Jean-Louis. *Our Fathers Have Told Us: Introduction to the analysis of Hebrew narratives*. Rome: Pontifical Biblical Institute, 1990.

Smelik, K. A. D. 'Ma'at.' Pp. 534–5 in *Dictionary of Deities and Demons in the Bible*. Ed. Karel van der Toorn, Bob Becking and Pieter W. van der Horst. 2nd edn. Leiden: Brill, 1999.

Smend, Rudolf. *From Astruc to Zimmerli: Old Testament scholarship in three centuries*. Trans. M. Kohl. Tübingen: Mohr Siebeck, 2007.

——. 'Julius Wellhausen and his *Prolegomena to the History of Israel*.' *Semeia* 25 (1982): 1–20.

——. *Yahweh War and Tribal Confederation: Reflections upon Israel's earliest history*. Trans. M. G. Rogers. Nashville, TN: Abingdon Press, 1970.

Smith, Mark S. *The Origins of Biblical Monotheism: Israel's polytheistic background and the Ugaritic texts*. Oxford: Oxford University Press, 2001.

——. 'YHWH's original character: questions about an unknown god.' Pp. 23–43 in *The Origins of Yahwism*. BZAW 484. Ed. Jürgen van Oorschot and Markus Witte. Berlin: de Gruyter, 2017.

Smith, Ralph L. *Micah-Malachi*. WBC 32. Waco, TX: Word, 1984.

Smith, Stuart Tyson. 'People.' *OEAE* 3:27–33.

Smylie, James H. 'On Jesus, pharaohs, and the chosen people: Martin Luther King as biblical interpreter and humanist.' *Int* 24 (January 1970): 74–91.

Song, Angeline M. G. 'Imaging Moses and Miriam re-imaged: through the empathic looking glass of a Singaporean Peranakan woman.' Pp. 169–82 in *Exodus and Deuteronomy*. Ed. Athalya Brenner and Gale A. Yee. TatC. Minneapolis, MN: Fortress Press, 2012.

Spencer, John R. 'Aaron.' *ABD* 1:1–6.

Sprinkle, J. M. *'The Book of the Covenant': A literary approach*. JSOTSup 174. Sheffield: JSOT Press, 1994.

Starling, David. 'Ephesians and the hermeneutics of the new exodus.' Pp. 139–59 in *Reverberations of the Exodus in Scripture*. Ed. R. Michael Fox. Eugene, OR: Pickwick, 2014.

Stavrakopoulou, Francesca, and John Barton, eds. *Religious Diversity in Ancient Israel and Judah*. London: T&T Clark, 2010.

Sternberg, Meir. *The Poetics of Biblical Narrative: Ideological literature and the drama of reading*. Bloomington, IN: Indiana University Press, 1985.

Surls, Austin. *Making Sense of the Divine Name in Exodus: From etymology to literary onomastics*. BBRSup 17. Winona Lake, IN: Eisenbrauns, 2017.

Taylor, John H. *Death and the Afterlife in Ancient Egypt*. Chicago, IL: University of Chicago Press, 2001.

Teeple, Howard M. *The Mosaic Eschatological Prophet*. JBLMS 10. Philadelphia, PA: Society of Biblical Literature, 1957.

Teeter, Emily. 'Maat.' *OEAE* 2:319–21.

Thompson, John. *The Ancient Near Eastern Treaties and the Old Testament*. London: Tyndale Press, 1963.

Thompson, Thomas L. *The Historicity of the Patriarchal Narratives: The quest for the historical Abraham*. New York, NY: de Gruyter, 1974.

Tigay, Jeffrey H. '"Heavy of mouth" and "heavy of tongue": on Moses' speech difficulty.' *BASOR* 231 (1978): 57–67.

Timmer, Daniel C. *Creation, Tabernacle, and Sabbath: The Sabbath frame of Exodus 31:12–17; 35.1–3 in exegetical and theological perspective*. Göttingen: Vandenhoeck & Ruprecht, 2009.

Tollerton, David. '"Hmmm . . . but LOVED the plagues": on engaging with Ridley Scott's epic and its audiences.' Pp. 1–8 in *Biblical Reception 4: A New Hollywood Moses: On the spectacle and reception of Exodus: Gods and Kings*. Ed. David Tollerton. London: Bloomsbury, 2017.

Tov, Emanuel, and Sidnie White. 'Reworked Pentateuch.' Pp. 187–351 in *Qumran Cave 4*: Vol. 8, *Parabiblical Texts*, Part 1. Ed. Harold Attridge, Torleif Elgvin, Jozef Milik, Saul Olyan, John Strugnell, Emanuel Tov, James VanderKam and Sidnie White, in consultation with James VanderKam. DJD 13. Oxford: Clarendon Press, 1995.

Trible, Phyllis. 'Bringing Miriam out of the shadows.' *BRev* 5.1 (1989): 14–25, 34.

——. 'Miriam 1.' Pp. 127–9 in *Women in Scripture: A dictionary of named and unnamed women in the Hebrew Bible, the apocryphal/deuterocanonical books, and the New Testament*. Ed. Carol Meyers. Grand Rapids, MI: Eerdmans, 2000.

Trimm, Charlie. *Fighting for the King and the Gods: A survey of warfare in the Ancient Near East*. Atlanta, GA: SBL Press, 2017.

——. *'YHWH Fights for Them!' The Divine Warrior in the Exodus narrative*. Piscataway, NJ: Gorgias Press, 2014.

Tropper, Josef. 'The divine name **Yahwa*.' Pp. 1–21 in *The Origins of Yahwism*, ed. Jürgen van Oorschot and Markus Witte. Berlin: de Gruyter, 2017.

Tsumura, David Toshio. *The First Book of Samuel*. NICOT. Grand Rapids, MI: Eerdmans, 2007.

Tuininga, Matthew J. *Calvin's Political Theology and the Public Engagement of the Church: Christ's two kingdoms*. Cambridge: Cambridge University Press, 2017.

Unger, M. F. *Archaeology and the Old Testament*. 4th edn. Grand Rapids, MI: Zondervan, 1960.

Uphill, Eric P. 'Pithom and Raamses: their location and significance.' *JNES* 27.4 (1968): 291–316.

Utzschneider, Helmut. 'Tabernacle.' Pp. 267–301 in *The Book of Exodus: Composition, reception, and interpretation*. Ed. Thomas B. Dozeman, Craig A. Evans and Joel N. Lohr. VTSup 164. Leiden: Brill, 2014.

Utzschneider, Helmut, and Wolfgang Oswald. *Exodus 1–15*. IECOT. Stuttgart: Kohlhammer, 2015.

Van Dam, Cornelis. *The Urim and Thummim: A means of revelation in Ancient Israel*. Winona Lake, IN: Eisenbrauns, 1997.

van der Steen, Eveline. *Near Eastern Tribal Societies during the Nineteenth Century: Economy, society and politics between tent and town*. Sheffield: Equinox, 2013.

van der Toorn, Karel. *Family Religion in Babylonia, Syria and Israel: Continuity and change in the forms of religious life*. Leiden: Brill, 1996.

——. 'Ilib and the "god of the father."' *UF* 25 (1993): 379–87.

——. 'Yahweh.' Pp. 910–19 in *Dictionary of Deities and Demons in the Bible*. Ed. Karel van der Toorn, Bob Becking and Pieter W. van der Horst. 2nd edn. Leiden: Brill, 1999.

Van Seters, John. *Abraham in History and Tradition*. New Haven, CT: Yale University Press, 1975.

——. *A Law Book for the Diaspora: Revision in the study of the Covenant Code*. New York, NY: Oxford University Press, 2003.

——. *The Life of Moses: The Yahwist as historian in Exodus-Numbers*. Philadelphia, PA: Westminster John Knox Press, 1994.

Vancil, Jack W. 'Sheep, shepherd.' *ABD* 5:1187–90.

VanderKam, James, and Peter Flint. *The Meaning of the Dead Sea Scrolls: Their significance for understanding the Bible, Judaism, Jesus, and Christianity*. New York, NY: HarperSanFrancisco, 2002.

Vaux, Roland de. *The Early History of Israel*. Philadelphia, PA: Westminster Press, 1978.

Velde, Herman te. 'Theology, priests, and worship in Ancient Egypt.' *CANE* 3:1731–49.

Velioti-Georgopoulos, Maria. 'Marriage.' *EAnth* 4:1536–40.

von Rad, Gerhard. *Holy War in Ancient Israel*. Reprint. Eugene, OR: Wipf & Stock, 2000.

———. *Old Testament Theology*, Vol. 1: *The Theology of Israel's Historical Traditions*. Trans. D. M. G. Stalker. New York, NY: Harper & Row, 1962.

Waida, Manuba. 'Miracles: an overview.' *ER* 9:6049–55.

Waite, Jerry. 'The census of Israelite men after their exodus from Egypt.' *Vetus Testamentum* 60 (2010): 487–91.

Walsh, Jerome T. *Old Testament Narrative: A guide to interpretation*. Louisville, KY: Westminster John Knox Press, 2010.

Walther, Ingo F. *Marc Chagall (1887–1985): Painting as poetry*. Düsseldorf: Benedikt Taschen, 1987.

Watts, John D. W. *Isaiah 34–66*. WBC 25. Waco, TX: Word, 1987.

Watts, Rikki E. *Isaiah's New Exodus*. Grand Rapids, MI: Baker Academic, 1997.

Weinstein, James. 'Exodus and archaeological reality.' Pp. 87–103 in *Exodus: The Egyptian evidence*. Ed. E. S. Frerichs and L. H. Lesko. Winona Lake, IN: Eisenbrauns, 1997.

Wellhausen, Julius. *Geschichte Israels*. Erster Band. Berlin: G. Reimer, 1878.

———. *Prolegomena to the History of Ancient Israel*. Gloucester, MA: Peter Smith, 1878. Reprinted New York, NY: Meridian, 1957.

Wenham, Gordon J. 'Aaron.' *NIDOTTE* 4:346–8.

———. *Exploring the Old Testament*, Vol. 1: *A Guide to the Pentateuch*. Downers Grove, IL: InterVarsity Press, 2003.

———. 'Sanctuary symbolism in the garden of Eden story.' Pp. 19–24 in *Proceedings of the Ninth World Congress of Jewish Studies*. Ed. David Assaf. Jerusalem: World Union of Jewish Studies, 1986.

Westermann, Claus. *Basic Forms of Prophetic Speech*. Trans. H. White. Louisville, KY: Westminster John Knox Press, 1991.

———. *Isaiah 40–66*. OTL. Philadelphia, PA: Westminster Press, 1969.

Wheeler, G. 'Ancient Egypt's silence about the exodus.' *AUSS* 40 (2002): 257–64.

Whybray, R. Norman. *Introduction to the Pentateuch*. Grand Rapids, MI: Eerdmans, 1995.

Wiener, Malcolm H. 'Dating the Theran eruption: archaeological science versus nonsense science.' Pp. 131–43 in *Israel's Exodus in Transdisciplinary Perspective: Text, archaeology, culture, and geoscience*. Ed. Thomas E. Levy, Thomas Schneider and William H. C. Propp. New York, NY: Springer, 2015.

Wilkinson, John. *From Synagogue to Church: The Traditional Design: Its beginning, its definition, its end*. London: Routledge, 2002.

Wilkinson, Richard H. *The Complete Gods and Goddesses of Ancient Egypt.* London: Thames & Hudson, 2003.

Wilkinson, Robert J. *Tetragrammaton: Western Christians and the Hebrew name of God from the beginnings to the seventeenth century.* SHCT 179. Leiden: Brill, 2015.

Williams, Joshua E. 'Promise and failure: second exodus in Ezra-Nehemiah.' Pp. 74–93 in *Reverberations of the Exodus in Scripture.* Ed. R. Michael Fox. Eugene, OR: Pickwick, 2014.

Williamson, H. G. M. *Ezra, Nehemiah.* WBC 16. Waco, TX: Word, 1985.

Willoughby, Thomas N. '"The Word became flesh and tabernacled among us": a primer for the exodus in John's Gospel.' Pp. 121–38 in *Reverberations of the Exodus in Scripture.* Ed. R. Michael Fox. Eugene, OR: Pickwick, 2014.

Wilson, Ian. *Exodus: The true story behind the biblical account.* New York, NY: HarperCollins, 1986.

Witte, John, Jr. *God's Joust, God's Justice: Law and religion in the Western tradition.* Grand Rapids, MI: Eerdmans, 2006.

Wood, Allen W. 'Enlightenment, The.' *ER* 4:2795–9.

Wood, B. G. 'The rise and fall of the 13th-century exodus-conquest theory.' *JETS* 48 (2005): 475–89.

Wood, L. J. *A Survey of Israel's History.* Rev. and enlarged by D. O'Brien. Grand Rapids, MI: Zondervan, 1986.

Works, Carla Swafford. *The Church in the Wilderness: Paul's use of exodus traditions in 1 Corinthians.* WUNT 2/379. Tübingen: Mohr Siebeck, 2014.

Wright, Christopher J. H. 'The Israelite household and the Decalogue: the social background and significance of some commandments.' *TynBul* 30 (1979): 101–24.

Wright, David P. 'The origin, development, and context of the Covenant Code.' Pp. 220–44 in *The Book of Exodus: Composition, reception, and interpretation.* Ed. Thomas B. Dozeman, Craig A. Evans and Joel N. Lohr. Leiden: Brill, 2014.

Wright, G. Ernest. *God Who Acts: Biblical theology as recital.* SBT 8. London: SCM Press, 1952.

Wright, N. T. *The Climax of the Covenant: Christ and the law in Pauline theology.* Minneapolis, MN: Fortress Press, 1993.

———. *The New Testament and the People of God.* Christian Origins and the Question of God 1. London and Minneapolis, MN: SPCK and Fortress Press, 1992.

Wright, N. T., and Michael Bird. *The New Testament in Its World: An introduction to the history, literature, and theology of the first Christians.* London and Grand Rapids, MI: SPCK and Zondervan, 2019.

Zakovitch, Yair. 'A study of precise and partial derivations in biblical etymology.' *JSOT* 15 (1980): 31–50.

Zevit, Ziony. 'The Priestly redaction and interpretation of the plague narrative in Exodus.' *JQR* 66 (1975–6): 193–211.

——. 'Three ways to look at the ten plagues.' *BRev* 6.3 (1990): 16–23, 42.

——. 'Timber for the tabernacle: text, tradition, and realia.' *Eretz-Israel* 23 (1992): 137*–43*.

Ziolkowski, Theodore. *Uses and Abuses of Moses: Literary representations since the Enlightenment.* Notre Dame, IN: University of Notre Dame Press, 2016.

Index of biblical references

Index of biblical references

Index of subjects

Aaron 7, 153, 170–2, 178; as high priest
    74, 133; leading the Israelites 147–8;
    as spokesman for Moses 5, 67, 69, 82
Abihu 7, 195
Abraham 1, 56
Abrahamic promises 1–2, 4, 59–60,
    127–8
adultery 123–4, 194
African spirituals 247–8
Albright, W. F. 152–3
Aling, C. 29
Allison, Dale 210–11
altar of incense 134
Amalekites 6, 178
Amarna texts 26
American civil rights movement
    250–3
American civil war 248–9
Amun (king of gods) 98, 105–6
archaeological record, in Sinai 31–4
Archer, G. L. 29
Aristotle 85
ark of the covenant 126, 131; in the Old
    Testament 197–200; parallels 139–40;
    and the Philistines 198–9
Assmann, Jan 238, 239

Baal 152
Babington, Bruce 236
Bailey, L. R. 152
Balogh, Amy 81
Bauckham, Richard 227–8
Beale, Gregory 217–18
Beecher, Henry Ward 248
Berman, Joshua 22–3, 105–6

Betz, Hans Dieter 223
biblical theology movement 21
Blenkinsopp, Joseph 16
Block, Daniel 191
blood 6, 7, 75, 83, 87; as metaphor 95–6;
    ratification of covenant 128, 210, 212;
    symbolism of 62, 137, 141, 219; see
    also sacrifices
Boling, Robert 72
Book of the Covenant 7, 73, 126–7, 150
Booysen, Rian 89
Bradford, William 242
Briggs, Charles 15
burning bush 5, 48, 80, 212
burnt offerings 153–4

call narrative 48, 80–2
Calvin, John 241
Canaan, conquest of 127–8
Canaan (Holmes) 249
canonical interpretation 19
Caruthers, Eli 245–6
Cassuto, Umberto 154
cattle cults 97
Chagall, Marc 231–2
Childs, Brevard 19, 81, 131
church music 239–41
churches, design 234–5
circumcision 41, 183–4
Coates, George 18
Code of Hammurabi 73
Code of Ur-Nammu 72–3
community, relationships in 122–5
Conzelmann, Hans 212
Cotton, John 242

Index of subjects

Index of subjects